# Women Migrants
# from East to West

# Women Migrants from East to West

Gender, Mobility and Belonging in Contemporary Europe

Edited by

*Luisa Passerini, Dawn Lyon, Enrica Capussotti and Ioanna Laliotou*

*Berghahn Books*
New York • Oxford

First published in 2007 by
*Berghahn Books*
www.berghahnbooks.com

©2007 Luisa Passerini, Dawn Lyon, Enrica Capussotti and Ioanna Laliotou

All rights reserved. Except for the quotation of short passages for the purposes of criticism and review, no part of this book may be reproduced in any form or by any means, electronic or mechanical, including photocopying, recording, or any information storage and retrieval system now known or to be invented, without written permission of the publisher.

**Library of Congress Cataloging-in-Publication Data**
Women migrants from East to West : gender, mobility, and belonging in contemporary Europe / edited by Luisa Passerini ... [et al.].
  p. cm.
Includes bibliographical references and index.
ISBN 978-1-84545-277-3 (hardback : alk. paper)
 1. Women immigrants--Europe--Social conditions. 2. East Europeans--Europe, Western--Social conditions. 3. Europe--Emigration and immigration. 4. Europe--Social conditions. I. Passerini, Luisa.

JV6347.W67 2007
305.48'96902094--dc22

2007012585

**British Library Cataloguing in Publication Data**
A catalogue record for this book is available from the British Library
Printed in the United States on acid-free paper

ISBN 978-1-84545-277-3 hardback

# Contents

| | | |
|---|---|---|
| **Acknowledgements** | | **vii** |
| **Editors' Introduction** | | **1** |
| **Part I** | **Subjectivity, Mobility and Gender in Europe** | |
| **Chapter 1** | On Becoming Europeans<br>*Rosi Braidotti* | 23 |
| **Chapter 2** | 'I want to see the world': Mobility and Subjectivity in the European Context<br>*Ioanna Laliotou* | 45 |
| **Chapter 3** | Transformations of Legal Subjectivity in Europe: From the Subjection of Women to Privileged Subjects<br>*Hanne Petersen* | 68 |
| *Intermezzo* | 'A Dance through Life': Narratives of Migrant Women<br>*Nadejda Alexandrova and Anna Hortobagyi* | 84 |
| **Part II** | **Subjectivity in Motion:**<br>**Analysing the Lives of Migrant Women** | |
| **Chapter 4** | Imaginary Geographies: Border-places and 'Home' in the Narratives of Migrant Women<br>*Nadejda Alexandrova and Dawn Lyon* | 95 |
| **Chapter 5** | 'My hobby is people': Migration and Communication in the Light of Late Totalitarianism<br>*Miglena Nikolchina* | 111 |
| **Chapter 6** | Migrant Women in Work<br>*Enrica Capussotti, Ioanna Laliotou and Dawn Lyon* | 122 |

| | | |
|---|---|---|
| **Chapter 7** | The *Topos* of Love in the Life-stories of Migrant Women<br>*Nadejda Alexandrova* | 138 |
| **Chapter 8** | Food-talk: Markers of Identity and Imaginary Belongings<br>*Andrea Pető* | 152 |
| *Intermezzo* | *Relationships in the Making: Accounts of Native Women*<br>*Enrica Capussotti and Esther Vonk* | 165 |
| **Part III:** | **Processes of Identification: Inclusion and Exclusion of Migrant Women** | |
| **Chapter 9** | Migration, Integration and Emancipation: Women's Positioning in the Debate in the Netherlands<br>*Esther Vonk* | 177 |
| **Chapter 10** | Modernity versus Backwardness: Italian Women's Perceptions of Self and Other<br>*Enrica Capussotti* | 195 |
| **Chapter 11** | Moral and Cultural Boundaries in Representations of Migrants: Italy and the Netherlands in Comparative Perspective<br>*Dawn Lyon* | 212 |
| **Chapter 12** | Changing Matrimonial Law in the Image of Immigration Law<br>*Inger Marie Conradsen and Annette Kronborg* | 228 |
| *Intermezzo* | *In Transit: Space, People, Identities*<br>*Andrea Pető* | 243 |
| **Conclusions** | Gender, Subjectivity, Europe: A Constellation for the Future<br>*Luisa Passerini* | 251 |
| **Appendix 1** | Summary of individual interviewees | 275 |
| **Appendix 2** | Summary of interviewees' characteristics by nationality | 304 |
| **Notes on Contributors** | | 314 |
| **Index** | | 317 |

# Acknowledgements

This book and the project from which it arises are the results of interdisciplinary and inter-national collaboration. The group of scholars who worked together are from seven countries – Bulgaria, Denmark, Greece, Hungary, Italy, the Netherlands and the UK – and from six disciplinary fields – history, philosophy, sociology, law, literature, and women's studies. We have all worked in languages other than our native tongue and have spent time in unfamiliar places for our research work and meetings. The process of the research has been very rich indeed, challenging, unsettling, and the sort of experience that takes you in new directions. Many thanks to all our collaborators in this research. Whilst almost all have chapters in this volume, we must add a special word of thanks to Borbála Juhász for her contribution in the fieldwork for this study.

In addition, the project engaged many transcribers and translators whose labours on the tape-recorded interviews transformed them into written texts in English so that we might have a common corpus of material. The Bulgarian interviews were transcribed and translated by Lora Boyadzhieva, Galina Chekurova, Nadejda Radulova, and Elena Stoyanova; the Hungarian interviews were transcribed by Ildiko Varga and translated by Ágnes Merényi, Nóra Kovács and Péter Valló, and additional work on the transcripts was conducted by Eszter Varsa; the Italian interviews were transcribed by Veronica Pellegrini and translated by Jacqueline Gordon; the Dutch interviews were transcribed by Marlies Drenth, Ruby van Leijenhorst, and Renate Schenk, and translated by Sonja Willems and Benoit Lhoest. In addition, many thanks must go to Giuseppe Lauricella, who took care of the construction of the on-line archive of the interviews; and to Aidan O'Malley for his excellent work in the language correction of this entire book.

The proposal for the research funding which made this project possible was originally suggested to us by the then director of the Robert Schuman Centre for Advanced Studies at the European University Institute in Florence, Yves Mény, now President of the EUI. We are grateful to him and to his successor at the RSC, Helen Wallace, for their support throughout the research. The research was done while the Gender Studies

Programme at the EUI was directed by Luisa Passerini and coordinated by Dawn Lyon; since its directorship and coordination too were based at the EUI, it also owes a great deal to the administrative and scientific support of the EUI personnel. In particular we owe much thanks to Roberto Nocentini, and Serena Scarselli for their financial management of the research. We also want to thank all the administrative and academic staff in the different partner institutions for their support with financial and organizational matters, especially Judit Gazsi and Antal Örkény.

The research funding was made available to us under the European Commission's Fifth Framework Programme 'Improving Human Potential and the Socio-Economic Knowledge Base' (contract number: HPSE-CT2001-00087). We gratefully acknowledge the support of the European Commission for this work, and especially thank Virginia Vitorino, our scientific officer, for her encouragement.

In the final stages of this work, we held three events to which we invited colleagues to critically comment upon our work in progress. The first, a conference hosted by the University of Sofia in March 2004, provided the setting for very productive exchanges. In particular we would like to thank our discussants: Anne-Marie Fortier, Eleonore Kofman and Helma Lutz, as well as all the participants of the panel discussion. The second event was a workshop hosted by the EUI in May 2004 where commentators once again helped us to move forward in our interpretations; as did our discussants at a third event, a conference hosted by the CIRSDe and the University of Turin in June 2005. We thank Jean-Pierre Cassarino, Frank Duvell, Mark Bell, Enrica Rigo, Ruba Salih, Bo Strath, and Giovanna Zincone. In addition, earlier versions of the chapters in this book presented as conference papers were greatly improved through the comments of discussants and participants, for which we are very grateful, notably to Jacqueline Andall.

We would also like to thank Marion Berghahn at Berghahn Books for her support for our work. In the preparation of this manuscript, we benefited from the professionalism of our publishers, in particular, Mark Stanton, to whom we are very grateful.

Finally, the greatest debt of gratitude goes to all the women who agreed to be interviewed for this research. The life stories and accounts of 110 women are the basis for this book. We thank them warmly for generously agreeing to share their time, thoughts and experiences with us.

Luisa Passerini, Dawn Lyon, Enrica Capussotti and Ioanna Laliotou
October 2006

# Editors' Introduction

*Luisa Passerini, Dawn Lyon, Enrica Capussotti and Ioanna Laliotou*

## Gender, Mobility and Belonging in Europe

This book is about women who move across Europe, specifically women moving from the European Centre–East to the West. Just fifteen years ago, before the fall of the Berlin wall, and the transformation of the Eastern bloc, mobility in eastern and central Europe beyond national frontiers was rare, requiring either political authorization or considerable risk. In present day Europe, migration from the East to the West is a very significant trend in international patterns of mobility. And, in a parallel change to the character of migration in the recent past, many contemporary migrants are women.

The research this book presents is an oral history of women who have migrated from Bulgaria or Hungary, to Italy or the Netherlands. Our aim is to identify new forms of subjectivity that are part of the contemporary history of Europe, and to explore how the movement of people across Europe is changing the cultural and social landscape with implications for how we think about what Europe means. The research assumes migrants to be active subjects, creating possibilities and taking decisions in their own lives, as well as being subject to legal and political regulation amongst others. We ask: How do people make sense of their experiences of migration? Can we trace new or different forms of subjectivity through present day mobility within Europe? What is the spectrum of contemporary forms of identification in Europe in relation to mobility? These latter questions are also relevant to native[1] women. Through interviews with native women in Italy and the Netherlands, we document and analyse the points of connection of friendship and empathy between native and migrant women, as well as mechanisms of exclusion and xenophobia expressed by native women, for what these allow us to perceive about the symbolic boundaries of Europe. In short, the contribution of this book is to explore migration for what sorts of subjectivity contemporary forms of mobility induce, in both migrants themselves and in native women, and to reconsider the complex set of representations and perceptions attributed to migrants and migration.

Our focus on the interrelation between gender and migration is grounded on particular historical as well as theoretical developments in the field of migration studies. Contemporary migration is marked by particular characteristics that distinguish it from past population movements (Koser and Lutz 1998) amongst which is the so-called feminization of migration. Social scientists have documented the marked increase in the number of women migrants in recent years, and the proportion of women in relation to the total number of migrants. This phenomenon is related to economic, political, social and cultural transformations of late capitalism; transformations that are taking place globally and have different effects on people's lives locally. The feminization of migration is also related to a theoretical re-orientation in the field. During the last decade the study of the relation between gender and migration has foregrounded the dynamic interplay of agency and structure in the organization and operation of the global economic, political and cultural processes that sustain human migration. Scholars have demonstrated how re-rethinking these relations through gender offers insight into the feminisation of migration flows and the establishment of transnational families whose networks expand globally and whose importance is fundamental for the operations of economy and culture in late capitalism (e.g. Sassen 2000; Parrenas 2001; Phizacklea 2003).

The testimonies of both migrant and native women confirm the central role of human mobility in the redefinition of relations between Central–Eastern and Western Europe post-1989. If new forms of encounters are shaped within the social, political and economic conditions of post-communism and through the intensification of a wide variety of social, political, economic, and cultural exchanges, mobility and migration between the East and the West play a central role in these exchanges whilst also giving rise to new transnational forms of subjectivity in Europe today. Gender relations have been at the core of these processes: first, the transition from state socialism to capitalism has had a huge impact on the lives and the position of women in Eastern European societies; secondly, the re-arrangement of gender relations is related to the modification of political and social practices, and to understandings of the private and public sphere in post-communism.

In these introductory remarks, we are using the language of migration, yet the concept of migration itself is problematic and warrants some discussion. The term refers to a wide range of movements of individuals and groups of people across regional and/or national borders. Migration has been largely connected to the pursuit of employment and the betterment of one's material conditions of life. Forced migration – as a result of political or religious persecution – has been located in a separate category of refugees. However, during the last two decades, and due to the intense diversification of population movements related to the economic and political processes of late capitalism, the concept of migration has expanded in order to include different forms of mobility across continuously shifting geographical, economic and political territories. The present research continues in this spirit by emphasizing the diversity and interconnections of processes and motivations through which migration takes place. This volume gives attention to the cultural and emotional underpinnings of the mobility, thus valuing a whole range of 'subjective' motives beyond the quest for material improvement, or political or religious freedom.

In addition, this project seeks to enrich the field of migration studies through an empirically grounded critique of understandings of the migrant as a dislocated and uprooted subject, either prey to forces of integration, or motivated exclusively by rational choices related to the betterment of living conditions. Taking as a starting point how women are moving across Europe immediately challenges the understanding of migration as a linear process of departure and arrival (loss and integration), in which places of origin and destination are singular and fixed and patterns of integration are assumed to follow several stages.

Indeed, the interviews provide us with input for a theoretical reconsideration of the assumptions attached to the term migration. For instance, since the early 1990s scholars of migration have stressed the importance of transnational movement and the establishment of transnational networks of interaction for the understanding of contemporary transformations in the practices of migration in cultural, political, civic and economic terms. The practices of mobility that are presented in the interviews challenge the conventional association between migrancy and loss of subjectivity (as a result of dislocation and uprooting) by suggesting that women transnational migrants develop new forms of subjectivity based on sets of relationships that develop in the context of the movement. Migration and mobility between the European East and the West is marked, enabled, motivated, and realized through the establishment of these relationships. Mobility is also often associated with the types of social, personal, professional and intimate relationships that the migrant establishes and maintains. Through relationships the physical movement of women between East and West Europe is related to the affective mobility that defines the migrants' subjectivity.

Overall, migration in the present research is envisioned as a contemporary form of mobility and a dynamic set of relations between places, cultures, people and identifications. And this has meant reconsidering simple categorizations of these women in terms of labour, family reunification, ideas of home and belonging, assumptions of happiness and satisfaction. For instance, migrant women may be transnational mothers, dividing their time between one site and country in which they work and another in which they share time and space with family members; or they may travel back and forth between different locations. Under these sorts of conditions any straightforward assumptions about sending and receiving societies are also challenged.

As we have already indicated, the study of migration presented here – from the European Centre-East to the European West – is part of a reflection on the repercussions of European migrations on existing ideas of Europe and Europeanness, which helps us to rethink forms of European belonging and to envisage new ways of being European. The contemporary historical context is marked by multiple processes of building a new European social, political and cultural environment that transgresses older divisions between the West and the East. Intra-European migration and the pursuit and establishment of relationships — personal, intimate, professional or collegial – across the European East and West, play a pivotal role in the consolidation of this emergent new European political and cultural space. Intra-European migration has been a constant process in the modern history of the continent and has contributed greatly to the making of European nation-states and the establishment of the European international state system (Bade 1987; Kussmaul 1981; Lowe 1989; Moch 1984; Wlocevski 1934). The intensification of migration from Eastern to Western and Southern Europe is a phenomenon inseparably connected with the post-1989 political changes in Eastern Europe and with the subsequent processes of EU enlargement to the East. Based on the post-Second World War division of the European geo-political space, Western and Eastern European migration systems were almost separate entities (see Hoerder 1990 on the concept of migration system). Post-1989 these two systems merged in a way that has led to the massive migration of people across borders (themselves often difficult to determine) between eastern and western parts of this continent, and this mobility has produced a phenomenon of major political and cultural significance, accompanied by a massive scholarly investigation.

Most studies of the relation between subjectivity and transnationalism trace the impact of the cultural logics of transnational networks on the construction of subjectivity. Aiwa Ong has argued that new modes of subjectivation are drastically shaped by the conditions of transnational mobility and consist of 'flexible practices, strategies and disciplines associated with transnational capitalism', themselves connected with 'new modes of subject making and new kinds of valorised subjectivity' (Ong 1999: 18–19). The expansion of transnational migrants' networks and communities and the intensification of transnational cultural, political and economic interaction in late capitalism have led to the emergence of new forms of subjectivity that enable the subject to act within different levels of local and global communication. The exploration of women's mobility and subjectivity between the European East and the West prompts us to consider how new and old practices of mobility re-configure political space, geo-cultural territories, and ideas of home and belonging.

While political and social transformations within the European Union as well as in single European states are at the centre of public debate, fundamental cultural aspects that shape political and social processes are marginal in EU politics. We do not wish to deny the importance of political, social and economic approaches to the significant moments and processes of the contemporary construction of Europe, e.g. EU enlargements on 1 May 2004 and 1 January 2007, however, we want also to stress the importance and gains of thinking through a cultural lens to analyse, understand and transform political, economic and social inequalities. Culture is often invoked in the context of official EU discourse in order to refer to top-down policies that aim at the bureaucratic engineering of European 'cultural identities'. Instead, the notion of culture that we invoke in this research refers rather to dynamic processes of production of meaning that enable the conceptualization of political, social and economic transformations on the level of everyday life and subjectivity.

The present research tries to open up ideas of Europe and Europeanness to include the experiences – in all their diversity – of being a woman moving between two or more countries, and to reconfigure traditionally established relationships between Eastern and Western Europe. It not only attempts to indicate the limits of the Western ways of being European and to criticize Eurocentrism on intellectual and empirical grounds; it also contributes to deconstructing stereotypes about Eastern and Western Europe and Europeans, interpreting the 'hints' at new forms of connection which emerge from the intercultural dialogue in daily life between 'migrant' and 'native' women. We therefore see it as a contribution to rethinking and redefining the very idea of Europe, and of belonging to this continent, into the future. In this perspective, focusing on Europe is a way of locating Europeanness in the world, seeing its specificity and giving up all claims to any alleged superiority and to all internal intra-European hierarchies. While we are aware that some of the problems we have been dealing with in this volume reappear virulently in relationships between European women and women from other continents, we think that the work we have done will constitute a platform for future approaches to intercultural dialogue in a perspective wider than the European one.

## *Methodological Choices*

The choice of the method of oral history in this research responds to two major considerations that we wish briefly to recall. The first is the unique opportunity that oral interviews offer as sources for history, allowing us to combine insights in individual experience at the same time as in the understanding of cultural changes in communities and the relationships between them. The second is the fact that oral history provides a privileged ground for a multidisciplinary approach. Indeed, the present research draws on the following fields of study: cultural history, philosophy, sociology, law, literature, and women's studies. While not all the participants in the research were specialists in the field of migration, their different expertises brought, we believe, innovative visions to this topic. Moreover the plurality of disciplines involved has had an impact on the language of the book itself. In the chapters of this book a multiplicity of vocabularies shaped by disciplinary and national conventions cohabit with the appropriation of specific theories, models and styles.

The research we present here is primarily based on the collection of life stories and interviews with migrant women from Bulgaria and Hungary, and native women in Italy and the Netherlands. This material is treated in different ways by the authors (single or multiple) of the different chapters. The interviews reappear in various configurations; this choice has been made at the risk of repetition, but it testifies to the possibility of viewing the same material from different points of view. One difficulty of dealing with the testimonies is that they are heavily loaded with projections and stereotypes, for instance based on nation or gender. The cultural stratifications of memory, ideology and experience converge to compose complex narrations that correspond in an indirect way to the complexities in the social processes of geographical mobility. The chapters in this book try to cope with this universe indicating various possible ways of interpreting it. The women's accounts are much more than personal stories. Through migrant women's narratives, we trace the processes (institutional and inter-subjective) which have shaped their strategies and their selves, their understandings of the past, and aspirations for the future, such that their narratives become a document of the contemporary phenomenon of migration in Europe.

We made several choices here which warrant further comment: to select women migrants, and not to include men; to conduct interviews with native as well as migrant women; and to do so in the specific countries chosen. First, our focus on women is connected to the feminization of migration we discussed above. Given the difficulties of managing the large quantity of materials produced in oral history research, we decided to privilege relationships between women as subjects. We set out to document the lives of these new social actors undertaking mobility, and to explore the repertoires of meaning through which they make sense of their trajectories. By asking women to tell us their own accounts, we effectively made it possible for them to position themselves as central actors in their mobility, in contrast to assumptions of their place in migratory processes as connected to family reunification, even though this has ceased to be the dominant reality. Whilst we made the choice to place the resources we had available for the research in the collection of women's testimonies – which has resulted, in addition to this book and other publications, in a digital archive of the interviews[2] – further research might adopt a similar approach to interviewing men. However, in the present research, men are not absent. They are frequently mentioned in the interviews (both in the questions and the answers) as interlocutors and partners, whose place in the decision to migrate, and more generally in the construction of new subjectivities, is crucial. They are often presented along nation-based stereotypical lines and they seem to be the target of a shared criticism. We acknowledge the necessity to give them the word on these matters and we look forward to future research taking up the suggestions from recent developments in men's studies and applying them to the study of migration.

Second, the interviews with native women have allowed us to trace contemporary forms of intercultural exchange through accounts of relationships between native and migrant women (and men), and broader perceptions and representations of migrants on the part of native women. This connects to our approach to migration set out above which emphasizes mobility as a dynamic set of relations between places, cultures, people and identifications, and thereby situates native and less mobile subjects in the frame alongside those who move. In other words, we explore migration as a set of acts and effects in the lives of women who are not necessarily mobile themselves but whose worlds are also marked by mobility. In particular this approach has allowed us to document and analyse different forms of encounter – experienced and discursive – between migrant and native women, which exposes both points of connection and empathy, and mechanisms of exclusion and racism. That we have been able to read the narratives produced in different national locations has given us greater purchase in the historical and cultural grounding of these processes.

This brings us to the third element we discuss here: the comparative design of the research. Comparative work illuminates processes specific to certain settings, in addition to those that have a wider resonance. Regarding the specific countries, the choice of Hungary and Bulgaria has made it possible to analyse a spectrum of different paths and patterns of migration. Migration during communism was a political act, irrespective of individual intentions, and a challenge to restrictions on freedom of movement. Within the interview sample, we include a sub-group of women who migrated for political reasons in the past 40 years. Their stories were collected both to document this mobility and to explore connections between the stories of women whose conditions of migration were very diverse, post-1989. Nevertheless, whether the explicit reason given for migration after the changes was love, work, education, or adventure, migration remains tightly bound with the ideas that brought about democratization and commercialization in the former communist block.

Bulgaria and Hungary can be seen as representing two different trajectories of communism. Whilst twentieth century Hungarian history is strongly marked by the events of 1956, in contrast in Bulgaria (a satellite of the Soviet Union), there were not strong anti-Socialist reactions. Today, Hungarian politics continue to be influenced by the 200,000 Hungarians who left after 1956 and formed a huge global diaspora of political migrants. Whilst some Bulgarians also migrated for political reasons during the 1944–89 period, this was not a general trend (Vassileva, 1999: 9) and has not left a similar legacy. Hungarian migrants in Europe nowadays still tend to form networks based on political, economic or intellectual ties, and the interview material evidences activism in preserving the language and traditions of the Hungarian diaspora. In contrast, Bulgarians abroad prefer to be part of informal networks that are not so strongly differentiated by background, education or political affiliations.

One dimension of the choice of these countries was to explore similarities and differences on the question of Europeanness, as viewed through their *central-to-eastern* locations. They offered a good field of observation, being both – at the time of the research – still out of the EU, but in the process of becoming part of it. The question of European belonging is immediately connected to considerations of gender relations. In addition to political independence, claims for equal opportunities for women and men in education were prerequisites for becoming European in Bulgaria; and in Hungary too Europeanness was explicitly equated with some level of gender equality. The history of the twentieth century and especially of the Socialist period brought to both countries similar discourses of women's liberation, equality and competitiveness between Eastern and Western Europe. Long before the end of the Socialist era, Bulgarians regarded Hungary as 'the 'West' of the 'Eastern Europe'[3]. In Bulgaria, women worked and had considerable property rights even in the context of the Ottoman empire. After independence was won, women from wealthier families continued to work: the middle-class family ideal in which women stayed at home was never a significant phenomenon, unlike Hungary.

With regard to the receiving countries, the Netherlands and Italy represent two of the variations within Europe in terms of their histories and politics in relation to migration, which makes their comparison significant. The Netherlands has shifted from being a multicultural society with a long tradition of tolerance, to one that is leading debate on the failure of multiculturalism, and as such opening the way for the acceptance of restrictive policy measures directed at migrants. Italy represents a new receiving country (characteristic of most Southern European countries), in which the category of 'the migrant' is used to redefine Italy's place within Europe from marginal to more central as boundaries of inclusion and exclusion are shifted, from Southern Europe to the East.

The discussion now turns to the research techniques we adopted and some of the issues we grappled with in managing the material and negotiating interpretation. The construction of the sample of migrant women was deliberately open-ended, as we sought to unpack categories of migrants built around singular motivations for migration, e.g. labour or marriage. Nevertheless, we sought to build a sample with internal variation along several dimensions:

marital status; sector of labour market participation; duration of stay (beyond the duration of a tourist visa); date of arrival (to include predominantly but not exclusively post-1989 migrants); age; family status in country of origin; religion; level of education; and location. We did not prioritize 'ethnic minorities' as a category but neither did we exclude it. In practice, too few interview subjects were found to belong to 'minorities' within Bulgaria or Hungary to do any comparative analysis in this respect. Neither did we seek out women who had been subject to forced migration or enslavement. In practice we found very considerable variation in these dimensions *within* women's lives. For instance, legal or illegal as tightly bounded and distinct categories did not make sense in the lives of some women who might pass between the different statuses as they were subject to changes in the law and their job situations.

To gain access to migrant women we used a 'snowball' sampling method. This involved making simultaneous approaches to potential interviewees through different channels, including informal contacts, associations, jobs agencies, and churches. The Bulgarian team established contacts with individuals, networks and organizations that could provide information about the location, occupation and status of migrant women. In practice, some interviews with return-migrants in Bulgaria were decisive for making initial contacts. Following the initial chain of connections, the researcher entered networks of women-migrants ('ex-dancers' in Italy, and workplace-based networks in the Netherlands). The Hungarian team contacted Hungarian embassies, cultural institutes and organizations of the Hungarian diaspora prior to commencing fieldwork, and initial contacts were set up through these organizations. In the Netherlands, the internet homepage of Hungarian immigrants and the mailing list of the Association of Young Hungarians were key sources for contacts: indeed almost all of the contacts came through responses to our call for interviewees advertised in these places. Finally, personal contacts within the sending countries, especially in the case of the return migrants, were also crucial.

All of the interviews were conducted in the first language of the interviewee by a native speaker who was a full member of the project team, and thereby involved in all stages of research design. Nadejda Alexandrova conducted all the interviews with Bulgarian women, and Borbála Juhász conducted the majority of those with Hungarian women; in addition, several interviews were carried out by Judit Gazsi and Andrea Pető. These interviews were semi-structured (by the interviewer) and followed the lines of the interviewee's narrative. We nevertheless sought to explore several themes: the decision to migrate, networks, the journey, employment, experience of legal and other institutions, relationships, customs, and aspirations for the future.

The interviews with native women followed a more structured set of questions: their relationships to migrant women from Eastern Europe; knowledge and images of countries of central andEastern Europe, including travel experiences; and ideas about social and cultural practices of migrants. Again, all of the interviews were conducted in the first language of the interviewee, by a full member of the project team. Enrica Capussotti conducted all the interviews with Italian women, and Esther Vonk conducted all those with Dutch women. The principal criterion for selection of women in this sample was to have been in contact with migrants from the East of Europe. In this way we opened the strictly geographical definition of the migrant sample (from Bulgaria and Hungary) and included in the sample of native women persons who had some connection to migrants from Poland, the Czech Republic, Romania, etc. We sought native women with different *forms of relationship* to migrant women: through employment – contractual or collegial; associative, e.g. in voluntary or other agencies; intimate, i.e. friendship or other close relationships. We also sought to include persons of various ages amongst the interviewees, and we decided to favour multiple locations within the country (urban and rural). Access was gained through informal contacts, suggestions from the migrants interviewed, and associations.

In both sets of interviews, the interviewer and interviewee shared a location within a common 'imagined' national community and were actively involved in the discussion (and construction) of a specific alterity: 'the native women' (Italians and Dutch, Western Europeans); 'the migrant women' (Bulgarians, Hungarians, Eastern Europeans). Although we acknowledge that positions and identifications are more contradictory and flexible than the categories used to conceptualize them, it is important to stress the presence of a common national background which was at the basis of the sample construction, and which shaped the interplay between selves and others within the exchanges. Overall, the project collected 110 interviews with migrant and native women.

**Table 1 Interviews by country** (n equals 110)

|  | In Italy | In the Netherlands | *Total* |
| --- | --- | --- | --- |
| Hungarian | 16+4return | 18+3return | **41** |
| Bulgarian | 15+2return | 17+3return | **37** |
| *Total* | 37 | 41 | **78** |
| Native | 18 | 14 | **32** |

The final part of this methodological discussion raises issues of interpretation and discusses the techniques and processes we put in place in our collaborative work. An important aspect of contemporary oral history is the question of the language, both in the interview and in the analysis of the transcript. All interviews were tape-recorded, transcribed and translated into English. Due to the different languages spoken in the research team, we chose English as the working language (the only language shared by all researchers). These various passages between form and language are relevant. If the transcription is already a transformation of form and meaning – from oral to written even though the transcript is as close as possible to the oral flow – the translation to another language is an additional intervention in the testimony. The texts which then form the data for our analysis are thereby constructed by multiple interventions: first, the construction of the sample itself through networks of different subjects, then the relationship between the interviewer and the interviewee, then the actions of transcribers and translators, and finally the viewpoints of the reader in trying to analyse the accounts. In our work, the researchers who share the same language as the interviewees continued to act as mediators between the different passages to help colleagues understand the resonances of meaning within the interviews. This was especially important as we sought to avoid single country-based analyses; instead we each worked across the corpus of interviews, and in some of the chapters, as joint authors.

The teams' geographical locations in different European spaces – South (Italy), North (Denmark and the Netherlands), Centre (Hungary), Balkans (Bulgaria) – have helped problematize within the group the very nature of geographical mappings and their implicit hierarchies. And the researchers' physical and intellectual movements through these different spatial constructions throughout the project (for meetings, seminars and conferences) have set in motion a deepened awareness of their artificial nature. Our different ways of interpreting the same corpus of material have generated exchanges (sometimes heated) across the particular epistemological assumptions, theoretical positions, and accepted practices of research associated with the different disciplines brought to this work. At the same time, each of our interpretations has been subject to scrutiny from multiple perspectives and locations. We sought to bring together our approaches, and expand our mutual knowledge of them, without reducing them to a single approach and agenda (Bommes and Morawska 2005). This has resulted in different viewpoints being brought to bear on the material analysed and presented in different styles in the chapters of this book.

Although the multiplicity of the methodological approaches in the analysis of the interviews which are interlaced in this book is part of its richness, we do not want to hide that it was sometimes problematic and challenging to combine differences. The first example of this is the dialogue between the opening piece by Braidotti, inspired by French philosophical studies, in particular of Deleuzian ascendancy, and the concluding one by Passerini, informed by the history of emotions, adopting the concept of inter-subjectivity from women's studies. These two essays represent two different lines of feminist studies, which do nevertheless interact fruitfully, converging on the idea of a new relationship between gender and Europe.

Another type of tension is created by the two essays that follow Braidotti's in Part I. Laliotou writes of women's mobility in a cultural perspective informed by a critical use of the category of gender in an essay that deconstructs the traditional conceptions of migration and links movement with new forms of transnational subjectivity. Petersen, in contrast, takes a legal perspective as a starting point to investigate the legal and normative aspects of subjectivity, which in contemporary Europe are linked to citizenship, at times producing what she terms *privileged subjectivity*.

In Part II, a multidisciplinary approach is brought to a series of key concepts. Building our analysis around these themes helped us to break down boundaries between oral history, literary studies, and the study of migration and mobility from social and historical perspectives. We had many discussions of the content of this part of the book and the concepts we settled on reflect the range of our view points. In the chapter on 'home' (Alexandrova and Lyon), the analysis draws out many aspects of the term connected with space and place, signifying the private and the public, the material and the metaphorical, the physical and the symbolic, all of which are linked through mobility and the capacity of the interview subjects to develop new senses of belonging. The analysis of 'love' (Alexandrova) informed by a multi-disciplinary approach, shows it to be a powerful mediator in and for migration, and a privileged site for exploring women's subjectivity. This is also the case for 'communication', in which Nikolchina explores the intercultural meanings of sharing and togetherness in daily conversation and rituals, as well as the stereotypes attached to different countries and peoples in the experience of migration. Other essays start from concepts which are key to certain disciplines, such as sociology and economics in the case of 'work' (Capussotti, Laliotou and Lyon). This chapter exposes the range of meanings subsumed in the term by the migrant women themselves – manual and intellectual, professional and unskilled, as well as informal care in the home – and highlights points of connection in the negotiation of subjectivity in relation to work. The last chapter of this part is concerned with 'food' (Pető), in which identity and otherness are understood on the basis of the type of socialisation made possible by food preparation and its narration.

The methodological choices and their connections in Part III are less complicated to trace. The first three essays create a field of comparison between two countries of arrival, the Netherlands and Italy, in which the native women's accounts are analysed using perspectives from contemporary history, media studies, and cultural sociology, each of which brings different insights to the interview material. The fourth adds a dimension that was present in its theoretical form since the beginning – the legal one – by offering a specific example in present day Europe which is a sort of warning of the possible negative transformations that democratic and tolerant countries such as Denmark can undergo faced with new pressures to respond to intercultural challenges.

Whilst all the writings refer to the corpus of interviews, they do this to different extents; some have more of a narrative form, others are more analytical. The three sets of narrations – what we have called *intermezzi* – that intersperse the three Parts of the book, give full voice to some of the interviewees, thus restoring the priority of individual memory in the study of subjectivity, whilst the Appendices document elements of each interviewee's biography.

## Structure of the Book

The organization of the book is intended to reflect the dynamic between individual and collective both at the level of authors and interviewees. It alternates between groups of chapters written individually or jointly, with *intermezzi* that bring the reader back to the narratives of several interviewees whose lives are particularly significant for the themes treated in the research. The analytic tone of the essay is therefore interspersed with the narrative one of the autobiographical testimony. The latter is constructed through a twofold inter-subjective exchange. The final version is the result of a montage of the oral narrations, together with a 'translation' of experience into writing.

Taking issue from three separate intellectual fields – history, philosophy and legal theory — the chapters included in Part I address the intersection of mobility, subjectivity and gender in contemporary visions of Europe. History, philosophy and legal theory are combined in this first part in order to evidence some of the interdisciplinary practices that formed this research project in its different stages of planning, interviewing, researching, analysing and elaborating the outcomes of the analysis. In addition, through the deliberate combination of these three fields we want to stress the multiplicity of the intellectual practices and traditions that are actively engaged in – as well as formed by – the process of imaging alternative forms of Europeaness.

In the first chapter, 'On Becoming Europeans' Rosi Braidotti emphasizes Europe's progressive potential. Against the grain of the simultaneous but contradictory celebration of transnational spaces on the one hand, and the resurgence of hyper-nationalisms at the micro-level on the other, Braidotti defends a process of the Deleuzean 'becoming-minoritarian'; in other words, of Europe as a way of both bypassing the global-local binary and of destabilizing the established definitions of European identity. Resting firmly on the belief in a post-Eurocentric vision of the European Union, she follows a philosophical orientation that is based on the practice of philosophy as the art of connection-making. Her aim in this chapter is to draw out a number of theoretical connections between different elements and themes which are discussed elsewhere in this book, such as the interrelation between identities, subject positions and affectivity or love relationships on the one hand, and issues of citizenship on the other. The conclusion of this argumentation, which is at once philosophical and political, is that the European Union as a progressive project means a site of possible political resistance against nationalism, xenophobia and racism – bad habits that are endemic to the old imperial Europe. It therefore follows that the question of the European Union no longer coincides with European identity, but rather constitutes a rupture from it and a transformation.

In Chapter 2, which is concerned with mobility and subjectivity in the European context, Ioanna Laliotou analyses practices of transnational migration as part of a wider phenomenon of mobility that includes physical, cultural, political, subjective and conceptual forms of movement. This analysis seeks to foreground mobility as a historical and theoretical concept that enables complex understandings of the interrelation between migrancy and subjectivity in contemporary history. The women migrants interviewed for this research were driven by a variety of factors, including the need for better material and professional resources, political and existential dissidence, personal and intimate relationships, love, curiosity, and desire. Their histories indicate that after their migration they were often implicated in life arrangements and conditions that exceeded or altered the plans, desires and strategies they had formulated prior to moving. Taking the interviewees' vacillation between distancing themselves from and associating with the position of the migrant as a historical and theoretical starting point, the chapter traces the implications of these migrant testimonies for the ways in which we understand the contemporary history of mobility. To that end, the author analyses the ways in which the interviewees envision mobility as a constitutive element of their subjective histories and circumstances *vis-à-vis* the contemporary theoretical constellation of notions of mobility, space, normativity, and affective relationships.

Hanne Petersen, in Chapter 3, addresses transformations of legal subjectivity in Europe tracing the changing ways in which legal theory conceives of subjecthood. European legal culture, she argues, is undergoing change as a result of the combination of geo-political developments in the European Union with processes of globalization. This is marked also by a shift from normative jurisprudence to cultural pluralism in contemporary legal studies. If European migration and mobility give rise to different and overlapping kinds of legal subjectivity, in practice what may emerge is a regime of special rights, general rights and different advantages. Petersen argues that a European legal culture has to deal with multiple selves in complex legal contexts and has to face an emerging regime of privilege which is no longer based in laws but rather in the market. Seen in this context, national immigration law and national marriage law in Europe today appear to legitimize certain forms of exclusion, and secure differentiated legal statuses, which exist in interaction with market law and market-based special rights and privileges.

The passage from the first to the second part of the book is punctuated by the first *intermezzo* comprised of two narrations from the migrant women interviewed, one by the Bulgarian woman, Jelisaveta, and the other by the Hungarian woman, Piroska. Jelisaveta tells the story of her experience in Italy, where she arrived in 1993 as a cabaret dancer, later married an Italian, and is now a professional bridge player. Piroska arrived in the Netherlands in 1990, and after many jobs now works as a kindergarten teacher in Amsterdam, and lives in Rotterdam with her second husband.

The collection of chapters in the second part of the book is primarily constructed around different and interconnecting dimensions of identification in the lives of migrant women. These chapters discuss the ways in which the migrant women create meaning in their lives and negotiate the categories in which they are positioned or through which they are called to account for themselves in everyday life. The themes we have selected for analysis emerged both from our *a priori* interests, and from what turned out to be significant in the women's interview accounts. Ideas about belonging is a theme which implicitly or explicitly underpinned much of the research, and is something which is echoed in several chapters – those on border-places and home, communication, and food, in particular. The centrality of relationships in the women's accounts is something that we highlight in the chapters on love, to some extent on work, and again on communication. There are doubtless other topics that we might have made the subject of a chapter here and our specific choices make no claim to comprehensiveness. What they achieve, we think, is to shed light on the ways in which women are moving into and within their new social worlds, through the parallel and complementary perspectives and styles of questioning we brought to the set of interviews.

In Chapter 4 Nadejda Alexandrova and Dawn Lyon discuss the first impressions of the migrant interviewees in the host country, and their memories of border-places such as customs offices, airports, and train stations. Crossing the boundary between home and elsewhere is regarded as a critical moment in the perception of the women as migrants, by themselves and others. The chapter explores liminal space, the 'in-between the designations of identity', and considers the extent to which migrant women create new, perhaps transnational, spaces of belonging, as well as how they sustain former affiliations.

Miglena Nikolchina – in Chapter 5 – analyses the role of communication in the narratives of women migrants. She demonstrates that, partly as a reaction to the painful history of isolation during communism, and partly as a reflection of the dynamics of contemporary life, communication emerges in many of the interviews as a central element of happiness. What she calls the 'turbulence of talk', i.e. filling one's time with people through spontaneous social interaction, is for the interviewees equalled to 'having a life'.

In Chapter 6, Enrica Capussotti, Ioanna Laliotou and Dawn Lyon take on a different element of everyday life: the extent to which migrant women construct their subjectivity in relation to work. The authors focus on the place of work in the contemporary forms of subjectivity that come about through processes of mobility and migration. They analyse the relations in which some women refuse non-professional work, whilst others accept low-status employment. Allied to this, they discuss the themes of dignity and discrimination as they emerge in the interviews, and the issue of the relationship between work and family life.

In Chapter 7, Nadejda Alexandrova explores another central theme, the role of love in the migrant women's accounts. The first part of her analysis describes classifications of literary motifs and plots which are echoed in the interviews and used for the justification of the decision to leave one's country and family, and to live with a partner from a foreign country. The second part of the chapter builds on this, exploring how romantic love becomes a source for 'legitimate' explanations of the migrant women's actions and moves. The third part of the analysis deals with the question of how identification with, or denial of, a romantic narrative can account for the migrants' sense of autonomy, for their capacity for decision-making, and for their own strategies of integration in a new society.

In Chapter 8, the final chapter in this part of the book, Andrea Pető discusses the constitutive and constructive functions of 'food-talk' in the interviews. Speaking about food is a marker of identity and a frame of narrating difference and belonging in the interviews. Analysing both the accounts of migrant and native women sheds light on the processes involved in the negotiation of identity between different food traditions and food systems in a context of migration.

As a bridge to Part III of the book, we have located our second *intermezzo* at this point, a piece which intertwines the voices of the Dutch woman Barbara and the Italian woman Angela. Barbara is a worker in the Jewish Social Service, and has the specific and relevant experience of being married to a Bulgarian; Angela, who now lives in Florence, has had her own migration experience, first following her father and then her husband, both officers in the army.

The interviews of the Dutch and Italian women are at the heart of Part III of the book. They are analysed through mapping out the circulation of images, discursive representations and practices in relation to migrant women in public and private. An analysis of Danish legislation dealing with cross-border relationships concludes this part of the book. Overall, it is here that we evidence and discuss the cultural repertoires and practices (from the legal to the everyday) present in three western EU countries regarding immigration in general and Eastern European women in particular. Esther Vonk, Enrica Capussotti and Dawn Lyon deal with the exchanges between two women with the same national background (interviewer and interviewee) who dialogically define the interviewee's relations with Bulgarian and Hungarian women amongst others; Inger Marie Conradsen and Annette Kronborg discuss the multiple influences of immigration law (public law) on family law (private law) arising from attempts by the state (or EU) to regulate immigration and cross-border relationships.

In Chapter 9, Vonk focuses on the interconnection between the discursive representations of Bulgarian and Hungarian women migrants in the interviews with Dutch women, and the current public debate on the 'integration of minorities' in the Netherlands. Her main interest lies in questioning if and how the interviewees reproduce, resist, or contest the political discourse on the 'failure of multiculturalism' that is dominated by exclusionary and racist perspectives. Oppositions between national and non-national, 'real' and 'fake', integration and non-integration connote the debate that occurs with the shift toward the closure of Dutch borders and the stigmatization of difference. If the interviewees echo these dominant paradigms to different degrees (e.g. evoking the distinction between 'real' and 'fake' marriages as ways to enter the country), both their testimonies and the public discourse suggest two main differences in comparison with Italy's public and political spheres. First, the centrality of the welfare state as a battleground for the struggle between inclusion and exclusion (to be a 'national' and to be a 'real' refugee is the precondition for state assistance). This concern seems less central in Italy due to the structural limitations and inefficiency of the welfare system. Secondly, the persistence of a grammar of 'multiculturalism' that is absent or weak in the Italian public discourse dealing with intercultural relations.

In Chapter 10, Capussotti evidences the Italian interviewees' difficulty in narrating their relations with women from the European East. In the Italian political and public spheres, lack of knowledge, repression and inadequacy of a collectively elaborated discourse are combined with the forced exclusion of immigrants' voices and self-representations. Instead, established stereotypes and prejudices offer resources to give images and forms to the relation with 'others': modernity opposed to backwardness, emancipation to traditional femininity, richness to poverty, sign the divide between Italian and Eastern European women. Capussotti interprets the use of these binary oppositions as Italian women's renegotiation of their position within contemporary transnational processes: women migrants are exploited for the self-representation of Italian women to finally become modern, emancipated and fully Western.

Similar discursive mechanisms shape both Dutch and Italian interviewees' relations to 'Eastern European women'. First, we see in both sets of interviews the notion of the 'exceptional' individual that allows for a positive evaluation of a single woman (usually a friend or an employee) in opposition to the rest of the national group. Secondly, we observe the centrality of gender and gender roles in native women's approaches to and opinions about migrant women – in relation to whom they position themselves as more emancipated – which confirms the centrality of gender in these discourses of 'others'. Thirdly, we note the importance of the nation, in articulation with transnational and global processes, as a basis for claims to belonging.

Lyon's comparative analysis of Italian and Dutch interviews in Chapter 11 further explores similarities and differences in the two sets of narratives, and relates these to the available cultural repertoires of the different settings. Using the concept of boundary-work, she analyses the place of moral and cultural boundaries in narrative constructions of self and other. The analysis disentangles different components of exclusion and racism on the one hand, and grounds for inclusion and solidarity on the other. Whereas employers tend to emphasize moral boundaries in their representations of migrant women, friends more often refer to cultural as well as moral boundaries as a basis for inclusion. The Dutch women voice moral boundaries less strongly than the Italians, and they emphasize cultural boundaries slightly more than moral ones. Furthermore, whereas the Dutch women talk about migration in terms of enrichment, openness, and universality, this vocabulary is absent in Italian testimonies.

Part III closes with an analysis of the Danish legislation concerning cross-border heterosexual relationships and marriage. Danish legislation to control immigration and cross-border relationships is a particularly interesting legal case study, both in relation to specific measures in Italy and the Netherlands, and as indicative of trends at the EU level. Conradsen and Kronborg discuss the growing importance of immigration law over other sectors traditionally identified with family and private law. The Danish conservative government's concern to limit immigration has focused on family reunification as one of the major channels of access to the country; inevitably the legislative effort entered the realm of public and private law transforming their traditional subjects and sphere of interests, and shifting family law into immigration law. Translating the moral panic constructed in Northern European countries around the figures of 'real/fake' refugees, in Denmark, State bio-power is articulated around the divide 'real/fake' marriage, in which love is opposed to instrumental marriage.

Between this collection of chapters and the concluding contribution to the book, the story of Edith appears as the third *intermezzo*. Bruck is a Hungarian woman who represents a sort of memory of 'old' forms of migration: she was the daughter of a very poor orthodox Jewish family deported to Auschwitz. From there, she was taken to Bergen Belsen, then in 1945 she went to Czechoslovakia, and later, in 1948, to Israel. She then made her home in Rome in 1954, where she became a successful published writer.

In the final and concluding chapter, Luisa Passerini opens discussion of a possible future configuration of European women's intersubjectivity. While any subjective formation found today – including those documented by the interviews in the present research – combines old and new forms of subjectivity, from ethnocentrism to interculturalism, this chapter tries to disentangle the new forms from the old. The new, promising ways of being European women point to multiplicity, openness and mutual collaboration, without forgetting the past experiences of women who felt European, such as those who created the group 'Femmes pour l'Europe' in the 1970s. At the same time, the stress put by many of the migrant interviewees on their belonging to 'Central' Europe as well as their insistence on the role of emotions within the process of mobility, contribute to the processes that de- and reterritorialize Europe. The testimonies of native women include both some uncertainty in defining Europeanness, and in some cases the capacity to enlarge their vision of Europe thanks to encounters with women from other parts of the continent. While no immediate optimism can ignore the elements of nationalism and Eurocentrism present in all the interviews – which often function to establish solidarity among European women through contrasting them with women from other continents (American) and/or other cultures (African, Islamic) – the research has nevertheless found in the interviews many elements that testify to the possibility of new ways of being European women, and new forms of belonging to Europe.

## Notes

1. We use the term 'native' to refer to those women selected for interview on the basis of their lifelong Italian or Dutch citizenship. We recognize that the term is problematic as it implies an essentialist belonging to nation, and thereby a strict distinction between native and non-native. However we intend it simply as a shorthand to distinguish between our different interviewee groupings. Amongst the repertoire of alternatives, e.g., host or receiving, we found nothing satisfactory.
2. The digital archive is accessible through the website of the European University Institute, which was the co-ordinating institution of the research. See: http://www.iue.it/RSCAS/Research/GRINE/.
3. However, in the 1980s the messianic theories about Bulgaria as 'the cradle of civilization', 'the land of the Thracians' were very widespread.

## References

Bade, K.J. 1987. *Population, Labor and Migration in 19th Century and 20th Century Germany*, New York, St. Martin's Press.

Bommes, M. and E. Morawska (eds.) 2005. *International Migration Research, Constructions, Omissions and the Promises of Interdisciplinarity*, Aldershot, Ashgate.

Hoerder, D. 1990. 'Migration and the International Labor Markets' in J. Puskas (ed.) *Overseas Migration from East-Central and Southeastern Europe, 1880–1940*, Budapest, Akademiai Kiado.

Koser, K. and H. Lutz (eds.) 1998. *The New Migration in Europe. Social Constructions and Social Realities*, London, Macmillan.

Kussmaul, A. 1981. *Servants in Husbandry in Early Modern England*, Cambridge, Cambridge University Press.

Lowe, W. 1989. *The Irish in Mid-Victorian Lancashire: The Shaping of a Working-Class Community*, New York, Peter Lang.

Moch, L.P. and L. Tilly 1984. 'Joining the Urban World: Occupation, Family, and Migration in Three French Cities', *Comparative Studies in Society and History* (27): 33–56.

Ong, A. 1999. *Flexible Citizenship. The Cultural Logics of Transnationality*, Durham and London, Duke University Press.

Parrenas, R.S. 2001. *Servants of Globalization. Women, Migration and Domestic Work*, Stanford, University of Stanford Press.

Phizacklea, A. 2003. 'Gendered Actors in Migration' in Andall J., (ed.) *Gender and Ethnicity in Contemporary Europe*, Oxford, Berg.

Sassen, S. 2000. 'Counter-Geographies of Globalization: the Feminization of survival', *Journal of International Affairs* 53, (2): 503–24.

Vassileva, B. 1999. *Bulgarian Political Emigration Since WWII*, Sofia, Sofia University Press.

Wlocevski, S. 1934. *L'Installation des Italiens en France*, Paris.

# Part I

## Subjectivity, Mobility and Gender in Europe

*Chapter 1*

# On Becoming Europeans

*Rosi Braidotti*

The notion of a 'new' European identity as a multicultural social space within the framework of the European Union (EU) is controversial to say the least, especially in the current political context of increasing Euroscepticism. The EU is positioned simultaneously as a major player within the global economy and as an alternative social space. In other words, the EU can be seen as perpetuating the theme of Europe, appointing itself as a centre which universalizes its own 'civilization'. However, it also constitutes a solid social democratic and hence progressive project, which not only counteracts the aggressive neo-liberalism of the U.S.A. on a number of key issues (privacy; telecommunication; genetically modified food and the environment), but also values human rights and world peace.

In this chapter I will emphasize the progressive potential of the EU. This project entails the re-definition not only of the interrelation of the member states, but also of the power-relations within them. This process of revision of identity triggers contradictory reactions. Not the least contradictory is the simultaneous celebration of trans-national spaces on the one hand, and the resurgence of hyper-nationalisms at the micro-level on the other. The global city and Fortress Europe stand both face-to-face and as two sides of the same coin (Sassen 1995). In relation to this, I want to defend a process of the 'becoming-minoritarian' of Europe (Deleuze and Guattari 1980) as a way of both bypassing the binary global–local and of destabilizing the established definitions of European identity. My position rests on the assumption of the decline of Eurocentrism as a historical event, and that this represents a qualitative shift of perspective in our collective sense of identity. Several political movements today, ranging from the Green Party to the European Social Forum, give top priority to a post-Eurocentric vision of the European Union. Some progressive thinkers, including the feminist scholars in this book, are also critiquing nationalism as a necessary step towards the construction of a new European citizenship.

My aim in this chapter is to draw out a number of theoretical connections between different elements and themes which are discussed elsewhere in this book, such as the interrelation between identities, subject positions and affectivity or love relationships on the one hand, and issues of citizenship on the other. My orientation is philosophical and I practice philosophy as the art of connection making. I follow both Foucault's redefinition of the philosopher as a technician of practical knowledge, and the feminist commitment to produce relevant knowledge claims that reflect the lived experience of women and of other marginal subjects. This philosophical practice is enacted through cartographic analyses of specific problem areas. My contribution, both in this chapter and in this project as a whole, focuses on the cluster: gender/subjectivity/Europe. The approach is meta-methodological, rather than meta-discursive. As a materialist cartographic practice, poststructuralist philosophy is well suited to the task of mapping out complex interactions among many structures, subjects and relations. I see it fundamentally as a critique of power, understood both in the negative sense of constraints (*potestas*) and in the positive sense of empowerment and the production of discursive practice (*potentia*). By stressing these interrelated elements, I hope to take forward the discussion on the progressive and critical possibilities of the 'new' Europe.

It is also the case that continental philosophy – prior to and including poststructuralism – is historically connected to the issue of European identity and 'civilization'. Since the end of the nineteenth century and the early decades of the twentieth century, the 'crisis' of European philosophy has both reflected and highlighted larger socio-political issues linked to the geopolitical status of Europe and to the growing sense of crisis about European identity. Nietzsche and Freud, then Husserl and Fanon, and later Adorno and the Frankfurt school are evidence of this trend. According to the poststructuralist generation – Foucault, Deleuze, Derrida and Irigaray – the crisis of philosophical humanism coincides historically with the decline of Europe as an imperial world-power, especially after the Second World War. Nowadays, wise old men like Habermas and Derrida and progressive spirits like Balibar have taken the lead in the public debate by stressing the advantages of a post-nationalist sense of the European Union.

In so far as Continental philosophy carries an in-built question about European identity, philosophical self-reflexivity – which in my case takes the form of a materialist cartography – has a unique contribution to make to the debate on Europe. It can help to de-segregate intellectual debates which tend to stay confined within set discursive communities. Philosophical reflection assesses and often resets theoretical lines of demarcation and thus it can produce discursive interconnections along areas or questions of common concern.

My argument is about the 'becoming-minor' of Europe, in the sense of a post-nationalist European space. This project rests on two sets of arguments: one political, the other historical. Politically, on the Continent, the opposition to the European Union is led by the authoritarian Right, which is nationalist and xenophobic. As Stuart Hall (1987; 1990) put it, the great resistance against the European Union, as well as the American suspicion of it, is a defensive response to a process that aims at overcoming the idea of European nation-states. The short-range effect of this process is a nationalist wave of paranoia and xenophobic fears, which is simultaneously anti-European and racist. I have argued that late postmodernity (Braidotti 2002a) functions through the paradox of simultaneous globalization and fragmentation. It is as if the law of the 'excluded middle' did not hold, and one thing and its opposite can simultaneously be the case (Appadurai 1994: 324–39). Thus, the expansion of European boundaries coincides with the resurgence of micro-nationalist borders at all levels in Europe today. Unification coexists with the closing down of borders; the common European citizenship and the common currency co-exist with increasing internal fragmentation and regionalism; a new, allegedly post-nationalist, identity coexists with the return of xenophobia, racism and anti-Semitism (Benhabib 1999). The disintegration of the Soviet empire marks simultaneously the triumph of the advanced market economy and the return of tribal ethnic wars of the most archaic kind. Globalization means both homogenization and extreme power differences (Eisenstein 1999).

Strong opposition to the EU is also voiced, however, by the nostalgic Left, which seems to miss the topological foundations for international working class solidarity. The cosmopolitan tradition of socialism militates against the European dimension: solidarity with the third world always carries a politically-correct consensus, whereas an interest in European matters is often dismissed as being vain and self-obsessive. Speaking as a left-wing feminist intellectual, I must say that the Left has often been unable to react with energy and vision to the historical evidence of the dislocation of European supremacy and the coming of the American empire (Hardt and Negri 2000). The Left has also been slow to understand the non-dialectical and schizophrenic nature of advanced capitalism (Deleuze and Guattari 1972; 1980). In this light, the feminist, pacifist and anti-racist movements can be of great inspiration in drawing more lucid and relevant political cartographies of contemporary power relations.

Historically, the project of the European Union originates in the defeat of fascism and Nazism after World War II. The moral and political bankruptcy of European 'civilization' was exemplified by the holocaust perpetuated against the Jewish, and Roma populations, as well as the persecution of homosexuals and communists by the Nazi and fascist regimes. The life and work of one of the initiators of the project of European federation – Altiero

Spinelli (Spinelli 1988; 1992) – testifies to this, as does his wife Ursula Hirschmann (Spinelli 1979; Hirschmann 1993), and Ursula's brother Albert Hirschman (Hirschman 1945; 1994). The project of the EU is consequently grounded in anti-fascism, anti-nationalism and anti-militarism (Spinelli and Rossi 1998). It was imposed on the European nation-states as a punishment for two Franco-German wars that spilled over into global wars. In the context of the Cold War, the new European community, as a showcase of Western superiority, also played the role of streamlining the reconstruction of Europe's war-torn economy.

The two branches of my argument – the political and the historical – converge upon a single conclusion: that the European Union as a progressive project means a site of possible political resistance against nationalism, xenophobia and racism, bad habits that are endemic to the old imperial Europe. It follows therefore that the question of the European Union no longer coincides with European identity, but rather constitutes a rupture from it and a transformation. The scholarship reflects this double-track: there is far more work on European identity, as such, than on the European Union. Feminists are especially notable for their absence from discussions on the post-nationalist project of the EU, and are prone to facile anti-Europeanism.

This view of Europe as a post-nationalist project is very attuned to feminist critiques of power. Europe as a world-power has practiced a form of universalism that has implied the exclusion or consumption of others. In a poststructuralist frame of reference, these constitutive 'others' are the specular complements of the subject of modernity. They are the woman; the ethnic or racialized other; and the natural environment, including animals, plants and forests. They constitute, respectively, the second sex or sexual complement of Man; the coloured, racialized or marked other that allows the Europeans to universalize their whiteness as the defining trait of humanity; and the naturalized environment against which technology is pitched and developed. These 'others' are of crucial importance to the constitution of the identity of the Same: they are structurally connected to it – albeit by negation. One cannot move without the other, therefore the redefinition of European identity intrinsically poses the question of the social and discursive status of 'difference', both in the sense of sexual difference and that of ethnic diversity.

The project of European unification involves a process of consciousness-raising, which in turn expresses a critique of the self-appointed missionary role of Europe as the alleged centre of the world. In an argument that runs parallel to feminist theory, this vision of Europe promotes a re-grounding of this pretentious and false universalism into a more situated, local perspective. As the work of feminist philosophers like Genevieve Lloyd (1985) has pointed out, universalistic claims are actually highly particular and partial. Feminist epistemologists, especially Sandra Harding (1991) and Donna Haraway (1990a), have produced some of the most significant critiques of the false universalism of the European subject of knowledge. They have also offered powerful alternative accounts of both subjectivity and of an enlarged sense of scientific objectivity. This process of epistemological revision runs parallel to new theorizations of the Subject. While it does not always result in such theorizations, it does however amount to a revision of the ethnocentrism implicit in a universalistic posture which positions Europe as the centre of the knowing subject: science as the white man's burden (Harding 1993). Such a dislocation of pseudo-scientific assertions of white superiority amounts to a re-grounding of Europe, no longer as the centre, but as one of the many peripheries in the world today. This process of consciousness-raising is a sober awakening to the concrete particularity of the European situation.

## The Politics of Location as Method and as Strategy

The politics of location is the method and the strategy which was developed (Rich 1987) and later theorized by feminists to account for consciousness-raising. It is also a way of making sense of diversity among women, understood as the binary opposites of the phallogocentric subject. This practice is coupled with that of epistemological and political accountability which is understood as the practice that consists of unveiling the power locations which one inevitably inhabits as the site of one's identity. The practice of accountability (for one's embodied and embedded locations) as a relational, collective activity of undoing power differentials is linked to two crucial notions: memory and narratives. They activate the process of putting into words, that is to say bringing into symbolic representation, that which escapes consciousness. In relation to migrant women themselves, the emphasis on remembering and narrating is central to the methodology of this project. Through all the chapters we see how these stories provide evidence of the plurality, ambivalence and contradictions of the subject. And through these analyses, we can see the richness and the complexity of these processes.

A 'location' in fact, is not a self-appointed and self-designed subject-position. It is a collectively shared and constructed, jointly occupied, spatio-temporal, territory. Because it is so familiar, it escapes self-scrutiny. The 'politics of location' consequently supports the process of consciousness-raising and results in a political awakening (Grewal and Kaplan 1994). 'Politics of locations' are cartographies of power which rest on a form of self-criticism, arrived at through a critical, genealogical self-narrative; they are relational and outside-directed. These 'embodied' accounts illuminate and transform our knowledge of ourselves and of the world. Thus, black women's texts and experiences make white women see the limitations of our locations, truths and discourses. Feminist knowledge is an inter-active and self-reflexive process that relies on networks of exchanges. It brings out aspects of our existence, especially our own involvement with power that we had not noticed before (Mohanty 1992).

'Figurations' of alternative feminist subjectivity[1] differ from classical 'metaphors' precisely in calling into play a sense of accountability for one's locations. They express materially-embedded cartographies and as such are self-reflexive and not parasitic upon a process of metaphorization of 'others'. The figurations that emerge from this process act as the spot-light that illuminates aspects of one's practice which were blind spots before. By extension, a new figuration of the subject functions like conceptual *personae*. As such, it is no metaphor, but acts rather as a cognitive map, i.e., it is a materially embedded and embodied account of one's power-relations. On the creative level, it expresses the rate of change, transformation or affirmative deconstruction of the power one inhabits. 'Figuration' materially embodies the stages of a metamorphosis of a subject position, which veers towards all that the phallogocentric system does not want it to become (Braidotti 2002a).

A range of new, alternative subjectivities have indeed emerged in the shifting landscapes of postmodernity. They contribute to the creation of a new social imaginary to replace established representations of women. They are contested, multi-layered and internally contradictory subject-positions, all of which does not make them any less ridden with power-relations. They are hybrid and in-between social categories for whom traditional descriptions in terms of sociological categories such as 'marginals', 'migrants', or 'minorities' are, as Saskia Sassen (1995) suggests, grossly inadequate. From the angle of 'different constitutive others' this inflationary production of different differences simultaneously expresses the logic of capitalist proliferation and exploitation, but also the emerging subjectivities of positive and self-defined others. It all depends on one's locations or situated perspectives. Far from seeing this as a form of relativism, I see it as an embedded and embodied form of enfleshed materialism. It is important to resist the uncritical reproduction of Sameness on a molecular, global or planetary scale by approaching differences in a non-dialectical and multi-layered framework which stresses their subversive potential.

The work on power, difference and the politics of location offered by postcolonial and anti-racist feminist thinkers[2] who are familiar with the European situation helps us to illuminate the paradoxes of the present. One of the most significant effects of late postmodernity in Europe is the phenomenon of trans-culturality in a pluri-ethnic or multi-cultural European social space. World-migration – a huge movement of population from periphery to centre, working on a world-wide scale of 'scattered hegemonies' (Grewal and Kaplan 1994) – has challenged the claim to an alleged cultural homogeneity of European nation-states and of the incipient European Union. Present-day Europe is struggling with multi-culturalism at a time of increasing racism and xenophobia. The paradoxes, power-dissymetries and fragmentations of the present historical context require that we shift the political debates from the issue of differences between cultures, to differences within the same culture. These are the shifting grounds on which periphery and centre confront each other, with a new level of complexity that defies dualistic or oppositional thinking. In this book, our research on the internal European migrations show what this approach can mean for Europe and European women.

Feminist theory argues that if it is the case that a socio-cultural mutation is taking place in the direction of a multi-ethnic, multi-media society, then the transformation cannot affect only the pole of 'the others'; it must equally dislocate the position and the prerogative of 'the same', the former centre. In other words, what is changing is not merely the terminology or metaphorical representation of the subjects, but the very structure of subjectivity, the social relations, and the social imaginary that support it. Again, the research presented within this project gives some indications in this direction. It is the syntax of social relations, as well as their symbolic representation, that is in upheaval. The customary standard-bearers of Euro-centric phallocentrism no longer hold in a civil society that is, amongst others, sexed female and male, multi-cultural and not inevitably Christian. More than ever, the question of social transformation begs that of representation: what can the male, white, Christian monotheistic symbolic do for emerging subjects-in-process? The challenges, as well as the anxieties evoked by them, mark patterns of becoming that require new forms of expression and representation, that is to say socially mediated forms which need to be assessed critically. Feminist theory is a very relevant and useful navigational tool in these stormy times of locally enacted, global phenomena, i.e. 'G-local' changes.[3]

The point of the matter is that we live in a world which is organized along multiple axes of mobility, circulation, flows of people and commodities (Cresswell 1997). Displacement is a central feature of the postmodern era, as critics like Probyn (1990) have also pointed out. Moreover, as Ernesto Laclau (1995) has argued, the point is that processes of hybridization and nomadic identities are neither marginal, nor self-chosen phenomena. It is rather the case, as Dahrendorf (1990) has argued, that advanced capitalism itself functions by organizing constant flows and displacements, in such a way as to erode its own foundations. The crisis of the nation state in the age of transnational capital flow is a significant example of this (Mouffe 1994); and contemporary technologies are accelerating this trend (Castells 1996).

Let me, however, make one point perfectly clear: I would never want to argue that rootlessness and homelessness, or constant mobility and displacement are universal features, although they have taken place, to different extents, in all periods of history. On the contrary, I do take shifts, mutations and processes of change as key features of the particular historical period we are going through. Precisely because of this, social critics need to be very situated in their approach to any analysis of the new subject-positions which have become available in post-industrial times – as we have sought to do here in the analyses of the subjectivities of the migrant women interviewed. The differences in degrees, types, kinds and modes of mobility and – even more significantly – of non-mobility need to be mapped out with precision and sensitivity. This cartographic accuracy is made necessary by the fact that non-unitary subject positions, hybrids, nomads and cyborgs are key elements of our historicity. They function as generic terms for the indexation of different degrees of access and entitlement to subject positions in the historical era of postmodernity. They situate subjects in one of the many poly-located centres which weave together the global economy. Power is the key-issue, and mobility is a term that indexes access to it. As such, power relations are internally contradictory and they require suitable politically-invested cartographies that account for them.

James Clifford (1994), who is more sympathetic to metaphors of travel and displacement than to nomadism, makes careful distinctions between different kinds of travel from the colonial exploration or bourgeois 'tour', to the itineraries of immigrant or indentured labourers. These differences need to be accounted for in such a way as to make the power differences explicit. These accounts are narratives of the diaspora, which, at the end of this millennium concern most communities, though in different degrees. The different narratives, however, have to be embedded in specific histories and geographies, thus preventing hasty metaphorizations. This goal echoes the aims of the feminist cartographic and materialist philosophies of the subject which I am defending. It is a way of avoiding universalistic generalizations and grounding critical practice so as to make it accountable. At both the micro and the macro-levels of the constitution of subjectivity, we need more complexities both in terms of genders and across ethnicities, class and age. This is the social agenda that needs to be addressed in the framework of the new European Union.

I want to propose therefore an alliance between two parallel but distinct projects and lines of argumentation, which also correspond to different forms of consciousness. They are, on the one hand, the deconstruction of the unitary idea of Europe as the 'cradle' of civilization – with its corollary implications of liberal individualism and universalism; on the other, the deconstruction of the unitary idea of gendered identities, fixed in the essentialist opposition masculine/feminine. In the same way that feminist theories after poststructuralism promote a split, multiple, hybrid, diasporic and nomadic vision of the subject-in-process, I see the new European Union as a framework for the transformation of Europe in the sense of our becoming-minoritarian.

This dual deconstructive strategy keeps the two axes of gendered and European subjectivities parallel but quite distinct and perhaps even a-symmetrical to each other. I think such distinctions are important because feminism and European consciousness are grounded in different political movements: the former in the many world-historical women's movements, the latter in the progressive potential of the project of European unification. Distinctions between these two parallel lines are important also on another score: these two discourses – gender and Europe – are separate at the institutional level and they suffer from an excessive segregation of discursive competences. European discussions on citizenship and feminist debates do not intersect easily and they seldom cross-reference each other. As a result, EU discussions on the social role of women hardly draw on the rather impressive amount of research compiled by feminists over the last twenty years on the question of alternative forms of political subjectivity. A new alliance is therefore needed between, on the one hand, a post-nationalist vision of European subjectivity based on the critique of Eurocentrism and, on the other, the multiple visions of the subject-as-process which stem from the rejection of feminine essentialism within feminism. This is an attempt to come to terms with the paradoxes and internal contradictions of our own historical predicament as 'post-Europe Europeans', just as gender theory has had to deal with the fragments, the deconstruction and re-construction of the 'post-Woman women' in the feminist processes of transformation (Braidotti 1994; 2002a).

## Re-grounding Europe

The European Union project has to do with the sobering experience of taking stock of our specific location and, following the feminist politics of location, adopting embedded and embodied perspectives. This is the opposite of the grandiose and aggressive universalism of the past: it is a situated and accountable perspective. It is about turning our collective memory to the service of a new political and ethical project, which is forward-looking and not nostalgic. Daniel Cohn-Bendit recently stated that if we want to make this European business work, we really must start from the assumption that Europe is the specific periphery where we live and that we must take responsibility for it. Imagining anything else would be a repetition of that flight into abstraction for which our culture is (in)famous: at best, it may procure us the benefits of escapism; at worst, the luxury of guilt. We have to start from where we are. This is a plea for lucidity and for accountability. We need both political strategies and imaginary figurations that are adequate to our historicity.

This is, however, only one side of the paradoxical coin of European deconstruction in the age of the European Union. The other side, simultaneously true and yet absolutely contradictory, is the danger of recreating a sovereign centre through the new European federation. That the two are simultaneously the case makes European identity into one of the most contested areas of political and social philosophy in our world at the moment. This reactive tendency towards a sovereign sense of the Union is also known as the 'Fortress Europe' syndrome, and has been extensively criticized by feminists and antiracists. They warn us against the danger of replacing the former Eurocentrism with a new 'Europism' (Essed 1991), i.e. the belief in an ethnically pure Europe. The question of ethnic purity is crucial and it is, of course, the germ of Eurofascism.

One concrete way to apply the feminist politics of location to the political analysis of gender relations in the new Europe is by singling out the issue of whiteness. Let me explain. For people who inherit the European region, 'the post'-condition translates concretely into the end of the myth of cultural homogeneity. As Michael Walzer (1992) has argued, this is the foundational political myth in Europe, as much as multiculturalism is the central myth in the United States. Of course, European history at any point in time provides ample evidence to the contrary: waves of migrations from the East and the South make a mockery of any claim to ethnic or cultural homogeneity in Europe, while the persistent presence of Jewish and Muslim citizens challenges the identification of Europe with Christianity. Nonetheless, the myth of cultural homogeneity is crucial to the tale of European nationalism.

In our era, these myths are being exposed and exploded into questions related to entitlement and agency. Thus, the European Union is faced with the issue: can one be European and Black or Muslim? Paul Gilroy's work on being a Black British subjectivity (1987) is indicative of the problem of how European citizenship and blackness emerge as contested is-sues. However, I want to argue that whiteness is also called into play. One of the radical implications of the project of the European Union is the possibility of giving a specific location, and conse-quently historical embeddedness or memory, to anti-racist whites. It can, finally, racialize our location, which is quite a feat because until recently in Europe, only white supremacists, naziskins and other fascists actually had a theory about the qualities that are inherent to white people. Like all fascists, all these groups are biological and cultural essentialists. Apart from this, whiteness was, quite simply, invisible, just not seen, at least, not by whites. It took the work of black writers and thinkers to expose whiteness as a political issue. Located in the lily-white purity of our universalistic fantasy, disembodied and disembedded, we actually thought we had no colour. Then Toni Morrison (1992) and bell hooks (1994) came along and painted us in, and forced white feminists to take race into account. But whiteness as such was already a political issue, as it had been criticized for providing the corner stone of European and Anglo-American political, cultural and economic hegemony.

In his analysis of the representation of whiteness as an ethnic category in mainstream films, Richard Dyer (1997) defines it as 'an emptiness, absence, denial or even a kind of death'. Being the norm, it is invisible, as if natural, inevitable or the ordinary way to do things (Ware 1992). The source of the representational power of white is its propensity to be everything and nothing, whereas black, of course, is always marked off as a colour. The effect of this structured invisibility, and of the process of the naturalization of whiteness, is that it masks itself off into a 'colourless multicolouredness'. White contains all other colours. This insight is strengthened philosophically by the work of Michel Foucault on the Panopticon (Foucault 1977) – the void that lies at the heart of the system and defines the contour of both social and symbolic visibility (Young 1990). Deleuze and Guattari (1972; 1980) also comment on the fact that any dominant notion – such as masculinity or race – has no positive definition: the prerogative of being dominant means that a concept gets defined oppositionally, by casting outwards upon others the marks of oppression or marginalization. Virginia Woolf (1943) had already commented on this aspect of the logic of domination when she asserted that what matters is not so much that He – the male – should be superior, so long as She – the Other – be clearly defined as inferior. There is no dominant concept other than that which acts as a term to index and patrol access and participation to entitlements and powers. Thus, the invisibility of the dominant concepts is also the expression of their insubstantiality – which makes them all the more effective in their murderous intents towards the many others on whose structural exclusion they rest their vampiristic powers.

Now, the immediate consequence of this process of naturalization or invisibility is not only political, but also methodological, namely that whiteness is very difficult to analyse critically. It tends to break down into subcategories of white-ness: Irishness, Italianness, Jewishness, etc. It follows therefore that nonwhites have a much clearer perception of whiteness than whites. Just think of bell hook's important work on whiteness as terror and as a death-giving force, and of feminist critiques of whiteness in mythology and fairy tales like Snow White (hooks 1995). The reverse, however, is not the case: black and other ethnic minori-ties do not need this specular logic in order to have a location of their own.

The experience of white European immigrants tends to confirm the lethal insubstantiality of whiteness. As cultural identity is external and retrospective, it is defined for Europeans in the confrontation with other – usually black – peoples. This was the experience of Irish, Italian and Jewish immigrants in countries like the U.S.A., Canada and Australia. Their 'whiteness' emerged oppositionally, as a distancing factor from the natives and blacks. Feminist critics like Frankberg (1994a; 1994b) and Brodkin Sacks (1994) have analyzed this phenomenon of a 'whitening' process by which Euro-immigrants – especially Jews and Italians – were constructed as 'whitened' citizens in the U.S.A. The extent to which this kind of 'whitened' identity is illusory as it is racist, can be seen by how divided the diasporic

Euro-immigrant communities actually are: they are all in their respective ghettos, antagonistic towards each other and locked in mutual suspicion. But all are equally 'whitened' by the gaze of the colonizer, bent on pitching them against the black population. By learning to view their subject positions as racialized white people, we can work towards antiracist forms of whiteness, or at least antiracist strategies to rework whiteness. This strategy has interesting new potential with respect to women from the East of Europe today. Comparable dynamics are also operating within the EU, which result in a new racialized hierarchy that polices access to full EU citizenship. Thus, for peoples from the Balkans, or the South-Western regions of Europe, in so far as they are not yet 'good Europeans', they are also not quite as 'white' as others. The whitening process expands with the new frontiers of the EU pushing outwards the 'illegal others'. An oriental or Eastern ethnic divide is operating which equates EU citizenship with whiteness and Christianity, casting shadows of suspicion on all 'others'. Joanna Regulska (1998) is one of the feminist scholars who has adopted the methodology of postcolonial theory to the study of Eastern European women. The research presented in this book also maps new forms of 'othering' that are made operational as a result of EU enlargement.

My political strategy in this regard is to support the claim of European identity as an open and multi-layered project, not as a fixed or given essence. A cultural identity of this kind is a space of historical contradictions which can be turned into spaces of critical resistance to hegemonic identities of all kinds. My own choice to rework whiteness in the era of postmodernity involves, firstly, situating it, in the geo-historical space of Europe and within the political project of the European Union. This amounts to historicizing it and de-mystifying its allegedly 'natural' locations. The next step, following the method of feminist politics of location, is to analyse it critically, to re-visit it by successive deconstructive repetitions that aim at emptying out the different layers of this complex identity, excavating it until it opens out to the new.

The third step consists in trying to re-locate European identity, so as to undo its hegemonic tendencies. I refer to this kind of identity as 'nomadic'. Being a nomadic European subject means to be in transit within different identity-formations, but, at the same time, being sufficiently anchored to a historical position to accept responsibility for it. The key words are: 'accountability' and the 'strategic re-location of whiteness'. It is also a way of positing the 'becoming-minoritarian of Europe' by dispelling the privilege of invisibility that was conferred on Europe as an alleged centre of the world. By assuming full responsibility for the partial perspective of its own location, a minoritarian European space opens up a possible political strategy for those who inhabit this particular centre of power in a globalized world marked by scattered hegemonies, and hence no longer dominated by European power alone.

The emphasis I place on situated politics of location echoes and supports the non-unitary structure of the subject. Locations are historicized and grounded contingent foundations that structure one's being-in-the-world, one's social modes of belonging and not belonging. In other words, being diasporic, nomadic, hybrid, in-between are not the same. They translate sociologically into different structural locations in relation to language, culture, class and labour, access to and participation in power in the broadest sense of the term. The 'post' in 'post-industrialism' is not the same as the post in post-colonialism or post-communism. Historically, however, these 'post' conditions resonate with each other and, politically, they are quite often mixed together and coincide on a number of targets and goals. The task of the social critic – and of this project – is to make relevant distinctions among these different locations, but also to map the points of intersection so as to contribute to a politically-invested cartography of the common grounds and moments that can be shared by multiply-located subjects who are committed to reconstructing subjectivities and not merely to deconstruction for its own sake. I call this the new materialism of post-humanistic subjects who are embedded, embodied, accountable but not unitary.

I want to describe the project of a post-nationalist understanding of European identity as a great historical chance for Europeans to become more knowledgeable of our own history and more self-critical in a productive sense. Nietzsche argued in the early on twentieth century that many Europeans no longer feel at home in Europe (Nietzsche 1966). At the closing of that same century many want to argue that those who do not identify with Europe in the sense of the centre – the dominant and heroic reading of Europe – are ideally suited to the task of re-framing Europe, by making it accountable for a history in which fascism, imperialism and domination has played a central role.

In nomadic European subjects lie the post-nationalist foundations for a multi-layered and flexible practice of European citizenship in the frame of the new European Union.

## On Flexible Citizenship

I would relate this post-nationalistic sense of identity to the political notion of flexible citizenship.[4] The focus is on the area of citizenship and multicultural identity in the framework of the 'new' European Union (Ferreira *et al.* 1998).

Avtar Brah's analysis (1996) foregrounds the emerging new diasporic and hybrid identities which challenge any assumption of monoculturalism in the new Europe. Diaspora is a space of transition and exchange which defines the indigenous peoples as much as the nomadic subjects of the post/colonial world order. Cross-referring to Gilroy, Brah defines diasporic identities as being both about roots and routes; that is to say, they are 'processes of multi-locationality across geographical, cultural and psychic boundaries' (Brah 1996: 194). These are accentuated under the impact of the new information technologies, which dislocate the relationship between the local and the global and thus complicate the idea of multi-locality. Brah adopts the feminist politics of location as the kind of cognitive mapping that can best do justice to the new web of diasporic identities and other new forms of ethnicities emerging in the new world order.

A radical restructuring of European identity as post-nationalistic can be concretely translated into a set of 'flexible forms of citizenship' that would allow for all 'others' – all kinds of hybrid citizens – to acquire legal status in what would otherwise deserve the label of 'Fortress Europe'. This would involve dismantling the us/them binary in such a way as to account for the undoing of a strong and fixed notion of European citizenship in favour of a functionally-differentiated network of affiliations and loyalties, which finally, for the citizens of the Member States of the European Union, leads to the disconnection of the three elements discussed above: nationality, citizenship, national identity. According to Ulrich Preuss, such a European notion of citizenship, disengaged from national foundations, lays the ground for a new kind of civil society, beyond the boundaries of any single nation-state. Because such a notion of 'alienage' (Preuss 1996: 551) would become an integral part of citizenship in the European Union, Preuss argues that all European citizens would end up being 'privileged foreigners'. In other words, they would function together without reference to a centralized and homogeneous sphere of political power (Preuss 1995: 280). Potentially, this notion of citizenship could therefore lead to a new concept of politics, which would no longer be bound to the nation-state. Of course, this notion of European citizenship is only a potential one and is highly contested at the national level, by both reactionary nostalgic forces and third-world-obsessed leftist political groups. I, however, see it as the most honest and pragmatic way to develop the progressive potential of the European Union, and also of accounting for the effects of globalisation upon us all. These effects boil down to one central idea: the end of pure and steady identities, and a consequent emphasis on creolization, hybridization, a multicultural Europe, within which 'new' Europeans can take their place alongside others (Bhavnani 1992).

In her recent work on European citizenship, Benhabib (2002) interrogates critically the disjunction between the concepts of nation, the state and cultural identity. Solidly grounded in her theory of communicative ethics, Benhabib works towards the elaboration of new rules of global democracy within a multicultural horizon. A self-professed Kantian cosmopolitan, Benhabib argues forcefully that 'democratic citizenship can be exercised across national boundaries and in transnational contexts' (Benahbib 2002: 183). She is especially keen to demonstrate that the distinction between national minority and ethnic group does very little to determine whether an identity/difference-driven movement is 'democratic, liberal, inclusive and universalist' (Benhabib 2002: 65).

Within the specific location of Europe, important work has been done on analyzing the on-going process of the European Union, both as a player in the global economy and as an attempt to move beyond the traditional grounds on which European nationalism has prospered, namely essentialist identities. Of great importance in this respect is the work of Etienne Balibar (2001; 2002) on Europe as a transnational space of mediation and exchange. This new European identity is internally differentiated and hence non-unitary and committed to trans-cultural hybrid exchanges. It is a situated perspective based on multiple border crossings, on confrontations with shifting frontiers and borders, and on a deep commitment to pacifism and human rights. I have stressed elsewhere (Braidotti 2002b; 2003a; 2003b), the relevance of this vision of the European Union for the feminist project of situating the critique of gender and power in the lived reality of our present geo-political locations. We need situated European perspectives on gender, feminist politics and social theory. This is a way of thinking locally and taking full accountability for the new trans-national European space. Becoming-Europeans in this critical mode is a process of actively re-grounding citizenship according to a more flexible model, which is related to claiming social rights on the European level.

## A New Social Imaginary

As indicated in the accounts provided by the interviews in this book, new images and representations of Europe do not readily appear. To produce a new imaginary requires the means of revisiting it, acknowledging it and understanding the complicity between 'difference' and 'exclusion' in the European mind-set. Repetitions are the road to creating positive re-definitions, in a progress of creative deconstruction. Communities are also imaginary institutions made of affects and desires (Anderson 1983). Homi Bhabha (1990; 1994), for instance, stresses the fact that common ideas of 'nation' are, to a large extent, imaginary tales, which project a re-assuring but nonetheless illusory sense of unity over the disjointed, fragmented and often incoherent range of internal regional and cultural differences that make up a national identity. Poststructuralist and anti-racist feminists have, moreover, developed a sceptical attitude towards the idea of unitary identity. We have also become painfully aware of the extent to which the legitimating tales of nationhood in the west have been constructed over the body of women, as well as in the crucible of imperial and colonial masculinity.

The project of developing a new kind of post-nationalist identity is related to the process of dis-identification from established, nation-bound identities. This dis-location can lead to a positive and affirmative re-location of European identities following the feminist politics of locations. I have stressed both the need for an adequate European social imaginary for this kind of subject-position, and the difficulties involved in developing this. There is no denying that such an enterprise involves a large sense of loss and is not without pain. No process of consciousness-raising can ever be painless. Migrants know this very well. In the research presented in this book, for instance in the analysis of border-crossing and home, we find multiple expressions of belonging. Home is lived both at the material and at the imaginary level, where it might be a destination, or something which is repeatedly deferred. It is not necessarily a place of 'origin', but can also mean belonging in multiple locations. In addition, my own experience in Australia has taught me to what an extent the process of dis-identification is linked to the pain of loss. This is not, however, the pathetic expression of a nostalgic yearning for a return to the past, but rather a mature, sobering experience, similar to the loss of illusions and of self-delusions of classical Greek tragedies.

A post-nationalist sense of European identity and of flexible citizenship does not come easily, and in some ways is even a counter-intuitive idea. It requires an extra effort in order to come into being, as it raises the question of how to change deeply-embedded habits of our imagination. How can such in-depth transformation be enacted? This question is made all the more urgent by the extent to which we are already living in post-nationalist ways and in a post-nationalist social space. This is partly due to the obvious effects of globalisation, and the conformism and homogeneization of cultures brought about by telecommunication. It is also related, however, to the impact of the European Union on the legal, economic and cultural structures in which most dwellers in Europe function nowadays. The impact of educational, scientific and cultural exchanges is very significant in this respect, and the implementation of the common currency has done the rest. I think that it is precisely the rather large role played by these post-nationalist instances in our social life that has generated the reaction against them in the form of various types of nostalgic identity-claims that are proliferating across Europe today.

What we are lacking is a social imaginary that adequately reflects the social realities which we are already experiencing, of a post-nationalist sense of European identity. We have failed to develop adequate, positive representations of the new trans-European condition that we are inhabiting in this Continent. This lack of the social imaginary both feeds upon and supports the political timidity and the resistances that are being moved against the European political project. More work is needed on the role of contemporary global media in both colonizing and stimulating the social imaginary of global cultures (Hall 1992; Shohat and Stam 1994; Gilroy 2000; Braidotti 2002b).

At least some of the difficulty involved is due to the lack of a specifically European – in the sense of European Union – public debate, as Habermas (1992) put it in his critique of the absence of a European public sphere. This is reflected in the rather staggering absence of what I would call a European social imaginary. Thinkers as varied as Passerini (1998), Mény (2000) and Morin (1987) all signal this problem, in different ways. Passerini laments the lack of an emotional attachment to the European dimension on the part of the citizens of the social space that is Europe. Elsewhere she has developed hypotheses on a possible critical innovation of what a 'love for Europe' could mean (Passerini 2003). For Mény the problem is rather the lack of imagination and of visionary force on the part of those who are in charge of propelling politically the European Union. For Edgar Morin, Europe is ill-loved and somewhat unwanted, 'une pauvre vieille petite chose' (Morin 1987: 23).

My question therefore becomes: how do you develop such a new European social imaginary? I think that such a notion is a project and not a given. Nonetheless, this does not make it utopian in the sense of being overidealistic. Even the contrary: it is a virtual social reality which can be actualized by a joint endeavour on the part of active, conscious and desiring citizens. If it is utopian at all, it is only in the positive sense of utopia: the necessary dose of dream-like vision without which no social project can take off and gather support.

Something along these lines is expressed with great passion by Edgar Morin, when he describes his becoming-European as the awakening of his consciousness about the new peripheral role of Europe in the post-Second World War era, after his years of indifference to Europe, in the tradition of Marxist cosmopolitanism and international proletarian solidarity. By his own admission, Edgar Morin overcame his own mistrust for the European dimension of both thinking and political activity in the late 1970s, when, like most of his generation, he took his distance from the unfulfilled promises of the Marxist utopia. This sobering experience made him see to what an extent the new world-wide binary opposition USSR/U.S.A. had dramatically dislocated the sources of planetary power away from Europe (Morin 1987).

The concrete result of this new consciousness-raising was that Morin started taking seriously the scholarly work connected to the research of European roots as both a cultural and political specificity. This is the paradox that lies at the heart of the quest for a new, post-nationalist redefinition of European identity: it becomes thinkable as an entity at the exact historical time when it has ceased to be operational as a social or symbolic reality. The process of becoming-Europeans entails the end of fixed Eurocentric identities and it thus parallels the becoming-nomadic of subjectivity.

The liberatory potential of this process is equally proportional to the imaginary and political efforts it requires of us all. The recognition of the new multi-layered, trans-cultural and post-nationalist idea of Europe in this case would only be the premise for the collective development of a new sense of accountability for the specific slice of world periphery that we happen to inhabit.

Let me make it perfectly clear, however, that this very definition of nomadic subjects is spoken from and speaks of the specific location I have chosen to make myself accountable for. It is an embedded European account of my own traditions or genealogies. In other words, it is only one of many possible locations which may apply to some of the people who situate themselves – in terms of genealogical consciousness and the related forms of accountability – with respect to the kind of power-relations that go with the continent of Europe. This is neither the only, nor is it the best of all possible locations. It merely happens to be the cartography that I acquired and chose to be accountable for. I want to present this kind of embodied genealogical accountability as my contribution to our discussions on gender and power. Through the pain of loss and dis-enchantment, just as 'post-Woman women' have moved away from compulsory gender dichotomies towards a redefinition of being-gendered-in-the-world, 'post-Eurocentric Europeans' may be able to find enough creativity and moral stamina to grab this historical chance to become just Europeans in the post-nationalist sense of the term.

## Notes

1. Instances of alternative feminist figurations are the womanist (Walker 1984); the lesbian (Wittig 1992); the cyborg (Haraway 1990b); the inappropriate (d) other (Trinh Minh-Ha 1989); the 'eccentric subject' (De Lauretis 1990); the mestiza (Anzaldua 1987); the nomadic feminist subject (Braidotti 1994).
2. Among them see in particular Gayatri Spivak (1987), Stuart Hall (1992), Paul Gilroy (1987), Avtra Brah (1993), Helma Lutz etal. (1996), Philomena Essed (1991), Nira Yuval-Davis and Floya Anthias (1989).
3. I owe this witty formulation to the discussions with my colleagues in the European Socrates Thematic Network ATHENA. See the website: www.athena2.org.
4. This term has gained widespread acceptance; I first read it in Aihwa Ong's work on Chinese migrants (Ong 1993).

# References

Anderson, B. 1983. *Imagined Communities*, London, Verso.

Anzaldua, G. 1987. *Borderlands/La Frontera: The New Mestiza*, San Francisco, Aunt Lute Books.

Appadurai, A. 1994. 'Disjuncture and Difference in the Global Cultural Economy', in Williams, P. and L. Chrisman (eds.) *Colonial Discourse and Post-Colonial Theory*, New York, Columbia University Press.

Balibar, E. 2001. *Nous, Citoyens d'Europe? Les Frontiers, l'État, le Peuple*, Paris, Éditions de la Découverte.

———. 2002. *Politics and the Other Scene*, London, Verso.

Benhabib, S. 1999. 'Citizen, Resident and Alien in a Changing World: Political Membership in a Global Era', *Social Research*, 66(3): 709–44.

———. 2002. *The Claims of Culture*, Princeton, Princeton University Press.

Bhabha, H. (ed.) 1990. *Nation and Narration*, London and New York, Routledge.

———. 1994. *The Location of Culture*, London and New York, Routledge.

Bhavnani, K. 1992. 'Towards a Multi-Cultural Europe?', met Nederlandse vertaling, Bernardijn ten Zeldam Stichting, Amsterdam.

Brah, A. 1993. 'Re-Framing Europe: En-Gendered Racisms, Ethnicities and Nationalisms in Contemporary Western Europe', *Feminist Review*, 45(Autumn): 9–28.

———. 1996. *Cartographies of the Diaspora*, London and New York, Routledge.

Braidotti, R. 1994. *Nomadic Subjects*, New York, Columbia University Press.

———. 2002a. *Metamorphoses*, Cambridge, Polity Press.

———. 2002b. *Nuovi Soggetti Nomadi*, Roma, Luca Sossella editore.

———. 2003a. 'L'Europe peut-elle nous faire rêver', interview with Antonella Corsani in *Multitudes Europe Constituante?*, Vol. 14: 97–109.

———. 2003b. 'La penseé féministe nomade', *Multitudes 12, féminismes, queer, multitudes*, pp. 27-47.

Brodkin Sacks, K. 1994. 'How did Jews Become White Folks?', in S. Gregory and R. Sanjek (eds.) *Race*, New Brunswick, NJ., Rutgers University Press.

Castells, M. 1996. *The Rise of the Network Society*, Oxford, Blackwells.

Clifford, J. 1992. 'Traveling Cultures', in Grossberg, N. and Treichler, P. (eds.) *Cultural Studies*, New York, London, Routledge.

———. 1994. 'Diasporas', *Cultural Anthropology*, 3: 302–38.

Cresswell, T. 1997. 'Imagining the Nomad: Mobility and the Postmodern Primitive', in Benko, G. and U. Strohmayer (eds.) *Space and Social Theory. Interpreting Modernity and Postmodernity*, Oxford, Blackwell.

Dahrendorf, R. 1990. *Reflections on the Revolution in Europe in a Letter Intended to Have Been Sent to a Gentleman in Warsaw*, London, Chatto and Windus.

De Lauretis, T. 1990. 'Eccentric Subjects: Feminist Theory and Historical Consciousness', *Feminist Studies*, 16(1): 115–50.

Deleuze, G. and F. Guattari 1972. *L'anti-Oedipe. Capitalisme et Schizophrénie I*, Paris, Minuit.

——. 1980. *Mille plateaux. Capitalisme et Schizophrénie II*, Paris, Minuit.

Dyer, R. 1997. *White*, London and New York, Routledge.

Eisenstein, Z. 1999. *Global Obscenities*, London, Zed Books.

Essed, P. 1991. *Understanding Everyday Racism*, London, Sage.

Ferreira V., T. Tavares and S. Portugal (eds.) 1998. *Shifting Bonds, Shifting Bounds. Women, Mobility and Citizenship in Europe*, Oeiras, Celta Editora.

Foucault, M. 1977. *Surveiller et Punir*, Paris, Minuit.

Frankberg, R. 1994a. 'Introduction: Points of Origin, Points of Departure', in *White Women, Race Matters*, Minneapolis, University of Minnesota Press, pp. 1–22.

——. 1994b. 'Questions of Culture and Belonging', in *White Women, Race Matters*, Minneapolis, University of Minnesota Press, pp. 191–235.

Gilroy, P. 1987. *There ain't no Black in the Union Jack*, London, Hutchinson.

——. 1993. *The Black Atlantic: Modernity and Double Consciousness*, London, Verso.

——. 2000. *Against Race*, Cambridge, MA, Harvard University Press.

Grewal, I. and C. Kaplan 1994. 'Introduction: Transnational Feminist Practices and Questions of Postmodernity' in I. Grewal and C. Kaplan (eds.) 1994. *Scattered Hegemonies. Postmodernity and Transnational Feminist Practices*, London, Minneapolis, University of Minnesota Press.

Habermas, J. 1992. 'Citizenship and National Identity: Some Reflections on the Future of Europe' in *Praxis International*, 12(1)(April): 1–34.

Hall, S. 1987. 'Minimal Selves' in ???? *Identity: The Real Me*, London, ICA Documents, pp. 44–6.

——. 1990. 'Cultural Identity and Diaspora', in J. Rutherford (ed.) *Identity: Community, Culture, Difference*, London, Lawrence & Wishart.

——. 1992. 'What is this 'Black' in Black Popular Culture?', in G. Dent (ed.) *Black Popular Culture*, Seattle, Boy Press.

Haraway, D. 1990a. 'Situated Knowledges', in *Simians, Cyborgs and Women*, London, Free Association Books.

———. 1990b. 'A Manifesto for Cyborgs: Science, Technology and Socialist Feminism in the 1980s', in *Simians, Cyborgs and Women*, London, Free Association Books.

Harding, S. 1991. *Whose Science? Whose Knowledge?*, Ithaca, Cornell University Press.

———. 1993. *The 'Racial' Economy of Science*, Bloomington, Indiana University Press.

Hardt, M. and A. Negri 2000. *Empire*, Harvard University Press.

Hirschman, A.O. 1945. 'Introduction', in V. Fry *Assignment: Rescue. An Autobiography*, New York, Scholastic Inc.

———. 1994. *Passaggi di Frontiera. I luoghi e le Idee di un Percorso di Vita*, Rome, Donzelli.

Hirschmann, U. 1993. *Noi senza patria*, Bologna, Il Mulino.

Hooks, Bell 1994. 'Postmodern Blackness', in P. Williams and L. Chrisman (eds.) *Colonial Discourse and Post-Colonial Theory*, New York, Columbia University Press.

———. 1995. 'Representations of Whiteness in the Black Imagination', in *Killing Rage. Ending Racism*, New York, Holt & Company.

Laclau, E. 1995. 'Subjects of Politics, Politics of the Subject', *Differences* 7(1): 146–64.

Lloyd, G. 1985. *The Man of Reason*, London, Methuen.

Lutz, H., N. Yuval-Davis and A. Phoenix (eds.) 1996. *Crossfires. Nationalism, Racism and Gender in Europe*, London, Pluto Press.

Mény, Y. 2000. *Tra Utopia e realtà. Una Costituzione per l'Europa*, Florence, Possigli Editore.

Minh-Ha, T. 1989. *Woman, Native, Other*, Bloomington, Indiana University Press.

Mohanty, C. 1992. 'Feminist Encounters: Locating the Politics of Experience', in Barrett, M. and A. Phillips (eds.) *Destabilizing Theory: Contemporary Feminist Debates*, Cambridge, Polity.

Morin, E. 1987. *Penser l'Europe*, Paris, Gallimard.

Morrison, T. 1992. *Playing in the Dark. Whiteness and the Literary Imagination*, Cambridge, MA, Harvard University Press.

Mouffe, C. 1994. 'For a Politics of Nomadic Identity', in Robertson G., Mash, M., Tickner, L., J. Bird, B. Curti and T. Putnam (eds.) *Travellers' Tales. Narratives of Home and Displacement*, London and New York, Routledge.

Nietzsche, F. 1966. *Beyond Good and Evil*, London, Vintage Books.

Ong, A. 1993. 'On the Edge of Empires: Flexible Citizenship among Chinese in Diaspora', *Positions*, 1(3): 745–78.

Passerini, L. (ed.) 1998. *Identità Culturale Europea. Idee, Sentimenti, Relazioni*, Florence, La Nuova Italia.

———. 2003. *Memoria e utopia*, Torino, Bollati Boringhieri.
Preuss, U. K. 1995. 'Problems of a Concept of European Citizenship', *European Law Journal*, 1(3): 267-81.
———. 1996. 'Two Challenges to European Citizenship' *Political Studies*, vol. XLIV: 534–552.
Probyn, E. 1990, 'Travels in the Postmodern: Making Sense of the Local', in Nicholson, L. (ed.) *Feminism/Postmodernism*, London and New York, Routledge.
Regulska, J. 1998. 'The New 'Other' European Woman', in V. Ferreira, T. Tavares and S. Portugal (eds.) *Shifting Bonds, Shifting Bounds. Women, Mobility and Citizenship in Europe*, Oeiras, Celta Editora.
Rich, A. 1987. 'The Politics of Location', in *Blood, Bread and Poetry*, London, Virago.
Sassen, S. 1995. *Losing Control. The Decline of Sovereignty in an Age of Globalisation*, New York, Columbia University Press.
Shohat, E. and R. Stam 1994. *Unthinking Eurocentrism: Multiculturalism and the Media*, London and New York, Routledge.
Soysal, Y. 1994. *Limits of Citizenship: Migrants and Postnational Membership in Europe*, Chicago, University of Chicago.
Spinelli, A. 1979. 'La vie politique d'Ursula Hirschmann, fondatrice de Femmes pour l'Europe', *Textes et Documents*, numéro spécial, Brussels, Ministère des Affaires Étrangères, du Commerce Extérieur et de la Coopération au Développement, pp. 11–15.
———. 1988. *Come ho tentato di diventare saggio*, Bologna, Il Mulino.
———. 1992. *Diario europeo*, Bologna, Il Mulino.
Spinelli, A. and Rossi, E. 1998. 'Per un'Europa libera e unita. Progetto d'un manifesto' in L. Passerini (ed.) *Identità culturale europea. Idee, sentimenti, relazioni*, Florence, La Nuova Italia.
Spivak, G.C. 1987. *In Other Worlds: Essays in Cultural Politics*, London, Methuen.
Walker, A. 1984. *In Search of Our Mother's Gardens*, London, The Women's Press.
Walzer, M. 1992. *What It Means To Be An American*, New York, Marsilio.
Ware, V. 1992. *Beyond the Pale. White Women, Racism and History*, London and New York, Verso.
Wittig, M. 1992. *The Straight Mind and Other Essays*, Hemel Hempstead, Harvester Wheatsheaf.
Woolf, V. 1943. *Three Guineas*, London, Hogarth Press.
Young, R. 1990. *White Mythologies. Writing History and the West*, London and New York, Routledge.
Yuval-Davis, N. and F. Anthias (eds.) 1989. *Woman-Nation-State*, London, Macmillan.

*Chapter 2*

# 'I want to see the world': Mobility and Subjectivity in the European Context

*Ioanna Laliotou*

Post-communist movements from Eastern to Western Europe are contributing greatly to the transformation of the ways in which we are currently re-conceptualizing the association between mobility, subjectivity and European history. The relation between Eastern and Western Europe after 1989 has been determined mainly by the social, political and economic conditions of post-communism and by the intensification of a wide variety of political, economic, and cultural exchanges between the East and the West. Human mobility plays a central role in these exchanges, as it transforms past definitions of the political space between the East and West and gives rise to new transnational forms of subjectivity in Europe.

In this chapter, I analyse practices of transnational migration as part of a wider phenomena of mobility that include physical, cultural, political, subjective and conceptual forms of movement. This analysis seeks to foreground mobility as a historical and theoretical concept that enables complex understandings of the interrelation between migrancy and subjectivity in contemporary history. While using the term mobility in order to describe the migrants' sets of experiences of transnational arrangements in Europe, one should remain aware of the liberal connotations of the term; connotations that do not necessarily apply to the historical phenomena of movement studied here. Mobility as a concept is often used in order to refer to the freedom of movement and the dissolution of political, family, social and economic constraints, and is more generally associated with nomadic practices as opposed to sedentary forms of existence and social being. The history of movement that is presented through the testimonies of women migrants from Eastern to Western Europe is not conducive to the validation of such a liberal take on the concept of mobility. The women whose histories of migration constitute the primary research material in this project were driven by a variety of factors, including the need for better material and professional resources, political and existential dissidence, personal and intimate relationships, love, curiosity, and desire. Furthermore, their histories indicate that after their migration they were often implicated in life arrangements and conditions that exceeded or altered the plans, desires and strategies that they had formulated prior to their decision to leave their countries of birth.

Among the plurality of often contradictory reasons that the interviewees give in order to explain why they left their countries, many of them stated that their movement was not planned as migration, but as a strategy for family unification, or that the purpose was to pursue personal relationships, or simply a result of their curiosity to 'see the world'. However, and despite the fact that this group of interviewees insist on drawing a distinction between themselves and 'migrants,' they describe the conditions of their lives after migration in ways that coincide with traditional narratives of migration, as these descriptions are organized around familiar themes such as adaptation to the new country, cultural incompatibilities, xenophobia, forced integration, nostalgia and homesickness, romanticization of the status of the exiled, etc. As Ana, who was born in Sofia, Bulgaria in 1962 and migrated to Italy as a member of a dance group in 1989, noted, some people never actually consciously decided to migrate. In her interview, Ana insists on the fact that although she had not thought of migrating *per se* she was driven to Italy by her desire to visit different places and countries (Ana, Bu/I). She is nostalgic for the period before the number of Bulgarian migrants increased, when 'people in Italy were interested in us', before they were faced with larger numbers of foreign migrants and became hostile and xenophobic. Like many others, Ana declares that she does not have relationships with other migrants, and she differentiates her position from the lot of the migrant. Despite her insistence on this differentiation, in her description of her social life in Italy, she also insists on her clear strategy of establishing relationships with other Bulgarian women, colleagues and friends. Interviewees who distance themselves from the category of migrants often base their argument on the distinction between having made a conscious decision to migrate on the one hand and of finding oneself in the condition of migrancy without having planned to be in this situation. This insistence is often expressed through extensive references to the role that personal relationships played in their decision to leave their country of birth.

Reflection on the properties of migrant subjectivity is common in the interviews with those who acknowledge the fact that the mobility of their lives is a particular characteristic that gives them a special position both in their homelands as well as in the countries where they reside. On the other hand, they feel that they do not fit comfortably in the traditional position of the migrant. Marina, a woman from Bulgaria, explains how migration was never in her plans, although travelling had always been her father's aspiration for himself; an aspiration that was never fulfilled 'because during the communist regime he wasn't allowed to do that' (Marina, Bu/I). Towards the end of her interview Marina makes a distinction between her mobility in Bulgaria, Russia and Italy and the forced migration of people who need to migrate in order to survive. She claims that forced migration is a global phenomenon which both expresses and is conducive to human suffering. Forced migration disrupts relationships and bonds of affection and is thus detrimental and cruel, whereas mobility creates possibilities for new relationships and for the expansion of one's horizon of connections and social networks. It would however be a mistake to relate the histories of movement and relocation that are documented in these interviews with cosmopolitanism, since such an interpretation would undermine the documented centrality of the conditions of migrancy in the experiences narrated. Reducing mobility to cosmopolitanism would impede us from understanding contemporary transformations of the practices and realities of migration. In using the term mobility in order to refer to these new practices of migration, I do not intend to undermine the difficulties and constraints that women are faced with in the processes involved in moving from one country to the other and the blockages – cultural, political and institutional – that determine their efforts to re-establish their lives in the countries of migration. Quite differently, the interviews demonstrate the multiplicity of points of departure, destinations, itineraries, strategies, practices and venues that constitute a large range of activities to which the term migration refers. The testimonies of women who state that their desire to 'see the world' defines their history of migration offer a starting point for a re-theorization of the concept of cosmopolitanism in the context of new *cosmopolitical* processes, as Jacques Derrida and others have put it, still in the phase of 'experimentation' (Derrida 2003: 3–23). In many cases women are motivated by an unspecified desire to move, 'to see the world' (Boyana, Bu/NL)

The interviews with women who have moved from the European East to the West are marked by a constant vacillation between distancing themselves from, and associating themselves with, the position of the migrant. Taking this vacillation as a historical and theoretical starting-point, in the following sections I trace the implications of these migrant testimonies for the ways in which we understand the contemporary history of mobility. To that end, I analyse the ways in which the interviewees envision mobility as a constitutive element of their subjective histories and circumstances vis-à-vis the contemporary theoretical constellation of notions of mobility, space, normativity and affective relationships.

## Movement and the Critique of Heteronormativity

The relationship between subjectivity and movement has been theorized in the context of many different disciplines and intellectual traditions including philosophy, psychoanalysis, cultural studies, history and post-colonial studies. Theorists, researchers and practitioners in these fields have employed notions such as hybridity and nomadism in order to conceptualise the subject-effects of physical, cultural or psychic transgressions. Hybridity and nomadism became key-concepts in the field of migration studies, especially during the 1990s, when new migrations to old metropolitan centres, including post-colonial and post-communist migrations – led to the creation of migrant communities, cultures and practices that could not be adequately analysed in terms of assimilation, integration, acculturation or parochialism. As has been suggested, migration in the era of postcolonialism created a 'third-space' in culture, a space inhabited by new subjects that enacted and embodied cultural hybridity in the metropoles.[1] Cultural identity was theoretically de-essentialised and re-worked as a terrain of constant negotiation on the level of everyday life and social interaction.[2]

On the other hand, the association of the migrant with the philosophical figure of the nomad gave rise to inspiring approaches to the psychic affects of migration and movement. Following the Deleuzean critique of the logo-centric and unitary subject of philosophy, attention was drawn to the always-becoming condition of subjectivity, and fragmentation and fluidity were recognized as its main characteristics.[3] Certainly, one should keep in mind the sharp distinction between the philosophical figure of the nomad and the historical and social figure of the migrant. Deleuze and Guattari have stressed this distinction with reference to the different sets of relations to the notion of origin,[4] while other theorists have stressed that the conflation of nomadism, migrancy and cosmopolitanism results in viewing the whole world as migrant, an approach that de-historicizes the experience of migration and undermines our attempt to understand the complexity of the history of mobility.[5]

Nomadic thought enables an understanding of the effects of movement and of the transgression of physical and symbolic borders on the ways in which the migrant becomes a subject. Migrants, as well as natives, partake in flows of desire that break away from codes of signification determined by the dominant assemblages of power, including community, family, nationhood, tradition and local belongings. Breaking away from certain familiar means –material, spiritual, mental or imaginary – of making sense of the world around us, is a necessary element of migration. In the same way, finding new practices of cultural re-coding is also part of the process of migration, leading migrants through recurring stages of reterritorialization. In the contemporary context of intensified mobility the relation between migrant communities and national homelands and between post-national processes and existing forms of nationhood are marked by different points of de- and re-territorialixation. One could even argue that migrant subjectivity is constituted within a sphere of cultural and political becomings, which allow us to study moments of crisis of established majorities and minorities, strategies of articulation of new subject-positions and alternative visions of self and community that do not necessarily historically evolve into fixed collective identities.

These new modes of subjectivation and new kinds of valorized subjectivity are currently being drastically shaped by the conditions of transnational mobility, and consist of practices and strategies and disciplines associated with late capitalism (Ong 1999: 18–19). The expansion of the transnational networks of migrants and communities and the intensification of transnational cultural, political and economic interaction in late capitalism have led to the emergence of new forms of being a subject that enable – and sometimes force – people to act on different levels of local and global communication. Post-1989 migrations and other forms of mobility have brought the concept and practices of citizenship into the foreground of public debates and theorization. Relating these emergences with the on-going political debate on European citizenship, many theorists have placed particular stress on the multi-layered forms of becoming a full member in a community in the age of globalization. On the basis of the varied and changing ways in which people's intimate lives, their families and their networks of friendship affect and are affected by their activities as citizens, theorists have endorsed the notion of 'transversal citizenship,' reflecting the varied forms of current political participation (i.e. national, European or dual citizenship, municipal political participation and residency rights, participation in community political organizations and associations, etc.).[6] This new form of transversal citizenship is linked to the new forms of subjectivity that have emerged as the result of the mass movements of people and to the consequent diversification of the social body in European societies.

The emphasis on the effects mobility has on the ways one becomes a subject is shared by studies of hybridity, nomadism and transversalism alike. This emphasis, however, encourages a unilateral conception of the relationship between mobility and subjectivity. Attention is focused on the subject-effects of mobility, whereas the possibility that particular forms of subjectivity might enable new practices of mobility is, in general, not considered. However, an important finding of our research is that many of the interviewees consider their migration from Eastern to Western Europe as a consequence of their character, their nature, their personal dispositions and their preferences. Character attributes, intimate relationships and desires, upbringing and family background, personal feelings are all factors that led the decision to migrate. No matter what the specific motivation was, the interviewees give accounts of how changes in emotions, psychic conditions and intimate relationships led to physical mobility. Preoccupied with the effects of migration on people and recipient societies, migration history and theory has, in general, undermined the bilateral nature of the relationship between subjectivity and mobility.[7]

Recently, this bilateral relationship has been addressed in a growing body of work that seeks to demonstrate the centrality of movement and mobility to the constitution of sexual and gender subjectivities, both historically and contemporarily (Stychin 2000; Binnie 1997; Binnie and Valentine 1999; Bell and Binnie 2000; Weston 1995). In recent years, queer theory has enabled scholars and students of migration to discuss mobility in relation to issues of sexuality and the constitution of sexual subjectivities in diasporas. In the field of Asian American studies in particular, mobility is currently used as a central concept in the study of the transnational citizenship in relation to sexual politics and the emergence of new forms of sexual subjectivities. The conceptual convergence between queer theory and diaspora studies derives from the shared preoccupation, evident also in the interviews of our project, with complicating and problematizing notions of home in order to make sense of conditions of movement. Accordingly, traditional points of departure and arrival, such as Eastern and Western Europe, as well as Asia and Asian America, become open-ended terms, i.e. they lack reference to a strictly defined territory. They represent transnational spaces defined by the movement and practices of people across large geopolitical areas, 'siteless locales' that inherently lack the territorial sovereignty that the geographical terms longingly invoke (Eng 1997). Home – both as origin as well as destination – is thus not limited in the territorial space of the nation-state, but is rather related to subjective practices and dispositions. In many of our interviews women relate home to affective relationships. Home is often detached from the normative association with domesticity or state-nationhood and is related to subjective moves and attachments. Women as subjects in migration are also subjects in exile, a de-domesticated home, an 'uninhabitable domain' (Eng 1997: 32; Eng and Hom 1998; Jackson 2000; Mackie 2001).[8] From the point of view of queer studies, exile is seen as an advantageous point from which to critique the normativity of heterosexual social and family orders. Queer diaspora studies can be taken as a useful framework and methodology for interrogating the normativity of cultural, political and social participation in the contemporary post-national, post-communist or post-colonial state. Focusing on the inside-out location of home and homeland in the context of sexual subjectivities, scholars have suggested that in order to explore the formation of subjectivity in exile we need to attend to the ways in which social normativities are embedded and embodied in citizenship and nationalism, circulated through capitalism, and mobilized in the discourses of postcolonialism. Exploring the relationship between subjectivity and social normativities of home and homeland presupposes a consideration of the circuits of desire within which home and homeland are conceived. This means attending to the multiple valences of desire, such as identification, national belonging, and affective relationships (Desai 2002: 85).

Studies in queer diaspora have indicated that the connections between travel, mobility and sexuality have a long and complex history. Thus, scholars have analysed the diverse connotations and experiences of home, that range from refuge to a place one seeks to escape from, to the building up of new communities within urban settings and imaginary homelands. The study of queer diaspora has problematized various normative and long-lasting assumptions of migration studies by tracing the multiplicity of definitions of home and origin and by challenging the notion that migrant communities are necessarily culturally homogenous and uniform (Sinfield 1996: 282). Moreover, queer diaspora studies, I suggest, may provide us with a starting point for re-theorizing the relationship between mobility and subjectivity by bringing into the foreground the dynamic nexus between migration and affective relationships.

## The Desire to Move: Personal 'Dissidence' as a Constitutive Element of Mobility

The dynamic nexus between migration and affective relationships is articulated in many of the interviews of this project through the invocation of the issue of personal dissidence. Personal dissidence appears in the interviews sporadically and often in inarticulate and contradictory ways. Elements of unruliness, disobedience and of a general disposition to follow a life path, which one was not expected to choose, often co-exist with political and cultural conformism and otherwise conventional outlooks. Even though inarticulate and sporadic, these references to personal dissidence are vital in helping us to understand the ways in which the interviewees conceptualize themselves as migrants in the contemporary European context. In this section, I trace these emergent conceptualizations of migrant subjectivity in order to explore the meaning that the interviewees attribute to the notion of mobility. In order to follow this line of exploration, I focus on points where personal dissidence is associated with an enacted desire and a will to 'move.'

This association is certainly more evident in the cases of women who left their countries of birth before 1989. Pre-1989 migrants often, but not always, identify themselves as political refugees, or as exiles. However, most of the interviewees are perplexed about the nature of their movement, as it appears to be very difficult for them to identify with one or the other of the categories often used to describe people who leave their native countries and spend a part of their lives elsewhere. The fluidity of these categories is manifested in the case of Rosa, a woman who left Bulgaria in 1968 at the age of twenty (Rosa, Bu/NL). After fleeing from Bulgaria, Rosa describes how, while at the refugee camp in Trieste, she had to choose if she were an economic or a political exile. According to migration policies of the time, a political exile ('azil politic' is the term used in the interviews) could get permission to stay in a European country. On the contrary, if a refugee identified herself as an economic exile ('azil economic') then she had to leave the continent and go to America, or Australia. Before leaving her homeland, Rosa was a dancer at a Bulgarian dancing group. She travelled and performed in many different places including Belgrade, Zagreb, Sarajevo, and Montenegro. While she was working at a resort hotel at Nova Gorica, she was asked by the Bulgarian authorities to return to Bulgaria. Rosa knew that that call meant the end of her travelling, at least for a while, and she was not ready to comply with the official request. So she decided to cross the border and become a refugee in Italy. She was a self-exiled refugee, although her interview makes it clear that she was not certain about the political or economic character of her exile. However, it is obvious in the interview that the driving force behind her movement across Europe was not resettlement, but rather a choice of going into exile instead of confinement in her home country. Rosa's exile led her to many different European locations including Trieste, Rome, Paris and The Hague. It is very difficult to understand the experience of mobility that is described by migrants such as Rosa through the conventional lenses through which migration and the need for resettlement in another country are viewed. The rigid categories used in official classifications and immigration policy documents do not make sense when the subjects narrate their life-stories. Apart from revealing the conventionality of the categories themselves, this ambiguity also registers the particular characteristics that mark population movements from Eastern to Western Europe after WWII. Pre-1989 migrants often emphatically insist on references to their personal dissidence as the main factor that made them move. 'I could not keep my mouth shut,' remarks an interviewee, and in this way she attributes her will to cross the borders to her unruly and independent character.

Although references to dissidence are to be expected in the stories of political refugees, they are also present in narratives that seem to belong to the more traditional migrant story variety. Personal dissidence – against that which different subjects define in their own terms as a norm – can be traced to the ways in which the interviewees present their will to 'see the world,' or 'to travel' in general, or to pursue professional success and education in other places, or simply to try one's luck outside the borders of the native land. In almost all of the interviews, migrants claim that it is their desire, their will and their envisioning of moving that eventually causes them to move. The desire and the will to move is an important element in all of the interviews. One could actually argue that the desire to move is the core element around which a plurality of other key referents are articulated which shape the migration story: love, relationships, nostalgia, professional pride, personal achievement, family obligations, the lure of the West, etc. Against the grain of the established assumptions that we have today about women's forced migration from Eastern to Western Europe – assumptions that are grounded in widely disseminated images of the Eastern European woman as a powerless sexual victim – almost all of the subjects insist that the decision to migrate was theirs and that this decision was grounded in the desire to leave their country and live for a certain period of time abroad. Even in cases where the overall narrative reveals the complexity of the structures of power within which women's movement takes place, the subjects insist on descriptions of their own desire and their will to migrate.

References to the desire to move are also very important for our understanding of the subjects' attitude towards Europe, the West and their native countries as well as to the countries of migration. One of the questions that came up in the interviews concerned the migrants' conceptualizations of Europe, and how their notions of European-ness relate to pre-existing images of the West. As expected, references to Europe and to the West were, in most cases, indirect and embedded in the migrants' descriptions of their experiences and their judgment of the countries of migration, as well as in their attitudes towards their native countries – in particular with regard to their positions on the issue of repatriation. These descriptions and attitudes are interdependent in the sense that we cannot understand the migrants' attitude towards Italy or the Netherlands unless we relate it to how they think about returning to their native countries. The reasons migrants give, in order to explain their desire to return to Bulgaria or Hungary, are related to their judgments of the countries of migration and their cultures, politics and everyday life. However, the ways in which they view Europe, the West and their countries (of origin and/or of migration) are influenced by the way in which they experience mobility. In almost all of the cases movement is presented as an on-going process. Moving from the one country to the other, from the one city to the other, back and forth between the native country and others is presented as a continuous process that should not be impeded by political and social factors and regulations. European countries, but also others that seem to be incorporated in the West, such as post-colonial Tunisia, seem to belong in a familiar territory within which movement does not represent a rupture in one's life's course. Even in the case of narratives that register nostalgia and homesickness, the physical movement away from the native land does not seem to represent a traumatic experience of separation. References to the notion of insurmountable distance, long or expensive journeys, long-term obstacles to communication are almost absent. Some exceptions can be found in the case of political migrants, when they refer to periods when, for political reasons, communication was very difficult with members of their families who had stayed behind. In general however, subjects seem to consider it common sense that they travel to their homeland at least twice a year and that they keep close relationships with family, friends and professional associates. Life in the homeland is not presented as a life left behind. In this respect, the narration of migration does not borrow elements of the rhetoric of loss and of death that we find in the study of other cases of migrant cultures. The chord between homeland and migrant land is alive and dynamic, and mobility between the East and the West is experienced as a continuous process of movement within a wider territory of Europe. As Marina, who was born in Sofia in 1967 and who left her country a few years ago after she fell in love with an Italian journalist, put it: 'it is trivial to talk about global world, but this is reality. I can see that my Bulgarian friends and I read the same books and we watch the same TV programs, we follow the progress of the same world events. So the distance between us is not so big' (Marina, Bu/I).

In this regard, the migrants' attitudes towards their homelands and towards their countries of residence are very ambivalent and fluid. Very rarely do we encounter fixed and wholehearted presentations of paradise either in descriptions of the homeland, or in descriptions of the country of migration. More importantly, it appears that migrants had not even expected to find in the countries to which they had migrated the actual materialisation of utopian visions of the West. The concept of the West that appears in the interviews has no strict territorial reference, but rather refers to the level of desire, objects, arrangements, ways of feeling and experiences that the subject desires or has desired in the past. Thus, the discrepancy between utopian visions of the West and the actual situation of the countries of migration is often not expressed as a form of disappointment. There are not many references in the interviews to the expectation of finding a utopian West in Italy or the Netherlands. Disappointment with the conditions of life in Italy or in the Netherlands is culturally defined in terms of national characteristics. Thus, Italy is often presented as being disorganized and bureaucratic, whereas Italian social life is often referred to as being too traditional and family-centred. Few of these critical representations of Italy reflect stereotypical Italian self-perceptions, while others follow typical European perceptions of culture and politics in the Mediterranean South. Similarly, the Netherlands is often presented as culturally reserved and emotionally 'cold'. Descriptions of the Netherlands and Italy are very mixed — critical and positive — quite inconsistent and contradictory, and sometimes even share elements that are used in the descriptions of Hungary and Bulgaria. In some cases, the descriptions of Hungary and Bulgaria are so positive that one may wonder why the subject chose to live elsewhere. These are the cases of subjects whose desire to move had become predominant and independent from territorial determinants. Dissidence in these cases is associated with mobility *per se*, because the latter presupposes disassociation from personal and social norms (i.e. what one is supposed or normally expected to do with their lives). Dissidence is thus expressed through the desire to move, both physically as well as subjectively. Boyana, who left Bulgaria to go to Tunisia, then to the Netherlands and back to Bulgaria in the pre-1989 period, after having been denied permission to study in the United States, admits that 'seeing the world' was her main goal, but then she concludes her interview by insisting that 'her feet are there,' meaning in Bulgaria. In many pre-1989 cases of migration, it is evident that restrictions on travel generated a general and overarching desire to move. Place did not always matter as much as the very experience and condition of being elsewhere (Boyana).

Political space is re-defined by this tendency to be mobile that is very often realized in gendered practices of mobility and in the transformation of gender relationships in Eastern and Western Europe. Through the association of mobility with personal as well as political dissidence, migrants conceptualize Europe more as a condition of aspired mobility than as a specific geopolitical territory or as a form of cultural identification. Eastern European migrants envision being 'Europeanly'[9] as being based on one's ability to move back and forth. This vision is very closely connected with a notion of the West as a utopian universe defined by one's ability to move, physically as well as psychically, and to pursue alternative life-courses.

## Curved Spaces

The association, made by the Eastern European migrants in these interviews, of the West, Europe and mobility has to be contextualized according to shifting conceptualizations of political space between Eastern and Western Europe. These interviews take place at a historical moment of transformation, marked by the processes of political, cultural and social transition in East Europe of the post-1989 period. During the last decade, gender relations have been at the core of these processes in many ways. First, the transition from state socialism to capitalism has had a huge impact on the lives and the position of women in Eastern European societies. Second, the re-arrangement of gender relations registers, and is indicative of, a wide range of changes that are related to the modification of political and social practices as well as understandings of the private and public sphere in post-communism (Einhorn 1993; Funk and Mueller 1993; Moghadam 1993; Rueschemeyer 1994; Corrin 1992; Reading 1992; Posadskaya 1994). Third, as political change has been accompanied by the intensification of multi-level communication between the European East and the West, gender issues have become particularly contentious and almost emblematic of the difficulties of communication and mutual understanding that exist between the two sides; ruptures that were powerfully and lastingly forged during the Cold War.

Since the early 1990s there has been a growing body of scholarship that addresses the relation between gender and political transition in Eastern and Central Europe. In many cases this scholarship has diagnosed a difficulty in communication about issues related to gender. Scholars have stressed how the presumption that political identities and categories under capitalist and communist regimes are fundamentally the same underpins the tensions in West–East transnational feminist debate. These tensions often concern the so-called 'paradox of (anti) feminism' in East Europe. This paradox is defined by two main elements: one, the realization that political transition has in many respects led to the deterioration of conditions in women's lives in the East (as indicated in less political participation, rising unemployment, the roll-back of social services, the masculinization of property, state intervention in reproductive practices, etc.); and two, the great apprehension felt by women in the East about unproblematically embracing feminism as an emblematic force of democratization (Watson 2000).[10]

This apprehension has been a common characteristic in countries where feminism was introduced early on, through state politics as part of projects which aimed at the modernization of traditional societies. State feminism has, in many cases, operated as a tool of political transition that marked the consolidation of modern nation-states and different projects of modernization in the twentieth century. State feminism in these cases developed a political agenda that aimed at the re-organization of the family and attempted to bring about changes in family law with the purpose of placing women in the role of the active and more efficient managers of the economics and the morals of the family unit. Moreover, it also aimed to promote the further introduction of working and lower middle-class women into the labour market – by endowing paid female labour with the aura of a means of emancipation – and to educate women so that they would undertake the task of being the interlocutors between Western ideas and methods of managing affective and family relationships on the one hand, and the traditional societies that had to be modernized on the other.[11]

The experience of the last decade has shown that, in the cases of political transition in Eastern and Central Europe and in the Balkans, Western feminism has often assumed the role of the promoter of Western values of liberal democracy and capitalist re-organization of society. More dramatically, since the early 1990s Western feminist agendas have been appropriated in order to legitimize and provide a moral background to practices of military intervention in the context of a series of 'just wars' conducted by Western countries in the Balkans and in the Middle East. Although feminists around the globe are very much aware that 'defending women and children from their own people's barbarity' has historically been used as an argument by colonizers and aggressors in order to legitimize the most cruel practices of territorial expansion and the establishment of coercive systems of control, in practice transnational feminist politics have not problematized adequately the different levels of complicity that the appropriation of feminist agendas today involves.[12]

It would however be a mistake to argue that the crisis in communication between Easterners and Westerners immediately after the changes of 1989 concerned exclusively feminists or the debates taking place within transnational feminism. As it has been pointed out, the late 1980s and early 1990s were marked by a generalized crisis in communication especially between partners whose intellectual engagement had anticipated the process of political transition. Interestingly, scholars who have attempted to analyse this communication failure have also pointed out that the incomprehensibility became even more apparent when post-communist Easterners were brought into discussion with Western Marxist thinkers. The communication failure was not in these cases attributed to cultural difference, but rather to the divergent meanings of homonymous concepts whose uses derived from differing political histories (Buck-Morss 2000).[13] If the communist regime has operated as a significant heterotopia for western democracies – including marxist intellectuals in the West – and *vice versa*, then the crisis of communication should be attributed to what Nikolchina terms an uncritical homonymic use of heterotopian signifieds. 'The trouble springs from the fact that the homonymy of signifieds, which, as in Foucault's specular definition of heterotopia, 'represent, contest, and invert' each other, has a neutralizing or even deadly effect when the mirror falls to pieces and the spaces on its two sides merge'.[14]

The more it becomes evident that, in order to explore and re-conceptualise the history of the European twentieth century beyond the Manichean terminology of the Cold War (i.e. beyond the fragmented vision of two Europes divided by the Iron Curtain), we cannot rely upon the obsolescent steadiness of heterotopian knowledge, the more we realize the need for new languages of communication and new concepts of analysis of Europe. Within this new project, the re-conceptualization of the space marked by the mobility of people whose lives transcend the changing borders between the East and the West is a first priority. Focusing on the association between mobility, visions of the West and Europeaness distances us from notions of an absolute space that does, or does not, accommodate the movement of social actors, identities and culture. The interviews analysed in this chapter indicate that it is the physical and psychic movement of people that defines space on different levels of interaction between the European East and the West. The understanding of subjective relationships between the European East and the European West as established by political/social actors in the pre-defined absolute space of post-communism leads to the deadlock of communication, which has already been described by theorists both in the East as well as in the West. Furthermore, presupposing knowledge of this political space just by naming it as post-communism – or as the European Union – and then trying to re-accommodate the history of a great part of the twentieth century under the reformist umbrella of western democratic normativity – in which feminism is then presented as a means of democratic reform – obliterates the challenge that historicity poses to our understandings of the world.

A return to historicity would direct our attention to the ways in which the space between East and West is constituted by the historical experiences and the visions of those whose movement defines – and is defined by and across – the political borders between the East and the West, in a period when these borders, as well as their imaginary functions, are intensively mobile and transitional. The ideas of Europe and the West that emerge in the interviews promote a notion of curved space, in the sense that political space between the East and the West is de-territorialized and re-determined by the physical as well as the subjective movement of actors. As has been argued, 'with political 'curved space" (…) political actors/identities, rather than acting 'within' political space, or being prevented from so doing by virtue of space's lack, instead *constitute, as they are constituted by* a specific political 'curved space' (Watson 2000: 197). As analysed in the previous section, dissidence towards normativity, the desire to move and the ability to maintain the distinction between utopian visions of the West as a condition of aspiring mobility and the migrants' actual experiences in Italy and the Netherlands, become factors that curve the political space between the European East and the West.

In the following section, I discuss how, in the process of migration, the political space between East and West is curved through 'moving relationships' that migrants pursue, establish and maintain.

## Relationships that Move You

Migration often entails the physical disruption of intimate relationships and, in some cases, it also involves taking a distance from one's own familiar territory, surroundings and social as well as family circles. In our interviews with Eastern European migrants to Italy and the Netherlands, mobility is most often either motivated by relationships, or has enabled the establishment of new relationships. We can understand this link between mobility and relationships in a twofold way. First, mobility can be motivated by relationships. The most typical examples of this are the movement that is subsequent to the establishment of relationships between people with different origins, and that which is involved in situations of family re-unification, caring for parents, children and other dependent family members. Secondly, relationships enable mobility on a more subjective level. Relationships provide the context within which the subject reflects on changes that are taking place in her personality, her desires, her general outlook and her plans for the future. In this sense relationships are associated with psychic and subjective forms of mobility. The subjects are thus both physically as well as psychically and subjectively moved *by* and *through* their relationships. In many cases, the interviewees emphatically insist on the inseparable intertwining between physical and subjective movement in a way that does not allow for any attempt to distinguish between the two aspects of mobility. This systematic insistence creates the impression that, for the interviewees, migration cannot be understood without a consideration of the relationships involved in the process, and also that the relationships necessarily result in personal transformation and movement. Relationships that are created prior to migration have an impact on the decision to move, whereas other relationships become important after the relocation to a new place, where they facilitate changes in the conditions of one's life and outlook.

Intimate and emotional relationships can operate both as motives for, as well as deterrents against, migration. In some cases, the migrant's relationships connect her with her place of origin, whereas in other cases relationships push her to transcend traditional bonds related to her social circles in the homeland. In many cases, relationships with people in the homeland remain un-named, as the interviewee refers to them using general terms such as 'family and friends' (Agi, Hu/NL). On the contrary, 'moving' relationships are named and exemplified. This is often expressed in contradictory ways (Boyana, Bu/NL), when for example migrants insist on the intimacy and closeness of relationships in East Europe while, at the same time, they also insist that it was an intimate relationship that made them move to the other country (Piroska, Hu/NL).

In many cases, relationships – or even the potential to establish relationships – redefine space, as they make geography and the psychic self intersect. Migrants often describe and evaluate cities and places of residence in terms of how suitable these places are for the establishment of personal relationships with others. This is more evident in the case of migrants who have followed a long itinerary of migrations. In these cases the experience of mobility is expressed though a constant evaluation of different places based on the subject's experiences of movement. Boyana, a 63 year-old Bulgarian violinist, left her homeland when she was very young. After completing her studies at the conservatorium, she worked for a couple of years in Bulgaria and then accepted a job as a performer in Tunis. Her ambition to continue her music studies in the U.S. was curtailed when her application for permission to accept a scholarship offered to her by the Boston Conservatorium was officially rejected. Thus, Boyana returned to Tunis where she stayed for eleven years, until she met her French husband and moved with him to Strasburg. Since then she has pursued her career and personal life in different European cities including Utrecht and Amsterdam. Establishing intimate relationships is presented as a major goal in this migrant's life, and the possibilities that a place offers for this become an important criterion for evaluating a city, a country, a culture, or a people. Despite her love for Amsterdam, Boyana refers extensively to the difficulties that she faced in establishing friendships there, which she attributes to the 'reserved' character of Dutch culture, as opposed to the 'adventurous' nature of people who, like herself, had been on the move. Intimacy and the potential for establishing close relationships is a constitutive element of subjectivity that emerges in the context of mobility. Relationships move the subject through different points of migration. The migrant's investment in the practices of establishing relationships enables reflection on the different sites of mobility and allows the subject to explain her choices, to argue for her own agency in the process of migration and to make sense of the long series of movements that would otherwise appear as totally circumstantial.

Apart from cities and cultures, there are also particular locations and spaces of social interaction – often related to certain professions and activities – that facilitate the establishment of relationships. As the migrant reflects on how she organizes her life in the context of mobility, special attention is given to the importance of places such as foreign language schools, training and immigration centres, social services and support networks, art centres and different kinds of welfare and sports associations. Even though most of the women insist on the fact that they avoid becoming involved in national associations which would possibly bring them in closer contact with other migrants from their own homeland, they actively pursue their involvement in activities that often attract international participants and publics. Apart from qualifications and expertise, language schools, training centres for women and migrants, and social services often also provide emotional refuge during periods of isolation and uncertainty. Through the relationships that are created in the context of these institutions, migrants share their experiences with others who are in a similar position and thus manage to recognize themselves in the lives of others. The migrants' reliance on social networks which have an international constituency is also reflected by the fact that many of the women who were interviewed often sought employment in sectors related to international professional activities: foreign language schools, universities, the arts, trade, sports and entertainment.

The interviews indicate a productive intersection between love relationships and the ways in which subjects understand and experience physical and affective mobility. This intersection is often articulated through the association between love relationships and the disruption of other social and affective bonds in the lives of women who migrate between Eastern and Western European countries. Let us take the example of Kamilla, who migrated to Italy in 1970. Kamilla was born in 1945 and raised in Budapest by Hungarian parents. At the age of sixteen she learned that she was in fact the out-of-wedlock daughter of a German woman married to a Hungarian man, with four children from that marriage. Having had music lessons at a young age, Kamilla took up singing in her early twenties and soon after that embarked on a performing career, first in Hungary and then abroad. As member of a Hungarian performing group she played music and danced in a number of Italian cities. During these years, however, Kamilla unknowingly became involved in a tax evasion scandal when the manager of the troupe withheld taxes from the artists but never turned money in to the Hungarian tax bureau. As a result of that Kamilla could not return to Hungary because of fear of being persecuted. She mentions that other members of the group who did return had their performing licenses withdrawn and were stranded in their cities of origins for as long as five years. The prospect of being stranded and being left in no position to perform seemed unbearable to Kamilla, who decided instead to stay in Italy under uncertain legal status both in Italy as well as in Hungary. She describes how she was drawn into the status of refugee against her own will, whereas her desire was simply to travel as a way of promoting her career.

For Kamilla, sliding into the status of illegal migrant–refugee involved an itinerary from Italy to South Africa, then Germany and back to Italy. She mentions that she kept touring around twenty-one different countries for about ten years before she relocated herself in Florence. In the process she attempted unsuccessfully to claim German citizenship and acquire legal documentation based on the fact that she was born in Germany. In the meantime, her communication with her family in Hungary had been disrupted, as her father had sent her coded letters warning her not to return in order to avoid persecution. She married an Italian and stayed in Florence with him, but the marriage ended shortly because of general failure in communication both between the couple, and between Kamilla and her husband's family. Kamilla's story is one of disrupted relationships. She presents disruption as a result of her original departure from Hungary. Defecting from her country, even though it was inevitable and beyond her own will or decision, represents in Kamilla's story an 'original sin', which has caused a series of disruptions and anxiety both about her own self and the lives of her loved ones. As she put it: 'since I left Hungary I've been fighting to overcome the difficulties of life. Nothing worked out the way it should've.'

Kamilla refers frequently to her worries about the family she left behind. She also describes mobility as a continuous cause of both further disruption and the establishment of new relationships. It is almost as if the flexibility and change of relationships comes to coincide with the physical mobility of the subject. Later in the interview she turns back to the issue of her biological family origins and at this point it becomes obvious that the 'original moment' of departure that led her to a lifelong experience of mobility has to be traced to the time before her own birth. Kamilla was born in Germany in 1945, the illegitimate child of a German army officer, and a German mother who was then married to a Hungarian soldier, who was at that time on the Russian front. After the war, the mother left the newborn child at the town clinic and returned to Hungary with her husband and her four children. Kamilla was taken under the protection of a Hungarian doctor who was working at the clinic and who, in 1948, decided to move back to Hungary and to bring the child with him. Kamilla was then given up for adoption to a Hungarian couple in Budapest, who raised her as their own child. She discovered that she was adopted when she was sixteen years old. Kamilla's life was marked by the disruption of relationships caused by various experiences of inter-European mobility. She understands her own life as a continuation of this tradition of operating within a geo-political space determined by a web of relationships, some of which are weaved beyond the subject's agency. Kamilla reclaims these relationships that are established and disrupted beyond her agency – such as her relationship with her biological mother – through her references to dreams and intuitive connections. Kamilla refers very often to her dreams, since she is convinced that she is warned by dreams whenever 'trouble is brewing' in her life. She mentions that she had dreamed of her migration before she left, and that later she dreamed of her father being ill when she was abroad. When she narrates her family history and the events of her adoption she does not refer much to her biological mother – although she was the one who played the most important role in the process. However, she concludes her reference to her half-siblings, whom she has never met and by whom she was never accepted, with a story that stresses the psychic connection between herself and her biological mother. According to this story, during a visit to Hungary in order to support her ailing foster mother, Kamilla happened to drive by her biological mother's house, which she vaguely remembered. Without making any further inquiry, she relied on her conviction that this incidental passing in front of the old house was a premonition that her biological mother was dead. Psychic connections, premonitions and instincts become means for reclaiming relationships that have been disrupted. By reclaiming these relationships, Kamilla manages to keep track of her long itinerary of movement and to make sense of her own story by recording her transformations and life changes.

In other cases, the subject experiences these changes through intimate relationships with her children. Relationships with children are particularly moving since the subject's transformation through mobility is reflected in what the children have become. The importance of child–parent relationships becomes more evident in those cases where the subject has particularly invested in the processes of social and cultural integration in the country of migration (Emilia, Hu/NL). For Emilia, a computer programmer, who was born in Budapest in 1958 and who migrated to Holland in 1988, social and cultural integration was achieved through her dedication to her children and their proper upbringing. Thus, her children became a strong link between Emilia and Dutch society and culture. This becomes evident when she explains how raising children in a foreign country motivates a parent to integrate into the new culture. As she put it: 'the moment you realize that this is the place where your children live, where they will grow up, the moment this flashes into your mind, *you have to* get down to it and start learning ... '. The relationship between Emilia and her children constructs a new universe that contains her life in her host country and renders her an integral part of this new universe. In this case, affective relationships become a means of integration and of establishing communication with a foreign culture.

Establishing, maintaining and reclaiming relationships are integral parts in the migration project. In most of the interviews with migrant women, relationships highlight various physical, psychic and subjective aspects of mobility. Through relationships, the physical movement of women between East and West Europe is related to the affective mobility that defines the migrants' subjectivity. From this point of view, the processes of establishing, maintaining and reclaiming relationships exercise a strong power on the 'curving' of political space between the East and the West. By addressing the connection between 'moving' relationships and the redefinition of political space, a new field of inquiry around issues of mobility, communication, participation and cultural emergences is opened up.

Approaching the history of migrants and contemporary migrations in Europe from the perspective of subjectivity, and enlarging the scope of migrant subjectivity through an emphasis on the role that affective relationships play in the context of mobility, goes against the grain of scholarly and other approaches that objectify the migrants by reducing the complex process of mobility to the movement of rational subjects driven solely by economic need, or to the coercive displacement of those who are trafficked or otherwise forcibly brought to the West. Such objectification deprives the social image of migrants in the Western European countries of important elements of agency, complexity and multiplicity. By foregrounding the notion of mobility, I propose an exploration of the physical as well as the psychic, subjective and cultural aspects of women's movements across Europe. Read from this perspective, the interviews offer us valuable lessons, especially because they provide points of critique that undermine normative notions of Europe, cultural territories, political space, home, homeland and migrancy. Through an analysis of the interviews that places emphasis on affective mobility, and consequently offers critique of normative understandings of culture and subjectivity, a ground is offered to us from which we might re-examine our definitions of Europe, the European East and the West, and the curvature of the political space between older definitions and the emerging understandings of people on the move.

*At different stages of conceptualization and writing, this paper has benefited greatly from exchanges and critical discussions with many colleagues at various institutions and academic settings at Ermoupolis (Summer Seminars), Florence, Volos, Mytilini (Department of History and Social Anthropology), Salonica (Conference on Balkans: Readings and Reflections), and Sofia (Gender Studies Program). I am particularly grateful to Athina Athanasiou, Eleonor Koffman, Miglena Nikolchina, Effi Voutira, and David Staples for generously offering comments and valuable suggestions.

## Notes

1. The literature in this field is vast. Here, I am referring mostly to the impact of the intellectual contributions of British scholars working in the field of Cultural Studies, such as Stuart Hall, Homi Bhabha, Paul Gilroy, Robert Young and others.
2. According to ethnographic, sociological and cultural analysis of hybridity, the creation of new migrant communities in the European metropolitan centres led to the emergence of new ways of being a migrant, that did not presuppose assimilation into the hegemonic culture of the country of destination, but which also defied the parochialism that characterized commitment to the norms of old country national culture. This process was also analysed from a different point of view by Etienne Balibar (Balibar and Wallerstein 1991).
3. This is another vast body of literature. Rosi Braidotti's intellectual contribution to the analysis of subjectivity via nomadic thought and ontology is a notable example of the richness and the strong impact of this approach on the study of migrant subjectivity (Braidotti 1994).
4. 'Whereas the immigrant leaves behind a milieu that has become amorphous and hostile, the nomad is the one who does not depart, does not want to depart, who clings to the smooth space left by the receding forest, whether the steppe, or the desert …' (Deleuze and Guattari 1987 [1980]: 381).
5. For a critique of this approach see Cheah and Robbins 1998.
6. With reference to post-1989 migrations in Europe, Nira Yuval-Davis has proposed the notion of multi-layered forms of becoming full member in a community in the age of globalization. She endorses the notion of 'transversal citizenship' in order to envision the possibility of new form of politics of difference. Transversal citizenship is grounded on the idea that 'difference encompasses equality and perceived unity and homogeneity are replaced by dialogues that give recognition to the specific positioning of those who participate in them as well as the 'unfinished knowledge' that each such positioning can offer' (Yuval-Davis 1999: 123). Transversal citizenship is thus based on an epistemological and political distinction between the notion of participation in and identification with a community. This new form of transversal citizenship fits with the new forms of subjectivity that have emerged as the result of mass movements and the diversification of the social body in European societies.
7. Elsewhere, I have analysed the role that the models of assimilation and/or integration have played in producing authoritative representations of the migrant as an uprooted subject whose history constitutes exclusively part of the national history of the recipient country. Research in the transnational history of migrants indicates that migration has historically played an important role in the consolidation of ideological

discourses on nationhood in countries of emigration. For such analysis in the case of Greece and Greek migration, see Laliotou 2004.
8. The scholarship on queer diaspora is extremely rich and diverse. For a comprehensive overview of such scholarship in the field of Asian American studies, see (Eng and Hom 1998; Jackson 2000; Mackie 2001).
9. By using the adverbial form of 'European' (unusual in English but present and sensible in other languages), I wish to stress and maintain the importance of the difference between being someone and enacting oneself in a particular way. Addressing the ontological aspect of this difference is much beyond the scope of this chapter, but I think the distinction has important implications for the ways in which cultural, political and intellectual mobility and exchanges between the East and West open up new possibilities for envisioning Europe beyond Eurocentrism today.
10. Peggy Watson describes this paradox by referring to the difficulties that Eastern thinkers and activists have encountered when trying to convey the different ways in which inequality is articulated in their countries to Western feminists. She argues that, from the beginning, much of the transnational literature on women in post-communism has reflected a need to account for the non-sequitur which anti-feminism after communism appeared to represent (Watson 2000: 191).
12. As Peggy Watson has suggested 'if feminism's raison d'être is specific to political exclusion in democratic regimes (...) how far is feminist discourse of transition actively reproducing the preconditions of its own existence, in naturalizing competitive democracy through a categorical focus on gender, and taking for granted the broader implications of the state-economy changes currently being put in place? Such considerations have been left outside the analysis of post-communism, where intellectual inquiry has been overly restricted to the excavation of the kind of communist legacies which will explain failed predictions, but leave presuppositions intact' (Watson 2000: 195).
13. Evidently, there is a notable lack of theorisation of the issue of East–West (mis-) communication on the part of Western European intellectuals and scholars. This lack is, I believe, indicative of how prone Western European intellectuals are to presume the commonality of language and terminology when it comes to engaging in debates with different intellectual environments and traditions. The Euro-centricity of such intellectual engagements is only conducive to the further deepening of the crisis of communication and the hardening of ideological positions that support the 'right' of the West to 'protect', 'educate' and 'develop' the European East and the Balkans.
14. As Nikolchina astutely points out, this neutralization and homonymy of unacknowledged differences resulted in a desematization of the signifiers, which then led to the evacuation of meaning and the disabling of communication that became apparent during the messy Yugoslav wars and which has migrated to subsequent conflicts, which are 'as bloody as they are inarticulate' (Nikolchina, forthcoming: 5–6).

# References

Balibar, E. and I. Wallerstein 1991. *Race, Nation, Class: Ambiguous Identities*, London, Verso.
Bell, D. and J. Binnie 2000. *The Sexual Citizen: Queer Politics and Beyond*,
Binnie, J. 1997. 'Invisible Europeans: Sexual Citizenship in the New Europe', *Environment and Planning A*, 29: 237.

Binnie, J. and G. Valentine 1999. 'Geographies of Sexuality. A Review of Progress', *Progress in Human Geography*, 175.

Braidotti, R. 1994. *Nomadic Subjects: Embodiment and Sexual Difference in Contemporary Feminist Theory*, New York, Columbia University Press.

Buck-Morss, S. 2000. *Dreamworld and Catastrophe: The Passing of Mass-Utopia in East and West*, Cambridge, MIT Press.

Cheag, P. and B. Robbins (eds.) 1998. *Cosmopolitics: Thinking and Feeling beyond the Nation*, Minneapolis, University of Minnesota.

Corrin, C. (ed.) 1992. *Superwomen and the Double Burden: Women's Experience of Change in Central and Eastern Europe and the Former Soviet Union*, Toronto, Second Story Press.

Derrida, J. 2003. *On Cosmopolitanism and Forgiveness*, London and New York, Routledge.

Desai, J. 2002. 'Home on the Range. Mobile and Global Sexualities', *Social Text*, 73(20)(Winter): 4.

Einhorn, B, ed. 1993. *Cinderella Goes to Market: Citizenship, Gender, and Women's Movements in East Central Europe*, London, Verso.

Eng, D.L. 1997. 'Out Here and Over There: Queerness and Diaspora in Asian American Studies', *Social Text, Queer Transexions of Race, Nation and Gender*, 52–3, Autumn-Winter.

Eng, D.L. and A.H. Hom (eds.) 1998. *Queer in Asian America*, Philadelphia, Temple University Press.

Funk N. and M. Mueller (eds.) 1993. *Gender Politics and Post-Communism: Reflections from Eastern Europe and the Former Soviet Union*, New York, Routledge.

Jackson, P.A. 2000. 'An Explosion of Thai Identities: Global Queering and Re-imagining Queer Theory', *Culture, Health and Sexuality* 2(4): 405–24.

Laliotou, I. 2004. *Transatlantic Subjects. Acts of Migration and Cultures of Transnationalism between Greece and America*, Chicago, The University of Chicago Press.

Mackie, V. 2001. 'The Transexual Citizen: Queering Sameness and Difference', *Australian Feminist Studies*, 16.

Moghadam, V. (ed.) 1993. *Democratic Reform and the Position of Women in Transitional Economies*, Oxford, Clarendon Press.

Nikolchina, M. forthcoming 'The West as Intellectual Utopia', in M. Todorova (ed.) *Remembering Communism: Genres of Representation*, New York: SSRC.

Ong, A. 1999. *Flexible Citizenship. The Cultural Logics of Transnationality*, Durham and London, Duke University Press.

Posadskaya, A. (ed.) 1994. *Women in Russia: A New Era in Russian Feminism*, London: Verso.

Reading, A. (ed.) 1992. *Polish Women, Solidarity, and Feminism*, London, Macmillan.

Rueschemeyer, M. (ed.) 1994. *Women in the Politics of Postcommunist Eastern Europe*, Armonk, N.Y. and London, M.E. Sharpe.

Sinfield, A. 1996. 'Diaspora and Hybridity: Queer Identities and the Ethnicity Model', *Textual Practice*, 10(2): 292–3.

Stychin, C.F. 2000. "A Stranger to its Laws': Sovereign Bodies, Global Sexualities and Transnational Citizens', *Journal of Law and Society* 27(4): 601–25.

Yuval-Davis, N. 1999. 'The 'Multi-layered Citizen'. Citizenship in the Age of 'Globalization', *International Feminist Journal of Politics* 1(1): 119–36.

Watson, P. 2000. 'Rethinking Transition. Globalism, Gender and Class', *International Feminist Journal of Politics*, Summer, 2.

Weston, K. 1995. 'Get Thee to a Big City: Sexual Imaginary and the Great Gay Migration', *2 Gay and lesbian Q:* 253.

*Chapter 3*

# Transformations of Legal Subjectivity in Europe: From the Subjection of Women to Privileged Subjects

*Hanne Petersen*

## European Legal Culture in Transformation: Towards Privileged Legal Subjectivity?

Modern European legal culture has been strongly influenced by the importance of national legal systems. For centuries, states have had a very strong role in lawmaking. Modern legislation has been understood as being equally valid for all citizens, and laws have been expected to be general and not to give special rights to special groups or individuals. Legislation, especially in Northern Europe, has been understood to be secular. Marriage has been assumed to be a voluntary monogamous union between a man and a woman, and legal restrictions on movement from one country to another have been usual. Family life has been protected legally, and foreigners (especially foreign women) who have married nationals have typically been granted easier (privileged) access to citizenship in a national jurisdiction. Europeans themselves have typically considered their own social and legal systems as superior to non-European systems, perhaps with the exception of American legal culture.

However, European legal culture is changing, partly because of the establishment of the EEC which has developed into an expanding EU, and partly because of the processes that are often described as globalization. There is a clear shift from normative jurisprudence to cultural pluralism in contemporary legal studies (Paasilehto 2002: 39). There is also an enormous general increase in studies dealing with globalization, a term that has only really been used since 1989, including some that deal with the consequences of globalization for legal theory (Petersen 2002).

It is not possible to give a clear picture of how these changes, at individual, national and European levels, will transform Europe's legal culture or cultures. But a number of indicators of change are already present. Much of what has so far been considered European *migration*, will, within an expanded Europe, be understood as legal and legally protected *mobility*. Mobility of privileged, resourceful Eastern Europeans will, in a longer time perspective, most likely not be restricted legally, regardless of gender. Many Europeans will in the future have different and overlapping kinds of legal subjectivity. In the process of becoming European subjects, a more instrumental approach to national citizenship may be developed. The role of states in the making of 'law in books' may decline. Europe's 'law' will consist of international law, EU-law, judge-made law, national law, and market law, to name the most important forms of law. These different legal regimes will not be equally valid for every European. Europe and Europeans will experience increasing legal diversity, although a different kind of diversity than that which was known in the period of the hegemony of state law. Under a regime of EU-law, legal diversity will probably originate from competing horizontal, as well as competing and combined hierarchical, sources of legality. State legal regimes may compete and coexist with other national legal regimes as well as with EU-law and international law, not least in areas of migration and marriage. In practice, what will emerge may look like a regime of special rights, general rights and different advantages. The most likely beneficiaries of this conglomerate of legal regimes will be those with the greatest bargaining power and access to market privileges.

The religious/Christian underpinnings of European (marriage) law may become a more strongly contested issue. Changes of migration law may undermine the assumption – stronger in some European legal cultures than in others – that European marriage law is based upon a love relationship, and not upon concerns about economic maintenance. The hegemony of marriage law which assumes that marriage is a legal union between a man and one woman is already a contested issue, both by homosexual groups and by Muslim migrants and European Muslims. Differential treatment of citizens with different ethnic backgrounds may become more usual. A jurisprudence of difference will challenge the twentieth-century's legacy of modern jurisprudence based upon the dominance of values of equal rights and freedom. Europeans may experience greater insecurity about their present social and legal systems. European identity may gradually become stronger but not necessarily more unified.

This chapter deals with some of the challenges which these transformation processes present to an emerging EUropean socio-legal and cultural research. It describes the increased necessity to transcend disciplinary and national boundaries of legal knowledge, and demonstrates how the research project has challenged methodological tools as well as the way we address our (new and different) audiences and readers. The research project has chosen 'subjectivity' as a core concept. It is discussed how in the pre-modern period the term was used to indicate a hierarchical relationship between ruler and ruled. Women were subjected to men, and regulations were differentiated through special rights and privilege. Now when the importance of Europe, culturally, legally and politically is growing 'new' forms of legal subjectivity are emerging. The chapter claims that a European legal culture has to deal with multiple selves in complex legal contexts and has to face an emerging regime of privilege which is no longer based in laws but rather in the market.

## European Interdisciplinary Research about Gender Relations: Methods and Definitions

The bulk of legal research and jurisprudence done in Europe in the twentieth century has dealt with positive law and with the systems of creation, administration and implementation of positive legal norms. From the beginning of the century national (democratic) legal systems became the focus of legal research in a struggle against the heritage of Natural law. The totalitarian heritage in (western) European law – what has been called the 'darker legacies of law' (Joerges and Ghaleigh 2003) – has not been part of mainstream research, either on a national level or on a European level. During the last part of the century, a focus upon EUropean law has gradually gained ground.

The dominant approach to the study of law, both on a national and on a European level, has been a uni-disciplinary approach. European *interdisciplinary* studies of law are not that usual, and studies involving a gendered legal perspective have only emerged within the last thirty years. In Northern Europe, Nordic Women's Law has, for a quarter of a century, attempted to work with transnational and, to a certain degree, also interdisciplinary approaches and methods, both at home and outside of Europe (Dahl 1987; Petersen 1996a; Hellum 1999; Nousiainen *et al.* 2001). This theoretical and methodological legacy is an important reason why Denmark provides us with a case which exemplifies the legal aspects of gender relations in Europe at the turn of the millennium. The studies of 'women's law' in the Nordic countries has been strongly influenced by socio-legal thinking within the framework of secularized, protestant, social democratic welfare states and welfare regimes – all influenced by international and Anglo-Saxon feminist jurisprudence (Olsen 1995). Nordic Women's Law has developed in a period which has been characterized by important changes in gender relations, important changes in women's work, which has gradually come to encompass both unpaid work in the home and a constantly growing participation in paid work for an ever large proportion of women, as well as a significant reconstitution of family life, where divorce rates have grown dramatically and where, as a consequence, the legal institution of marriage has lost its former social function as a legal frame of a stable and enduring intimate union. Processes of individualization supported by legal regulation have been particularly strong in the Nordic countries and in Denmark. Several of the developments in Northern Europe may be more comparable to the situation in what is no longer called 'Eastern Europe', than to the situation in Southern Europe. Nousiainen writes that 'the Nordic model differs from the Continental one because it favours women's opting out of families and family dependency whereas the conservative Continental regime favours their opting into family' (2001: 36).

The development of a field sometimes called 'feminist jurisprudence' is not only linked to so-called Western countries including Europe, but, as is well known, also has had global expressions (Armstrong and Welshman 1987; Stewart and Armstrong 1990; Mehdi and Shaheed 1997). The work of the organization known under the acronym WLUML (Women Living under Muslim Law) is especially important in this respect. There are, however, probably distinct European traits to the emergence of this international field of knowledge, which are related to the strong importance of nation state positive law and legislation, especially in continental Europe. In order to understand the normative principles and values, which inform the choices and actions of European women in a reconfigured Europe and an expanding European Union, interdisciplinary European research, which includes a socio-legal and gendered approach, is important.

In this interdisciplinary research project, the bulk of the work which has been done has consisted of collecting sources of oral history – individual stories about women, who have moved from one European country to another and/or married there. Decisions to change place and establish relations of a personal, social, cultural, economic and legal nature are individual, but they are also influenced by contexts, expectations and traditions. They take place within a European context at the turn of the millennium, where important social, cultural and legal transformations are also taking place. These transformations influence both personal considerations and resources, but the reverse is also true. The accumulated effects of wo/men's choices influence general political and legal considerations. Time and space matter, as do patterns of uncoordinated but combined and similar actions. The interviews give an idea about both differences and similarities in the reflections, motivations and concerns of women moving from the eastern part of Europe to Western European countries. They also give an idea about how women's expectations and decisions have clear normative implications and thus have relevance for legal systems and thinking.

The legal approach taken here has involved a combination of a case study and a study of socio-legal cultural developments, informed by both the biographical approaches and the legal case study. From a legal perspective, the case study serves as a method which illustrates the general and common research questions of the project in at least two ways.

The *first* and most important approach has been to study *one* example of a European national legal system more closely, namely the Danish legal system. The Danish case study presented by Conradsen and Kronborg in this book illustrates how one national legal system attempts to manage the changes and limitations of its legislative and state powers, due to globalization processes of increased global mobility of human beings, money and goods, and to the expansion of the European union. The case study thus gives an idea about how changing understandings of national and European identities and values influence local and supranational law-making and legal cultures. The Danish case study may also give a sense of the more general – and often very restrictive – legislative climate emerging in EUropean countries today in matters regarding trans-national marriages and third country migration.

This case study is not meant to be a 'traditional' legal *Länderbericht*, in the sense in which this concept is used in comparative legal theory, which usually compares *national* legal systems to each other, and sometimes clusters them in what is called *legal* families (see also Petersen 1996b). It can rather be seen as an attempt to map a corner of the European legal landscape by combining a normative or legal dogmatic approach with a legal cultural approach. The points of orientation of this process of mapping are *marriage*, *migration* and *subjectivity* seen from legal perspectives. The Danish case can also be seen as an example of a 'radical case'. It is an example of a national community with a self-understanding as being equality minded, liberal and tolerant, but as other Nordic countries it has difficulties dealing with contemporary diversity (Svensson *et al.* 2004). National regulation, which may be understood as discriminatory from outside, is not necessarily viewed as such in Denmark, and recent changes of immigration law have not been opposed strongly internally. These regulations may be at odds with traditional legal values (protecting women via their status as spouses), but they are not necessarily opposed to emerging (post) modern values or to an emerging (Nordic) legal culture, where marriage has lost its importance, but loyalty towards the welfare state and the legislator may still be strong (see also Nousiainen *et al.* 2001: 15–20).

The *second* use of the case method relates to the legal insights which may be gained through taking legal perspectives of the interview-material. To use the term of the Dutch legal anthropologist J. F. Holleman (1994), the interviews may generally be described as '*trouble-less cases*'. These are cases which have not necessarily resulted in formal legal conflicts. In very few of the life stories described in the interviews have serious legal conflicts arisen in connection to relationships. Nonetheless, the cases may contribute to a broader understanding of some of the normative processes through which a new European legal culture and new legal regimes may be emerging. We may find indications in this material of guiding normative principles and values, which could be important in a broader 'range of socio-legal traffic' taking place in Europe at the turn of the millennium. And as Holleman also claims 'it is the common trouble-less cases of normal practice that usually constitute the normative frame of reference by which trouble-cases themselves are being judged'. That is, the legally – and politically – *relatively* uncontroversial cases of trans-national movements and legal migrations of ('Eastern' and 'Western') European women and of trans-national marriages between Europeans – serve as the normative frame of reference by which trouble cases involving mobility and marriage of Europeans as well as non-Europeans may be judged.

In an interdisciplinary research project, another difficulty stems from the fact that we use terms and concepts which have different histories and different meanings within different disciplinary traditions of knowledge. This is especially striking with regard to the concepts of *subject* and *subjectivity*. The use of the term differs from one field of knowledge to another as well as from one national and professional language to another. That we are dealing with an elusive term is indicated by the fact that a general search for the term 'subject' in Oxford Reference Online displays 98 results of understandings of the term 'subject' and of its use in specific relations.

In the project, the term is used in at least two important ways, one more related to social theory in a very broad sense and one related to legal theory in a more narrow sense. This paper will deal primarily with the legal understanding of the term, and with its developments.

The Danish and German contemporary understanding seem to be very similar: 'the legal subject describes all persons who are bearers of rights and obligations. Besides natural persons (human beings) these are also legal persons in their different legal forms such as associations, corporations, companies with limited liabilities and by public law bodies' [author's translation].[1] In English, the term 'subject' may be used to describe somebody, who 'is under the dominion of a sovereign', and it may also refer to the term 'citizen'. In German and Danish, the first understanding of 'subject' is translated in ways which underline the hierarchical relations between the sovereign and the ruled. The imperial as well as colonial heritage of the term is underlined in the way Oxford Reference Online explains the term 'British subject'.[2]

A contemporary, differentiated, legal subject-hood both within the individual European nations and member states of the EU, and within the EU itself, opens the doors to social relations of great complexity, as well as to legal relations of great complexity. We may envisage a future, where legal and social relations could be characterized by individuals, whose *statuses* are becoming more and more different, and where the change in economic and legal status will have serious implications for the rights and obligations of individual subjects.

## Pre-modern Privileged 'Subjectivity' and the Legal Subordination of Women

Not so terribly long ago, before modern democratic constitutions and systems became the dominant mode through which to exercise power in Europe, subjects were actually subjected or subordinated – often to absolutist kings or princes. Political and legal relations were organized hierarchically in societies, as in marriage. Men and women were legal subjects with different duties and obligations towards superiors and rulers. However collective entities could also be legal subjects organized according to territory, as in the German 'Kommune' (municipality), or in the Renaissance, as in the autonomous cities of Northern Italy. Companies, foundations, charitable institutions, guilds and other such entities were examples of functionally organized forms of legal subjects. These kinds of legal subjects were socially constructed entities, created often for specific purposes and often also through specific privileges (Dübeck 1991). To give a contemporary example, the EU has been struggling to become a legal subject especially in international relations and in international laws for some time. The EU constitution is, amongst other things, an instrument meant to achieve this goal. Depending upon the power of the superior – the King or sometimes Queen – the privileges of these subjects could be withdrawn or the subjects / 'undersåtter' could be given or contracted away, as was the case with 'the bishoprics, dioceses, and provinces which make up all of the kingdom of Norway, *including all its inhabitants*, cities, ports, fortresses, villages and islands on all coasts of this' [author's emphasis]. In a peace-treaty in 1814 – after the Napoleonic wars – the king of the double monarchy of Norway and Denmark, was forced to surrender Norway – including inhabitants as well as all 'privileges, rights, and advantages' to the Swedish king.

Privileges were *special* rights – either favourable or unfavourable (privilegia *favorabilia, privilegia odiosa*) given to individuals, groups of people or other legal subjects by the sovereign ruler – originally, often because these groups or entities carried out specific tasks which were considered to be of general interest. This system with special rights for specifically identified social groups created very complex legal situations. When the Danish jurist Ørsted, in 1828, published the third volume of his handbook on Danish and Norwegian legal skills, his chapter on 'privileged persons' took up 107 pages out of 568 pages. Other chapters dealt with citizens of market towns and with peasants (1828). The nobility and the church were estates and institutions which enjoyed special favourable rights (especially tax exemption) in most European countries. The Reformation abolished ecclesiastical privileges in protestant countries, and after the French Revolution, special favourable rights for the nobility were gradually abolished in Europe and special unfavourable regulations regarding copyholders and slaves were also abolished. In 1861 a few years before slavery was abolished in the U.S., John Stuart Mill published his modern classic, *The Subjection of Women*, a thorough argument in favour of legal equality between women and men. He claimed then: 'that the principle which regulates the existing social relations between the two sexes – the legal subordination of one sex to the other – is wrong in itself, and now one of the chief hindrances to human improvement; and that it ought to be replaced by a principle of perfect equality, admitting no power or privilege on the one side, nor disability on the other' (Mill 1986: 7). Mill – and many others – described 'the peculiar character of the modern world' as being that 'human beings are no longer born to their place in life, and chained down by an inexorable bond to the place they are born to, but are free to employ their faculties, and such favourable chances as offer, to achieve the lot which may appear to them most desirable' (1986: 22).

In today's processes of European social, cultural and legal change, it should perhaps be remembered that less than 200 years before the 'reunification' of Europe in 1989, the legal culture of Europe was *dominated* by legal regimes based upon special rights and privileges, combined with general rights. Two hundred years ago, these special rights were primarily legal rights granted by a sovereign, an absolute monarch or an emperor. European legal history is thus a history of different rights for different groups (estates and classes) of people including different rights for men and women. Contemporary European legal culture may still be more influenced by this legacy than we might think. With the expansion of the EU to include a very large number of new member states, the diversity of the historical and cultural legacies becomes more clearly seen and felt. It may also be expected that the diversity of the legal traditions and cultures within the enlarged EU will have an influence on cooperation between member states and in the EU. The legal situation of individuals in the new member states will most likely gradually undergo a number of changes. And the actual legal positions of the millions of individuals who feel they 'belong' to Europe and the European Union will most likely not become equal in any near future. The socio-legal diversity will continue – the EU-constitution speaks about a Europe *'united in diversity'*. It may however be a reconstructed and restructured diversity, with new winners and most surely also new losers – new subjects experiencing favourable and unfavourable privileges.

## Modern Citizenship: The 'Unencumbered Citizen' as Subject of Equal Rights

With the change in Europe from monarchies to constitutional monarchies, republics, and democracies, the legal relationships between authority and subject slowly changed. Loyal subordinates gradually became formal legal citizens of the new and emerging states, and acquired rights. Differential legal treatment was, however, not promptly removed by the new bourgeois democracies. In 1861, John Stuart Mill described how 'the law of the strongest' seemed to be then at least partially abandoned:

> We now live – that is to say, one or two of the most advanced nations of the world now live – in a state in which the law of the strongest seems to be entirely abandoned as the regulating principle of the world's affairs: nobody professes it, and, as regards most of the relations between human beings, nobody is permitted to practice it. When anyone succeeds in doing so, it is under cover of some pretext which gives him the semblance of having some general social interest on his side (1986: 12).

The legal concepts of subject, citizen, person and people were and are fictitious and (re)constructed concepts, which have never related to what we would today consider empirical understandings of these concepts. Special rights granted to white, land-owning men were little by little removed and/or expanded to men without private property, as well as to women and black men. In the middle of the twentieth century, political rights were granted to what was earlier called 'primitive' human beings – often nomadic people, who since have been called indigenous peoples (especially in North America and Northern Europe). This legal and political development was closely related to the change of legal status of the colonial legal subjects, who continued to be subordinate and without equal rights, until they gradually acquired formal rights within post-colonial states, established especially after the Second World War. It was also linked to changes in the legal status of women in several European countries, including France. At least formally, gender, race and ethnicity were no longer meant to influence the rights of a citizen towards the state. However, in practice, not everybody became what the Australian law professor, Sandra Berns (2002), has called the 'unencumbered citizen'. Here she underlines that, to a lawyer, citizenship is embedded in notions of domicile, residence, suffrage and possession of appropriate documents (Berns 2002: 33). She asks a rhetorical question about who is the unencumbered citizen, the bearer of rights, and answers the question in the following way:

> The unencumbered citizen is devoid of markers denoting particularity. The social *indicia* that accompany racial, ethnic and religious background have nothing to do with the subject of rights. *In theory* [author's emphasis], the brute facts of race, ethnicity and religion neither facilitate nor inhibit participation. The unencumbered citizen is neither black nor white, neither Catholic nor Muslim nor Jew. Those facts are irrelevant to her status as the subject of rights. The unencumbered citizen is able to access the 'infrastructure' required to participate fully and as an equal in the public sphere. Thus, the unencumbered citizen has a wife, or behaves as if she does. If she has religious beliefs, she wears them lightly and is prepared to subordinate them to the requirements of public sphere participation. If she has family, she relies upon others for care work and all of the other services that facilitate single-minded concentration upon tasks at hand. She is, in short, 'unencumbered': by interpersonal obligations, by responsibilities, by beliefs (2002: 43).

This understanding of an 'unencumbered citizen' may – perhaps – suit the self-understanding of a European man, and perhaps that of a Dutch or Nordic European woman, better than the self-understanding of several of the interviewed Bulgarian and Hungarian women, who have lost the 'infrastructure' which earlier had enabled many women to combine work and family. The 'demand' in the Western world, where the family structure is changing and the welfare state is weakened, for 'unencumbered citizenship' seems to lead to an important demand for 'non-indigenous' migrant women who can perform the caring work of the 'wife'.

## Emerging Forms of Legal Subjectivity in Late Modernity

In *practice* – also in the practical legal relations of an expanding Europe in the twentieth century – the 'brute facts' of race, ethnicity, religion and gender, matter. But not only *facts* also *relations* matter for the interviewed women. Relations to places matter, as do relations to human beings. Relations to a country, a city or a 'home', matter, and relations to (grand)parents, family, lovers, spouses, children, and friends, clearly matter. These relations are valued, and this value influences behaviour and decisions, including decisions of clear legal relevance. Relations underline and sustain felt, though not necessarily formally and legally binding, obligations and responsibilities. Such relations are the basis for the emotional ties and 'bonds of affection' that interact with contractual relations, marriage relations and relations to immigration authorities.

In his second edition of *The Politics of Jurisprudence*, Roger Cotterrell writes that:

> When Austin's writings speak of subjects of the sovereign, or Hart's speak of citizens and officials who view legal rules from internal or external standpoints, it is no longer possible to imagine that these abstract persons conceptualised in normative legal theory can also be thought of in any simple way as representing real human beings engaging in actual social practices (2003: 228).

Some of the real female human beings engaging in actual social practices in Europe today move between cities, and countries, establish families, seek work, adventure, and new experiences, as well as meaningful activities, and possibilities for community and communication with other human beings in their shifting environments. The 'citizeness' of today may feel at home in several places, and seek to nourish her bonds of affection, but she may also feel excluded and lost.

The difficulties which the EU-court seems to have had in dealing with *pregnant* working women demonstrates the difficulties legal institutions have had when they have to sort out the challenges stemming from what has been be called 'the intersectional self' (Powell, 2003). What kind of legal subject is a pregnant women – how many legal subjects are encompassed in the pregnant woman? Is she a 'normal' legal subject, or is she in some ways 'impaired', should she be considered sick or healthy, in need of special or general rights and treatment? How can she be 'discriminated' – that is distinguished or differentiated legally – from other 'normal' legal subjects? What rights will the child or children have, once born? When they are constrained from entering the country where they are legal citizens, because of the lack economic means, as in the case of the Dutch children of one Hungarian interviewee, what seems to emerge is a European subject who is experiencing an unfavourable legal status. The former link between citizenship and rights is deteriorating.

What has become clear in the last part of the twentieth century is that the changing understanding of the legal subject is something which has been especially felt as a challenge for courts (Foblets and Dupret 1999: 57–71). This can be seen as a development which brings Europe closer to the American experience. Porsdam (2002; 1999) claims that the important role of courts in American legal culture reflects the multicultural composition of American society, where different cultural minorities and individuals may find it easier to address courts than legislators in order to secure their rights. The important and dynamic role which the European Court of Justice (ECJ) has played in relation to the process of European integration is well known, and could be linked to a similar rationale although more aspects are probably at play here. The growing importance of the lawmaking role of courts in Europe, (both national courts, the ECJ and the European Court of Human Rights of the European Council), is related both to the challenge to reconcile different national legal systems within an expanding, reunifying and changing Europe, and to dealing with changing legal environments within European countries, which have within the last generation become gradually more multicultural and multi-religious societies. Such legal developments may thus also be seen as a result of global migration processes. These changes are, of course, a challenge not only to courts, but also to legal theory and legal philosophy, which increasingly has to deal with consequences of pluralism, polycentricity and difference (Petersen and Zahle 1995; Soeteman 2001).

## Multiple Selves in Complex Legal Contexts

John Powell (2003) comments that by rejecting the modern, unitary, stable and transparent self, postmodernism strikes at the very foundation of modern jurisprudence, the legal subject: 'there are a number of ways that acceptance of a fractured, multiple, and intersectional self would change the way we think about the law. The issue of agency and choice would clearly be altered by moving away from the unitary self'. Within an expanding European Union, a number of systems of national law coexist together with EU-law and international law, as well as with local norms and customs and different legal cultures. This means that the legal context within which the – emerging European – multiple self operates becomes a very complex one, as can also be seen from the interviews. There is thus complexity both in relation to the postmodern individual herself, as well as within the postmodern legal environment in which she operates.

A Hungarian/Bulgarian woman in Italy or The Netherlands may be considered as a migrant, as a (traditional) woman, as a spouse, a mother, a colleague, a professional, as Christian, as a white person, as a foreigner, and as a so-called Third Country National. She is in a position which shifts from subordination and discrimination (understood as unequal and un-legitimized different treatment) to a privileged and favourable situation (compared to other third country nationals, to illegal immigrants in EU-countries, and in some respects to Muslim immigrants, etc.). It is clear from the interviews, however, that it is not always that easy for a married and migrated woman to make friends and create 'bonds of affection' with other people in the 'host' country, apart from her own family. The need and wish to uphold continuous and relatively strong relations with other places of 'home' and to maintain earlier, close emotional relations, however is not dependent upon whether a person has bonds to a new home.

Powell uses the concept of subordination, when he speaks about 'subordinate gender and racial status', and when he writes that '[if] we accept that the self is relational and multiple, our efforts to address oppression must focus upon the privileged as well as the oppressed. From a pragmatic standpoint we must acknowledge that subordination affects the position of the dominant and the dominated'. The forms of subordination and/or privilege experienced by migrating and/or married women are not (necessarily) a consequence of formal and legal differences *within* one national legal system. In the cases we are dealing with, they may also be the result of intersections and overlapping of a number of different legal systems and cultures. In the EU-European context, issues of 'whiteness', religion (Christianity), formal education and qualifications, as well as economic income are amongst the markers of privilege. 'Traditional' (un-modern) gendered lifestyles and religious affiliation (especially to Islam) may be reasons for, or markers of practical and legal forms of subordination in other situations. Thus, some, or even several of the interviewed women can be seen as privileged in some respects and less privileged or even subordinated in other respects. When I use the term 'privilege' here, I presuppose a changing understanding of the notion of privilege along the lines of the development of a changing understanding of the term 'monopoly'. Monopolies were, in earlier centuries, granted by sovereigns as exclusive legal rights, but today they are mainly understood to originate from market conditions. In the same way, today's privileges – special rights – no longer necessarily originate in legal rights granted by a sovereign power, be it a monarch or a legislator. Most contemporary privileges – special rights – will probably originate from different forms of bargaining power of individuals or groups of individuals, who may thus produce 'negotiated law' in the form of contracts and thus become beneficiaries of market privileges – maybe even beneficiaries of privileges in marriage markets.

Security issues, concerning both states and individuals, as well as issues of how to secure global power relations, have gained overriding prominence in the Western world in the beginning of the twentieth century. It is not a new concern for (European) states. Nonetheless, in a changing Europe, these issues affect both national and European legal policies and regulations, and at present they also seem to legitimize restrictive legal regimes towards so-called 'third country nationals', especially with regard to family unification, work permits and reasons for extradition. This development may also legitimize or give rise to *general forms* of legal regulation and administration, which deliberately have *different effects* upon different groups of citizens, depending upon their ethnic background and affiliation. The case study of the Danish legal regime is an example of this. It may also indicate and illustrate a relative shift of values in European states and perhaps in Europe at large, where values of equality and freedom are yielding to, or being supplemented by, values of security and difference. The ambivalence towards or even 'unattractiveness' of upholding a mono-valent 'universal' ideal of legal equality amongst human beings is expressed in a quotation from one of the interviews:

If someone comes here [The Netherlands] with a refugee status because there is God knows what regime in Africa and he's being pursued, the same person [in the administration] will decide whether this refugee can stay or not who will decide about me coming here with a college degree to further improve their economy (Annett).

The Polish (legal) sociologist, Grazyna Skapska, has drawn attention to what she calls 'a dangerous development of liberal democracy: either focussed on the standards of technical rationality, or limited to the well-being of the individual' (2001: 157). Within this development 'civic society and civic virtues give place to the recipients' passivity' (Skapska 2001: 163). She further describes situations and cases where 'democracy is rather perceived as aimed at consolidation, a defence of a *status quo*, as a support of social homeostasis, and not as a challenge to governmental practices' (2001: 165). In several respects, this description seems to fit the development of democratic law-making in Europe, especially in relation to regulations concerning the combination of marriage and migration. We may now live in an age, where (some) cross-national bonds of affection between women and men are sometimes becoming as difficult to establish *legally*, as they once were in status societies, where relations across class and status could not be established or where the poor (or the colonized) were not always allowed to marry. But today the obstacles to the legal recognition of marriages may originate from lack of economic means, from 'unsuitable' national legal status, or from 'unsuitable' 'non-European' religious marital practices (e.g. Shah 2003), and not (necessarily) from membership of social class by birth, as was the case when Balzac wrote about the *'Lost Illusions'* of feudal France at the beginning of the nineteenth century. National immigration law and national marriage law in Europe today seem to be legitimizing certain forms of exclusion, and establishing certain forms of differentiated legal statuses, which exist in interaction with market law and market based special rights and privilege.

## Notes

1. Mit Rechtssubjekt werden alle Personen bezeichnet, die Träger von Rechten und Pflichten sein können. Neben den natürlichen Personen (also Menschen) sind dies auch die juristischen Personen in ihren vielerlei Rechtsformen, wie z.B. Vereine, Aktiengesellschaften, Gesellschaften mit beschränkter Haftung, Körperschaften des öffentlichen Rechts u.a. (Wikipedia, die freie Enzyklopädie).
2. Under the British Nationality Act 1948, a *secondary status* that was common to all who were primarily citizens either of the U.K. and Colonies or of one of the independent Commonwealth countries. This status was also shared by a limited number of people who did not have any such *primary citizenship*, including former British subjects who were also citizens of Eire (as it then was) or who could have acquired one of the primary citizenships but did not in fact do so. Under the British Nationality Act 1981 (which replaced the 1948 Act as from 1 January 1983), the status of

British subject was confined to those who had enjoyed it under the former Act without having one of the primary citizenships; the expression *commonwealth citizen* was redefined as a *secondary status* of more universal application. The Act provided for minors to be able to apply for registration as British subjects and for British subjects to become entitled to registration as British citizens by virtue of U.K. residence [author's emphasis]. See 'British subject', Martin, E.A. (ed.) 2002. *A Dictionary of Law*, Oxford University Press and *Oxford Reference Online*, http://www.oxfordreference.com/views/ENTRY.html?subview=Main&entry=t49.000401 [19 June 2003].

# References

Armstrong, A. and N. Welshman (eds.) 1987. *Women and Law in Southern Africa*, Zimbabwe Publishing House.

Berns, S. 2002. *Women Going Backwards. Law and Change in a Family Unfriendly Society*, Aldershot, Ashgate.

Cotterrell, R. 2003. *The Politics of Jurisprudence. A Critical Introduction to Legal Philosophy*, LexisNexis TM UK.

Dahl, T.S. 1987. *Women's Law. An Introduction to Feminist Jurisprudence*, Oslo, Norwegian University Press.

Dübeck, I. 1991. *Aktieselskabernes Retshistorie*, Copenhagen, Jurist- og Økonomforbundets Forlag.

Foblets, M.C. and B. Dupret 2002. 'Islam som Retskilde i et Pluralistisk Samfund. Belgiske og Egyptiske Dommere Kontronteret med Islamiske Referencer', in Petersen, H. (ed.) *Globaliseringer, ret og retsfilosofi*, Jurist- og Økonomforbundets forlag. (Translated from B. Dupret et al. (eds.) 1999. *Legal Pluralism in the Arab World*, pp.57–71)

Hellum, A. 1999. *Women's Human Rights and Legal Pluralism in Africa. Mixed Norms and Identities in Infertility Management in Zimbabwe*, Tano-Aschehoug, Oslo, Mond Books.

Holleman, J. F. 1994. 'Trouble -Cases and Trouble-less Cases in the Study of Customary Law and Legal Reform', in A. Dundes Renteln and A. Dundes (eds.) *Folk Law: Essays in the Theory and Practice of Lex Non Scripta*, New York, Garland.

Joerges, C. and N. S. Ghaleigh (eds.) 2003. *Darker Legacies of Law in Europe. The Shadow of National Socialism and Fascism over Europe and its Legal Traditions*, Oxford and Portland, Oregon, Hart Publishing.

Mehdi, R. and F. Shaheed 1997. *Women's Law in Legal Education and Practice in Pakistan. North South Cooperation*, Copenhagen, New Social Science Monographs.

Mill, J.S. [1861] 1986. *The Subjection of Women*, Prometheus Books.

Nousiainen, K. 2001. 'Transformative Nordic Welfarism: Liberal and Communitarian Trends in Family and Market Law', in Nousiainen *et al.* (eds.) *Responsible Selves. Women in the Nordic legal culture*, Aldershot, Ashgate.

Nousiainen, K., A. Gunnarson, K. Lundström and J. Niemi-Kiesiläinen (eds.) 2001. *Responsible Selves. Women in the Nordic legal culture,* Aldershot, Ashgate.

Olsen, F.E. 1995. *Feminist Legal Theory I and II (Foundations and Outlooks; Positioning Feminist Theory Within the Law),* Aldershot, Ashgate.

Paasilehto, S. 2002. *Constellations. A New Approach to Legal Culture and European Integration of Private Law,* Helsinki, University of Helsinki Printing House.

Petersen, H. 1996a. *Home Knitted Law. Norms and Values in Gendered Rule-Making,* Aldershot, Ashgate.

———. 1996b. 'Famiglie di donne e famiglie guiridiche. Le esperienze dei paesi nordici', in G. Maggoni (ed.) *Come il diritto tratta le famiglie,* Urbino, Istituto di Sociologia, QuattroVenti.

———. (ed.) 2002. *Globaliseringer, ret og retsfilosofi,* København. Jurist- og Økonomforbundets forlag.

Petersen, H. and H. Zahle (eds.) 1995, *Legal Polycentricity. Consequences of Pluralism in Law,* Aldershot, Ashgate.

Porsdam, H. 1999. *Legally Speaking: Contemporary American Culture and the Law,* Amherst, MA, University of Massachusetts Press.

Porsdam, H. 2002. *Fra pax americana til lex americana? En diskussion af dansk retliggørelse som en påvirkning fra USA,* Århus, Magtudredningen.

Powell, J. 2003. *The Multiple Self: Exploring Between and Beyond Modernity and Postmodernity,* www.usyd.edu.au/su/social/papers/powell.htm [17 January 2003].

Shah, P.A. 2003. 'Attitudes to Polygamy in English Law', in *International Comparative Law Quarterly,* (52) April.

Skapska, G. 2001. 'Law, Rights and Democracy After Totalitarianism', in Soeteman A., ed. *Pluralism and Law,* Kluwer Academic Publishers.

Soeteman, A. (ed.) 2001. *Pluralism and Law,* Kluwer Academic Publishers.

Stewart, J. and A. Armstrong (eds.) 1990. *The Legal Situation of Women in Southern Africa. Women and Law in Southern Africa,* (II) Harare, University of Zimbabwe Publications.

Svensson, E.M., A. Pylkkänen and J. Niemi-Kiesiläinen (eds.) 2004. *Nordic equality at a crossroads: Feminist Legal Studies Coping with Difference,* Ashgate.

Ørsted, A. S. 1828. *Haandbog over den danske og norske Lovkyndighed med stadigt hensyn til Hr. Statsraad og Professor Hurtigkarls Lærebog,* Kjøbenhavn, Tredje Bind.

*Intermezzo*

# 'A Dance through Life': Narratives of Migrant Women

## *Nadejda Alexandrova and Anna Hortobagyi*

*Jelisaveta is a Bulgarian woman who went to Italy in 1993 at the age of 18 and joined a group of Bulgarian cabaret dancers who travelled and performed around the country. In 2002, at the time of the interview, she was married to an Italian referee of bridge and had become a professional bridge player and referee herself.[1]*

*The interview was conducted in her newly-furnished flat in a Florentine neighborhood. Her husband served us coffee and left. A cat was quietly present. Jelisaveta appeared to feel relaxed. Her body language during the whole interview was spontaneous – sitting 'turkish style' on the sofa, proud of her passion for cards, showing me photos of bridge tournaments and special sets of cards. After the end of the recording she told me more about the rules of the game, which make it so serious and exceptional. She talked about the philosophy of the game in which the partners are not direct enemies and every game is unique.*

How did I come up with the idea to come here to Italy? It happened by chance. It was a question of luck. One day my father asked me if I wanted to go to Italy to learn Italian. I said I did, and as he had already met the dancers from the ballet group, who were working in Italy at the time, he got in touch with them. Then he prepared my papers and finally he came to me and said, 'If you want, I'll go and buy you a ticket, and you leave for Italy right away'.

My first impression? Oh, it was wonderful. We arrived on 26 November. At that time in Bulgaria there had already been a snowfall and everything was so grey. But, as the plane was flying over Italy I saw all, lots of greenery;

everything was green. And that made a great impression on me because I was used to seeing snowy and dark winters. That was the first impression Italy gave me. I liked the scenery very much. It was quite similar to Bulgaria, but perhaps in later spring there. Especially here, in Tuscany, it feels like the Balkans, there are a lot of similarities. But I was worried when I got off the plane. Quite worried, actually, because I hadn't met this person who came to pick me up at the airport. He was a ballet dancer in that group and I hadn't met him before. But he recognized me and I didn't have any problems.

I started to work soon after I arrived, within a month, maybe even in less than a month – in two weeks. Everything was just fine. I could rely on the family who first put me up, and there were other friends too, there were a lot of Bulgarian women. Moreover, I came here at a young age and I was lucky to learn Italian really fast. It's very easy to learn Italian, I mean it's easy for everybody. In the beginning I had no difficulties at all. Maybe later. I had some when I decided to change my job and look for something different. In the ballet group we didn't do classical ballet dancing, and of course I used to perform simple things, I was never a solo dancer in the group. [...]

I initially came here for one year. Nine months later I fell in love with an Italian [*laughter*] and I decided one year was not enough. Five years later I decided to change my job by chance. I'd broken up with my boyfriend and I just needed to make a complete change in my life. I had some friends who were in the coffee business. They used to sell *Lavazza* coffee here, in Italy, so I became a trade representative of *Lavazza* by chance ... Again by chance [*laughter*] with my friends.

My job was to sell coffee to people and companies. I always liked this job. Then, for the next two years, I was employed in a private company, selling books. I even set up my own office in Prato, which is a town near here. But right now Italy is going through a crisis in every respect, and of course, the tradesmen are the first ones to suffer the effects of the crisis in a country. So, naturally, when matters had been getting worse for a year, I decided to close down the office before I went bankrupt.

This had been my occupation up to now. I am pleased with it, as it was a useful experience, and I enjoyed it a lot because I like meeting people and starting relationships ... I don't mean just the customer–seller relation, but also making friends and so on. I still meet some of my ex-customers now and then. And, without a doubt, I needed to go through all these things to gain some experience. Now I've taken up something I really enjoy, and it's Sports Bridge. Anyway, I must admit I've always been engaged in activities I enjoy. Besides, I also like changing jobs, so ... [*laughter*]. Only this time I hope to get on with bridge because it requires a lot of learning and willingness and hard work.

Sports Bridge is a real sport, not just a game of cards, as many people might think. Tournaments are held regularly. In Florence there are four tournaments every week, and apart from these, you can play in the club every day. Bridge is a sport in which you keep developing and improving because it involves logical thinking, not just repeating things over and over. It is interesting. I've had some ... well, I wouldn't like to boast [*laughing*] ... I have achieved some good results in Italy and bridge experts have made favourable comments on my category in public ... I mean the category I used to have before. Now I've moved into a higher category and it is a bit more difficult to win the games ... .

There is a chance to make a career, there is a chance to make a change [*in high spirits*]. It happened to me – I came here to work with a ballet group, then I was a tradeswoman and then right now I'm a bridge referee [*laughter*]. There is a chance for a change, as long as you're willing to make it. Bulgarians are willing and they are able to make a good judgment in any situation. [...] And I met my husband in the bridge club. It was by chance that I joined the Bridge sports club, Italians are among the best bridge players in the world today. And in this club, since I am a very communicative person, I find it easy to make a lot of acquaintances. As soon as I joined the club, I made some new friends, of course, and I met my husband by chance. He is a good player, but his main occupation is organizing bridge tournaments and so on, as he is a referee. [...] We became very close in less than a year [*laughter*]. We got married shortly after we met, eight months later I think, and everything was just brilliant. He took me on a one-week boat trip for our honeymoon and I had a chance to see Spain and France. Now we get along nicely. I think that in the beginning he felt sharply the cultural differences between us. We [Bulgarians] are a little more serious than them [Italians] in some respects. That's why, in the beginning he found it hard to get used to the fact that I was closely bound to my family back in Bulgaria and I wanted to return there frequently or, at least, to meet my parents. But now he has already visited Bulgaria a few times and he has met everybody there. He speaks a little Bulgarian and he can understand almost every word we say. He enjoys these visits. [...]

Will citizenship make my life easier? Well, it will be helpful. It won't affect me personally because I've always had a work permit. I've never been out of job and, thank god, I've never had any problems with papers either. It's my family in Bulgaria that I'm concerned about. My father and his wife and two of my brothers would like to come and live in Italy and my youngest brother is interested in sports, especially Karting, and he is training here now with an Italian Karting club. He is fourteen and of course he can't live in Italy only with me, away from his parents and so on. That's why all my family decided to join us here. Another reason is my father's business here. Many people here want to use his service because he's a good professional [*he works as a cargo truck driver*]. Few people are good at this job. So I want to prepare the papers for them and invite them here. By the way, it has become difficult to get a visa for sports activities, which would officially permit my family to live here. They can stay here only on condition that I have Italian citizenship. So from this point of view I'm happy I'm going to have Italian citizenship because it will make it possible for my relatives … for my parents to stay in Italy until my younger brothers finish their education. Afterwards, of course, my parents want to go back to Bulgaria. So, my major concern is to sort out this problem. It's a matter of time because my parents would like to return to Bulgaria afterwards. If everything comes out right, I hope my husband and I will be able to move to Bulgaria too. […]

Plans for the future? We own a small flat in Sofia already. And we have achieved some brilliant results in Sports Bridge. So, my husband and I would like to organize some kind of education practice, to establish some courses for the younger generations because Bulgarians are very good at this sport and it should be promoted. Our ambition is to establish a certain bridge standard, a list of rules that defines and rules out the irregularities. In this way it will become possible to hold bridge tournaments on a larger scale. Every summer there is a two-week international tournament in Bulgaria. It is held in Varna and my husband and I are going to participate in it. I hope to go there next year. […]

Home for me is something very intimate. This is my home. My home has been created with lots of love. We've made it all together and I can sense this in every little bit of it. And we've created it willingly, just the way we want it to be. Of course, it will take some time to have children and bring more joy in it. This is what I'm looking forward to – joy, cosiness … home. When I think about home, I always recall that I grew up living with my grandparents, my parents being divorced and so on. I can recall those evenings [*laughing*] we used to spend together, the whole family, perhaps watching TV. My grandfather would often tell me stories, he was a brilliant narrator. And we used to talk together a lot, we used to share a lot. This is my idea of home and I hope to create my own home just the way I experienced it as a child. I hope my children will grow up in the same atmosphere, surrounded with love. My grandfather used to take care of my grandma, he used to massage her; he used to tell stories and play with us. Even studying was a kind of game to us because he made it feel like it. This is my home. Home involves the family values which existed in the past. I hope these values haven't been lost even today. My vision of home might be a little old-fashioned, but this is the way I picture it in my mind [*laughter*], home means coziness and love … lots of love.

*Piroska was born in 1963 in Szolnok, a provincial town in rural central Hungary. After three years of acquaintance, she married her Dutch husband, and they moved to the Netherlands in 1990. They later divorced and Piroska is now living with a Dutch partner, has a son by this partner and was expecting her second baby at the time of the interview. In Hungary she worked as a secretary, then for years as a physical education teacher in the local school. She has also been a professional Hungarian folk dancer. In the Netherlands she has worked as a taxi driver and as a post office employee. Now she is a kindergarten teacher in Amsterdam. She teaches Hungarian folk dance as a hobby.*

*The interview took place in her home, which is a seventeenth century house on the canal in downtown Rotterdam, a sort of communal house. The flats are not locked in the building. She is boyish, with cropped hair and brown eyes. Her partner is silent and kind, and he offers us herbal tea and some cakes, and takes the kid out while we talk. He is a doctor of natural medicine. The house is full of objects, for instance, candles and arrangements of pebbles. Piroska is like a professional storyteller, and she shows me many photos from home: Piroska in the dance group, Piroska as a pioneer. The interview situation is very pleasant.*[2]

It was in 1990 that I came to live here. I got married here. I met my husband[3] in Hungary at a folk dance course. I taught and was in charge of various dance groups. It was not easy. We were separated after two and a half years of marriage. It is difficult to speak about it as according to the law here in the Netherlands you have to be married for three years in order to stay here, or you need to have a residence permit for five years, without interruptions. We fell short of three years, so my passport had stamped into it twice that I was to leave the country in thirty days. [...]

If I returned home after the divorce? No, I did not ... Initially, I wanted to return, then I thought, well, if I don't try to live on here in the Netherlands, I might regret later on that I had returned home. If I try and I fail, I'll have a clear conscience returning home [...]. In Hungary I was a drawing teacher; it was a good, reliable, permanent job. Teaching drawing, to 10–14-year-old children. I had six years of teaching behind me. I lived with my parents, travelled around with the dance troupe, 'been there, done that'.

I left behind a solid existence to be able to accompany my former husband and for the sake of what was to be our future together. I'm not so sure everyone would have left it all behind just like that. When I started to live here, I felt I wasn't getting the kind of support from my husband that I needed. On the other hand, a lot of things thrilled me, things that I found interesting. Still, the new tasks to cope with here egged me on, sort of. And I had enough backbone, you see, as I had to realize that my former husband wasn't any help, nor did I get the kind of support from his parents that I needed, so I'd have to go it alone, my way of doing it. This self-supporting attitude of mine turned out to be a disadvantage, causing my husband to sue for divorce. [...]

The time of the divorce was a time when I simply could not get into the flat, as my husband had replaced the lock after he put me out – all my stuff, all my belongings were there. I simply could not get in. I then went to sleep in a place in the neighbourhood.[4]

During the two and a half years that I had spent in the Netherlands I had been involved in working for a dance troupe, a Dutch one. I had taught Hungarian at a school. So I had achieved many things. I had many friends through my ex-husband, also through the school and my other work stuff, etc. I felt that I had achieved quite a lot in that two and a half years and I did not want it to be taken away from me because of my husband. [...] I went to work for a taxi company. I was a bus driver ... I took children to a kindergarten where they were given health treatment. This was my job. I enjoyed it a lot. I was in touch with a lot of people. It was there that I learned how to live from day to day. It was then, when I had these appeals pending, that I learned how to be happy about even the smallest things ...

What eventually helped me to stay was that I had a Dutch family whom I knew – I had taught them Hungarian for three years, husband and wife. The relationship was quite close between us. When they found out about my situation they tried to help me by all possible means. They had this idea along the lines of 'if you are so keen to stay, we will ask our son if he would take care of you for this three years ...' The son was still a student so he could not do it, but they also had a daughter. She said it was not a problem at all. All in all, it was a protracted process with the appeals and all that, but I had been here almost four years, so they said, well, it is only one year to go, we will manage somehow. That was how it was done.

*You were living together with the daughter as if you were partners? Because this is possible to do in the Netherlands?*
Precisely ... Well, I have asked myself a couple of times since, would I have the courage to do it? Seriously. We are still very close with the family. The daughter then got married, she has a son, she is expecting her twins, so they come to see us regularly, and we are still good friends. This is how I managed to make it last for five years.

If you come to live here, you have the impression, something they otherwise make a point of demonstrating to you, that Dutch people are very tolerant. Tolerant they are, up to a point ... The moment you come up with your own problems, they immediately shut you out emotionally. Now and again, I would chance upon one or two Dutch people whom I could in fact talk to about my problem. In most cases, though, it was the Hungarian women who helped me... There are five Hungarian women in Eindhoven who got to know each other in some way and managed to get in touch with each other in twos or threes. As long as I lived in Eindhoven, we had a get-together every three or four months. It was a nice atmosphere there ... it was the attention that we paid to what had been happening to the others. People in Hungary knew about what was happening in here. Everyone knew about everything. You know what I think was an interesting thing to witness? Although it was hard for my parents to realize that my life here was turning into a failure, they said to me 'Give it a try. Do not come home just now. If you succeed, fine, if not, you come home.' My sister said 'Why not try it first.' And I succeeded! [...]

Another love. ... There was this birthday party, my friend's husband – I went there and had a good time. Then I saw a young bloke, I said to my friend 'Wow!' But after or during a divorce you are in this 'thanks a lot, I have had enough' kind of mood. But a year later my friend's husband had a birthday party. He was there again and I was there again. And from that very moment the relationship between me and my present boyfriend has been an exceptional one. [...] Something was set in motion in me and in him, too, and then we got talking. [...] Then, you see, he phoned me up and wrote me letters. You feel tempted to say 'yes' right at the beginning, but somewhere deep inside my answer was 'no'. No rushing headlong into any relationship. We could have a chat, we might date, but I should be careful because I had a lot to put behind me at that point. In the meantime we started to see each other on a more regular basis, plus I came to Rotterdam – he came to Eindhoven.

My boyfriend gave me precisely what I missed in the relationship with my ex-husband, something that I never had in that relationship. So this second relationship got off to a fast and smooth start, given the fact that I could speak good Dutch by then and we could communicate properly with each other. Here we are, we have a little boy now. In this relationship I have learned to... fight for the other person. Fight for each other, maybe? To give and to get – it is an important equation ... In my marriage I greatly depended on my husband. In every possible way. One problem was that if I said something that was not right, or did something that was not right ... he became aggressive, angry, he shouted at me, called me names. He beat me up.

After the relationship had lasted for one and a half years we shacked up together. We are not married, we do not live together, no contract of cohabitation, nothing. But he has a father's rights. Why these decisions? Dependence is something I can hardly stand to this day. Probably that's why we have these two officially separate flats, if something goes wrong between the two of us, I won't have to end up in the street, homeless.[5] This house has a peculiar history. This is a leased-out property of some sort, whatever the word is. This – BB is the word for it back home. Everyone lives his own life ... We have, instead, sporadic get-togethers where we sort out problems along the lines of 'time to clean the staircase'. All the tenants in this house are on good, friendly terms with all the other occupants. This staircase thing is the only unique characteristic of the house. Anyway, I like it here a lot. I have always said that Rotterdam was the centre of the world. We rent a seasonal plot close to the sea, a campsite. So if the weather permits and if we are OK for leisure time, we spend some time out there ... This is where we go hiking. It is good for Karl [her son] and good for us, too. Compensates us a bit for this lack of city space.

When I moved to Rotterdam I worked as a substitute staff in a kindergarten for a month; I stood in when someone of the staff left or was on a sick leave or quit the job for some reason. We had a phone call from another kindergarten saying that they needed someone for two months as they were in trouble due to staff shortage. I started to work there for two months. In the meantime my diploma got the stamp of approval, so I stayed there for two years... And I ended up in a lovely place where I work even today. I have been doing it for four and a half years. I have opened up a lot, I am a drawing teacher in a kindergarten ... I love doing it! I work four days a week, which is a lot, but our family is getting bigger: I am two months pregnant. I am having a good time here and I can really enjoy a freedom of expression in this job. When I say I am stuck with this place, I mean I was going to go on to further education this year to become a senior kindergarten teacher. Now that things are shaping up the way they are, I have put that idea off until some time later. Next year perhaps, or later.

## Notes

1. This interview was conducted by Nadejda Alexandrova.
2. This interview was conducted by Borbala Juhász.
3. With whom Piroska previously spent three years together, spending four-five months a year in Hungary.
4. She moved to a convent for six months, and after that she rented a room.
5. They live in two adjacent but separate flats, sharing numerous common rooms. In practice, they live together in two flats.

# Part II

## Subjectivity in Motion: Analysing the Lives of Migrant Women

*Chapter 4*

# Imaginary Geographies: Border-places and 'Home' in the Narratives of Migrant Women

*Nadejda Alexandrova and Dawn Lyon*

> This is another interesting question, the question of the home. Well, where does one feel at home? What is home? Is this a geographical concept? Or does this refer to a person? Or to a house? Or to objects? Or the air? I do not know.
> (Emma, Hu/I)

## Introduction

The narratives of the migrant women interviewed in this research can be considered as maps of imaginary geographies, charted from their stories of mobility from Eastern Europe to Italy or the Netherlands. This chapter looks at these geographies, and especially at the migrant women's images of 'border-places' and 'home', to analyse their relations and politics of belonging.[1] In the analysis, these claims for belonging are connected to the dominant available ways to make sense of migrants' social locations in contemporary Europe.

A prototypical immigration narrative is one in which 'immigrants' are supposed to move from one 'culture' into another (e.g. Yuval-Davis 1993). In this way of thinking, cultures are assumed to be distinctly bound in space, and home is assumed to emerge through a linear transition from one place to another, a process through which migrants are 'integrated'. In contrast, multicultural perspectives emphasize migrants' communities. In effect, this reinscribes home in the country of origin, as a kind of essentialism from which there can be no escape. A third alternative, much discussed in recent years, are transnational perspectives.[2] Transnational identities emphasize new forms of belonging and social embeddedness, where networks span more than one location, and migrants are not reduced to any one belonging – national origin or present location. The resultant amalgamations of identities are celebrated by some commentators and academics as novel and liberatory forms of subjectivity.

This chapter seeks to engage critically with this thinking through the analysis presented here of what migrant women say about their own sense of place and belonging in the worlds they inhabit, and to what extent this sense of belonging might be related to a sense of autonomy and control in their own lives (Anthias and Lazaridis 2000: 37). The discussion is organized in four sections. The first considers the legal regulation of belonging through stories of giving up and/or re-gaining a passport or other identity documents. The second part considers key moments in becoming a migrant through memories of crossing the border, and how belonging is spatially constituted. Following on from this, there is a discussion of first impressions of the new country in terms of landscape and infrastructure, and the creation of home through private space and objects. Finally, we trace the migrant women's claims of multiple belonging and explore where the limits to this might lie.

## Crossing Borders: The Sanctity of the Passport

That the border-place may be experienced and imagined in many different ways (Yuval-Davis and Stoetzler 2002: 331) means that narratives of border-crossings can be considered as key moments in the subject's construction of the meanings of transition and reincorporation. What makes the border-place so important is its liminal status, 'as a threshold between more or less stable phases of social processes' (Turner 1987: 75), a site which is literally and symbolically 'in-between', a place from which new life possibilities can be imagined. The passage through a passport office for non-EU citizens requires many kinds of identifications, proofs and guarantees of identity. Reasons and explanations and all other accounts of the migrant's decision to cross the national border are, in that moment, representations of the self, repeated and reconfigured according to time, place, location and questioner. The border-place is a threshold in the lives of the migrant women who are the focus of this study, and their narrations of this experience bring into evidence their agency, self-reflexivity, and forms of belonging, both achieved and imagined.

The passport is a major object of concern and care in the migrant women's interviews, a guarantee of possible return in both directions. The women without identity documents felt acutely the precarious nature of their situations, which made the drama of return very immediate, as they were fearful that the border would never be successfully crossed and that a liminal phase would continue indefinitely.[3] Women with dual citizenship, or two identification documents, are comforted by having them in their possession, fully aware of the flexibility they permit: the possibility of changing one's formal identity and belonging, according to the requirements of the national border to be crossed. Whatever their personal situations, all the migrant women insist on the importance of keeping their documents in order and of respecting the sanctity of the passport.[4]

An exemplary story of the centrality of the passport in underpinning a sense of self is that of Rosa, a Bulgarian dancer who illegally crossed the frontier between Yugoslavia and Italy in 1968. She then stayed for two years in a refugee camp, re-emigrated to France and later married a Dutchman, and moved to The Netherlands. In her description of her preparations to jump through the barbed wire to the 'free world' in 1968, she emphasized the importance of her suitcase full of clothes, an object of material and symbolic concern. With the help of the smuggler who arranged the trip, the suitcase went to Italy some days prior to her departure. Rosa then followed. She recounts very clearly how she felt insecure without a passport, and immediately upon arrival in Italy, she wanted to obtain new identification documents. Possessing no stable legal status, she describes herself as having no identity except that provided by the unfamiliar word *profuga*, the description of herself she gives to the policeman in Trieste, and that she carried the only thing left from the past – her suitcase. Her account of this time is very expressive, with many exclamations and interjections.

> Do you understand? These were my thoughts. That was the way I thought at the time. I was talking to myself, I was making a decision. And I set out. The first time I went to have a look, the second time ... [I thought] if somebody stops me I'll say I'm going to have a look at the train schedules, and now you see, I was with my passport, 'cause you can't go anywhere without a passport, a card.

In short phrases, with many repetitions, Rosa describes her actions in the liminal space between the known and the unknown. In her memory, she is absorbed in her action and does not recall seeing or hearing anything at the moment of jumping through. The only clear idea she conveys is that there was no chance of return, the only way to go on was to go ahead, and the only way to reach a secure place was to run. At the same time, she begins to gather her first impressions of the area beyond the border: 'There were some old broken cars, parts, and things like that. Oh God and you get to Italy.

And downwards when you cross these dead fields ... you know where waste is thrown, after the barbed wire, there are some trees, things like that, hills and Udine!' There is gradual change in the appreciation of the things Rosa sees upon crossing the border. First, the horrifying image of the dead field, a profane space, a hostile space of the 'beyond', then as she runs, the ugly images of the border space change into more intelligible sites – trees and hills. Indeed, this natural greenery comes out as a positive first impression of the country of migration in many interviews (an element to which we will return later).

Still, as Rosa insists, reaching the town was just a first step in her journey. She confessed to the great insecurity she felt at not having a passport, a fear which is vividly expressed in the descriptions of her emotions upon getting the train to the refugee camp in Trieste. During the trip she was constantly worried that the train might actually go in the opposite direction and that she was not moving forwards but backwards. She arrived safely in Italy and went to live in a refugee camp. However, two years had to pass before she achieved her goal of getting a passport, which she felt to be the basis for a more secure identity. The traumatic memory of the train going backwards seems to have been overcome by the time she embarked on another important event in her life story, which she vividly captures in recounting the moment when she arrived at Gare de Lyon, in Paris, willing to start her life anew. Her new passport gave Rosa confidence, and she felt comfortable in her new identity.

A different kind of story, this time of flexibility, emerges in the case of Marina, a Bulgarian journalist married to an Italian. Marina openly acknowledged that she had experienced problems with documents or visas when crossing borders: before the 1989 changes, when she was still studying in Prague, she was regarded with suspicion and was once detained at the Italian border because her identification document was issued in Prague and not in Bulgaria. The situation changed once she obtained Italian citizenship. Still, she humorously recounts a number of situations she has encountered at borders, such as when she was travelling to Russia. She used to have two passports, Bulgarian and Italian, and so would select the one she found more appropriate for the requirements of the country she was entering.[5]

> The funny thing was that I always entered the country and passed through the passport office with my Bulgarian passport, because Bulgarians didn't need a visa to go to Russia. But whenever we flew from Moscow to Italy, I'd leave the country with my Italian passport. And the Russian officers would always say: 'How come that you're leaving for Italy and you don't have a visa legalizing your stay here? How did you enter the country?' And I answered I had a Bulgarian passport too, and showed it to them. Then they would say, 'Alright, but in your Bulgarian passport, you don't have a visa which allows you to go to Italy'. And I had to explain that I had an Italian passport as well.

And so, after I had shown them both my passports a few times, they would finally leave me alone and let me go.

Changing passports was a way for Marina to claim different national belongings, and crossing the liminal space became a source of comic stories. Marina took pleasure in the role of a trickster, one who could just change a costume, 'put on a new gown' and enter through the right gate. She remembers how she had to think in advance about her actions, of how she had to take the risk of confusing the passport officers and then finally convince them of her legitimate, two-faced, identity: 'I remember that whenever I was crossing a border, I had to concentrate and think about which particular border it was, and hence which passport I was supposed to show and what explanation I had to give in order to avoid any trouble.' Nowadays, the symbols and entitlements of citizenship allow her to feel secure in her belonging: 'I do enjoy returning to Bulgaria with my Bulgarian passport and I can still feel I am Bulgarian. I am glad I haven't been rejected.' She goes on to say: 'I always declare I am Bulgarian and I do it with great pleasure …', which she does against a backdrop of ignorance and prejudice about Bulgaria in Italy. Still, she recognizes the discretion of the passport officer in these situations of transition, the 'gate-keeper' authorized to represent the Law of a certain country with whom one must negotiate claims to identity.

In other interviews, there are accounts both of positive impressions of welcome and of treatment based on suspicion and disdain. For instance, Monika, a Hungarian migrant to the Netherlands, was treated with disrespect by the officer who arranged her visa documents. She felt this negative attitude sharply, all the more so because she had made financial and professional sacrifices for the sake of her marriage. Upon coming to live with her husband in the Netherlands she was accused of having a fake marriage: 'Whatever I told them, they never believed it and kept threatening to expel me. It was as though I had been a prostitute, the way they treated me. […] This was a policeman who apparently had negative experience.' Finally, after a long period of mistreatment and rejection, and with the help of another official, Monika obtained her new ID. However the trauma of this treatment remained and added bitterness to her account of her experiences in Dutch society generally.

## Transition and Non-places

For the migrant women from Eastern Europe who fly for the first time to the West, the walk, on arrival, along the long curved corridors between airport terminals and gates has often left a powerful impression. Many included descriptions of airports in accounts of their journeys, especially the airports at Amsterdam, Milan and Rome.[6] When asked what was their first impression of the country of migration, several directly replied 'the huge, enormous, airport' (Alena, Eva, Mina, Teodora). Some describe their feeling of astonishment when they encounter the glitter of the airport shopping zone, especially those who migrated before 1989 or in the early 1990s. The airport gives the impression of an enormous, clean and regulated transit space, where it seems that the passing strangers cannot do harm. The airport buildings, built around strictly measured landing strips, tend to grow in the accounts in dimension and brightness. These buildings symbolize the cleanliness and order of the West, and the shelves full of luxury goods and perfumes are enticing symbols of wealth and abundance.

Some of these travellers, those on the verge of becoming migrants, might use their identities (those they hold in formal ways, through passports and other documents) to pass over the border and to become partially freed of those identities, capable and ready, in the mix of the colourful, consuming crowd, to see themselves anew. Indeed, in Marc Augé's description of border-places such as 'airports, railway stations, hotel chains, [and] leisure parks' as 'non-places' (1995: 79), their primary purpose is to be a transit place between different destinations and identities. At the same time, these are spaces in which others realize the loneliness of their journey (e.g. Mina). Some of the interviewees talk of feelings of confusion when they lose themselves in the labyrinth of halls and escalators. Indeed, Eva, arriving from Bulgaria, got lost at Schiphol airport in Amsterdam and recounts asking a policeman to show her the way out. No one was waiting for her, which made her subsequent journey into the countryside very difficult. This is quite a typical story in the accounts of those who do not recognize or are not able to follow the signs and rules of their new locations. However, arrival in such a place is also connected with entering into a world that contains the images and hopes for better life, order and maybe emotional enrichment. Overall, the airport is a confusing threshold of the space 'beyond, which signifies spatial distance, marks progress, [and] promises the future' (Bhabha 1995: 4); a non-space for some, and for others a place of transition to a new beginning.

The airport was often recounted as the first gate to social and the cultural life of the country. For instance, Mina recounts her first impression of Italy: 'I thought it was a beautiful country … although I couldn't see much of it from 'Leonardo da Vinci' airport in Rome …'. The name 'Leonardo da Vinci' airport is enough for her to call Italy beautiful, a name which represents the art and beauty of the European/Italian Renaissance. While this name is given to a modern building which does not have much history, the name nevertheless functions as a metonymic link that transfers *beauty* from art to national territory, thus producing meaning for the migrant familiar with the figure of Leonardo. Similar dreams and expectations are expressed by other women who transfer their knowledge about Italian language and culture onto their own migration experience, perhaps also in order to justify the decision to come to Italy. Marina finds it easy to understand Italian she says, because she already knew Latin and she was familiar with Italian history and culture before coming to Italy, and she further justifies her decision to continue her studies in Florence, rather than in another Italian city, because of the special sense of 'Italianness' that she felt it contained.

Not all migrants fly to their destinations. So the places of transition also include train and bus stations. The Venice train station appears in two stories in powerful ways. Nona and Olga are both Bulgarians who went to Italy in 1990 to become 'dancers'. They both recounted their long journeys to Venezia on an international night train, but their memories and first impressions of the country of migration differ considerably. Both were worried and without clear ideas of their goals and their future occupations. But, from her present perspective of a well-married rich wife, Nona regards that episode of border-crossing as 'fun', whereas Olga remembers crying all the time for the loss of home. She considers that traumatic memory of home, and the fact that her daughter was in Bulgaria, as decisive reasons for her breakdown and her return some time later. It is a memorable moment, the first real touch with the space beyond. For Nona, the waiting for someone to meet her and her companions for hours at the train station has left nothing but the memory of 'Venice as a fairy-tale'. It is just the opposite for Olga, who tells nothing about the charm of Venice and describes instead the painful and anxious moment of waiting for 'no one knows who'. The Venice train station functions as a transit place, which has a positive image in the account of Nona – a place that integrates earlier dreams and expectations and is the premise of a successful personal history. On the contrary, for Olga the same transit place is full of strangers, it is threatening and is effectively the starting point of her painful journey back home.

## Landscapes, Space and Objects

In the interviews of Jelisaveta and Alena, Bulgarian women migrants who went Italy and the Netherlands respectively, the green land, seen from the window of the plane or train which took them to their destinations, was the first impression they remember. 'Lots of greenery and everything remains untouched' is Alena's description of the space 'beyond' (i.e. the other side of the liminal zone, Bhabha, 1995) in the Netherlands. The greenery is not unfamiliar for Jelisaveta. In fact it reminds her of Bulgaria: 'I liked the scenery very much. It is quite similar to Bulgaria, but maybe later in spring ... It's great ... Especially here, in Tuscany, it feels like the Balkans, there are a lot of similarities', inverting the usual hierarchies within Europe. Other interviewees mention different features of the landscape and infrastructure as points of divergence from the sending countries. 'Terrific superhighways' (Plamena) are amongst the things one has to get used to, as are tidiness, cleanliness (Reneta, Alena), and 'the abundance of everything'[7] (Albena, Mina, Angelina).

Whilst the geographic characteristics are similar to those of the place she has left, Jelisaveta next has to create a more private space in her new location. Indeed, one of the most self-evident ways in which home is talked about is in terms of the physical space that it occupies (Finch and Hayes 1994). Specifically, on the question of what home means to her, Ana is first of all taken aback, then reiterates the sense of non-belonging in the present and home as material: 'Pardon? *Home, what is home for you?* That's another tough question [*laughing*], as I haven't had a home for many years now. Maybe it's the house I live in now and that's all.' In this and other cases, home is a minimal expression of belonging. However, sometimes this is linked to the investment in property in a different location. Ana and her husband started building their own house in Bulgaria while they were working and travelling around Italy, initially as performers. What is interesting in this and similar accounts (e.g. from Irena, Angelina and Jelsiaveta) is the investment in a home elsewhere and into the future, and which involves the flow of significant financial sums to Bulgaria, whilst everyday work and life takes place in Italy. In these cases home is both destination and return, and deferred into the future.

Other women talk explicitly about a more laboured creation of home. Eva, a Bulgarian migrant, lives with her Georgian boyfriend in the Netherlands. When she is asked if she has found her home or still looking for it, she replies: 'I'd say I am creating it. I am rather creating it than looking for it. Because I have this flat and I'm going to make it my place. At least while I'm here …'. This evidences what Avtar Brah calls 'homing desires' (1996: 180) – 'the desire to feel at home by physically or symbolically (re)constituting spaces which provide some kind of ontological security in the context of migration' (Fortier 2001: 410). In addition, the space of home is also used as a starting point from which to voice what has been left behind in a register of escape. One Hungarian woman in Italy remembers 'the bedroom that I shared with my sister' and how as an 'adult woman' she wants to avoid the return to childlike comforts and constraints at all costs. Furthermore, a relationship and another's family history can mediate the process of belonging. Joanna, a Bulgarian migrant in the Netherlands, is beginning to assume the attachment her partner feels for a specific house: 'What home is to me? Well, I think that it's beginning to become a more and more important part … because Paul has an emotional connection to this house exactly and to this village, because he used to come here very often as a child and so on; and, yes, it's beginning to become my own.'

The place of objects, both within and between the spaces of home, and the symbolic value they carry, also offer very interesting insights into expressions of belonging (see Salih 2003). In the interviews, we did not ask directly what the migrant women buy or take with them when they visit their relatives or friends in their countries of origin and vice versa. Still, they spontaneously talked about food as a site of belonging – explored in depth in a separate chapter – and they sometimes also referred to the 'peopling' of their workplaces and homes with images and icons of their 'home' countries, or with objects and fragments of their lives through which they could feel secure (as in the biography of Edit Bruck). In the case of Karolina, a journalist and translator, this practice is one conducted by several women in her workplace. It might be that their work, as experts in the language or current events of their countries, strengthens their sense of belonging and constructs in them stronger national identities than might otherwise have been the case. Indeed, as Bruno Riccio (2002) has argued, some forms of transnational connections reinforce the sense of national identity, and are expressed through symbols of home.

> On our desk, next to the portrait made by my father-in-law, which I'm very proud of, a portrait of Botev,[8] we put a wonderful picture of King Simeon I[9]– taken for 'Slavyani' magazine … What is left for us, my colleague and me, [is] our pride […] the Hungarian woman has put their St. Stefan. … So I think it's a great working place.
>
> And again, in my house [is] the portrait of Botev and Levski.[10] My husband had already bought the *History of Bulgarian Literature* in Italian and 'Baj Ganjo'[11] translated in Italian, when I came here.

## Multiple Belonging and Its Limits

In this part of the chapter we analyse the ways in which migrant women claim to belong to more than one place or grouping. First, we hear from those who consider themselves to be firmly socially anchored in the receiving country on the one hand, and also speak in reified terms about belonging to their nation of origin on the other, but without any view to return. The second set of voices comes from those who feel that their home is in two locations and who emphasize the importance of mobility between them, as well as technologies of communication in the everyday. Finally we hear about the limits to belonging, expressed first through legal regulation, then in cultural terms.

Karolina, a Bulgarian migrant who now works as a part-time journalist and translator in Italy and is married to an Italian, speaks of her long-standing patriotism, a sense of national belonging inculcated by the communist regime she says, and undiminished by her 'fully democratic' ideas and her Italian citizenship. She puts it strongly: '... despite the fact that I'm an Italian citizen, I've always stood up for my fatherland. My fatherland remains in my heart'. However, in response to the question of whether she would return to Bulgaria she is very direct:

> Well, frankly said, no. I mean when I get on the plane or travel by car to Bulgaria there is this ... as the old women say, shivers all over your spine, because after all you go home.[12] But this long period of staying[13] in Italy, nearly thirty years, made me get accustomed. I got accustomed to the Italian environment and to my greatest happiness I feel well in the Italian environment.

Others also idealize the country of origin, reifying national belonging, for example, Boyana who discusses her return to Bulgaria after 23 years in the Netherlands in these terms: 'But my roots are here [Bulgaria], my feet are in this land'. Frequent trips to the sending country during the time of living away make the integration of central figures and places of life possible, notably through repeated visits to symbolic sites: 'He has visited the Rila Monastery maybe 25 times and every time we come back', Karolina remarks about her husband, implying that through the re-enactment of these processes of incorporation, the idea of home is encapsulated in specific locations. In these orientations, home remains 'sentimentalized as a space of comfort and seamless belonging' (Fortier 2001: 412) such that the movement away from home contributes to the production of it as ideal.

Albena speaks powerfully in the register of multiple belonging, where physical presence and symbolic attachment to both locations – Bulgaria and the Netherlands – are essential, although these forms of attachment might be better described as pluri-national rather transnational (Salih 2001: 669). This is also the case for Violeta who, in her rendition of attachment, inverts the more usual representation of home: for her, home as the place where her parents live is a site of change, whilst the home she has created in the Netherlands is the place of familiarity.

> Every year I go from one of my homes to the other. Recently my colleagues asked me where I was going during the holidays. I said 'I'm going home'. And when you leave that home, you come home here. Both these places are 'home' for me. Since I came to the Netherlands, it's almost 15 years, every year I've been going home in Bulgaria. *How do you feel at home?* I feel all right both here and there. I can't do without that trip in the summer, usually a month and a half, the children and me. (Albena)
>
> In the narrow sense of the word, home is our home, where my husband and I live. In the broad sense both Bulgaria and the Netherlands are home for me now. Home is in both of the countries. [...] The moment I am in Bulgaria I feel at home. *Do you go back often? How do you feel, when you go back to Bulgaria, and then when you are on the way back to the Netherlands?* Well, now I

try to go back to Bulgaria at least two times a year. [...] I feel at home there. When I am here I feel at home too, because everything is already familiar to me. (Violeta)

It is very clear from these and other excerpts that for many women, mobility is a prerequisite for comfort and well-being in the country of migration.[14] In particular, women migrants living in the receiving country for longer periods (more than 10 years) emphasized their knowledge and experience in obtaining new documents which legalize and secure their stay and guarantee their mobility, and reducing the drama of crossing borders.

Technologies are understood to bridge distance very clearly, making places more accessible and lifestyles more mutual (e.g. Morley 2001). Emma talks about mobility as a 'feeling' related to the opportunity to come and go, which she counterposes to definitive exile. There is no strong distinction in time between one place and another, she says. For Marina, the sites of her longing are also multiple: 'I feel a little homesick about Moscow, although I lived in it only six years and it isn't my native country. Nevertheless I miss living in Moscow sometimes, just like I feel homesick about Bulgaria.' But she does not consider herself to be an 'emigrant', a phenomenon which in her view 'has a relative meaning in 2002'. As she explains, 'It only takes one hour and forty minutes to get from here to Bulgaria. If I had married somebody who lived in Burgas,[15] perhaps I would visit my parents even more seldom than I do now. As soon as I make up my mind, I can make a flight reservation and the next day I can be having lunch with my friends in Sofia.' Csilla also refers to time-space compression: '1000 kms is not that far after all ... you can get into the car in the morning and you're there in the evening'. In addition, some of the migrant women emphasize cultural proximity in a 'global world'. For instance, Marina explains, 'I can see that my Bulgarian friends and I read the same books and we watch the same TV programs, we follow the progress of the same world events. So the distance between us is not so big.' The circulation of 'symbolic goods' (Lash and Friedman, 1992, cited in Morley, 2001: 426) mediates affective connection, and can sustain belonging.

However, multiple belonging is not so fluid for all the migrant women. Its limits are also frequently expressed, not least in relation to legal status. Boyana, who is shortly to retire, wants to feel like a European citizen who can cross borders without fear and settle in whatever place she finds convenient. Similarly, Angelina, a 30-year-old migrant in Italy, considers the possibility of return, but only when she finally gets Italian citizenship. And there is the traumatic experience of Reneta, a migrant in the Netherlands, who made her first effort to cross the Bulgarian-Serbian border illegally in 1988. She and her husband were arrested and repatriated 'home' as prisoners, and it was only after 1989 that her fixation to go to 'the clean space' in the West was satisfied and she went to the Netherlands. Only after marrying there and saving money for her retirement is she confident of enjoying the rights and the documents to return to Bulgaria and, at the same time, to use the income saved in the Netherlands.

Individual accounts are often contradictory. Amongst Marina's orientations, she expresses what a number of migrants fear – the loss of any kind of home, the danger of becoming 'a kind of rootless tree', sometimes implicitly pointing to cultural practices as exclusionary. 'I guess it comes to this … I suppose the other emigrants feel it too … All of a sudden, you feel like you don't belong anywhere. The longer you stay here, the more you lose your connections with Bulgaria. On the other hand, you are never quite … of course, here you remain a stranger until the end.' (Ana) 'I am as fully integrated as I could be, because one can never be absolutely integrated in a foreign country.' (Victoria)

> I am not a Hungarian any more back at home and Hungarians in Hungary say that this is the Italian Vali. And here I am not and will never be an Italian. It is difficult to explain. I lost track of the things that go on at home, I don't feel that they are mine any more. And here … no matter how well Italians accept foreigners, I'll never be an Italian and I will never really feel at home here. This is a strange thing but this is how it is. I have talked to several Hungarians who married Italians just like I did. Many say [they feel at home] neither here nor there. (Vali)

## Conclusion

The women migrants interviewed from Bulgaria and Hungary for this research have a particular experience – as do others whose early lives were spent in countries of the former communist block. Mobility under the communist regimes was strictly regulated and travel abroad was only possible in specific circumstances and with specific authorization (marriage, professional engagement, education). Amongst the interviewees, those who 'left home' before 1989 often (but not always)[16] did so in a spirit of finality, exploration, and desire. For these women, home was immediately thought to be elsewhere. Leaving was escape from constraint and the lack of possibility, although it was also loss.[17] Estrangement was both voluntary and unavoidable, as sustained contact for instance through letter-writing could be problematic for family members or friends who continued to live in the countries they had left. At the same time, a sense of un-belonging already in the country of origin is part of what makes for a story of exit, and in these early cases, exile.[18] In contrast, post-1989 migrants could undertake the journey to another country with much more ambivalence. Indeed, the option to return was underlined by several interviewees who had enough money or a pre-paid ticket to keep the lines of connection and belonging open (e.g. Jelisaveta).

This chapter has analysed the ways in which the migrant women interviewed narrate attachment to place. The approach has sought to de-reify border-crossing, home and belonging. The analysis underscores their indeterminacy (Fortier 2001), and brings attention to some alternative formulations of home (beyond home as origin): for instance, how home is imagined, either into the future – as a destination – or as an ever-present latent possibility, often connected to an imagined return, which is repeatedly deferred. The analysis evidences a dynamic relation to 'home' such that different temporalities of remembering and wishfulness are in operation in the interview.

The legal regulation of formal belonging, and its implications for feeling a sense of entitlement to place, is powerfully underlined in the narratives. Not having documents is the source of considerable anxiety. Who is and is not entitled to gain legal residence, or other legal statuses, is a central question for the possibilities of belonging. Dual citizenship permits relatively easy mobility and participation in the life of more than one location. So for those within European Union countries,[19] the persistent salience of nation states in the regulation of everyday life is *less* significant than for some other migrant groups or contexts where 'naturalisation' requires the surrendering of one's former citizenship. However, notwithstanding the importance of legal regulation, residence permits or citizenship rights are not by themselves sufficient to secure belonging.

To return to the point at which we began, we can ask what the forms of belonging we have presented tell us about transnational or other practices in the lives of these migrant women. Certainly some of the women report activities which are embedded in their lives and which require sustained contacts and travel across national borders – an accepted understanding of transnationalism (Portes *et al.* 1999). These range from the economic (traders, e.g. Jelisaveta), the political (e.g. those who go to vote), the cultural (teaching exchanges, job secondments, translation and journalistic work), and the personal (the many interviewees who regularly spend summers and other extended periods in the sending countries). Yet amongst those who meet these criteria, their felt attachments vary considerably. As we heard in the last section in particular, some of the interviewees have a sense of self as fundamentally belonging to the country in which they grew up. At the other end of the spectrum, no one claims that they wholly belong to the cultural groupings they talk about, e.g. Tuscan or Roman, in the countries in which they have come to live (whatever their legal status, or linguistic competence). Finally what is interesting is that accounts from the two contexts – Italy, an emigration country until recently, and the Netherlands, noted for its successful multi-culturalism and tolerance until recently – do not differ significantly.

# Notes

1. The term belonging was foregrounded in the edited collection of Andrew Geddes and Adrian Favell (1999). Two sorts of materials are used from the interviews. One is the spontaneous reference to forms of belonging, or tensions over attachments and identifications, for instance between generations. The other is the set of responses to a direct question about the meaning of home – 'What does "home" mean to you?' This latter material especially should be used carefully as the question itself prompts a reflection of home that is 'attached, fixed into place, in acts of remembering "what it was like"' (Fortier 2001: 413). Given traditional thinking about women's roles and their association with the domestic, and the extent of women's work in the creation of the physical and symbolic dimensions of homes, it might be said that the narratives analysed here of migrant women produce an analysis of home which would not directly apply to migrant men.
2. Transnationalism has many sites of usage, here it is intended in a limited way for its relevance to migration only, where it is understood to refer to activities which are anchored in but transcend more than one nation state (Al-Ali and Koser 2002: 2).
3. The drama of return occurs especially in the case of trafficking, which is not a subject of discussion in this paper.
4. There are many examples here. Some reveal the bureaucratic circles the migrants are caught in. For instance, in the case of Emma, who needed to get a copy of her birth certificate from her birthplace to be able to renew her Italian identity card, something which she said paralysed her for seven years.
5. According to Bulgarian law, Bulgarian citizens can enjoy dual citizenship. However, often the Bulgarian citizens abroad are requested to give up their Bulgarian citizenship in order to gain a new one, depending on the national law of the accepting country. So, in the case of Marina the Italian law allowed her to retain dual citizenship.
6. In fact, nine women of the Bulgarian women.
7. The variety of food is often mentioned as something that made a great impression on the interviewees.
8. Hristo Botev is one of the most distinguished Bulgarian poets, who sacrificed his life in the revolt against Ottoman domination in 1876, at the age of 29.
9. Simeon I (893-930) was one of the most powerful Bulgarian kings, who enlarged the territories of the country and introduced Christian Orthodox religion as the predominant religion for the Bulgarian State.
10. Hristo Botev and Vassil Levski are the two most cherished national icons – revolutionaries and poets.
11. Another text from the literary canon of the Bulgaria Literature. 'Baj Ganjo', a parody of the pseudo-civilized Bulgarian who travels around Europe, was written in 1895 by Aleco Konstantinov.
12. This sentiment is echoed in many interviews, e.g. Victoria's claim: 'I don't visit Bulgaria as a tourist.'
13. Interestingly, she uses the verb which signifies waiting rather than living or being.
14. This position is also voiced by Irena, Ralica, Nona, Jelisaveta, Marina, Bea, Scilla, Emma, Juli and Karolina – in Italy – and by Kalina, Eva, Albena, Boyana, Monika, Emilia, Agi and Kremena – in the Netherlands.
15. Burgas is the biggest port and resort on the Southern Bulgarian seaside. The distance between Sofia and Burgas is close to 400km and the journey time is more than five hours.
16. Rosa, a dancer who left Bulgaria in the 1960s for instance states: 'And ... I didn't have any, ... well ... any special idea to go somewhere and not to come back.'

17. Kamilla recounts how she couldn't return for six years, which made her suffer and weep: 'I even missed the word 'Hungary'.'
18. This might be similar to the 'equation between leaving and becoming' that Fortier discusses for queer subjectivities (2001: 410).
19. Hungary and Bulgaria joined the EU (in May 2004 and January 2007 respectively) since the fieldwork for this research was conducted.

# References

Al-Ali, N. and K. Koser 2002. 'Transnationalism, International Migration and Home' in N. Al-Ali, N. and K. Koser (eds.) *New Approaches to Migration? Transnational Communities and the Transformation of Home*, London and New York, Routledge.

Anthias, F. 2000. 'Metaphors of Home: Gendering New Migrations to Southern Europe' in F. Anthias and G. Lazaridis (eds.) *Gender and Migration in Southern Europe, Women on the Move*, Oxford and New York, Berg.

Augé, M. 1995. *Non-Places. Introduction to and Anthropology of Supermodernity*, London and New York, Verso.

Bhabha, H.K. 1995. *The Location of Culture*, London and New York, Routledge.

Brah, A. 1996. *Cartographies of Diaspora: Contesting Identities*, London and New York: Routledge.

Finch, J. and L. Hayes 1994. 'Inheritance, Death and the Concept of the Home', *Sociology* 28(2): 417-33.

Fortier, A.M. 2000. *Migrant Belongings: Memory, Space, Identity*, Oxford and New York, Berg.

———. 2001. "Coming home', Queer Migrations and Multiple Evocations of Home', *European Journal of Cultural Studies* 4(4): 405–24.

Geddes, A. and A. Favell (eds.) 1999. *The Politics of Belonging: Migrants and Minorities in Contemporary Europe*, Aldershot: Ashgate.

Gurney, C. M. 1997. "… Half of Me was Satisfied': Making Sense of Home Through Episodic Ethnographies', *Women's Studies International Forum* 20(3): 373–86.

Lash, S. and J. Friedman (eds.) 1992. *Modernity and Identity*, Oxford, Blackwell.

Morley, D. 2001. 'Belongings: Place, Space and Identity in a Mediated World', *European Journal of Cultural Studies* 4(4): 425–48.

Portes, A., L.E. Guarnizo and P. Landolt 1999. 'The Study of Transnationalism: Pitfalls and Promises of an Emergent Research Field', *Ethnic and Racial Studies* 22(2): 217–37.

Rapport, N. and A. Dawson (eds.) 1998. *Migrants of Identity, Perceptions of Home in a World in Movement*, Oxford and New York, Berg.

Riccio, B. 2002. 'Senegal is our Home: The Anchored Nature of Senegalese Transnational Networks', in N. Al-Ali and K. Koser (eds.) *New Approaches to Migration? Transnational Communities and the Transformation of Home*, London and New York, Routledge.

Salih, R. 2000. 'Shifting Boundaries of Self and Other, Moroccan Migrant Women in Italy', *The European Journal of Women's Studies* 7, 321–35.

———. 2001. 'Moroccan Migrant Women: Transnationalism, Nation-states and Gender', *Journal of Ethnic and Migration Studies* 27(4): 655–71.

———. 2002. 'Shifting Meanings of 'Home': Consumption and Identity in Moroccan Women's Transnational Practices between Italy and Morocco' in N. Al-Ali and K. Koser (eds.) *New Approaches to Migration? Transnational Communities and the Transformation of Home*, London and New York, Routledge.

———. 2003. *Gender in Transnationalism. Home, Longing and Belonging among Moroccan Migrant Women*, London and New York, Routledge.

Yuval-Davis, N. 1993. 'Gender and Nation', *Ethnic and Racial Studies* 16(4): 621–32.

Yuval-Davis, N. and M. Stoetzler 2002. 'Imagined Boundaries and Borders: A Gendered Gaze', *European Journal of Women's Studies* 9(3): 329–44.

Turner, V. 1987. *The Anthropology of Performance*, New York, PAJ Publications.

*Chapter 5*

# 'My hobby is people': Migration and Communication in the Light of Late Totalitarianism

*Miglena Nikolchina*

## Which Communication?

The word communication exists in Bulgarian: *komunikatsia* refers to the transmission and exchange of thoughts, messages, or information by any type of sign system. It can and frequently does imply some sort of technological framework (as in 'means of mass communication'). In its uses, the aspect of interpersonal rapport or togetherness is not essential: hence, in everyday occurrences, the word is usually purged of the implications of intimacy, empathy, or emotional identification. *Komunikatsia* is not a word one would normally use to refer to what happens between lovers, between friends, at a party, in a café, or in a pub.

For cases like that, one would use the Bulgarian correlatives of the term: *obshtuvane* or the slightly archaic *obshtenie*. Like communication, these words are derivatives from the root of a word meaning 'common' (in the sense of 'shared by,' 'belonging to all,' 'general'). Unlike communication, they can never be used in a combination like 'mass communication'. *Obshtuvane* and *obshtenie* presuppose togetherness, rapport, and, figuratively if not literally, being face to face. If there is a goal in the act of *obshtuvane*, it cannot be reduced to the transmission of information as a one-way trajectory that begins with the sender and ends with the recipient; the goal of *obshtuvane*, if such a goal can at all be conceived as something transcending the act itself, can happen only in the horizon of togetherness and reciprocity.

The recurrent emphasis on the latter understanding of communication, on the joy of conversation as its major vehicle and on its little rituals (like having coffee or *rakia* with salad) is what struck me in the interviews with the Bulgarian women-migrants. Although Hungarian migrants do make observations in a similar vein, pointing out, as Agi does, the higher intensity of social life in their country of origin, it seems that only in the Bulgarian migrants' interviews does communication emerge as the figure of a specific understanding of happiness as essentially a good positioning in a fluctuating group where you can talk! Talking to other people, being talked to by other people forms the curious core of this understanding of happiness. 'I always want to talk. I love talking.' (Kremena, Bu/NL)

We are not necessarily speaking of friendship here – we are not necessarily speaking of deep mutual understanding, of loyalty, or durability. It is not a question of being helpful and supportive, either: one Hungarian interviewee makes a fine point about the helpfulness of the Dutch as opposed to what she sees as their lower levels of 'intensity' and 'emotional drive' in communication. 'Social life, friendly get-togethers, these are all much less in fashion here [in the Netherlands], life is a hundred times more turbulent there' (Agi). Agi's distinction is valid for the understanding of *obshtuvane*: what matters in the *obshtuvane* is the turbulence, the event itself. It is not a question of usefulness and it is not a question of fine moral attitudes but, rather, of a certain easy-going availability of people to whom one can talk.

> If I enter a big store where thousands of people go – everybody knows me! 'Ciao, Irena!' If I don't go there for a day: 'What's the matter? Is someone sick?' My husband's sister, she, the Italian, never goes shopping without me because I know everybody! (Irena, Bu/I)
>
> I dare say I have a very broad circle of acquaintances, with whom I, so to say, fill my free time. It sounds vulgar but this is it: I fill my time with people! (Plamena, Bu/NL)

This effortless, easy-going aspect of 'filling one's time with people' is essential. *Obshtuvane* should not be planned, negotiated, prepared. Its indispensable component is spontaneity – the option of meeting someone in the street and deciding to have coffee together immediately, without the other one taking out his/her calendar and saying:

> 'What about next Friday?' It is very important for me … to be able to drop in at a friend's for coffee without me calling first and she taking out her calendar 'I'm busy tomorrow.' If she is in, in you go to have coffee, if not – on you go. […] Just like this – let's go have coffee, let's have a smoke. (Alena, Bu/NL)
>
> Just go out, go there, in Bulgaria, meet this female friend, that male friend, go out, have coffee, closeness, warmth. (Reneta, Bu/NL)

A life full of such sparkling occurrences 'just like this' is the life. In a number of the interviews, in terms of the praise it gets, this vision of happiness where you can have coffee with people without taking out your calendar looms larger than love, larger than the chance to follow one's vocation, and larger than economic success. The absence of the perpetually open horizon of spontaneous interaction seems to make other achievements insufficient: 'I always wanted to have a life. If there is no one to meet and discuss my pictures … I don't feel good' (Kremena Bu/NL). Marriage does not seem to assuage such an absence, although work – any work that involves being with other people – might. As Nona, whose 'golden cage' marriage seems to create precisely this type of dilemma, points out, she would prefer to work – in spite of her being abundantly provided for – 'as a shopkeeper or in a tourist agency just for the sake of being for at least four hours among people'. 'I preferred working rather than staying at home … just to have a reason to go out of the house and then come back.' (Violeta, Bu/NL)

This vision of the spontaneous interactive being with people as equivalent to 'having a life' is frequently articulated in terms that oppose it to economic rationality (Max Weber would certainly endorse this). The 'just like this' emphasizes the refusal to quantify being with others. The massive horror of the 'agenda' when it comes to 'having coffee' springs precisely from the fact that the agenda places communication in the register of what can be measured, calculated, and planned.

> Unless they go shopping, they never go out *just like this*, to have some contact. It seemed to me so horrible … If someone says: come and visit me or let's meet, they both, even if they want to go out, take their calendars and arrange to meet in six weeks at the least. (Kalina, Bu/NL)
>
> Here comes a Dutch woman, she wants to communicate with me, she opens her agenda – it is, let's say, March – and she says: Let's meet in September. Well, I do not know whether I will be in the mood in September, whether I will be here in September, whether I will be alive in September, but she says: can we meet on September 18? Well, I do not know! … I hate this agenda thing and until this very day I have no Dutch woman-friend. (Kremena, Bu/NL)

In her elaborate and comic disquisition on the issue of 'agenda' Kremena explicitly links what she sees as the communicative inadequacies of the Dutch to their firmly closed wallets. When you visit them they offer you some treat and then they take it away: they 'leave nothing on the table.' Bulgarians are poorer but you always find money in the streets. In the Netherlands 'you cannot find a cent'. In ten years she found a couple of coins and kept them like relics. 'It's a mystery how they keep their wallets closed' (Kremena, Bu/NL). The propensity to 'save' and 'stinginess' around the table (this motive appears also in the interviews with Hungarian migrants) is hence explicitly opposed to communication.

> They don't communicate. And … if they have one cent, they want to make it two. (Reneta, Bu/NL)

Always busy, what are they so busy with? True, they do sports, and, then, they have hobbies. They ask me: What is your hobby? (Kremena, Bu/NL)

I have only one hobby ... I fill my time with people. (Plamena, Bu/NL)

## Culture as Communication

It is like listening to mono or to stereo – when you are in the Bulgarian language, when you are with your own experience, you hear everything stereo ... (Joanna, Bu/NL)

At first I heard, in the groping language of this metaphor, the utopia of the migrant as the stereo of hearing: one listens to the foreign language through the native language and, due to the layering of the sounds of two languages, two cultures, two sets of collective experience, one has the effects of spatial, in-depth communicational acoustics. Then I realized that Joanna was trying to hit upon the words with which to describe her own communication failures in the Netherlands. The mono effect was precisely what happened in communicating in the other language, in the other culture: somehow the perspective was lost, the additional dimensions of one's meanings disappeared and misunderstandings ensued.

The interviewees tend to state the presence or absence of the 'stereo' effects of communication in explicit cultural terms. The Bulgarians are warmer than the Dutch and as warm as the Italians – or, perhaps, as warm as the South Italians in the case when Italians in the North will not do.

> Like most Dutch people my husband is a big enthusiast about this Bulgarian warmth, hospitality, broadmindedness, whatever you call it ... It just flows out of me! (Plamena)
> 
> Unfortunately, the Dutch are very reserved and we have very few contacts here. (Violeta)
> 
> The Dutch are weird people in the sense they are cold people. (Alena)
> 
> They are cold. (Reneta)
> 
> There is coldness, a barrier ... The Dutch are like this ... We Bulgarians are warmer, more forthcoming, more spontaneous in our contacts, more expressive. (Julia)
> 
> They are not like Bulgarian women. (Alena)
> 
> At first, it seems that they are 'friendly, warm, merry, smiling' – they start talking to you in the train, in the tram, anywhere! But in six months you realize that they don't know how to love and are afraid of being loved! (Boyana)
> 
> Nothing spontaneous can be done here. (Joanna)
> 
> Is anybody living here at all? (Kremena)

There is no doubt that the attitudes of the migrant-women are amalgamated with the representations and the self-representations that are current in their receiving countries. Quoting a Dutchman – 'Maria, do you know why our windows are open? Because our doors are closed' (Boyana). In contrast to the grievances about the 'low intensity' of Dutch social life (the issues of agenda, hobby, and leaving nothing on the table form the prominent points of convergence between Bulgarian and Hungarian interviewees), the Dutch are often praised about their responsiveness in professional and institutional settings – as being helpful, understanding, having a sense of humor, not being formal. In at least one case, in fact, there is a complaint that they spend their time at work having coffee and chatting! (Violeta). But 'they never become friends in their work' (Kalina). Even the famous Dutch tolerance is not spared and is attributed to indifference:

> The other word for tolerance is indifference. (Plamena)
> In spite of the tolerance of the Dutch, it is mostly superficial and this nation has as much trouble accepting the others as all other nations … it helps us that we are white. (Violeta)

The disparity between the perception of Italy and the Netherlands in the interviews of Bulgarian migrants reinforces the cultural perspective, especially if we take into consideration the fact that complaints about loneliness and personal failure in communication may still accompany the conviction that Italians are open and communicative.

> Italians are very open. Their manner of contact does not differ much from what we are used to. (Emma)
> Italians are very open and especially if you are introduced through friends the distance is shortened very quickly. (Marina)
> Very responsive people, the moment they consider you as friend … Bulgarians and Italians are very similar in their mores. (Olga)

In spite of her belief in the responsiveness of Italians, Olga who had to return to Bulgaria in a state of psychological breakdown offers one of the most dramatic narratives of communicative deficiency. Tellingly, in her account – or, rather, in the pauses and syntactical ruptures of her account – something like the Real of communication emerges: the Real of its ultimate failure and impossibility.

> People there are strange. In these clubs, I think, this is my opinion … they are clubs where people go […] who need some big unburdening which … they cannot share it with anyone. This is what I mean. And then, a number of these people that are there they simply have problems. But problems that are … [Interviewer, trying to help: Family, personal?] Family, even personal … or problems that they are too reserved, they cannot communicate. That is, out there they are very, you see … it is difficult for them to know people, difficult … [she breaks off]. (Olga)

It is not the Real of communication that I want to question here by bringing forth the obsession of Bulgarian migrants with communication, nor the truth of national or ethnic, nor cultural communicative capacities pitched up against this Real. The question, rather, is the complicity between the migrants and the native women in conceiving differences as cultural, ethnic, or national. Today, this complicity is reinforced by current theoretical perspectives with their various emphases on multiculturalism, on ethnicity, or on the local versus the global. If, however, we unpack the migrant women's emphasis on communication through an approach that takes into account certain comparatively recent contingencies we might be able to uncover a dynamism that is not reducible to issues of cultural identity. Communication became a dominant preoccupation in the last decade of communism in Bulgaria – in theoretical terms but also as a *modus vivendi* that simultaneously incorporated and kept its distance from traditional practices in a conscious effort to differentiate itself from the discursive monopoly of the state. I will briefly turn to this aspect of the communist legacy that had its complicated dealings with attitudes perceived as Eastern or Balkan.

## On Good Conversations

Communication (as *obshtuvane* and *obshtenie*) and conversation emerged as important theoretical preoccupations in Bulgaria in the late seventies and in the eighties. Although titles like *Culture as Communication [obshtenie]* (Stoyanov 1988) and *Communication [obshtuvane] with the text* (Angelov 1992), as well as the issue of the journal of philosophy *Filosofski pregled* (1991) dedicated to the dialogical settings of Plato's *Symposium* (a telling topic, as I will try to show) appeared comparatively late, they comprised essays written earlier and reflected upon the previous decades. The reception of Bakhtin and his ideas of dialogism which had begun before the first Bulgarian translations of his work appeared in the 1970s was certainly a factor in the escalation of this problematic. A less evident but more poignant incentive for these preoccupations was the premature death in 1971 of a major Bulgarian literary theoretician, Tsvetan Stoyanov. The posthumous publication of his mostly unfinished work took more than two decades and was accompanied by the mournful attempts of his circle to convey to the public the true stature of his achievement. The ensuing writing on and about Stoyanov was a mixture of memoir and interpretation that invariably emphasized the impossibility of the task of passing on Stoyanov's Rabelaisian magnitude to the wider audience since, no matter how important his written work might be conceived to be, the truly great part of his thinking had materialized, according to his literary friends, in his conversations: in 'the voice that articulated the thought' (Zhechev 1988: 5). 'I cannot resist the conviction that the true complexities of his tastes, partialities, ideas, critical positions and essayistic inspirations cannot be easily grasped by people who did not know him personally' (Zhechev 1988: 9).

It was a pity Stoyanov could not accomplish his projects but 'he himself used to say that for an intellectual product it made no difference whether it would be realized and live for centuries, or whether it would be consumed in a conversation. In the perspective of eternity, these terms are equivalent' (Kuiumdjiev 1978: 17). Far from being a simple expression of mourning ('I feel that I need the man more than his books'), such claims were accompanied by the belief that the cultural legacy, when deprived of the 'flame of its initial life and of its improvisational element', was just a corpse (Zhechev 1988: 5). There was unquestionably much in Stoyanov's own writing, a considerable part of which was in the form of a dialogue, that worked towards the idea subtending such interpretations, the idea of the primacy of the spoken, of 'culture as communication.' As Stoyanov himself put it in an essay significantly entitled 'On good conversations,' which, according to his publishers, was written in 1959 but, most pertinently, appeared for the first time in print in 1978, good conversations 'are perhaps worth more than the hundreds of hours when we imagined we were doing something useful' (Stoyanov 1988: 68).

If the reception of a contemporary figure brought forth the primacy of conversation, of what did not accede to writing – for, after all, 'the claim that good conversations are ephemeral does not correspond to the truth' (Stoyanov 1988: 69), it is noteworthy that the concurrent intensification of the interest in a figure as long dead as Plato focused with the same fervor on 'dialectical communication' and the 'complete unfurling of the element of speech.' The years during which Stoyanov was produced by his publishers, biographers, and interpreters as the master of conversation and the genius of the unwritten were also years of intense theoretical problematisation of Plato's 'unwritten doctrine,' which centred around the privileging of the oral versus the written. Very much in the spirit of the praise that Stoyanov received – 'With ease he guessed and sometimes even more eloquently expressed our own objections [...]. In the multifaceted, orchestral organization of his spirit there lived simultaneously both his and the other's point of view' (Zhechev 1978: 10), – it was important to demonstrate that Plato's 'dialogism' privileged 'dialectical communication' not only against writing but also against silence and monological speaking. 'Plato's ideal is not mystical silence but the complete unfurling of the element of speech [...]. The most profound knowledge is not achieved through mystical illumination in solitude but through an intense cognitive effort, which is always carried out with the other' (Boiadjiev 1984: 20–1). And yet, 'the Philosopher defends traditional oral culture but he upholds one type of oral communication against other types [...] the opposition to the pompous public medium for communication is perhaps even more important [than the opposition to writing]. Although he defends the oral speech of Hellenic tradition, Plato is against the noisy and affected speaking which moves the human multitudes but leaves them unchanged' (Bogdanov 1985: 216).

If both the reception of a contemporary figure and the intensification of the interest in a classical figure focused on the act of enunciation *per se*, the Bakhtinian impact on these trends, sometimes discreet, sometimes explicit, received thereof a rather specific twist. The irreducible presence of the voice, of the phoné, in Bakhtin's ideas of polyphony and dialogism is conceptualized for and in writing. When it comes to the emphasis on the unwritten that surfaced in the 1980s discussions of Plato and Tsvetan Stoyanov and that, in fact, comprised a field exceeding these two representative figures, the penchant was to render Bakhtin's ideas *literal*: dialogue was no longer an internal aspect of the written word but an epitome of the 'good conversations'. What remains unwritten in *this* 'doctrine,' in the written defence of the unwritten, is the tacit knowledge that the recourse to orality, to speaking rather than writing, to the art and the 'element' of conversation, to the voice that articulates the thought and is equally good in presenting its own position and the position of the other, was motivated by a censorship that could still control publishing but no longer controlled speaking. Among his 'good conversations' Stoyanov places 'the conversation of the oppressed and the tortured, above whom there weighs the shadow of a gloomy tyranny and for whom it would be dangerous to even dream together – and yet, there is hope in each syllable they utter …' (Stoyanov 1988: 69). What was impossible in writing took place in talking.

Dialogue was hence not only valorized theoretically but was also – or, perhaps, predominantly – enacted as conversation. It thus returned to the cultural substratum where – its theoreticians were perfectly aware – it had its immediate support. But not unchanged. While, in the 1960s, the conversations for which Stoyanov was praised by those who remembered him were still informal and took place in selected cafes and private apartments, from the late 1970s on – which happened to be the time of the first publication of 'On good conversations' – dialogism turned into an increasingly deliberate practice. As Angel Angelov (1997) put it, 'Dialogue was a humanitarian mind-set, normative and unattainable, that was cultivated in intellectual circles in the 1980s against the complacent and monological institutionalized discourse of the state. This mind-set presupposed the self-discipline of listening to the other while simultaneously neutralizing the noise of your internal authority.'

The cultivation of dialogism took the form of what came to be designated as *the* seminar (Nikolchina 2002). The seminar, which began in elitist groups discussing Plato's distrust of writing or Wittgenstein's critique of language, grew through proliferating circles of people and events and emerged as a major feature of the last decade of the communist regime in Bulgaria. By the end of the 1980s it spilled over from University auditoriums into street action involving hundreds of thousands of people. This was as much as Tsvetan Stoyanov had hoped for: 'How often, since there are human beings and human history, have good conversations gone beyond their microcosm and turned into a huge social force! Now close by, now far away, the fires of good conversations are flickering all over the globe today … . Conversations are weapons … . Nothing was ever done without a good conversation – neither the building of the Parthenon, nor the tearing down of the Bastille' (Stoyanov 1988: 70-1).

## Written and Unwritten

A little change of perspective – be it temporal, or spatial, or both – is enough to screen the relevance of good conversations in the precise *topoi* where it was formerly charted. In her charade of Tsvetan Stoyanov as Dan in *Les Samouraïs*, Julia Kristeva (1990: 55ff., 400ff) turns him, from her Parisian perspective, into an agent of the chivalry of writing rather than of speaking. The present day students of the 1980s proponents of dialectical communication have uncovered ample evidence for Plato's reservations with regard to speech (Panova 2000). While no Bulgarian intellectual today seems to be particularly concerned with the 'complete unfurling of the element of speech' or, indeed, with the virtues of dialogism, the belief in the value of communication seems to have accompanied migrant women. Are they keeping the traces of the political past of the home country? Some of the migrants do mention in their interviews the ban on communication and the isolation imposed by the *ancien régime* in order to 'keep people in ignorance and disinformation' (Irena, Bu/I) and prevent them from being seduced by the 'capitalist idea' that could stick to them 'like shells onto a ship' (Boyana, Bu/NL). This ban had foreigners as one of its specific targets and turned the foreigner into an exotic creature and an object of ardent fantasy. Migrant women are aware that the ban was dictated by the regime's fear that free communication would open one's eyes – and 'it is good when people open their eyes, isn't it?' (Irena, Bu/I).

In a further echo from intellectual attitudes in the 1980s, there is an awareness of the 'dialogical' aspect of communication and a keen perceptiveness to the lack of dialogism as an internal component of thinking. 'I always try to think not only my own thoughts but also the thoughts of the other. I don't think it's good to be blind to other positions and believe only in your own' – says Ana whose pet shop in Pisa brings her in frequent debates with animal rights activists. She is worried not by their particular ideas but by their unwillingness to assume that the other's position might have legitimate claims to what is right. 'I cannot believe my own beliefs with such absolute conviction that I wouldn't allow for the possibility that the other might be right. But am I right in being like this?' – she asks.

Or is there, perhaps, something in the situation of the migrant that carries on preoccupations already forgotten in the home country? Are the lightness, the ease, the grace in the general attitude of new migrants to migration enacting the fantasy of the eighties, the fantasy of being 'logged in' to the now close, now distant fires of conversations flickering all over the globe? 'Emigrant? I do not feel an emigrant. I am a Bulgarian who lives here. Tomorrow I may decide to live in the States, what's the problem?' (Joanna). This easy-going, serene perception of movement is typical of new migrants for whom 'patriotism' (unlike older emigrants, they never use the word) is not a country but the attachment to a certain type of sociality, to 'just having coffee with people.' 'How did I decide to migrate? Oh, it was a joke.' There is a sharp difference in this respect between these attitudes and the attitudes of older emigrants for whom deciding to live somewhere else was the result of dramatic choices and frequently involved cutting off of connections to the home country. Most new migrants emphasize the *ad hoc* nature of their decision to first go, then stay, then keep open the possibility of frequently commuting, and, perhaps, of going back one day. The awareness of the 'mono' and 'stereo' effects of understanding might be the specific gift, to a world in flux, of this light-hearted mobility which voices its plea for 'dialectical communication.'

Last but not least, in the face of new challenges, could communication be the Bulgarian migrant's 'weapon' (to go back to Stoyanov's claim that 'conversations are weapons') in times of need? There are cultural differences, all right. The question, the vital question that looks to the flexibility of the future rather than to the sediments of the past, is what mobilizes these differences and to what ends it summons their shifting meanings.

## References

Angelov, A. and A. Kiossev 1992. *Obshtuvane s teksta*, Sofia, Sofia University Press.
Angelov, A. 1997. *Dialog i Dialogizm*, Literaturen vestnik, 9 April.
Bogdanov, B. 1985. *Mit i Literatura*, Sofia, Nauka i izkustvo.
Boiadjiev, T. 1984. *'Nepisanoto Uchenie' na Platon*, Sofia, Nauka i izkustvo.
Kristeva, J. 1990. *Les Samouraïs*, Paris, Fayard.
Kuiumdjiev, K. 1978. 'Tsvetan Stoyanov', in Stoyanov T., *Nevidimiat salon*, Varna, Georgi Bakalov.
Nikolchina, M. 2002. 'The Seminar: *Mode d'emploi*. Impure Spaces in the Light of Late Totalitarianism', *differences* 15: 96–127.

Panova, N. 2000. 'Platonovite Dialozi za Dialoga', in V. Gerdjikova (ed.) *SUMPOSION ili Antichnost i Humanitaristika*, Sofia, Sonm.

Stoyanov, T. 1988. 'Za hubavite razgovori', in *Kulturata kato Obshtenie*, Sofia, Bulgarski pisatel.

Zhechev, T. 1978. 'Tsvetan Stoyanov i Negovata Posledna Kniga', in T. Stoyanov (ed.) *Geniat i negoviat nastavnik*, Sofia, Otechestven front.

———. 1988. 'Tiga po Tsvetan Stoyanov', in T. Stoyanov, *Kulturata kato Obshtenie*, Sofia, Bulgarski pisatel.

*Chapter 6*

# Migrant Women in Work

*Enrica Capussotti, Ioanna Laliotou and Dawn Lyon*

## Premise

The theme of work[1] is a site through which migrant women negotiate their sense of self, and reflect on their social position. The heterogeneity of the interviewees of this research (see Appendix for details) means that they express a range of relations to work, determined by their occupational and educational background, their social status and varying connections between work and other dimensions of their lives (sociality, communication, affective relationships, home, social recognition). This chapter focuses on the place of work in the development of forms of subjectivity arising through mobility and migration.[2]

The women we interviewed are migrants in the context of global processes which make certain kinds of work available and desirable in certain locations (Sassen 1991; Scrinzi 2003). These global processes change the availability of work, its conditions, and its value (in monetary and social terms). At the same time, the women are subject to the norms and conditions of national and local labour markets, including, especially in Italy, informal and unregulated ones. There are some significant differences in the labour markets of Italy and the Netherlands. Notwithstanding these structural features, the sectors in which the interviewees tended to work were quite similar and we did not find major national differences expressed in their accounts, which are more strongly marked both by local conditions and by general problems in the two countries (e.g. childcare arrangements and the structure of the working day).

Two-thirds of women are in the labour market in the Netherlands, where a central feature of women's employment is the high proportion who work part-time: three-quarters of those employed.[3] Whilst they enjoy a wide range of social rights and provisions notwithstanding this status, the Netherlands is nevertheless characterized both by high labour market participation for women, and by traditional gender relations in terms of the division of domestic labour, something which is reflected in the interviewees' accounts of the structure of the school day for instance. Italy has the lowest proportion of women in the labour market of all the twenty-five European Union countries; little more than two-fifths of women are in employment. In contrast to the Netherlands, women who work tend to be engaged in full-time employment, with less than one fifth of those in work working part-time.[4] Traditional gender relations predominate in the division of domestic labour. For example, Italy is noted for the presence of migrant domestic and care workers in Italian homes (Andall 2000). This is associated with limited provision of social services in the public and private sectors. Whilst it supports the participation of some women in the labour market, it does not alter the organization of domestic labour between native men and women (Phizacklea 1997).

This chapter is organized in five sections. The first is concerned with the interviewees' emphasis on self-realization through work. In the second section work is articulated as a sphere through which affective relationships can be built and where intersubjectivity can develop. The third section focuses on the ways in which migrant women claim dignity as workers. A fourth theme is a discussion of work and family; and in the final section, we explore how the women interviewed reflect on exploitation, and gender and race discrimination in their work environment.

## Sustaining Professional Identities

This part of the discussion analyses the ways in which work is a source of a positive sense of self and a basis for satisfaction. It is work – or more specifically, the market valorization of skills and competences for work – that underpins the women's capacity for mobility. These interviewees are mostly in (or looking for) professional positions, for instance in teaching, information technology (IT), and translation. Work is associated with a sense of possibility and openness – notably for those with computer and IT training in the Netherlands (Kalina), and for those working in intellectual fields in Italy.[5] The analysis shows how these women define what work they would and would not accept. This is connected to their sense of self-worth in terms of their social/occupational status, or in some cases, have an explicit economic basis, notably related to the possibility of 'return'. At the same time, they are subject to specific pressures and constraints as non-native workers, marked both as women and as migrants. Their abilities are viewed through these positions, as a result of which they are channelled in particular directions.

Plamena, a Bulgarian woman living in the Netherlands, refused to apply for lower-level jobs even when her initial and repeated applications for training programmes with banks were unsuccessful, because of her inadequate language proficiency, she said. Finally, her persistence was rewarded with a traineeship in which she could develop her language skills whilst working in a 'huge organization that is known all over the country. This is very important to me.' She evidently seeks recognition through her work and cannot contemplate a lower-status position, because of the effect it might have on her self-image and relationships with others. Her decision to migrate was a definitive one – 'I came here with the idea that there is no coming back'. At the same time, her only possibility of returning to Bulgaria is by earning money: 'It sounds very pragmatic, but I can't go back to Bulgaria without money'. Both building her life in the Netherlands in the present and keeping open the possibility of return in the future mean that she will only consider work of a certain status.

Marina, a Bulgarian migrant in Italy who works as a journalist, considers return as an ever-present option: 'it feels good to know I can do it any time I wish to'. However, the logic informing her decision not to return in a more permanent way is expressed through her professional activity: 'I'd go back if I found a job which is more interesting or which I can do better than what I do now. So far I haven't discovered such a job and that's why I don't consider returning to Bulgaria'. Whilst the reality of economic and professional opportunities is highly relevant[6] – as Kalina expresses it, 'I just can't smile with such a salary' – prioritizing work over country of residence is not a given. Yet occupation functions in the interview accounts *as if* it were wholly determinant; rather than constraining, this might be read as allowing another life which is hard to claim on other grounds.[7] Moreover, in the context of present economic conditions, it is a highly legitimate mode of justification for life choices. An effect of this orientation, however, is that it is necessary to have a reason to return, rather than a rationale to stay.

In a third example, Kristina also refuses low-level work. She explicitly states that she migrated for work, and not for a relationship. She was a performer in a Bulgarian circus, which she joined after working in a disco in the former Yugoslavia. When the circus moved to France, she stayed in Italy. This was in early 1989, prior to the collapse of communism, when it was possible to obtain a residence permit valid for two years. Nowadays, her orientation is to stay in Italy 'as long as it gives me opportunities to work' – but not just any kind of work. She has become a fitness instructor and a drama teacher and 'wouldn't stay in Italy if I had to work as a cleaner or a housemaid'. She has always 'pray[ed] to God to let me work only in jobs I enjoy [laughter]. I guess God must exist because so far I always worked in what I've wanted to'. Work gives her a wider sense of belonging in the world, and she can imagine living in many locations. She is 'closely bound up with my job' and would move for it as it is work that 'brings me satisfaction and keeps me happy'. In her own estimation, she is 'not the kind of woman to settle down with a family'. As in other cases, there is an emphasis here both on self-realization and on a middle-class status.

If the above examples evidence the limits some interviewees fix on their choice of work, in what follows, we see another pattern, that is, how migrant women in (semi)professional occupations are 'channelled' in their work. The story of Henrietta, a Hungarian woman who migrated to the Netherlands to be with her partner, is very telling of the ways in which the context of a migrant woman's life constructs her professional possibilities. Henrietta was a lecturer in a Hungarian university, teaching Dutch. She and her future (Dutch) husband met when he visited the university. They decided to pursue their relationship in the Netherlands, she left her job and migrated. In the interview she recounts, at length and with feeling, the different jobs she has held since her arrival. She has settled, for the time being, into a secretarial position for a university professor. She feels 'truly relieved' that she 'might after all be able to survive all this!' she says. Still, she misses teaching and feels some discomfort at 'being a secretary with a university qualification.' In her search for intellectual activity in her life, she has recently undertaken some translation work. Translation emerges in this context as a possible profession, and one can trace in Henrietta's narration the channelling of interests and energies to this point. Paradoxically, the Dutch context effectively robs her of the capital that was valorized in Hungary – her capacity to teach Dutch. What is notable is how translation work comes to be seen as a resolution.[8] However, within this, it is through her 'being Hungarian', and her command of her native tongue, that she is now valorized.

Similarly, Anett, a Hungarian woman who went to the Netherlands to be with her partner, energetically sought a job, sending out 20–25 copies of her CV a day. She was finally contacted by an agency looking for Hungarian, English-speaking, people. Whilst she retains ambitions to start her own company, or to do an MBA, one can see how the structure of opportunity also channelled her to move towards translation.[9] Women in these positions are effectively valorized for what we call their 'national capital' – competence in their native language, and local knowledge.

In this section, we have drawn attention to two orientations to professional work. The first is the refusal to accept low-status work. Here, work is the site through which the women gain a sense of place in the receiving country, within which social status registers as very important. This might indicate that particularly in a new geographical location and one in which some forms of belonging are difficult to achieve, status and position become more significant for creating a sense of self (Olwig and Sorensen 2002: 8). In the second set of examples, we have seen how one's positioning as a migrant gives rise to specific 'choices' (e.g. translation work) as some capacities are foregrounded and valued over others in new ways in the new context.

## 'Doing something for myself': Creating Social Bonds through Work

The migrants' accounts present us with an enlarged understanding of work, encompassing the affective relationships the workplace makes possible, as well as work as an activity (of service, production, etc.). Many interviewees talk about social isolation as an aspect of living in a foreign country, and for some the need to break out of this is more significant than the intrinsic satisfaction they might get from work. Indeed, the connection between work and relationships is most explicit when the interviewees describe employment as a means of social integration in the new country. Work provides opportunities to create social relations and friendships, and is a reason to go out – just 'not to stay at home'. Kalina, for example, is 'motivated to start working, because of the isolation ...' Annet takes this further, suggesting that work is also linked to autonomy within a partnership: 'I had no job, no nothing at the time, just him [her partner]'.[10]

Furthermore, the context of work itself provides emotional stimuli for establishing relationships – although for the migrant women it may also at times be a site of discomfort. Henrietta talks of her fraught experience of looking for work in The Netherlands. She starts positively, also echoing Annet's point:

> I didn't want to stay at home at all. I thought if I wanted to get integrated in this society it wouldn't do just to make some sandwiches in the morning for my friend and then to stay here waiting for him to return at 6 p.m., watching TV and reading the papers. That wouldn't help make me feel at home. I thought, well, I still do, that the best way to establish relations is to find a job and work together with others and then you get to know the Dutch.

The narration which follows is of trials and difficulties and is charged with emotion and strong language. After starting to work as a secretary in a company producing bread-making machines, an experience she describes as 'a disaster', she loses confidence in her ability to operate in Dutch, as she 'just couldn't cope'. The technical vocabulary used in the company and the need to deal with people from different parts of the country who spoke with strong accents or in dialect, sent her into a spiral of uncertainty. She became shy and implies that her relationship suffered as a result. However, a new job provided the basis for new forms of social relations: 'After I changed my job, it got much better, I started to feel alive. Joined a sports club, joined a choir last September, so now I do plenty of things and feel all right.'

The association between work and socialization reflects an attitude that does not exclusively concern migrants, but characterizes contemporary post-industrial societies more generally. The blurring of boundaries between work and 'free' time, and between work-space and home-space, is congruent with the experiences of many people who create social networks and bonds from within their work environment. This attitude is accentuated however in the case of the migrant women interviewed here, as they made a more general evaluation of types of employment according to the opportunities specific environments offered for the establishment of relationships. This emphasis is telling of the importance of social bonds for survival in the receiving society, and helps us understand why some of the interviewees argue that they are pleased with their employment in low-qualified low-paid jobs. The pleasure of work needs to be read against a context in which it is difficult to find one's 'place', to achieve a sense of belonging.

Lubomira and Teodora are both highly-trained women who claim to be satisfied with their current employment in a supermarket mostly because of their 'friendly colleagues and the atmosphere that gives you the chance to develop in one way or another without feeling ignored'. Teodora is a graduate in Slavic philosophy who speaks with remarkable equanimity about this shift in her life. She is learning Dutch and fits her work around her classes. Her friend, Lubomira, relates positively to her work experience because she is treated in a way that does not make her feel like a second-rate person, 'just because I am not Dutch and I do not come from a Western European country', something which often happens in other contexts, she says. Lubomira attributes this friendly atmosphere to the Dutch work-culture, commenting, 'the well-known distance between a boss and a worker, which is characteristic for Bulgaria, does not exist.' According to Teodora, there is relief from the patriarchal styles of supervision that the women are more familiar with in Bulgaria:

> As for the distance between a boss and a worker in the Netherlands, no one tolerates people who try to dominate by power and shouting ... So you will never come across the 'chorbadja'[11] type of boss. You will never have a boss of the 'fatherly' type either: that is to say 'I do everything for you and you have to be grateful to me.' So I don't feel discriminated in that sense.

The self-fulfilment that these migrant women seek through work has many dimensions and, is not exclusively related to content, status or pay.[12] An important dimension is the opportunity to 're-make oneself'. Teodora finds dignity in her supermarket job because she sees in it a demonstration of the rejection of a source of discontent for her in Bulgaria.

> I even had a conversation with my boss once, he had by chance read my application file and he asked me: 'Lubomira, I can see what kind of education you

have.' And I said to him: 'It doesn't matter what kind of education I have, because I am not used to sitting at home doing nothing; so I like my job at the moment and what is important to me is that I am satisfied that I am doing something mainly for myself'. [...] Because I was 42 and I wasn't married back in Bulgaria to some extent I felt underestimated as I was a woman and I was not married. You can never see that here. Under no circumstances. And I simply relaxed.

When Teodora and Lubomira talk about the future, they offer different visions of the development of their lives. Whilst Teodora, for the time being at least, is settled in her low-status work, Lubomira envisages a professional future, and considers her job in the supermarket as a short-term solution. The difference in these orientations is explicitly connected to what they both perceive to be *viable*. After arriving in the Netherlands, Lubomira needed to wait for her diplomas to be approved in order to apply for a higher-level position in her field (engineering), something she refers to repeatedly, and about which she is hopeful. If that does not work out, she says that she will pursue her education in the Netherlands 'to get a master's degree and to look for an appropriate job. Not that I am having any financial problems, but I just don't want to turn my back on those six years of studying, to forget them as if nothing had happened [laughing].' In contrast, Teodora has 'no illusions that I will be able to find a job here', because the dominant interest in the Netherlands is in modern languages, which means western languages. Even if she tried her hand in this area, she would be competing with native speakers which would be 'very hard' she says.

> As for the financial side of the question I have accepted the possibility that I will work till I am 65 years of age, as it is here, if I am safe and sound, as a cashier: that is what I work as now. Because my salary is enough to finance, together with my husband's, four trips abroad every year. That is what I am interested in, being able to travel to neighbouring and remote countries, and to buy books. My salary covers that completely and I have the chance to save something: 'to put something by for a rainy day' [laughing]; I could never do that back in Bulgaria ... The money simply goes so fast in Bulgaria. That's it.

Despite the differences in their future plans and their work-related ambitions, Teodora's and Ludomira's accounts indicate that they have a high degree of emotional and psychic investment in their work, especially in terms of establishing social networks and relationships within the receiving countries, and between receiving and sending ones.

## Demanding Dignity

In contrast to these accounts, many women migrants are disconcerted about the content of their low-paid and low-social-status work. Dignity, a traditional dimension of self-representations of working, reoccurs repeatedly in the interviews, taking various forms: a claim, a hope, an ambition, or an absence. These women insist that their work environment does not provide them with opportunities to develop relationships and is thus a source of discontent as an activity and an image. For example, Rosa, a fifty-three year-old woman from Bulgaria who lives in the Netherlands, explains how difficult it is to find a fulfilling occupation: 'I don't have any work, I get social benefits; meanwhile I work on the black market. What can I say, I go to clean people's homes. When somebody asks me what I do, I say, I look after old people, 'cause I don't feel like saying I clean houses'. Rosa wanted to train as a dental assistant, but was rejected because of her age, and she was forced to take whatever work she could find in order to support her teenage son. Her testimony evidences the social stigma attached to cleaning, whilst eldercare ranks more highly. Even though she is in a very difficult position, the image of dignity in work remains significant.

In another case, Reneta, a Bulgarian migrant who works at a social care centre, uses her work environment as a starting-point in her criticism of Dutch society. She clearly relates her criticism of the lack of communication in Dutch culture generally to the fact that she feels very constrained and underestimated in her job. Her account, which contradicts those of Teodora and Lubomira, nevertheless confirms the importance of the quality of intersubjective interaction and social relationships in the subject's experience and understanding of work, positively or negatively. Furthermore, feeling isolated from Dutch employees and the work culture are juxtaposed with the apparent naturalness of her relationships with other migrants. Reneta emphatically argues that she has contacts with other migrants all the time; she identifies with migrancy, which she sees not only as a condition of being in another country, but as the only condition within which sociality can develop, underlining positive complicity between migrants:

> I told a friend of mine who is an Indonesian woman – I told her: 'it's better to have a team, to work in a team, which would consist of people from the lowest class of other countries, but not in a Dutch team'. Because they [migrants] are, they are like us – natural people. You can tell them absolutely everything, you can joke with them, while you can't do this with Dutch people. No.

Reneta's disposition towards work is strongly marked by the way in which she conceptualizes her status as a migrant woman, which has itself arisen through her being constituted as a migrant in the Netherlands. Now a fifty year-old woman, she originally left Bulgaria in 1988, illegally crossing the border into

Serbia, where she was arrested, and sent first to a Serbian prison, then to a refugee camp, and finally back to Bulgaria. She managed to migrate after the amnesty in 1989, and ended up in the Netherlands, where she has succeeded in securing permanent residency: however, she is now contemplating retirement in the 'warmth and sorrow' of Bulgaria. In her present world, dignity and recognition are things she can only claim from other migrant workers and friends. And dignity – from within social relationships – is presented as more important than the status, pay or content of work.

## The Relationship between Work and Family Life

The 'feminization' of the labour market – the massive entrance of women into the paid economy, and capitalism's higher evaluation of attitudes and competencies historically perceived as feminine (care, reconciliation, mediation, etc.) – is the context in which migrant women seek work. In spite of this trend, the women's testimonies articulate the persistent divide between the private and the public, and the gendered dimensions of labour relations. They refer specifically to women's experience of having to combine productive work with family care. The frequency of references to the care system – inside and outside the family, private and public – points to the enduring division of labour between the sexes: most of the women interviewees who are also mothers undertake the major responsibility for care.[13]

In the Netherlands, some of the women who are not in formal employment comment on how the structure of the school day makes it practically impossible to combine work and childcare. For instance: 'Well, for example in the morning I have to take my little girl to the school at a quarter to nine, after that I have to pick her up at twelve, after that I have to take her back again at half past one and pick her up again at half past three, which actually completely divides up the whole day' (Alena, Bu/NL). Others lament the good professional opportunities that existed under socialism (Victoria, Bu/I), or explain how the situation of migration with limited resources makes them reliant on men and thereby in part reproduces traditional gender relations (Jelisaveta, Bu/I), which is a reversal of their previous situations of equality.

The limitation of workers' social rights (e.g. maternity leave) is navigated by women through various forms of resistance. Motherhood can mean entering a terrain of negotiation and conflict with one's employer, since a working mother is a stigmatized figure in both Italy and the Netherlands:

> I didn't tell my boss I was pregnant. [When] I really couldn't do up my skirt and trousers, I told him. He was speechless when I confessed my 'sin' of being pregnant ... I felt very much ashamed, my face was burning, you can imagine, because I also felt I betrayed him.' (Emma, Hu/I)

Lying, for Emma, registers as a negative action that leaves her with the sense of having betrayed her own values, because she believes that for 'human relations to be fair and open, we all tell what we think. I don't like to carry secrets …'. Alena's outlook towards work and motherhood is critical of specific versions of womanhood in Bulgaria. Differentiating herself from the 'ambitious' model of womanhood, she enlarges the idea of work, so that it includes the labour required to take care of oneself and others. Other interviewees claim that studying, caring for children, and 'dreaming' of what else they might want to do is also valuable work, and no less ambitious than being employed. In a shift in Alena's ideas about work, she now believes that self-fulfilment can also come from investing time and effort in herself and not just from offering her labour in the form of employment and expecting acknowledgment from the work environment. Caring – for herself or her family – is part of her new understanding of herself and is presented as a form of emancipation. After introducing the typical opposition between motherhood and ambition for a career, Alena refers to a new dimension, that is the perception that her ambitions will however be frustrated by job market conditions in the Netherlands. This declaration casts light on another dimension of the ambivalent relationship between desire, satisfaction and opportunities: when the job market is unable to sustain and meet women's ambitions (because of persistent hierarchies and power relations based on gender, class, racial and ethnic dimensions), the private sphere emerges as a possible, positive location. Subjectivity is articulated around both a previous time – the one devoted to the self-realization one found through work in one's own country – and a present time, which is marked by motherhood and the family, in the context of migration. Employment is then presented as an impediment to the fulfilment of true relationships, such as love and parenting relationships. Alena comments,

> I don't think there is anything nicer that paying attention to your own child and watching her grow. And few women have this opportunity in Bulgaria, very few women. Now the truth is that Bulgarian women are morbidly ambitious and they want to work actually. And I was like that. I was like that until the moment I found out it was much nicer and much more enjoyable to be busy with my kid than going to work! Because no matter what kind of job I find here, most probably it will not be on my specialty, or what I have always dreamed of or wished for …

Similarly, in Bori's narrative, her lack of interest in a career coincides with her condition of being a Hungarian living in Italy. She has a university degree in Italian and Hungarian languages, and she was a teacher in Hungary, but when talking about the job market in Italy she can only be generic and ironically refers to 'selling ice-cream':

> I'd like to have some type of job, which doesn't make me nervous as my reasons are, first of all, I want to have something to do, and we also need money. But in Hungary I worked a lot in my job, which brought me a lot of satisfaction, so I'm not motivated by any desire of self-realisation. For me, that is in the past tense. [...] I'll have to work, no question about that. I have no idea, though, because what I am qualified to do is not relevant here at the moment. Anyway, things will sort themselves out somehow. I do not feel any particular commitment to, say, selling ice-cream, but I'll come up with something, I'm sure I will, only I don't know what it will be.

The contribution of this section is to show how subjectivity is shaped by the conditions in which the migrant women deal with motherhood and work. They argue that the very concept of work should be expanded to include care activities in the home; and their accounts illustrate how the private sphere emerges as a space of potential satisfaction in the face of frustration in the labour market. Whilst these points are relevant for women more generally, migrant women face particular forms of discrimination and exclusion.

## Discrimination and Solidarity

> It was very interesting but I worked illegally. Because in the capitalist system a workforce costs much less if one works illegally. [...] Capitalism was something new for me. Things were changing at home in 1991 but we were taken very good care of. If you work illegally nothing is secured for you. You can't be sure whether you get your salary at the end of the month or not, whether you can still continue next Monday. So it was a very new and hard life style for me. Very hard. Because I realized how vulnerable you are when you have virtually nothing. (Emma, Hu/I)

In response to the question of whether her precarious work conditions are due to her being a foreigner, Emma continues to stress the superimposition of class, gender, national and geographical discrimination and prejudice:

> No, this is quite usual. And it makes things worse if you are a foreigner. A foreigner but not an American, English, French ... Coming from Eastern Europe means they look down on you. You have to do twice as much to be appreciated, just as it is between men and women. ... They are afraid that Eastern European people hunting for jobs will pour in. They are afraid of criminals and prostitutes. This is what they are afraid of. So it is not simple, not simple.

Insecurity, openness, self-employment and creativity are the fundamental concepts of current hegemonic discourses about the labour market: if jobs are not offered, they can somehow be invented, so the ideology which underpins current discourses about work goes. Yet, despite this dominant discourse, migrant labour is, in general, considered to be much more predetermined and less open to negotiation and creative invention. Migrants are seen as being almost 'natural' providers of cheap, flexible, unskilled and mundane work, with their labour being deprived of creativity and inventiveness. We can understand the ambivalent references we encountered on this subject as a direct reaction to the pressures that migrant women feel to accept work as unskilled workers in low-paid jobs despite the fact that they are often highly qualified. In many of the interviews, the women migrants counteract the pressure on them to provide flexible and low-paid labour in the receiving country by claiming their right to reflect inventively on their position in the labour market.

Violeta (Bu/NL) takes an explicit position on the discrepancy between the migrants' qualifications and their employment. According to her, the migrants' troubled relation to qualified employment is determined by the perspective of the more economically developed countries of migration as a social problem. New as well as old cultural, political and economic divisions between migrant and native labour determine the politics of discrimination and solidarity in contemporary European societies. She recounts,

> It's unreasonably difficult for foreigners to find work, in spite of their qualifications and experience. It's true for all kinds of foreigners – it doesn't matter if they are from Eastern Europe, from America, from Western Europe. In spite of the fact the Dutch are tolerant, it's almost on the surface, accepting others is still a problem of this nation, as it is a problem for all nations.

The forms of discrimination that these women encounter, both in Italy and the Netherlands, due to the fact that they come from Eastern Europe, are often denounced by the interviewees in ways which stress the negative consequences not only in term of material conditions but also as psychic costs: 'so my self-esteem here [Hungary] was always turned on and there [Italy] it was rather turned off' (Gyöngy). Uncertainty, harsh competition, and self-promotion are the key elements used by Gyöngy to describe the labour market in Hungary after the transition. Although she is happy to be back in her job as a teacher of English in Hungary (she is a return migrant), she notes the context of uncertainty: 'whatever you have you can lose it overnight, so you're supposed to renew yourself all the time. [...] You have to keep fighting to do the job. Fighting! ... You have to sell yourself! So that's how it is here, too ...'. In fact Gyöngy felt herself to be a successful teacher of English in Hungary, while she was someone with 'no place there [Italy]'. Not being a 'native speaker' prevented her finding a job; but she feels that 'the [schools of English] were biased against Eastern Europeans, their pronunciation or whatever. So I wasn't given a chance. What's more, when my son was in kindergarten, I offered them to give English lessons for free ... They refused even that. I felt myself to be a kind of failure ...'.

This kind of discrimination is also felt by other migrant women who live, like Gyöngy, in a city in southern Italy. Gyöngy recounts two examples of extreme exploitation, the case of a baby sitter from South Africa, and a domestic helper from Romania, who were both treated as 'servants': 'It irritated me no end the way she [the Romanian woman] was exploited. I think it irritated me because I saw her as oppressed and felt myself oppressed at the same time. Well, she came from Romania, from poverty. And then people here wanted to take advantage of her'. Although there were many differences between these women lives (in terms of education, job opportunities, and material conditions), Gyöngy stresses her sense of empathy based on the connections to her own experience (the frustration of her ambitions). Nonetheless, she defines the possibility of solidarity at an emotional level, which can be sustained by the common experiences of being abroad, being migrants, and being women. Overall, this section has evidenced discrimination faced by the migrant women, its effects at the material and symbolic levels, and, more positively, how it can be used as a basis for solidarity.

## Conclusions

In this chapter we have traced various ways in which women migrants relate to work and the impact it has on how they conceive of themselves in the context of migrancy. We have focused on the ways in which they negotiate their professional identities and occupational choices, and we have explored how the women migrants position themselves in the work environment and evaluate forms of sociality that emerge there. We have analysed the migrants' positions *vis-à-vis* discrimination at the workplace, claims for dignity, and the relationship between work and family life.

Recent research in the field of labour studies has approached work – particularly low-paid, low status and often, but not always, migrant work – from the point of view of the biopolitical formation of subjectivity with a varying degree of success (Felstead and Jewson 1999; Parrenas 2001). In order to distance themselves from approaches that uncritically overemphasize the notion of control over migrant and labouring subjectivities, and women's subjectivity in particular, scholars have pointed out that such approaches tell us only part of the story, since they erase 'the linkage to the circuitry of power that is to be found, increasingly throughout the globe, in the multi-face of what many have been otherwise calling 'control' inside the network comprised by the homeworker, the state social worker, the NGO advocate, the organizer, the academic, and the policymaker' (Staples 2003; see also, Clough 2002). Resituating the politics of labour at the core of the analysis of this global circuitry of power makes it necessary to turn our attention to the appearance of new types of working subjectivities that could be characterized as 'turbulent' rather than as 'revolutionary' in the old sense.

The new turbulent politics of labour that has been traced by other researchers emerge through the contradictions that mark the relation between migrant subjectivity and work in various ways. Migrants invest and pursue professional identities, but at the same time they endow low-paid and low-status employment with great expectations in terms of social recognition, dignity and the establishment of social relations. Women migrants view work as an important site for the achievement of self-fulfilment and personal development; but on the other hand, they often deconstruct and enlarge the very notion of work by disassociating it from employment and occupational activities. They reflect on discrimination as a core element of the condition of migrancy, but they also insist on the liberating potential of working in a country other than their own. These sets of contradictions echo overall transformations of the role and the concept of work that concern not only migrants but contemporary late-capitalist societies more generally. Nevertheless, the emergence of these contradictions in the interviews with migrants indicate the complex and multifaceted role that work plays in the formation of the migrants' sense of self and thus go against the grain of uncritical approaches that assume a direct, self-evident and homogeneous association between migration and labour.

## Notes

1. We use the term work broadly to refer to employment and other forms of labour, paid or unpaid, in the formal, informal or voluntary sectors.
2. We do not address the full range of concerns which can be found in the rich bibliography on work, migration and gender. Over the last two decades scholars in the field have conducted in-depth research into the role played by gender divisions and migrations in the formation of labour relations in post-industrial societies. Strong emphasis has been put on the study of home-based labour and the transnational structure of informal sectors of employment (Fuentes and Ehrenreich 1983; Benería and Roldán 1987; Kofman et al. 2000; Lutz et al. 1995; Phizacklea and Wolkowitz 1995; Borris and Prügl 1996; Koser and Lutz 1998; Parrenas 2001; Ehrenreich and Hochschild 2002). This body of scholarship has provided us with empirical evidence as well as conceptual formulations that solidly ground the position that the gendered organization of contemporary migrations is at the core of complex processes that determine the role, the form and the politics of labour in late capitalism.
3. 65.8% of women in the Netherlands are in the labour market in 2003; 74% of them work part-time which usually means less than 20 hours per week (Eurostat, http://europa.eu.int/comm/eurostat/).
4. 42.7% of women in Italy are in the labour market in 2003; 17.2% of them work part-time, an average of 23 hours per week (Eurostat, http://europa.eu.int/comm/eurostat/).
5. However, there are also stories of the non-recognition of qualifications, especially in the 1960s and 70s.
6. This orientation is repeated by several other interviewees, e.g. Poly, Irena, Kristina.

7. Indeed, in the case of Marina, her parents were unprepared, scared and saddened, as well as glad for her at the news of her departure. The shock or grief of parents is also a common motif in the interviews.
8. She is also considering doing a Ph.D. on the history and politics of translation between Hungarian and Dutch.
9. This is the case for most of the women who work as translators in our sample.
10. Independence is a theme echoed in other interviews, in such a way that work becomes the pre-condition of migration for some women (Erzsébet, Hu/NL).
11. A feudal type of governor in Bulgaria during the Ottoman times.
12. Catherine Casey (2004) argues in the case of temporary work that 'some women are striving to practise their own preferential employment patterns in ways that actively challenge conventional economic assumptions of employment behaviour and traditional trajectories of women's lives'. However, she also goes on to suggest that these orientations may be an oppositional strategy to the acceptance of degraded jobs and employment relations.
13. There were some cases of transnational mothering, and this is certainly a widespread phenomenon (Parrenas 2001).

# References

Andall, J. 2000. *Gender, Migration And Domestic Service: The Politics Of Black Women In Italy*, Aldershot, Ashgate.

Benería, L. and M. Roldán 1987. *The Crossroads of Class and Gender: Industrial Homework, Subcontracting, and Household Dynamics in Mexico City*, Chicago, Chicago University Press.

Borris, E. and E. Prügl (eds.) 1996. *Homeworkers in Global Perspective: Invisible No More*, New York, Routledge.

Casey, C. 2004. 'Just a temp?', *Work, Employment and Society* 18(3): 459–80.

Clough, P. 2002. 'Technoscience: Three Shifts in Critical Theory.' Paper delivered at the Humanities Center, University of California at Irvine, January.

Ehrenreich, B. and A. Hochschild (eds.) 2002. *Global Woman: Nannies, Maids and Sex Workers in the New Economy*, New York, Metropolitan Books.

Felstead, A. and N. Jewson 1999. *In Work, At Home. Towards an Understanding of Homeworking*, London, Routledge.

Fuentes, A. and B. Ehrenreich 1983. *Women in the Global Factory*, Boston, South End Press.

Lutz, H., A. Phoenix, and N. Yuval-Davis (eds.) 1995. *Crossfires. Nationalism, Racism and Gender in Europe*, London, Pluto.

Kofman, E., A. Phizacklea, P. Raghuran, and R. Sales 2000. *Gender and International Migration in Europe. Employment, Welfare and Politics*, London, Routledge.

Koser, K. and H. Lutz 1998. *The New Migrations in Europe. Social Constructions and Social Realities*, London, Macmillan.

Olwig, K. F. and N.N. Sorensen 2002. 'Mobile Livelihoods: Making a Living in the World' in K.F. Olwig and N.N. Sorensen (eds.) *Work and Migration, Life and Livelihoods in a Globalizing World*, London and New York, Routledge.

Parrenas, R. 2001. *Servants of Globalization: Women, Migration and Domestic Work*, Stanford, CA, Stanford University Press.

Phizacklea, A. and C. Wolkowitz 1995. *Homeworking Women: Gender Racism and Work*, London, Sage Publications.

Phizacklea, A. 1997. 'Migration and Globalisation: A Feminist Perspective' in K. Koser and H. Lutz (eds.) *The New Migration in Europe. Social Constructions and Social Realities*, London, Macmillan.

Sassen, S. 1991. *The Global City*, Princeton, N.J, Princeton University Press.

———. 1998. *Globalization and Its Discontents. Essays on the New Mobility of People and Money*, New York, The New Press.

Scrinzi, F. 2003. 'The Globalisation of Domestic Work: Women Migrants and Neo-domesticity', in J. Freedman (ed.) *Gender and Insecurity, Migrant women in Europe*, Aldershot, Ashgate.

Staples, D. 2003. 'No Place Like Home: Organizing Home-Based Labor in the Era of Structural Adjustment', Ph.D. Dissertation, The City University of New York, NY.

*Chapter 7*

# The *Topos* of Love in the Life-stories of Migrant Women

*Nadejda Alexandrova*

### Topographical Mapping of the Concept of Love as a Mediator

One possible way to locate *topoi* of love in the life-stories of migrant women is to regard their narratives of migration as journey narratives,[1] which offer to the self the possibility of taking a multiplicity of paths in the course of its construction. The specific place of a certain topos of love depends on the relation of love to other feelings and emotions, and on the connections between the story of love and various aspects of the story of migration, such as legal status in the country of migration, relationships with the local people, relations with the country of origin, etc. The sense of change and mobility, which the interviewed migrant women develop during their journey can become a way of developing agency, of producing knowledge about the migrant's own self and her capacity for actions.

Plato's definition of Eros as *'leading to knowledge'* can be elaborated with regard to these ways of developing subjectivity. *'It is love that both leads the way and is the path. A mediator par excellence'* (Irigaray 1993: 21). This image of love as mediator is helpful in identifying the topography of love in the journey narratives. It is productive for a research that seeks to explore forms of self-reflexivity in women who migrate, adapt (and marry), and reformulate their experiences in a story. In view of this definition, if we regard the life-story as a 'path' which contains active emotional investments, such as love, then a further step in our interpretation is to show how the story of this love experience 'leads the way' towards understandings of broader social regimes of power. In other words, through the means of the discourse of love, the migrant expresses her knowledge of her own self, of others, and of the power relations that influence her personal life when she adapts to the new space of the country of migration. The 'spatial story' (de Certeau 2002: 173) which includes or denies love as part of the story of migration is a reflection of the migrant's positionality in a world full of cultural and social norms, and stereotypes.

One of the most rigid one of these norms is that marriage should be based on love.[2] This analysis will not concern itself with tracing the concrete literary and cultural sources which have grounded this assumption. Instead, the first part of the analysis describes already existing classifications of literary motifs and plots, which can be found in the interviews. They form the apparatus of the romantic regime of love that is used for justification of certain actions, for instance the decision to leave their country and family, and start living with a partner from a foreign country. While the first part of the analysis searches out romantic schemes and plots in the narratives of Bulgarian and Hungarian migrant women, the second part will pay attention to the ways through which the romantic love becomes a source for 'legitimate' explanations of the migrant women's actions and moves. Thus, this paper seeks to explore how the regime of romantic love is most often preferred as a way of proving the existence of 'true emotional attachment' in a transnational heterosexual relationship between an East European woman and a Western male partner. There is an awareness of the social stigma attached to transnational intimacies, which are often perceived as being based on economic and pragmatic grounds; therefore the migrant's story of marriage needs legitimization from the society by a story of 'true love'. Romantic love can serve as means for gaining such legitimization, especially when intercultural relationships are discussed. In Giddens's terms, precisely the regime of romantic love 'provides a narrative within which the individual can make sense of the unfolding of his or her life' (Gross and Simmons 2002: 535). The assumption that the notion of 'true love' entails a life-long heterosexual marriage creates a secure narrative which does not oppose 'powerful constraints such as common sense, religious tradition and jurisprudence' (ibid.).

The third part of the analysis will deal with the question of how identification with, or denial of, the romantic love-story can account for the migrants' sense of autonomy, for their capacity for decision-making, and for their own strategies of integration in a new society. It will use examples of life-stories which, while they contain romantic narratives and plots, are related more to other aspects of the migrant's life, such as work, career, and adaptation to the local society. Without embracing the full set of characteristics of the opposition 'romantic love/pure love relationship', as offered by Giddens,[3] the paper will try to illustrate how the regime of 'romantic love' gives way to that of 'pure love' in cases where the intercultural relationship is regarded as means for self-development, and as a 'reflexive project of the self' (Giddens 1992: 9). These features are especially visible in the migrants' stories of separation, in their stories of several consecutive relationships, or in those cases where the women claim that love is not part of their story of migration.

## Romantic Motifs and Plots in the Migrants' Stories of Migration

When the sources of knowledge about love are discussed, one of La Rochefoucauld's maxims is often quoted 'there are those who would never have been in love, had they never heard about love' (de Rougemont 2003: 175). Literature has proven to be a great source of exemplary love stories, where love is measured by the human capacity to act in the name of Eros. 'Exquisite mixture of destructive possession and idealization, crest between the flow of desire and the boundaries set up by prohibition, love crosses the threshold of modern times only in literature' (Kristeva 1992: 12). Perhaps the notions of love that the interviewees express in the material are influenced by much more complex sources, such as cinema, media and the filter of their own experience, but whatever the concrete source is, the material contains mental topologies of love, which are based on elements and schemes from the discourse of courtly/romantic love, on the Enlightenment notion of love as a passion, and on the notion that 'every marriage must have 'falling in love'. This may be due to the circularity in culture, as has been observed by scholars such as Carlo Ginzburg (1989) and Peter Burke (2001), between various levels and types of cultural phenomena (such as between 'low' and 'high', according to different temporalities, and a belonging to various social groups and agents, such as those based on class, gender, generation, nationality and so on).

The most frequent motif used in describing the story of a transnational intimate relationship is the motif of *love at a distance* ('*amor de loing*'). The real geographical distance offers possibilities of developing that motif by combining it with the motif of *love as a passion*, a driving force which overcomes distance, and the *motif of separation* and suffering, caused by leaving or giving up the object of love.[4] According to the interview material, marriage or cohabitation, based on 'true love', are also means for overcoming that distance, therefore the scheme of falling in love (at first sight) and getting married to the partner from another nationality is the most common one in the sample (51 percent). To broaden the view of the variety of *topoi* of love in the sample, I will pay attention also to the mimicry of the *motif of the quest*, which can be connected with the migrant's strategy of travelling and learning, and in which love experiences and marriage are regarded as part of the road to personal accomplishment and success.

In what follows I will try to provide some concrete examples, which illustrate the usage of these motifs in the interviews with Bulgarian and Hungarian women in Italy and the Netherlands.

A typical feature of the motif of love at a distance is a long period of courting. In a number of these life-stories, the partners were in correspondence for years before they finally decided to get together (the Bulgarians – Teodora, Marina, Irena, Albena; and the Hungarians – Emilia, Monika, Rozika, Teri). The love-letter as a means for the expression of emotional attachment appears quite often in the accounts of these women. The letters can be regarded also as *topoi* of love, and can be approached from a double perspective – one is the love-letter as a *topos* in the 'spatial story' – the presence and importance which the letter exchange has for a relationship with a partner from another country; the other approach is connected with the love-letter a literary *topos* and as a figure of condensed emotional expression. In such kinds of written communication, the sender expresses her/his individuality through the text but, at the same time, the letter keeps a dialogical regime as it always presupposes an addressee. It is a projection of a phantasmic other, a sublime object of love, similar to those of the troubadours. It is an object of desire whose distance purifies the relationship from all the inconveniences which daily communication might bring out.

In the story of the Bulgarian woman Teodora, the exchange of letters with her present Dutch husband continued for 23 years with one short interruption. Teodora, who graduated from university with a degree in literature, was the interviewee who most openly addressed her story of migration as an exemplary 'romantic' story of love. This is visible not only in her description of the longevity of the relationship but also in her claim that all her decisions are guided by love. Love in her account is the power that can stand against 'everything else':

> And we convinced ourselves that love is what one has to follow and love is what determines one's personal legend, if I could use Paulo Coelho's term, and my ... my life centre is love. So I keep on being the same (laughing): I keep on giving out love!

A very interesting example of such a relationship is the case of Monika – a Hungarian migrant in the Netherlands. She had only three days in a religious summer camp to get to know her future husband, who on the other hand, later confessed that he knew from the very beginning that Monika would become his wife. This love relationship was emotionally intensified by their exchange of letters: 'I had this postcard from X and the question he asked was 'how we can we continue from now on?' It was the start of our exchange of letters'.

Monika remembers that the image of the lover 'was kind of blurred' and that she had to 'fancy the person, this being also part of the game'. The letters became topoi of love in Monika's spatial story and they were also a means for a projection of the images of the sublime other on to the real person, whom she had met only once.

The dominant classical configuration in the romance plots containing the motif of love-at-a-distance, is that the noble Lady is the object of love and the troubadour is the speaking subject (Hadzikosev and Vagenstein 1990: 5–18). Sometimes, as in the small amount of literary works left by female troubadours,[5] in their love stories the women-migrants reproduce that configuration in a reversed and more complex manner. The interviewees possess the authority to speak from the position of the subject of love, choosing appropriate images of themselves and of their loved ones. Yet the situation can become more complex if the interviewee decides to retell also the love-story from the perspective of the partner who had fallen in love. Then the speaking subject presents herself also as the object of love. Such is the story of the Hungarian migrant Sharlota, whose Italian admirer wrote her 'beautiful poems and letters that really pleased her injured soul'. In the case of the Bulgarian migrant (to the Netherlands) Kremena, the interviewee tried to integrate the husband's perspective into her own in reproducing the love-story. Their casual acquaintance at an open market for arts and crafts in Bulgaria sprang into love when the man started sending postcards. He told her later that after meeting her, he kept writing down his memories of their meeting. Kremena was trying to give the point of view of this man in love, placing herself in the position of the love object.

The woman as a subject of love who objectifies her intimate relationship can be discussed also in view of the interconnection between the motif of distance and the motif of separation. Usually this is a separation initiated by the woman who, after migrating to Italy or the Netherlands, decides to break up with her boyfriend or get a divorce from her husband (Eva, Mina, Yana from Bulgaria and Emma, Piroshka from Hungary). Several reasons were pointed out to justify the migrant's decision to separate – the distance itself, the new environment, the career opportunities or the new 'real' love she had found in the country of migration. The stories, which reproduce this motif of separation, contain broad emotional investments, but also suffering and desperation, guilt and remorse. A sense of remorse can be felt in the account of Mina, whose story of separation with her ex-boyfriend in Bulgaria occupies large part of the narrative. When she left to study in Italy her boyfriend tried to follow her journey to the West but went to France to continue his studies in French philology. However, the distance remained and Mina blames it for her decision to break up with the Bulgarian. The romance had a tragic end because the man was traumatized and had a nervous breakdown, as a result of all his efforts to convince her to become his lover again. From her present perspective, Mina tries to find justifications for her actions and decisions that make her reflect on her own needs and her affection and demands towards another person. She confessed that the process of adaptation had changed her and had set different goals and priorities in front of her. The denial of this love also mediated experience and knowledge which helped her to clarify her point of view on her future relationships. Mina, as well as many of the above-mentioned migrant women, regards her previous love experience and separation as a possibility to establish new criteria on her new love objects. The migrant women are willing to initiate new quests for love, but this time it is for a 'pure love relationship' in Gidden's sense – a quest which follows the trajectory of the woman's own self-improvement, a spatial story which involves also accomplishments in the migrant's work or studies.

There are several such life-stories in which love is regarded as a driving force that controls the actions of the women and helps them to overcome language, bureaucratic and national barriers. Several Bulgarian interviewees (Boyana, Teodora, Marina, Irena, Albena) and some Hungarian (Emilia, Monika, Rozika, Teri) expressed their willingness to leave behind their life in Bulgaria in order to stay with their beloved. A typical initiation of such love-stories is the claim that 'love came at first sight' (Brigi, Emilia, Monika, Teri, Henrieta from Hungary, and Adela, Kremena, Yana from Bulgaria). This usage of the romantic notion of love as a passion that strikes like thunder and blinds rational thinking, can be interpreted as a way of resisting the guilt that might be felt for leaving one's family or partner in the country of origin. The cliché 'to listen to the voice of the heart' is an expression of such a justification of one's decision to leave, to migrate, to move from one place to another. An appropriate example is the story of Emma from Hungary who, after meeting her Italian lover, decided that her first marriage with a Hungarian had been entered into for the sake of convenience, whereas in her second relationship with the Italian she had found her 'true love': 'I fell in love with my husband and I left everything behind and came to Italy, as simple as that'.

As is visible in the examples, the narratives of these migrant women from Bulgaria and Hungary contain a large spectrum of emotions, from love as passion to love as suffering. The regime of romantic love operates by inserting these motifs, plots and stereotypes in their proper places – *topoi* of love – in the migrants' journey narratives. That is how the regime of romantic love can provide justification for the present sense of belonging and social position of the interviewee. In many of the interviews such sense of social position and belonging is associated with marriage.

## Love Legitimizing Marriage and Migration

This part of the paper will give examples from the sample of the way in which the regime of romantic love is used as a social legitimization for the intercultural heterosexual relationships between East European women and Western European men. The discourse of romantic love is employed to guarantee the authenticity of a transnational marriage and to enhance the understanding of larger cultural stereotypes and attitudes.

One such stereotype, which acts as a defence of the romantic nature of love, is expressed by the claim that only 'true love' should lead to marriage or (re)union, and that all marriages which are based on other (financial, economic) reasons should be condemned. The construction of this stereotype is part of a complex and multidimensional debate on love in the European tradition, which among other things includes the impact of eighteenth and nineteenth century romance novels and their later movie and soap opera duplicates. At present, this stereotype often functions in the assertion of transnational marriages as legitimate relationships. The echo of the Western public debate about fake marriages, which East European women enter into in order to have a better life in the West, seems to be heard in the migrants' efforts to convince the interviewer of the authenticity of their feeling.[6] According to Dutch immigration policy, for instance, the authenticity of the relationship should be proven by certain artifacts. A declaration is issued on the basis of those artifacts, which asserts that the marriage is 'real' and not 'fake'. Therefore, letters, diaries and signs of mutual affection often assume, in the stories of the interviewed women, the roles of proofs that their story of marriage and migration is a based on 'true love'.

A love relationship that led to marriage (living on family terms with a Dutch or Italian partner) was the reason for migration for more than 50 percent of the Hungarian and Bulgarian interviewees. When asked directly if love were a part of their story of migration, more than one third of the Bulgarian women answered positively.[7] Love comes 'at first sight', the husband is idealized, and there is a substantial period of courting, but there is also the awareness that marriage, and not just friendship, will give security to the women (Yana, Nona, Kremena, Plamena, etc.). The decision to marry was taken 'suddenly' or 'urgently' (Jelisaveta, Yana), however from answers to other questions, it is visible that the interviewees regard their family status with much more rationality and caution.

Most of these women are aware that there is an 'instrumental' usage of such mixed marriages as a way of getting EU citizenship, so they need to underline that this is not the case with them. This can be regarded as a way in which the romance becomes a source of their narrative. Both in the Bulgarian and Hungarian cases, such an instrumental attitude to marriage is treated as risky and is denounced. Carolina, a Bulgarian woman who has been married to an Italian for 30 years, says:

What does marriage to a foreigner mean? Is the economic reason a myth?

I think that it is ... you said it right ... a chimera, a myth to think that coming to Western Europe, to those countries which are in Western Europe, and we are from the southeast Balkans, they think that their way of life will change. Or they think that they will cross their legs in a café and everything will be served on a silver tray. And it's not like this. Dreams and aims are one thing, reality sometimes – quite different, bitter, and from that point the [problems] appear. I remember the words that my husband told me in the beginning when we met. That was a quick platonic meeting, without any kind of sentimental depths he said: I do not want a fire, which comes from straw and burns quickly, but a small fire which burns ... forever.

In some of the interviews the women who eagerly retell the love story of their marriage with a foreigner, express clearly their distance from and disdain towards those 'other' women who came illegally, who can be labelled 'migrants' rather than 'wives'. Albena, Teodora, Carolina, Kristina from the Bulgarian sample and Csilla from the Hungarian are just a few of the interviewed women who prefer not to know or interact with economic migrant women, especially if they have come to enter into a fake marriage. Here is Lora's attitude to those migrant women who enter into fake marriages in The Netherlands:

> I have to tell you that I, as a woman, take the following position: if a Dutchman gets married to a Bulgarian woman, I'd rather think it could be out of love, that our Bulgarian women are beautiful, pretty women, intelligent women. But a Bulgarian woman who marries a Dutchman because she loves him: no!
> 
> *No?*
> 
> No, definitely. [...] I know a lot of stories, when they come to the Netherlands; they leave them [the husbands] and marry a Bulgarian, or some other guy! Or they do whatever they want to! Yes.

Another usage of the regime of romantic love can be observed in the interviewees' conviction that 'true love' is the necessary prerequisite for overcoming cultural differences between two partners from different countries. When distance is overcome in such a transnational marriage, the process of learning the ways of the other becomes difficult, because cultural differences become visible in the everyday life of the couple. The women account that marriage involves a long process of accepting the reactions and attitude of the partner and only romance and 'true love' can provide the necessary patience for such an intercultural relationship.

Violeta, who met her Dutch husband through an agency, claims that she definitely fell in love, and gives the following advice to women who want to marry a foreigner: 'I would advise them to look for love as a base, because only this could help them to survive in a foreign country'. Romance comes as a means for overcoming 'the insurmountability of cultural differences and the need to preserve one's own identity from all forms of mixing' (Flesler 2004). Sometimes, as a comment on and explanation of this experience, the migrant expresses stereotypical points of view like this remark of the Bulgarian Jelisaveta, who is married to an Italian:

> I think that in the beginning he felt sharply the cultural differences between us. We [Bulgarians] are a little more serious than them [Italians] in some respects. That's why, in the beginning he found it hard to get used to the fact that I was closely bound to my family back in Bulgaria.

The love relationship in marriage can facilitate understanding and knowledge not only about the partner but also about the local culture, mentality and social order. The interviewed women often reproduce more general social positions and stereotypes, such as the alienation in the Dutch society, or the laziness and backwardness of southern Italians, etc. For example, some of the Bulgarian interviewees who are married to rich Italians from the north of Italy (Irena, Nona) are in favour of the policy of governing party of Berlusconi, which does not tolerate immigration, and would introduce restrictive migration policies, even though they once had to face bureaucratic obstacles in order to stay and marry in Italy. Another example is the attitude to southern Italians, which in most of the cases is not based on personal contacts but on a deeply rooted stereotype in the Italian society about the lack of order and the laziness of people in southern Italy (Irena, Angelina, Yana).

The examples given so far are illustrations of the way the discourse of romantic love is infiltrated with dominant public discourses about immigration, marriage, nationality, etc. The inscription of the *topos* of love within the *topos* of marriage is thus not only a way of positioning oneself in the new intimate space – that of the romantic relationship – but it also signifies positioning oneself within larger regimes of power in the new social space of the country of migration. The love-story is a means for interpreting social norms, and the reproduction of stereotypes; and as a whole, it is a means for revising the progress of the 'reflexive project of the self'.

## The Quest of Love as Part of the Story of Self-improvement

When Anthony Giddens discusses the romantic view of love, he pays attention to the portrayal of life in romance novels as 'quest[s] in which self-identity awaits its validation from the discovery of the other' (Gross and Simmons 2002: 535). Such vision of life as 'quest for the discovery of the other', which inevitably concerns rediscovery of the self, is valid also for the narrations of the Bulgarian and Hungarian women. There are cases in which the topos of love is central for this quest of self-discovery, yet there are other cases in which love is present in the narrative of self-improvement but is not its central part, and sometimes love is even consciously excluded from the story of migration. The latter will be discussed in this part of the paper.

If the love episodes are not considered central to the life-story, the emphasis in these spatial stories is placed on other aspects of life in the country of migration such as job opportunities, career, strategies of adaptation, future plans and visions. The migrants wish to be more autonomous. They present their experiences of entering or quitting a relationship as having been without much suffering and with mutual content. Although romantic figures and plots can be noticed on a rhetorical level, the regime of 'pure love relationship' is preferred in the description of intimate relationships with local heterosexual partners.

The accounts of a group of interviewees for whom 'love' is present in the narrative but was not perceived as a direct reason for coming to Italy, can serve as example for this kind of attitude to the *topos* of love. These interviewees were not 'brought on the wings of love' but point to job opportunities or education as their reasons for migration. During their period of adaptation, these women had intimate relationships with local partners and they state that this experience was significant in their decision to remain in the country. The *topos* of love is not central for their story of migration, but wherever it appears it contains such romantic motifs and plots as those which were already discussed above. In several interviews with Bulgarian women in Italy (Angelina, Yana, Kristina, Mina, Jelisaveta), the romance with the first Italian boyfriend and the strength of the feeling towards him was mentioned as a reason to stay in the country. That part of the migrants' love-stories, and especially the separation with that first love object in Italy (Jelisaveta, Mina, Kristina), must have had an emotional impact on the women because they refer to it without especially being asked about it. However, at present, they do not put a strong emphasis on the topos of love in their recent migration history, and prefer to describe other quests for self-improvement.

Angelina met her first love in Italy on the seventh month after she came from Bulgaria to be an assistant in a circus. Her Romeo was some kind of a *mafioso*, who treated her with respect and chivalry and took care of her. She didn't know about his life of a criminal, because he said he was a dentist, but even when she understood that this was a lie, she accepted it as a benevolent gesture of care for her. That man was the most handsome and clever she had ever met, and it was he who quit the relationship only to protect her from what might happen to her by being with him. The scenario of the gangster with a romantic heart is not alien either to literature or to cinema, and for Angelina it is an important story of her past migration experience. The relationship did not lead to marriage but was pointed out as a significant moment in the story of this Bulgarian woman. Angelina claimed that the recovery from the separation with the noble gangster, made her more independent and self-assured. She started improving her skills as a hairdresser, which was her profession in Bulgaria, and she tried to emphasis her priorities at present -the satisfaction she gets from her work and her good chances for profit.

Although without such an intense romantic scenario, the stories of several other of the Bulgarian women in Italy do contain such plots. It is especially valid for the cases of the 'dancers' in Italy (10 cases). They had different backgrounds and professions in Bulgaria in the early 90s, and used the opportunity of legal entrance to Italy as *ballerine* to come and try to make a living in the West. While they were once *ballerine* (Ana, Jelisaveta), or 'actresses in circus' (Kristina, Angelina), or night club companions 'with consumption' (Olga, Nona), some of these women are now married to Italians, and some remain single, but almost all of them speak with seriousness and concern about their present job. Kristina is a theatre director, Yana is a cook, Angelina is a hairdresser, Jelisaveta is a bridge player, Ana has a pet shop, and Ralica is a sales manager.

In all the interviews, the migrant women had the chance to place the topos of love at a moment they found appropriate, and to make it central or peripheral to their story of migration. Most of the interviewees from the Bulgarian sample also had a direct opportunity to locate the *topos* of love in relation to their experiences of travelling, when they were asked: 'Is love part of your story of migration?'. From the answers given, it is clear that the directness and suddenness of the question sometimes disrupts the continuous flow of the carefully prepared therapeutic story. It provokes laughter (Eva, Ana, Mina, Joanna), signs of misunderstanding (Olga, Lora), confusion (Alena), avoidance (Emma), and approval of the idea (Angelina, Yana, Kremena, Albena).

There were positive answers to this question, and they are usually connected with the usage of the romantic regime of love. The women answer positively in all cases in which marriage was a reason for migration, and so love was considered as a necessary prerequisite for such a union. What is interesting with regard to the quest of self-improvement, and the presence of the *topos* of love in it, are the negative answers to this direct question. There are several possible reasons for such negative answers. Of course, there can be technical reasons related to the preparation of the questionnaire and sample, and the influence of the neighboring sections of questions, which were focused on other spheres of life. On the other hand, one can suggest that the regime of romantic love is not used as means for justification in those interviews in which the women emphasize 'work', 'career', or 'politics'.[8] Their stories of migration include various intimate relationships, some of which were mentioned in the interviews, but their negative answers show that consciously they do not link their stories of migration with what they see as 'love' (Kristina, Reneta, Rosa, Adela, Ana).

Similar attitudes to 'love' can be seen in all the cases which discuss the family reunification of Bulgarians in the Netherlands. Those Bulgarian women who came to join their husbands in the Netherlands (Alena, Poly, Kalina) deserve special attention because they show variations in the perception of love. They make a distinction between the motif of passionate love and their kind of emotional attachment. Their move across boundaries was more for the sake of their family than for the sake of love. It seems that their marriage also does not need legitimization through a romantic love story. For these Bulgarians, following their husbands was a rational decision, which did not always relate to love as 'a strong emotion', and they even reject the idea of love as part of their story of migration. Here is Poly's answer to the question: 'Is love a part of your migration story? No. Not in the sense that there was a kind of a very strong emotion that made me leave Bulgaria and be with someone! I just followed my husband'.

The negation of love is also a product of the work of love as a mediator of experience. The process of positioning oneself far from one's notion of 'love' tells of the ways in which the meaning of love is perceived. Despite the migrants' different experiences, they can acknowledge the stereotype of marriage based on love and mutuality, but they cannot identify with such a romantic plot.

The 'quest for the discovery of the other' in the accounts of these interviewees seems to be linked more closely with the discovery of the capacity of positioning the self in new spatial (and social) realms. The interviews offer an opportunity for the women to reflect and determine how much they rely on themselves and how important to them are their intimate partners. Many of those who give negative answers to the 'love question' claim that they have learned to rely mostly on themselves, that they have successfully learned to undertake various social positions – 'the lover', 'the professional', 'the mother', 'the friend', etc. Their love experience is acknowledged as useful and constructive in their strategies of adaptation to the local environment. However, their sense of autonomy and equality in the relationship is not explicitly linked with issues of gender and feminism. The 'reflexive project of the self' does not include explanations of the social conditions that have made their emancipation possible.

Both those interviewees who include romantic plots in their narratives and those who claim not to relate their experience of migration to love prefer to explain their decisions in terms of their own personal qualities and characteristics, rather than through references to larger social phenomena, such as feminism, male domination or heterosexual hegemony. One of the possible ways for the gender relations to come to the fore and be analysed, is through analyses of the expression of emotions. The regimes of love relationships transgress the field of the personal and have long been incorporated within larger regimes of power. Therefore this chapter tries to analyse the interview material with regard to the 'affective investment' (Passerini 2003: 21–35) of emotions such as love, which the migrant women make in the course of their processes of adaptation and integration to their new intimate and social space in the country of migration.

From the cases that have been observed, it is clear that the *topos* of love can appear and occupy different places in these journey narratives. The romance, encompassing many literary exemplary love motifs, is regarded as a means of articulating a legitimate explanation for the interviewee's actions and moves across space. It also became apparent that romantic love, whether embraced or denied as part of the story of migration, is envisioned as a mediator of experience from which the women learn more about their own selves in a new environment and about their relation to others, to their object of love. Furthermore, the usage of the regime of romantic love is a means for analyses of new types of subjectivity formed by the intersection between mobility and affective investments.

## Notes

1. In Michel de Certeau's terms, narrative is introduced as a practice that 'organize[s] the play of changing relationships between places and spaces' where the animated space of/in the narrative is 'a frequented place" (de Certeau 2002: 173). See also Augé (1995).
2. Anthony Giddens (1992) calls a 'pure love relationship' 'a social relation entered for its own sake, for what is derived by each person from a sustained association with another; and which is continued only insofar as it is thought by both partners to deliver enough satisfaction for each individual to stay within it' .
3. See the comments of Luisa Passerini (1999) on the genealogy of this statement.
4. An inspiration for usage in the characteristics of these motifs is derived from an anthology of Provencal Lyrics published in Bulgarian. See Hadzhikosev and Vagenstein (1990).
5. The tradition includes also the opposite case, in which a trobairitz, such as countess Biatriz de Dia, Countess de Provenza Gardensa, Maria de Ventadorn, etc. speak to an aloof knight who is in the position of the love object. The scant literature of the trobairitz only consists of between 23 and 46 works, compared to the some 2,500 poems coming from the male troubadours of about the same period. See Liz Hale, Trobairitz at http://www.vanderbilt.edu/htdocs/Blair/Courses/MUSL242/s02/trobar.htm [November 2004].
6. On the fake marriage debate in The Netherlands see Esther Vonk's contribution in this book.
7. From the total of 37 interviews the question was asked in 31 of the Bulgarian cases and produced extremely interesting results about the women's perceptions of love and marriage. The material contains 14 positive answers to that question, and nine negative answers. The other 15 cases are placed in between affirmation and negation for a number of reasons.

8. There is only one such story in the Bulgarian sample – the political migrant Rosa who in 1968 sought asylum in Italy and then re-emigrated to France and the Netherlands.

# References

Augé, M. 1995. *Non-Places. Introduction to and Anthropology of Supermodernity*, London New York, Verso.
Burke, P. 2001. *New Perspectives on Historical Writing*, Philadelphia, Pennsylvania State University Press.
Certeau, M. de 2002. *The Practice of Everyday Life*, Berkeley, University of California Press.
Flesler, D. 2004. 'New Racism, Intercultural Romance, and the Immigration Question in Contemporary Spanish Cinema, *Studies in Hispanic Cinema* 1(2): 103–18.
Giddens, A. 1992. *The Transformation of Intimacy: Sexuality, Love and Eroticism in Modern Societies*, Palo Alto, Stanford University Press.
Ginzburg, C. 1989. *Clues, Myths, and the Historical Method*, Baltimore, John Hopkins University Press.
Hadzhikosev, S. and Vagenstein, S. (eds.) 1990. *Snegyt zelenina sanuva. Anthology of Provancal Lyrics*, Sofia, Narodna Kultura.
Irigaray, L. 1993. 'Sorcerer Love: A Reading of Plato, Symposium, Diotima's Speech', *An Ethics of Sexual Difference*, London, Athlone Press.
Kristeva, J. 1987. 'Manic Eros, Sublime Eros: On Male Sexuality', *Tales of Love*, Columbia University Press.
———. 1992. 'Parole et sujet en Psychanalyse', *Au Commencement était L'Amour. Psychanalyse et foi* (Paris, Hachette, 1985, trans. I. Ditchev, Kritika i humanizm, Sofia).
Passerini, L. 1999. *Europe in Love, Love in Europe. Imagination and Politics in Britain between the Wars*, London and New York, I.B.Taurus.
———. 2003. 'Dimensions of the Symbolic in the Construction of Europenness', *Figures d'Europe. Images and Myths of Europe*, Brussels, P.I.E.-Peter Lang.
Plato, 1971. *The Symposium*, trans. W. Hamilton, London, Penguin Classics.
Gross, N. and S. Simmons 2002. 'Intimacy as a Double-Edged Phenomenon? An Empirical Test of Giddens', *Social Forces* 81(2): 531–55.
Rougemont, D. de. 2003. *L'Amour et l'Occident*, trans. Lilia Staleva, LIK publishing house.

*Chapter 8*

# Food-talk: Markers of Identity and Imaginary Belongings

*Andrea Pető*

## Introduction

A Hungarian woman made a comment once. She lives in the Netherlands and she is married to a Hungarian, too. She said that she had always known that she wanted to have a Hungarian husband, because 'I want to talk Hungarian in the kitchen and in the bedroom'.

This quote from Erzsebet, a Hungarian migrant to the Netherlands, illustrates the point I would like to make in this chapter: how talking about buying, preparing, and consuming food – what I call 'food-talk' – is part of what constructs identity and imaginary belongings. This chapter explores food-talk as an indicator of the social relations of belonging in the interviews conducted in this research.[1] First, the study of food has become a significant topic of research: 'food is life, and life can be studied and understood through food' (Couhnihan and Esterik 1997: 1), emphasizing the social dimension of food (Douglas 1997: 36). More broadly, the production, preparation, consumption, attitude, and symbolism of food operate in time and space defined by gender, class, ethnicity, beliefs and cultural context.[2] Second, analysing interviews of migrant and native women in the receiving countries of this study sheds light on the processes involved in the negotiation of identity between different traditions of food systems in a context of migration (Glants and Toomre 1997: xii).

Food-talk has different social functions and encodes social events (Barthes 1961). Speaking about food (processing and consuming) is used as a marker of identity and as a frame of narrating forms of difference and similarity. This is a meta-discourse: everybody knows and seemingly understands food, i.e. we all have to eat to survive, so it is an 'easy' vocabulary to use when important issues are described. Food-talk is also a frame for constructing imaginary belonging, as the food-talk frame with its topical and emotional flexibility serves as a site for the construction of self and other. In addition, food has productive and regulative functions. Insofar as women are mostly expected to prepare food and it is consumed as a part of a community, the rituals, arrangements and myths constructed around food underlie some forms of resistance and oppression. In this chapter I analyse some aspects of the conflicting traditions of systems of food in Hungary, Bulgaria, Italy and in the Netherlands, and through this explore the implications of changing power relations in a migration context.

## Conflicting Traditions of Food Systems

The two receiving countries in our project, the Netherlands and Italy, represent two divergent points in a north–south contrast as far as cuisine is concerned, which opens up space for comparison (Goody 1998: 128). The imperial tradition, which is not as present in Italian history as it is in the Netherlands, influences the food culture differently: in Italy, so-called 'ethnic' cuisine is just recently becoming popular while there is no space yet for ethnic cooking from the former Italian colonies, such as Ethiopia and Albania, at the tables of today's Italians – while in Netherlands a wide variety of ethnic cooking is available. Italian cooking is experienced by migrant women as being the dominant and hegemonic cuisine in spite of the fact that the regional dimension is still largely present. Fusion between Italian regional cuisine and other national cuisine has begun to appear in the last decades of the twentieth century (e.g. with Chinese cooking, and also with Arabic, Indian and Pakistani). However, the vast majority of homes and restaurants still offer only regional variations in their cuisine. In the Netherlands, there is no difference as far as regional cooking habits are concerned.

In addition, the ways in which women generally organize cooking, meals and social life are different in the two countries. In the testimonies, a stereotypical picture survives that attributes the small, enclosed nuclear type of family to the Netherlands, and the open families, consisting of distant relatives and friends who all go out to eat together in Italy. These situations help us to understand the constructions of difference experienced by migrant women who arrive in these countries from Hungary and Bulgaria.

Women migrants who come from the culture of 'state feminist' emancipation were acquainted with the ideology and practices that removed this domestic burden from women. During the 'state feminist' period, the culture of the communal kitchen was set up, and activists of women's emancipation rewrote cookbooks in order to promote healthy and easy ways of cooking. This process transformed the symbolic understanding of cooking in the former Communist countries into something that was not considered to be a duty nor a female achievement, but rather, a required service (Rothstein and Rothstein 1997: 180). Italian 'good housewives' are portrayed in the interviews as those who earn appreciation through domestic labour. This picture is particularly strong in the testimonies of women who arrived in Italy during the 1970s and who describe having found an Italian society dominated by patriarchal rules, especially regarding family law and gender roles. A simple differentiation between an emancipated 'East' and a backward Italy that is contradicted by Mari's description of her family gendered division of labour (see Mari's excerpt in the following pages).

Another dimension of eating together is as a process through which intimacy might be constructed. The functionalist approach to food underlines how the consumption of food fosters ties in the community. It reflects and reinforces social hierarchies and diminishes social distances. The intimacy of eating together used to be a part of the women's social life at home, before migration. In the oral stories, a number of the migrant women describe home as a site of friendly gatherings and consumption. They have to learn, as migrants, that eating together in a restaurant constructs different social distances and bonding. In Bulgaria and in Hungary there is a serious division between the public form of eating, which is connected to work and to the 'official state', and the private sphere, which was a site of resistance wherein one is expected to foster private networks (Pető and Szapor, 2004). As Mina (Bu/I) put it, describing her bitter experiences of her social life in Italy: 'Finding a job was the hardest part because frankly, Italians can be very polite and invite you to lunch and dinner and pretend to be your friends but when you really need their help, they just disappear. I mean… that's terrible, it turns out that you can't trust anybody.'

Rozika (Hu/NL) has not found her place in the Netherlands either. She complained about the emotionally empty social events with so-called friends. Her long description of the ritual and choreography of the Dutch social event highlights the lack of intimacy.

> We hardly ever go visiting any of them [meaning the Dutch friends of her husband]. Mark's friends are very formal. It's a strict scenario – we phone each other, fix a date three months in advance, the date gets jotted down in our respective diaries, and the actual event unfolds by ceremonial procedures. One time, it's them coming to our place, next time it's us going to theirs. It's always the same time, 5pm, chatting time first, then we have a drink and some peanuts to go with it, then a hors d'oeuvre, a main course, dessert, coffee to follow, a little more chat, and then off they go. All this means damn all for me … Chatting along the lines of 'how are the children doing?' 'they're doing fine' 'and your job?' 'that's OK, too'.

In the case of migrant women, family bonding can be fostered through eating, but this is rarely the case. Teri (Hu/NL) feels at home only with her mother-in-law, because of the way she prepares her table.

> But their hospitality and spontaneity ... I mean that when they eat they are not like the Dutch who would not say to you to take a plate and eat with them. They would say that it was a bad moment for you to come because they were eating and you bother us, and stuff like that. So very much like this. If two of them eat they would only prepare two pieces of meat and not three or five pieces, only two. At my mother-in-law's it is very much like at home where we have a lot of everything on the table. I felt at home in their house very quickly.

In contrast, the Bulgarian migrant woman, Kremena speaks about her in-laws' economy with food as a meta-story for being not accepted in the Dutch family, and as a complaint about the way they economize their love towards her.

> Yes, they don't leave – because I was invited to houses where they would serve something, the Dutch serve, they take the box they serve coffee, tea, they would ask you, they would serve what you'd like – but they would serve and then they would take back the box. They don't leave it on the table ... Well, and when they hid it, I said to myself, 'Well, these people, are they mean, are they stingy with sweets?' And, you know, they serve things which we didn't have in Bulgaria, a little bit different, some sweets or cookies, different things, after all, why aren't they on the table? I said, 'These people are real mean'. That's what I thought in the end.

The women who left Bulgaria and Hungary after 1989 did so mainly for economic reasons. In Bulgaria, economic difficulties made life difficult there and food was rare and undifferentiated. Leaving Bulgaria meant that they had gone to a different situation, one in which they still had little money but had a variety of choices. Monika's narrative is marked by her anger against those who were, and still are, wasting food, which might be read in part as a cover for her own financial problems to buy food. She started off 'at the bottom of the social ladder' she says, a 'Miss No One'. The contrasts between her poverty in Scotland where she lived in a castle as a teacher in an elite school, but with very few resources, and her former life are stark.

> Back in Hungary, food and all that was never a problem, my parents provided all that for me. Here, on the other hand, I couldn't afford anything, not even a piece of clothing, not even second hand, during the first two years, 75 guilder, which is 7,500 forint (25 EU now), was all I could spend a week on food, clothes, household money, everything. That kind of money will get you nowhere, even if you're in Hungary.

Similarly, Albena (Bu/NL) constructs a narrative in which it appears to have been her own choice to eat less, to cover her embarrassment at being poor. At the same time, the poverty of Bulgaria is manifested in the few brands of food which were available in the market.

> At that time in Bulgaria when you wanted a soft drink in a bar you do not specify what exactly ... because they usually have only one kind of soft drink. And it was quite difficult at the beginning – when my husband asked me 'Do you want something to drink?' 'A soft drink' 'What exactly?' 'It doesn't matter' 'It does matter, because there are fifteen kinds of soft drinks. We have to tell the waiter what to bring' [*they both laugh*]. So these were the things that impressed me most.

Similarly, in the case of Todorova, the economic and cultural richness of Italy is narrated as the rich tradition of Italian cuisine. The missing vocabulary of Italian seafood in Bulgarian is a reference to the poverty of Bulgaria.

> But Italy was always my dream ... Italy has this ... the good cuisine – I claim that their cuisine is very good, different from ours ... And there is more to their dishes than pasta – spaghetti, macaroni – everything is called pasta. I love eating fish and fish delicacies, fresh crabs ... [...] I know them in Italian, but in Bulgarian I don't know how to translate, because this is seafood – they don't live in our sea, so I can't translate their names, but they are good.

Mina, on the other hand, reacted to her new environment by over-eating and she gained weight as she consumed too many sweets which were unknown to her before coming to Italy: 'In the beginning I had money of my own, which was very important to me ... and I used to spend most of it on sweets [*laughter*]. You can't find sweets like these in Bulgaria.'

If a common experience for the Hungarian and Bulgarian migrant women was that they came from a culture of need to a culture of consumption, the receiving women are aware of the fact that the first impressions of those arriving in a new country are related to food. In the Netherlands, Annette and Inge accept that their puritan environment can be narrated as being strange – this type of emotional distance and self-reflection can indicate an opening of the culture.

> They were very critical of the Dutch lunches. Some things happened, we were in a youth hostel for some kind of introduction weekend and then there was a pot with a pouring spout for the *hagelslag* and there was this Russian from the Ural and he poured it into his tea, he thought it was sugar ... things like that. Then your eyes open up like: 'That's so weird'. Yes, but the food was really boring, you wouldn't gain any weight in the Netherlands in a year. A filled pastry was the only thing that tasted good sometimes.
>
> At my grandma's, it's still, coffee at 10, sandwiches at 12:30, tea at 3 and a warm meal at 5:30, that's imprinted so deep, you can't change that. And

now, in our generation, you start seeing ... we hardly eat potatoes anymore, it all changed ... see that cover, but that took a long time and you can't change that anymore. And then I think: they're habits and that has to do with your cultural background and your inherited ideas ... and I think that's really hard to change.

## Food-talk Marking the 'Self' and the 'Other'

Food serves as a site of self-identification and expresses ideas about the relationship between the 'self' and the 'other'. Speaking about different types of food and different ways of preparing food is a way of marking differentiation and, as such, it is very much connected to describing migration processes. For some, the expression of subjectivity of migrant women takes the form of finding comfort in the process of adapting to a new food culture, and at times, difference is overcome by imitating the food culture of the receiving community. At the same time, the preservation of an imagined culinary tradition as a link with the homeland is a key factor in securing a form of attachment for migrant women to their homeland. Food–talk is a site where identity is negotiated, and where the constraints of subjectivity become apparent. The interviews with migrant and receiving women illustrate the relationships between food practices and identity construction.

That food is a site of identity is clear from the excerpts about the different Hungarian cultural events which were organized in Italy or in the Netherlands, arranged around ritual ethnic 'food consumption'. Processing the same food in the same ways as 'the Hungarians', sets up an imagined ancestral link with the homeland, which offers emotional security. The cooking of ideal-typical dishes also serves as a form of memory; as a reconstructed memory of the homeland. As Mary Douglas has pointed out: 'each meal carries something of the meaning of other meals: each meal is a structured social event which structures others in its own image' (Goody 1982: 31). Returning home to enjoy the previously 'imagined (and remembered) meals' with family members and friends who represent home is a joy to many migrant women.

Processing the food also means maintaining the cultural norms of the community: the process of preparing exactly a certain type of food at a certain date of the year constructs belonging. When Albena speaks about giving up the habit of preparing the traditional Bulgarian New Year's Eve dish, this is also a story about her redefining what Bulgarian identity means for her now. Rituals around food are the means of preserving national identity, and the first signs of acculturation and integration can be evidenced when one stops celebrating holidays and cooking the traditional meals, as described by Plamena (Bu/NL).[3]

I meet Bulgarians, I read newspapers … And of course, at home, in the garden … I have a great husband who works a lot, long days. So I also dedicate some time also to him – I cook some Bulgarians meals for him – well, you know, I buy some clothes for him. And of course my family in Bulgaria. I think about them a lot and I am preoccupied with them.

The 'food-loving Italian' is a stereotype which is used as a narrative frame for describing Italian ignorance about other peoples and other nations. Csilla dreams about opening a Hungarian restaurant, but she confesses that possibly it will not be a big success, since she assumes that the Italians would not like to eat regularly food other than their own. This narrative frame of 'ignorant Italians' is used to describe the abandonment and lack of interest she experiences from the Italians: 'true, Italians are more interested in the food, I'm aware, when we had our Márai[4] evening, very few people turned up. When there is a dinner, many more people come along'.

Paulette Kershenovich, in her research on Syrian Jewish cooking in Mexico, talks about amalgamation, preservation and innovation when she describes the processes through which Syrian Jewish cooking has been transformed (Kershenovich 2002: 106). The Hungarian and Bulgarian women of the present research speak about the preservation of their cooking tradition, maintained by frequent visits home and contact with relatives, and they sometimes find a form of power in the self-identification which comes with their own 'national' food. At the same time, they seek to perform 'Dutch' or 'Italian' cooking but without any interference from the food culture they were born into. Marina, for instance, uses the recipes of her Bulgarian mother to impress her Italian guests. It is obvious from the interview that learning how to cook was not an important part of her socialisation. So when she was expected to perform her 'Bulgarianness' – as the exoticized other – she returned to her mother. She did not mention in the interview whether the guests were really impressed by the Bulgarian food, but she does emphasise that she is also able to cook Italian-style: 'Italians are very curious about cooking, so they often ask me to cook Bulgarian traditional dishes for them and I had to turn to my mother's recipes. But now my friends know that I can cook Italian food too.' The well-known phenomena of ethnic cooking or of 'fusion food' are nowhere to be found in the stereotypes dominating these interviews: there is no interaction in the interviews between the different 'food-talks'. This is in contrast to the case of Syrian Jews living in Mexico, where food is a place for hybridity. Amongst the Bulgarian and Hungarian migrants there is no mention of the combination of different ingredients, nor of the difficulties involved in buying 'real' ingredients for ethnic cooking.

In order to come to terms with the ways in which the receiving women construct the 'Other', a good starting-point for such an analysis can be found in the structuralist approach to food, especially that of Lévi-Strauss

(Counihan and van Esterick 1997). His binary division of cooked and raw food is very useful to understand the differences in food preparation, evidenced in the way in which the receiving women marked out the migrant women as those who eat fried (Carla) and canned food (Orietta). Consuming fresh food is a class privilege (Goody 1998).

> Yes, always fried things, I don't know, fried things ... they always buy whatever is on sale, they try to save on what they eat ... Eating, I don't know, I don't see what they eat, well, I don't understand. The cooking would be out of the question for us Italians, but how can you say anything about how other people eat? [...] Then I don't know what they eat, I really don't know how they cook, what they eat. I don't think they eat very well. [Carla]
>
> For food, I see that they don't know a lot, for example pasta, they eat a lot of canned food, vegetables, tomatoes more than anything, but a lot of canned goods, sandwiches, they don't really cook ... for example, at lunch I make pasta, or meat, well, they eat meat, yes, they buy a lot of it. [Orietta]

In Italy, the expression of love for Italian cooking may be read as a manifestation of the will to assimilate into Italy. It is an expression of appreciation towards a constructed imaginary belonging. For the receiving women, liking the food of the other is an important step towards forming intimate relationships. The Italian receiving women (e.g. Angela) never made any self-reflective comments about Italian culture or its food traditions.

> She's an excellent cook and she makes both Italian and Hungarian food, she can do both of them well, she's special, she's a special woman. Then my mother met her, and she had the same impression, that she knows how to do everything. I've tasted her cooking, because I like to eat, [*laughs*] and I like everything, even what she cooks, she also made some Hungarian dishes I can't remember what they're called but I liked them, I really did.

Speaking about food is also a way of expressing feelings which are related to the new environment. Magda speaks with disgust about the food the Dutch have at breakfast, despite the fact that a breakfast of bread and jam could be labelled as being French or Hungarian as well. But, in the next sentence when she refers to the easy ways of adaptation, when there is a 'must', she uses food as a meta-text, specifically in connection with children, who are sometimes positioned as the carriers of cultural practices.

> Consequently the kid grows up in a family after all, except not in his own but in someone else's. Which is for me, as a Hungarian, quite strange, I'd find it strange because obviously I would like my own child to receive something of my own culture, that is not to grow up in a Dutch family and ask for such things for breakfast that's ... oh my God! Where did he get the idea? Impossible! Like bread and butter spread with chocolate. Oh, what the hell! That couldn't be helped. You can get used to everything, though.[5] [Magda]

## Food and Power

Consuming food fosters and maintains social connections, and reinforces hierarchies through power. As Jack Goody has pointed out 'the analysis of cooking has to be related to the distribution of power and authority in the economic sphere' (Goody 1982: 37). Power is manifested in who is being served and who is serving the food. Mari described how in her family her father was served first and how she was shocked by this brutal manifestation of patriarchal hierarchy. She was faced with the problem that the emancipated values of the society and her own egalitarian values were not present in the home of her parents, who belonged to a different generation.

> Even now when I go home I keep making my mom rebel against my dad. [...] I cannot put up with it. I can't tolerate that my dad sits down at the table and waits for the food to appear. And he is not able to grab his plate and take it to that stuff. I simply can't put up with it. I can't. The whole world turns around my dad. My mom's life turns around my dad. A lot of women step into this role. And they drag their crosses around like martyrs. [Mari]

At the same time, women gain symbolic power from controlling cooking. It is not only a question of financial control, when women are in charge of the household money, but it is also through their ability to decide what to cook that they influence the behaviour of the whole family. Plamena discovered that buying food is economic power and that in the context of migration, control over the purchase is a form of disciplining power exercised by the receiving community – men and women:

> You're in the supermarket and you don't know what direction to take! I go to my father-in-law, who is pushing his trolley, and I follow him like ... a sheep, you know. And ... I want to buy a kind of a jam, but he tells me: well, no, it's very expensive. We eat the other one in our family, don't we?

Preparation of food in the kitchen constructs intergenerational connections and/or strengthens the position of some people, as they gain a power they can exercise over others, for instance in some cases of mother-in-laws and daughter-in-laws. Gyöngy (Hu/I) described her relationship with her Italian mother-in-law in terms of her constant intervention into her most private sphere, into her cooking. In the interviews, speaking about a disruption in an intergenerational link fostered in the kitchen is a sign of interiorizing the outsider position.

> Well, she's [mother-in-law] kind of pushy, one who bosses the whole family around. She's well-meaning and helpful and all, but she keeps interfering in my business. It started, you know, with what to cook, say we went to see them, and then she packed loads of things up to give me so that I cook this or that on Monday. That's helpful but it really drove me crazy!

For Ella (Hu/NL) 'cooking Dutch' is a way of defending herself against her intrusive mother-in-law. Her comment about the simplicity of cooking secures her status as an outsider and an empowered position in a household where she had to endure the power of her mother-in-law: 'She stayed with us for a very long time. I am cooking and baking. Sometimes I like to do it and sometimes I do not. If I do not feel like it, then I cook very Dutch. That is so very simple.'

Steeped in relations of kinship, food processing is narrated in a self-sacrificing and self-destructive frame by women, and this often serves as a form of emotional blackmail. Csilla (Hu/I) and Mari (Hu/NL) reject that pattern, used by their mothers and by some Italian housewives, possibly because their generation was brought up in communist Hungary at a time when the influence of religious patterns of self-sacrifice were not present in the public discourses, which were instead shaped by women's emancipation. Csilla refuses to follow the prefabricated self-destructive patterns she encounters in her environment, but instead she transforms them for her own emotional needs.

> I like being at home, playing with the children or doing my things. But I hate being at home just to do the cleaning and the cooking. Understand? There are lots of Italian women for whom that is the top thing, you know, that I'm at home and the house is in tip-top shape condition and then – see, that's terribly important – unfortunately many of those, like those girls who come here, Italian wives we see, learn this …

Mari, a young woman, also speaks about rejecting the self-sacrificing strategy of her mother, and about how she is trying to construct her autonomy by opposing her mother.

> For example my mother has always said to me when I visited her at home, and she was talking about cooking, one of the central conversational topics 'look how well I do this, I always do the cooking while Lilike is asleep'. She always did the cooking while the baby was asleep. Because that was when she had time for it … And then I told my mom that I never cooked. We eat in the evening and not during the day. I never cook while she is asleep because I use that time for myself and read. My mom looked at me in a way … I think it never occurred to her that she could spend that time on herself.

Preparing food is also a means of exercising control between partners. In the case of Piroska (Hu/NL), she recognized that there was a problem with her marriage when her husband started not to like the food she prepared, as it was 'Hungarian'. It is quite a different matter liking the food of another country as a tourist than having that very same food at 'home'. In some cases, women are identified with the food they are preparing as 'the Other', who is not liked through/because of the food she is putting on the table.

The fact of the matter is, I did it both ways, but he made faces at the food quite often when we had Hungarian food on the table. I didn't understand how it was, whenever he had been in our place [in Hungary] he had liked everything, everything had been delicious. And here [in Italy] I cooked a meal, and he keeps asking: 'What's this?' Why doesn't he eat it? I felt offended by this, too. If it happened now, I wouldn't be offended, now I look at it from a different perspective: OK, I've cooked this meal. You don't like it? It's not me he doesn't like, it's the meal. I've changed a lot. If you feel that your very personality is being offended, you'll get more cross that way or you'll respond in a different way. These things lead to more serious differences. This is one reason why I saw life here differently. [Piroska]

## Conclusions

Food is a tool for women's socialization: food processing, exchanging recipes, 'gossiping' in the kitchen were always important parts of women's social life. For migrant women in their new homes, this social support and networks are missing and the previous experience of community and intimacy becomes an individual struggle for acceptance on the most intimate level. They have to learn how to cook 'according to the taste' of their partners, or sometimes their mother-in-laws. Eating, like talking, is a patterned activity (Douglas 1997: 37). In Kristeva's work, *Powers of Horror*, food symbolically competes with words (Kristeva 1982), which has a special resonance here in terms of the experiences of migrants, who are also struggling with language problems. This isolation makes this pattern of food processing an achievement, and a product of integration. At the same time, there is also an expression of imagined belonging to home in the narratives through the preservation of ethnic cooking.

Consuming food together strengthens family bonds. Should a couple represent different cooking traditions, the question of whose cooking becomes the dominant one is a manifestation of power. These migrant women have given up their 'gate keeper' function and often try to match their performance to the expectations of the receiving community. However, not liking the food processed by the other can also be a form of resistance, since it represents 'the other'.

A history of non-understanding between receiving women and migrants is manifested in narratives about food. Migrant women do not speak the language and they are not familiar with the customs and the traditions of the receiving country's patterned activity of cooking. The first level of experiencing 'otherness' is through purchasing, preparing and consuming food. Therefore, food-talk is an important site where identities and imaginary belongings are manifested. The belief that there is a choice for these women during food-talk is illusory: they can adopt a narrative strategy of negotiation in which to construct agency, but there is very limited space in which to negotiate women's work as a work of care, due to the complex function that food has in social, economic and cultural contexts, which this chapter has only started to explore.

## Notes

1. On the different functional, structural, and cultural approaches to food, see Goody (1982: 12–33).
2. A tentative summary of the cultural history of food can be found in Montanari (1994).
3. Joyce Toomre analyses the transformation of Armenian cooking when it was a part of the Soviet empire, and points out that the swallowing of the small landlocked republic into the empire led not only to an increase in the variety of food available in the market, but the religious holidays and the eating rituals around those also disappeared. However, based on oral histories with women, she concluded that behind their closed doors Armenians kept on following their practices of preparing 'traditional' Armenian food for New Year's Eve and in their modes of preparing food without any real interference from the Soviet policy makers (1997: 210–11).
4. Sándor Márai (1900–89) is a Hungarian writer. He was born in Kassa (now Kosice in Slovakia), and opposed both Nazism and communism. He emigrated in 1948, worked for Radio Free Europe as a journalist. He died in the U.S.A. He had something of a renaissance, after the changes in Hungary, as a 'bourgeois' writer who stood for the civic order of values, something highly praised after 40 years of socialism. He is also known abroad, and has been translated into Italian (see for instance, *L'Eredità di Eszter*).
5. For Hungarian tastes, a sweet breakfast (such as, for instance, nutella on toast) is alien. An average traditional Hungarian breakfast would be a roll or other type of bread with ham, sausage or cheese, boiled or scrambled eggs, and only afterwards would there be some jam or honey. In the countryside it might even be simply white smoked bacon with onion. Vegetables or fruit are usually not eaten for breakfast.

## References

Barthes, R. 1961. 'Towards a Psychology of Contemporary Food Consumption', *Annales E.S.C*, Sept–Oct., n. 16.

Couhnihan, C. and P. van Esterik 1997. 'Introduction', in C. Couhnihan and P. van Esterik (eds.) *Food and Culture. A Reader*, London and New York, Routledge.

Douglas, M. 1997. 'Deciphering a Meal', in C. Couhnihan and P. van Esterik (eds.) *Food and Culture. A Reader*, London–New York, Routledge.

Glants, M. and J. Toomre 1997. 'Introduction', in M. Glants and J. Toomre (eds.) *Food in Russian History and Culture*, Bloomington, Indiana University Press.

Goody, J. 1982. *Cooking, Cuisine and Class. A Study in Comparative Sociology*, Cambridge, Cambrige University Press.

Goody, J. 1998. *Food and Love. A Cultural History of East and West*, London and New York, Verso.

Kershenovich, P. 2002. 'Evoking the Essence of the Divine: The Construction of Identity through Food in the Syrian Jewish Community in Mexico', *Nashim. A Journal of Jewish Women's Studies and Gender Issues*, n. 5.

Kristeva, J. 1982. *Powers of Horror: An Essay on Abjection*, New York, Columbia University Press.

Lévi-Strauss, C. 1997. 'The Culinary Triangle', in C. Couhnihan and P. van Esterik (eds.) *Food and Culture. A Reader*, London and New York, Routledge.

Montanari, M. 1994. *The Culture of Food*, Oxford, Blackwell.

Pető, A. and J. Szapor 2004. 'Women and the 'alternative public sphere'. Towards a new definiton of women's activism and the separate spheres in East-Central Europe', *NORA. The Nordic Journal of Women's Studies*, 4: 172–82.

Rothstein, H. and R.A. Rothstein 1997. 'The Beginning of Soviet Culinary Arts', in M. Glants and J. Toomre (eds.) *Food in Russian History and Culture*, Bloomington, Indiana University Press.

Toomre, J. 1997. 'Food and National Identity in Soviet Armenia', in M. Glants and J. Toomre (eds.) *Food in Russian History and Culture*, Bloomington, Indiana University Press.

*Intermezzo*

# Relationships in the Making: Accounts of Native Women

*Enrica Capussotti and Esther Vonk*

*Barbara, 29, lives and works in Amsterdam. She is a social worker in Jewish Social Work. Barbara is married to a Bulgarian man – they met three and a half years ago, and, at the time of the interview, have been married for one year; he was already in the Netherlands when they met. Andreas, Barbara's husband, came to the Netherlands for work, through which he also, eventually, received his residence permit. Barbara contacted me through bulletin board of 'Bulgarije pagina', a portal containing links to sites of interest for Bulgarians in the Netherlands and those interested in Bulgaria, where I posted a message calling for contacts with Bulgarian as well as Dutch women who were willing to contribute to our research project. When Barbara called me, she told me that she thinks she has a lot to say about Bulgarian women, Dutch women and the relationships, similarities and differences between them. She knows a lot of Bulgarian women here, and has a couple of very close friends among them. Barbara comes to Utrecht at the end of the afternoon, after a day of work. We conduct the interview at the university, and go for a drink and a talk to the cafe around the corner after we are finished with the interview. The interview proceeds smoothly; Barbara thinks a lot about the relationships she is involved in, her position in society and in relation to other people, in her personal life as well as in the context of her work and in her neighbourhood. She has a great interest in other people's lives and experiences, and reflects on her own way of life and desires in relation to those of others. She is also interested in my opinion on what she has to say; she asks me questions, asks for agreement or disagreement, and once during the interview she corrects herself: 'Oh no, you're asking the questions'.*

I have a lot of contact with migrant women, especially Bulgarian women because I'm married to a Bulgarian. And I live in a neighbourhood in Amsterdam where many migrant women live and I sometimes have contact with them, but that's not more than a chat on the street while I'm walking my dog in the park. I suspect that these women are mostly from Morocco and Turkey. The ones I talk to, well, I don't always ask, but I did hear several times that they're from Morocco, from the north of Morocco, they often add. But the younger girls were mostly born in the Netherlands. And through my work, I have a lot of contact with Israeli women: regularly, as clients. […] I feel most connected to migrant women from Eastern Europe, because, before I met my husband, I coincidentally knew – well, I don't know if it was coincidental – friends living in Hungary and the Czech Republic. And especially in Hungary, I was there often and I had a lot of contact with Eastern European women, Hungarian women. And furthermore, I can, for the most part, understand how women from Israel think, what they're like. How they keep their heads above water here in the Netherlands, because I hear a lot at work. I work for the Jewish social work. So they tell me about what their life is like here in the Netherlands. So yes, 'connected' might be a big word, but I can identify with them, because I hear their stories. And I have to say, honestly, the women that I see in my neighbourhood, I always feel a distance. I will always try, that is probably the 'socio' in me so to say, to make contact, as it intrigues me a lot. But it doesn't always work. It's often very closed, they're often together, it's easier with the younger girls than with the older women. It's something I think about a lot. […]

I feel connected to Bulgarian women, because I think I know what they have to deal with in their life, especially in their relationships with men. I am married to a Bulgarian man, so yes, I know firsthand what are the expectations of a Bulgarian man of his wife. Now, my husband, he's from a so-called intellectual circle and has learned to think things through, but it's also sometimes stronger than he is. He did live there for twenty-seven years and sometimes I notice that he has different ideas about the roles of men and women, ones that I absolutely don't agree with, and that causes, in our case, friction. I see, with Bulgarian women, I can see similarities. They have to deal with the same things as I do. But they handle it differently from me. It is, after all, a very macho culture, the Bulgarian culture, and the Bulgarian women have been raised in it; they have seen how their fathers and mothers interacted with each other and they know what is expected of them. And from some Bulgarian women I definitely hear – well, maybe I'm jumping the gun, but … I do notice that it's different for Bulgarian women here in the Netherlands, because they of course see what's going on around them and come into contact with Dutch women and start to question who should be determining what in their lives. Should they, or their husband? Or the circumstances, which often predominate. Coming from a poor country, always having to work hard and so on. […]

Among the Bulgarian women I know, I have two very good friends. And the rest, it varies from very good acquaintances to people I sometimes see at parties. If I see similarities between them and myself? I mostly see a lot of differences. Yes. I see that they have such a different background, and building up a life here in the Netherlands takes so much of their time and attention, while my bed has been made here. I have my education, the language already makes a big difference, I have a fun, good job here. The only similarities I see are, well, there is one similarity, and a very important one, really: it's that I think Bulgarian women are often very interested in politics. Bulgarians in general, but Bulgarian women as well. I speak with them a lot and I'm interested as well. And they're involved in what happens around them. And also, I find, also with those two friends of mine in mind, but not only them, they are very involved in the Netherlands and not just the Netherlands […]. Of course, that's all new for them. I like to talk to them about it, anyway. Of course, that's very subjective, because those are the people I choose as friends. So I could also name a lot of Bulgarian women who don't have a clue. Those are women who have only come here for one reason, because their husband is here. And that is the reason nine out of ten times: their husbands came to the Netherlands and they followed them.

In terms of relationships between men and women, what do I find striking? Women have, it's very clear, they have so many different tasks that it's almost impossible to do them all, indeed, I don't know where they get that energy sometimes. You notice, they're often drab and look tired, grey. But think about it, you have to be a mother and work hard and look sexy. It's so much. And that's what I hear from women in Bulgaria too, that it's a very hard life for women. They're often a little bitter, mad at the men that do that to them. It depends a lot on what kind of environment you're from, because of course not all Bulgarians are the same. My friend Milena, she was always stimulated by her family, to develop and to think about herself and to be as independent as possible, and she's brought that with her here in the Netherlands. One of my friends came here for her study, got a residence permit that was linked to her study, for which you have to have this much money and prove that you can support yourself and so on. It was a very complicated and long story, but it worked in the end. So she came here on her own. So there are also women like that, but they're the exceptions, I think. I think that most women who come here just adapt to the life of their husbands, and that means with or without a child, sitting between all these Bulgarian men, because there are a lot more Bulgarian men here than women. And do what is said and don't whine. I see a lot of that around me, and I hate it. I'm really disturbed by that. I'd rather not interact with those people. […]

I see the women who have learned to think for themselves a little, you see them rebel here in the Netherlands. Like Milena. OK, it took two and a half years. I got very impatient in that period. I don't know how she got through that, but anyway. She did bite the bullet and said, while her husband wasn't happy with it at all, she said: 'I'm going to try to find my own job here', she is still doing that. 'And as long as that has not succeeded, I'm going to study, because I want to invest in myself'. But she's an exception. And the other friend is now studying law here. But she did it all on her own, she didn't have a relationship. So she was happy to get rid of those Bulgarian men. She also says: 'I will never, in my whole life, want a Bulgarian husband, how can you, as a Dutch woman, choose a Bulgarian husband'. She says: 'here in the Netherlands, I'll make sure that I, it doesn't matter which, the best would be Dutch, but never Bulgarian'. [...]

I think the most sensible thing you can do as a Bulgarian woman in the Netherlands, is to try to become one of the guys. So don't expect them to treat you like a woman. If I see which women they like, those are women who participate in what they do. Don't expect too much. I notice it with my husband too, he likes me most when I go along with those friends and he thinks it's a pain when I say yes, but I also want to spend time together, just the two of us. I understand that it's very important in Bulgaria to be with your friends every night, and to just walk in without having made any plans, but I'm a Dutch woman and I expect something else.

I want to feel special, I don't want to be one of the guys. That's the bottom line. I don't want it to be like, it's fun whether I'm there or not, it hardly makes a difference. Friends are so important. And a woman is ... nice, easy. That's it, easy. And I see that I sometimes walk into that trap with my eyes wide open, because I also tend to organize things and make sure that everything keeps running. And of course I'm also the Dutch woman and he's the Bulgarian. So that brings in another dimension, because he sometimes doesn't understand things, how things work here. And I feel very responsible, I'm like, 'I'll do it, so it will be done right'. I also notice that he tends to pretend to be very dependent, a little dumb. How does this work and where is that ...? And in the beginning, I would get up and get it, but now, even if I know where it is, I say, I don't know, go look for it yourself. And I keep fighting for that. That's a big difference between me and Bulgarian women. Bulgarian women never learned to fight for their position in a relationship. They just let it happen and I think, I will keep fighting for what I think is important. And I keep saying that they're not unreasonable or strange expectations. That it's normal in a relationship.

What I learn from my Bulgarian friends, what I find positive ...? I don't find a lot of positive things. As positive characteristics for women I hear devotion a lot, and caring and things like that ... And I don't like it, I find it a little threatening when I hear women say things like that. Maybe because I have to fight to prevent that I'm pushed into a specific box. But what I do think, that's true not just for Bulgarian women, but also for men, is that for them making contact is a lot easier. It's also very much deeper more quickly than with the Dutch.

Why my friends and my husband are spending time with the Bulgarians here, even if they disagree with how to handle things? My husband says that here you're kind of sentenced to each other. Because you have the urge to speak your own language and to feel safe, to know what's going on. Because, look, my husband works as a psychotherapist and he speaks Dutch fluently. He's working in a Dutch organization, he has a lot of Dutch friends, but he says that it's still all unpredictable and you never know if you're doing well, what people think about you. While, even with those stupid Bulgarians there in that squat, it's very clear. He says: 'I know what I can say; I know how to present myself. I know that if we get into an argument, that it's an argument for a short period of time, but that we can make up again, and I know how to make up'. I also see how he interacts with colleagues, that's all much more complicated. I say, 'why do you socialize with them if you don't really like them?' And he says 'I don't know many other Bulgarians in the Netherlands'. It's the largest group, the illegal guys who have illegal jobs here. There are others, but where do you meet them? It also came about because he used to be illegal himself and so on.

For example, a lot of them live in squats in Amsterdam, many of them in one place. In one of the Bulgarian squats here there is one woman, the rest are ten or twelve men. And her husband doesn't allow her to work, because she has to take care of the child, so she's either with the child or with all those men. And I tried to say, 'come with me, we can go to the park, we can go to the playground with the boy'. But, well, then she says, 'yes, let's have some fun', but it never really happens. I think she knows that that's not appreciated there. They see me as a troublemaker anyway. God, if your wife is in contact with Barbara, then … and everyone thinks that my husband has no say in our house and so on. Yes, I'm 'that Dutch woman'. [...]

I've got the feeling, I don't know if it's true, that some Bulgarian women, especially in the squatter clan, so to speak, aren't allowed to associate with me or something, I don't know what it is. But they also think, I mean Andreas and I have, publicly, in front of everyone, had big fights. It's unthinkable that a woman can just, when the other men are there to see – there was even one who said, you must have married her for the residence permit, how else could you marry such a *kenau*.[1] But it's a struggle. I think I didn't make it easy for myself by marrying a Bulgarian. But we love each other very much and we both try our best. I don't insist on making everything into a problem. It's all right that way; it's finding a compromise. He too, he has changed a lot. He has a nickname in the Bulgarian group: the Dutchman. They think he has become Dutch. Because of the way he treats me, I think. If they invite him somewhere, then he'll say, I have to check with Barbara first. And that's really strange; he's the only one who does that, even with his friends who, let's say, have a higher education, they don't even do that. They don't have to ask their wife. Their social life is completely separated from what they do with their wives. But Andreas does. He always calls me, he always lets me know where he is. And he always says, 'I have to check with Barbara'. They think that's ridiculous, he's a wimp.

My Bulgarian friends think that Andreas is very special. They always tell me that I should appreciate to have met a very special Bulgarian man. I think that also has to do with what we have both invested. He wasn't like that when we first met. He has changed, so have I. But well, we talk a lot. I think it's practical that he's in the care sector and I'm in the social sector: we're both verbal, we automatically talk a lot.

I think that people I'm closer with also see that it's not easy for me. My Bulgarian friend, she's like, 'why don't you just stop complaining, and be happy with what you've got'. But they do see it. And my Dutch friends, they think that Andreas can be really difficult. It's so funny, to them, I have to keep explaining: he's from Bulgaria, he's used to other ways of being in a relationship, of treating women, and he does think about it, he does his best. But it's the upbringing and a socialisation that you can't just flatten out or erase. I don't have that illusion at all.

I want to say something else. What might be strange is that, as a Dutch woman, you yourself are part of a subculture, that's a strange realization. It's also very interesting, enriching. I also work for a Jewish organization while I'm not Jewish, so that kind of is a part of my life. With my family, we used to live as townsfolk in Lunteren, a small village, where we never really fitted in. We have always been the outsiders who do and who don't belong.

*Do you find that a comfortable position?*
I can deal with it. It's always been like that, actually. And yes, I like it because it's very, without wanting to sound pretentious, very enriching. I don't have a boring life, not at all. But, moreover, I'm not stuck in a specific box. I'm learning to look at the world in a much more balanced way.

*Angela lives in a block of buildings facing a barrack in the outskirts of Florence. She is in her early forties, wife of an Italian soldier and mother of a eight-year-old girl. The apartment is large and new, sparsely furnished and with many empty spaces. We sit in the living room which is dominated by a huge TV. The colours and the apartment design seem to confirm Angela's self presentation of being a homebody, a quiet person, a housewife who likes to stay inside although she does not like to perform the typical duties of her role (e.g. cooking). Yet the peripheral location of the building as well as the apartment furnishings mirror a petit bourgeois lifestyle. Nevertheless, as a housewife within a middle class setting, Angela identifies with emancipated, autonomous and affluent women. Csilla, intervieweed by Borbala Juhasz, informed Angela of our project and asked her to participate. When I first called her, Angela expressed concerns about her appropriateness for the research. She said, 'I don't know enough, I don't know what to say'. Other Italian interviewees expressed this form of apprehension; a self-deprecating stance that could fade during the interview or remerge within the story. Different hypotheses could be introduced to explain this reaction to the request of being interviewed: a lack of self esteem which might be spurred by the awareness of leaving a public testimony on a tape recorder; the insecurity caused by the loss of control over the testimony itself; and the awareness of being asked to talk about relations that have strong implication. But self-deprecation can also be a rhetorical formulation independent of any judgement about one's self.*

*Angela's worries were coupled with curiosity about the project and the use of her testimony. She begins the interview asking,* 'What are you going to do with these tapes?' *Later, her question resurfaces:* 'I thought you were supposed to ask me a lot of questions. The main point is how you get along with foreigners, is this what you want to get at? But what is it good for? How can this kind of interview be of any use?' *Despite Angela's scepticism and her portrayal of a limited life within a small area, she has many stories to tell about women from different locations; accounts that are based on her past experiences as well as on her present one, and which are connected with her life within the military environment.*

The woman who lives on the top floor is Hungarian. But to me it doesn't matter where people come from even if they are foreigners. My father was in the military and I was abroad during middle school. I studied in an international school where I met people from northern Europe, Dutch, Swedes, Norwegians, French. None from the east, I've only met people from the east since the wall went down, of course within NATO it was impossible to have contact with them, no? [*laughs*] So when I meet someone I don't have any preconceptions, I try to really get to know them.

Most foreigners that I've met are wives of my husband's co-workers, it seems as if Italians like foreign women. And Italian women really like American men, at least from what I've seen. I was in Gaeta[2] and a bunch of girls from there married American men and moved to America. My downstairs neighbour in Tarquinia[3] also married an American man; it was a beautiful love story because she was turning into an old maid, than he came along and they fell in love, really in love, and now they live happily in America with a baby. So by my own calculations Italian women like American men, while Italian men love women from Eastern Europe, Central America, the women who are in more desperate circumstances, so we women go with those who are better off [*more laughter*].

Italian men haven't really been able to follow the women, the Italian woman liberated herself while the Italian man has been left a little bit behind. When an Italian meets one of this women who comes from a country where women are still women they fall in love more easily. If you take an Eastern European woman caught in these circumstances, think of the Albanians poor things, who live under such bad conditions, even though I've never met one. But what happens to these poor women? They adjust more to the man. Italian women are too emancipated, women here have been liberated, they are free woman, they have really an open mind.

Do you want me to talk about my friend Csilla? She isn't like other women from Eastern Europe. She's done well, economically, she is very intelligent, modern. Sincerely, I've met more women who are really more like us, almost exactly like us, European like we are, we have the same attitudes, the same ways of thinking, because the Finnish woman thinks more or less just like we do, so does Csilla, even if she's from the East she's like us, then the Americans too. The people I've met have been more or less like us, with our way, our perspective, Western, it's really more or less a Western mentality. [...] I think Csilla comes from the upper classes, from what I can tell she seems privileged compared to what I've heard about life in Eastern Europe, at least from what I know, but once again I've never been there and I can't really say, my husband was there and he told me that there was a lot of poverty.

As a friend Csilla is the only one who isn't Italian. We talk and visit each other. If there's a birthday, a holiday, we hear from each other, things like that. I like to stay at home, I'm a real homebody. We talk about everyday things, about what happens to us during the day, things like that. We have the same ideals, the same values, we're not really very different, how shall I put it, the same ideals and values, I think I've said enough. And then there are other cultures much more different from ours and so I can say that at least we see eye to eye on most things, that's it. I really trust her. Of all the people who I know here I think she is absolutely, the number one, for me she's my number one, truly, for me she is special. [...] She is special because she's good with people, she always knows what to say, she says the right thing at the right time. I've seen how she is at home, she's a perfect housewife, she is an exceptional mother. I see her and right away I feel, how can I put it, it's as if I have a sister. Because I'm alone here and without any relatives around, she's a person I can count on, even if we don't talk to each other every day. She's an excellent cook and she makes both Italian and Hungarian food, she's a special woman; it's the same story, she knows how to do everything! [*laughs*] Then my mother met her, and she had the same impression, that she knows how to do everything. I've tasted her cooking, because I like to eat [*laughs*] and I like everything, even what she cooks, she also made some Hungarian dishes I can't remember what they're called but I liked them, I really did. I don't like to cook, I only like to eat [*laughs*]. I could really develop an inferiority complex but ...

It's not that I'm comparing myself to her, it's that she really is better at these things ... She's a little bit better at everything, it's not like all people are alike! Really, this is why we get along so well. Because together we make ... the circle is complete [*laughs*].

What do I think about mixed marriage? Mixed marriages are fine with me, the important thing is that they love each other and get along together. Mixed marriages are fine if they have the same affinities, it's the same problem that two Italians would face. I'm in favour of it, of course, they have to be the ones to judge, if they are happy together, if they are compatible why shouldn't it work? Maybe sometimes there are more surprises in mixed marriages, just from what people say, unfortunately the Muslim culture with the Catholic culture, for example. This comes to mind because I once heard about some people that got married, then later on they had trouble with the children, because they have a different culture from ours. There the women have to submit to their husbands, and so the woman may not be entitled to her own children. The other day I heard about that little girl who has been living in the embassy. I don't know if it's the Tunisian or the Algerian embassy. She's been there for two years, and she can't go out or else her father will take her. Things like that make you think, I have to say that before you get married, you should take a little time to get to know the family, their world-view. If they have the same values, then it's fine, but if their values are really different, that could threaten the marriage. That's what I think, but personally I've never met anyone in that situation. The mixed marriages I know about are between Protestants and Catholics, so they're really more or less from the same faith, but with Muslims, no, I don't know any. Jews, I've met some Jews, you find them, married to Catholics and there isn't any problem, but I don't know any couples ... But I don't really get out much, I have my routine, always the daily routine with the children, you go to the park to meet other mothers, that's how I've been able to make friends, you make a lot of friends through your children.

*Angela recalls her experience abroad as a child to introduce contradictory comments about supposed Italian identity. She defines Italians as 'tarallucci[4] and vino' (wine), referring to an attitude that prefers to avoid conflicts in favour of a simple and naive life. Angela's words echo images historical associated with Italians by commentators located both outside and inside the country.*

I experienced discrimination myself! I experienced it because in Belgium I lived in an area with lots of Americans but it was a German bus that came to get us for school. The Americans [*lapsus*] hated me because I was Italian! I've had some experiences that I really can't [*emotional voice*] ... the Belgians would try to hurt my feelings by shouting 'get out of our sight' but the Germans were the one who really hated us [*said in muted tones, as if to keep the Germans from hearing*]. The Germans don't like us because we betrayed them twice. Maybe I should say that no one likes us! It is that Italians aren't trustworthy, Italians are *tarallucci e vino*, you scratch my back and I'll scratch yours, *pasta* and *pizza* ... And after having lived abroad I can't say that it's a wrong impression, because foreigners are more serious about things that we are. I'm sorry to say so, I'm Italian, but I'm more of a serious person. I see Italy as a kind of Montecarlo, that is, a beautiful place to visit, with beautiful things to see, beautiful women; beautiful objects, fashion, if you're talking about fashion, aesthetic is another thing, on that we are the best in the world at least. Because really, even with all of these missions abroad, all of these things that they do, I can't see Italy ... please! [...]

When I go to visit my American friend, she's got the American flag there in the house. Oh goodness, not me but most Italians like whatever is somewhere else, everything else abroad is better than Italy. I for one would send the whole lot abroad! Because it is true in Italy there are a lot of deficiencies but travelling and travelling and just looking around I still feel lucky to be an Italian. The American, the Finnish women, all of them speak very well of their own countries and we Italians speak ill of our own country, it's really crazy. [...]

The Finnish woman once told me that they never go out up there; they never stand in line at counters, they do everything via computer, even old people know how to use computer. We go and stand in line at the post office, at the bank, they are much more advanced in this sense. [...] I've been in Germany with my husband and my goodness it's cold there! [*said nearly in a whisper, as if amazed*]. Belgium is pretty cold too, isn't it? It's humid, they are Catholics but they're still colder than we are, we're more sunny; they're much more reserved. The farther North you go, the more reserved the people are. I don't know why but it is true. [...] And there is a big difference between Italy's north and south for goodness sake! I was in Naples in Easter, they're different, how the sun purifies! I have the impression that the temperature dawn there clears everything away. I don't know, it is hot and you go out more, you see more, there are more contact with people, you socialize more. [...]

When we were living at Arcofelice[5] we had American friends there too and we used to go to Bagnoli. That just shows that I don't have any problem with foreigners because I feel foreign. I don't feel, how can I say because when someone asks me where I'm from I don't know the answer anymore, I say that I'm Italian and I feel Italian but even though I was born in Rome I'm not Roman, I'm not Neapolitan even though my parents are from there, I'm not from Tarquinia and I don't feel like a Tarquinian because I'm different from them. I don't feel like a Florentine ... So when they ask me 'where are you from?' Italian I say.

## Notes

1. A vitago. The word *kenau* refers to Kenau Simonsdochter Hasselaar, a woman who joined in the fighting during the siege of Haarlem in 1572–73 and became famous for that. However, it is supposed to be disgraceful for the woman to be called *kenau*, as it signifies a mannish woman, a battle-axe.
2. Gaeta (24,000 inhabitants) is a seaside city northern of Naples. The city hosts the permanent location of the U.S. Sixth Navy (flotta).
3. Tarquinia (about 15 thousands inhabitants) is a small town north of Rome.
4. *Tarallucci* are a sort of salty round cracker typical of Italy's south (the most famous are from the Puglia region) made with flour, olive oil, salt, yeast and fennel seeds.
5. Small village close to Naples.

# Part III

## Processes of Identification: Inclusion and Exclusion of Migrant Women

*Chapter 9*

# Migration, Integration and Emancipation: Women's Positioning in the Debate in the Netherlands

*Esther Vonk*

### Introduction

In November 2003, the then Minister for Social Affairs and Employment, Aart Jan de Geus, who is responsible for emancipation policy, gave a speech at an event to celebrate twenty-five years of emancipation policy in the Netherlands. He used this opportunity to state that the emancipation of the Dutch woman is accomplished – a statement which had been made before, but had never officially been declared by a government representative. However, de Geus hurried to footnote his declaration adding that, when he says 'Dutch women' in this context, he means 'native' Dutch women – so-called *autochtone vrouwen*. There are other groups of women in the Netherlands, for whom emancipation is still necessary. The minister, from then on would, therefore focus on the process of emancipation of what he called 'some of our *allochtone* (non-native) fellow citizens'.

This chapter discusses the possibilities for feminist interventions in the current public debate on 'the integration of minorities' in the Netherlands, with a particular focus on the issue of women's emancipation, and its discursive role within this debate. This debate has everything to do with gender, ethnicity and power relations, and the ways in which the debate takes shape calls for critical feminist analysis and contributions.

## Contextualizing the Discourse: The Debate on 'Integration of Minorities' in the Netherlands

In the current public debate around the 'integration of minorities' – the most recent chapter in an ongoing debate on the Netherlands as a multicultural society – the idea that multicultural society has failed is predominant. This idea is not new. Feminist philosopher Baukje Prins (2000) has thoroughly documented the ways in which articulations of this idea have developed since the early 1990s. She groups the different *genres* of discourse that have declared the multicultural society to have failed under the heading of 'new-realist discourses'.

What is new in the recent debate is, first, that the new realist discourse around immigration and integration has been radicalized. Secondly, it has wider public support to the extent that it is no longer necessarily viewed as being racist or of the extreme-right, but as simply realistic, as 'seeing things for what they are'. A wave of publications in the popular as well as in the serious press on the 'problems' of multicultural society and the lack of integration of second and third generation Turks and Moroccans are illustrative of this tendency. So are the critiques of government policies that seek to enable immigrants to 'integrate' in Dutch society: a commission of politicians, with the help of a team of researchers, investigated the results of thirty years of 'integration policy'.[1] The report they delivered – which was mildly critical, with an overall conclusion that most migrants did integrate, either thanks to, or despite, the policy – was trashed by many politicians, scientists and opinion makers, even before it was published, and from some sides even before the investigation stated. This illustrates the shift that has taken place in the arena of the debate on migrants and minorities: the accusation of 'political correctness' is easily and often made by new realists, who are very present in the public debate, challenging anyone who is critical of the idea that integration has failed and that multicultural society is bankrupt.

The reason to characterize 'new realism' as a discursive genre is based on Prins' choice to focus on the performative effects of the discourse that is employed. Rather than simply pointing out how a certain discourse *describes* reality, Prins is interested in how the discourse *generates* reality. According to her, the four dominant tropes which characterize this new realist discourse, are its use of a vocabulary of truth, of common people, of reality, and its anti-leftism.[2]

New forms of the new realist discourse are both the hyperrealism of the late populist politician Pim Fortuyn and his followers, and the new realism 'with a social face' initiated by the journalist and commentator, Paul Scheffer. The current debate is marked by an emphasis on national identity, and by the homogenization of the notion of 'culture', which refers to both 'Dutch culture' and the cultures of ethnic or religious minorities in the Netherlands.

Public debates not only describe and comment upon reality, they are also dialectically linked to this 'reality'. Public opinion, policy-making and relationships between individuals and between and within groups are also shaped by the debates that are taking place in the media. The interviewees' accounts of their relationships to each other can be seen as a site where the influence of public debates on relationships between people in their daily lives – the ways in which discourses in public debates are influencing and shaping 'reality' and practices – operates. The discursive space within which the current public debate on the integration of minorities takes place works as an 'enabling constraint' on the kind of stories that can be told about immigration and integration.

Critical discourse analysis looks at the different levels of what is being said. Teun van Dijk has extensively studied the ways in which white majorities speak about immigrants and ethnic 'others' (Van Dijk 1984, 1987; Wodak and van Dijk 2000). Interestingly, when comparing the findings of his analysis of everyday conversations and interviews with spoken and written texts used in media and parliament, he found significant similarities at the level of topics, semantics, narrative, style and rhetoric. The interviews discussed here are examples of women who belong to the white majority speaking about women who belong to a minority: immigrant women from Eastern Europe. It is relevant to situate the interviews within the context of recent public debates, as these can help clarify and interpret some of the issues voiced in the interviews.

I will focus on the question of how the Dutch interviewees, in their accounts of their relationships with Eastern European women and their representations of 'self' and 'other', negotiate their position within or against the public discourse. The Dutch women I interviewed are involved in relationships with Hungarian and Bulgarian women in different ways: in close friendships; as acquaintances whom they got to know through work, relatives or in their neighbourhoods; as colleagues; and, in a few cases, through working with migrant women's groups. How do they represent themselves, the other women, and the relationships they are involved in? How do their stories relate to the 'stories' that come to the fore in the public debate? In which ways are dimensions of gender, ethnicity and cultural identity articulated? How do Dutch women, as representatives of the 'neutral' majority group, relate to representatives of the 'marked' minority? How do they identify with them? What is the function of signifiers of sameness and difference in their stories? 'Difference' sometimes creates a fundamentally ambiguous position for those in the majority position in relation to those in the minority position, especially when personal interests are involved. How do the interviewees deal with this? I am particularly interested in the strategies that are used to deal with, and counter, hegemonic discourse. People are also active subjects, who can resist the 'call' of discourse upon them. By analysing the respondents' stories around 'integration in Dutch society', I will explore the above questions, and assess the strategies employed by the respondents to resist hegemonic discourse.

## Real or Fake? Preoccupied with Truth and Authenticity

The current debate on the failure of multicultural society can be seen as a symptom of nostalgia, a longing for a single truth, identity and authenticity. This nostalgia shows up in the 'new realist' discourse around the failure of multicultural society, in the call for a return to 'authentic' Dutch norms and values, the revival of national identity, and the homogenization of 'culture'. The difficulty of breaking loose from fixed narratives is also evident in the narratives of the interviewees and their attempts to resist these and create their own stories. The overarching reason the Dutch interviewees identified for women to move from Eastern Europe to Western Europe is articulated in terms of the desire to 'build a future here'. In this context, career opportunities, economic advantages, and educational opportunities are specifically mentioned. This is often linked to the situation in the (former) home country, where people in general, or the particular woman concerned are thought to have had fewer chances to obtain a good or well paid job, a good education, or the kind of career to which they aspired. Personal professional aspirations can be distinguished from a general quest for a 'better' or 'easier' life, as the latter are more strongly linked to economic advantages in the new country, and the former to 'self-realization'. Generally, the governmental distinction between different 'types' of migrants, which distinguishes 'economic migrancy' from other forms, does not resonate in the interviewees' stories. This distinction mostly operates in the debate about asylum seekers. Asylum seekers are divided into 'real refugees', who were forced to flee because of circumstances outside their control, such as war or oppressive regimes in the home country, and 'economic migrants'. Only a minority of the interviewees mentions refugees or asylum seekers when they speak of migrants. This indicates that they see 'migrants' and 'refugees' as two distinct categories. The difference, then, is mainly based on the 'force' versus 'choice' distinction when it comes to the causes of migration.

Although most interviewees do not talk about refugees when they talk about migrants, the political discourse on asylum seekers, and the changes in asylum policy which has become more restrictive over the last years, nevertheless do resonate in the images of migrants that come to the fore in the interviews.

> I don't have the image of migrants as really uneducated people who see golden mountains here ... no, I don't have that image, because I think ... or I'm very naïve to think they don't know that yet, but I think it's come through in those countries that the Netherlands has a much stricter asylum policy and that it's not all golden mountains here. At least, that's the worldview I have: I have that image now that that has come through, that they don't come to the Netherlands as gold diggers.

Inge, a 31 year-old researcher at a technical university, refers to the image of immigrants as 'uneducated people who see golden mountains here', stating that this is not the image she has of migrants. Why does she make reference to it then? Where does it come from? And what is the function of her reference to it? The image of the 'gold digger' is a typical image that is referred to in the media, in order to justify new restrictions in asylum policy. The majority of the asylum seekers, in this frame, who enter the country are not 'real refugees', on the contrary, they come here to benefit from 'our' social security system – the 'golden mountains' to which she refers. This, Inge stresses, is not the image she has, yet her apparent attempt to undermine the image of migrants as 'gold diggers' has the opposite effect: by adding that she might be 'very naïve', she implies that it is very well possible that the majority of immigrants are indeed that which she has just stated they are not, but that it is her virtue of 'naïvety', her specific 'worldview' that makes her believe otherwise. She makes no reference to the source of this image. This indicates that she is aware that she and I share a certain context, where the image of migrants as 'gold diggers' is well known and can be spoken about without 'footnoting'.

Along with economic reasons, marriages and relationships are mentioned as the reasons for migration. Interestingly, this is sometimes also linked to 'building a future here', in the same terms as 'building a future here' based on economic or educational reasons.

> What brings the women I know to the Netherlands, is that it's apparently attractive, from the foreign point of view, to build a future in the Netherlands ... whether it's for a relationship, mostly from the Polish point of view ... and from the Romanian point of view, it's to build up an income and to return after a period of time to be able to carry on with their lives again.

In describing why women would move from Eastern Europe to the Netherlands, Wilma, a self-employed health and nutrition consultant who works with women from many different national backgrounds, both as colleagues and as clients, states that 'apparently' it is attractive, 'from the foreign point of view', to build a future here. She goes on to distinguish different reasons for this attractiveness according to different Eastern European national backgrounds: for a relationship, or to build up an income and return. The underlying reason for migration, thus, is the attractiveness of the Netherlands. By mentioning the immediate reasons in one sentence – relationships and the aim of making some money – these two become interchangeable, depending on the nationality of the woman concerned. Polish women will come because of relationships; Rumanian women will come to make money and return. By mentioning the immediate reason only after stating that the main reason for women to migrate to the Netherlands is its attractiveness, the immediate reason appears to be instrumental and secondary.

Closely linked to ideas about reasons for migration are knowledge of, and ideas about, the possible ways of entering the Netherlands as a migrant woman from an Eastern European country and of obtaining a residence permit. Against this background, some interesting articulations of 'marriage or love as a reason for migration' come to the fore in the interviews. Wilma says this about her friend Jirina:

> She first came for a test period to see if it would work, so not with the clear goal of I'm going to hook this man … that's not how it went. But just to come to the Netherlands as a kind of 'pilot' to see if it works. And because her husband also already had two teenage children when she came, it was doubtful if it would click, because then you get bombarded to be kind of a mother.

From this excerpt, it seems that Wilma feels that she has to state explicitly that Jirina did not come here 'with the clear goal to hook this man'. At different points in the interview she emphasizes that Jirina moved to the Netherlands 'to be with her love'. Wilma is not the only one who emphasizes that 'love' was the reason for their friends to come to the Netherlands in cases where they were married to a Dutch man; many interviewees mentioned this several times. This can be seen as an implicit reference to the notion of the 'fake marriage'.[3] In 1994, the 'law on prevention and combat of fake marriages' was introduced in the Netherlands. Before that the term *schijnhuwelijk* was already used within the field of migration law but had not been officially introduced. The first official appearance of the term is in the 'guidelines on not-real marriages':[4] 'a marriage with the apparent aim of staying in the Netherlands by means of this marriage'. A marriage is a fake marriage in the case where the aim of the partners, or of one of them, is not 'to fulfil the duties attached to the marital state', but instead to obtain legal entry to the Netherlands. *Schijnhuwelijk* is an immigration-juridical construction: it only exists in the context of immigration law. It is in direct contradiction with civil law in which 'marriage' is defined as follows: 'there is a marriage when the formal requirements for a marriage are fulfilled' (i.e. when the marriage is performed by the registrar). The law 'distances itself from affection and love of the respective spouses towards each other' as the essence of marriage. From this definition it follows that a *schijnhuwelijk* is, in fact, a contradiction in terms: when a marriage is performed, it is a marriage, as marriage itself is a formal, juridical construction. However, in this case – and only and exclusively in case of marriages involving a partner who does not have Dutch citizenship – migration law overrules civil law. Moreover, another field of law comes into the procedure that was invented to prevent 'fake marriages'. The registrar, before performing the marriage between a Dutch citizen or a citizen with a permanent residence permit, and a 'third-country national' who would, on the basis of this marriage, gain residence rights in the Netherlands, is obliged to 'check' whether this marriage is 'fake' or 'real'. The basis of this 'check' is a declaration signed by the immigration police. With this procedure 'fake marriages' are criminalized.

I read the instances where the interviewees state that a marriage was made 'out of love' and explain that the purpose of the marriage was not to obtain a residence permit, as references to the artefact of the fake marriage. In this way, the interviewees not only show that they are aware that there is such a construction as the 'fake marriage', but they also confirm implicitly that indeed, marriages *are* made for instrumental reasons, i.e. to obtain a residence permit. Moreover, by emphasizing the importance of 'love' as a leading principle, they implicitly agree with the judgement that marriages based on grounds other than 'love' are illegal and, moreover, immoral. They do not criticize the fact that certain marriages are constructed as illegal; they only insist that their friend's marriage is of another, better, kind. The difficulties of maintaining clear boundaries between images of Eastern European migrant women in general, and the specific woman that is spoken of, are illustrated when Wilma, later in the interview, speaks about the ways of obtaining legal status in the Netherlands, and states: 'From the Polish point of view, I've noticed that they often come here illegally, without speaking of prejudice. Um… Jirina did that via the relationships.' This implies that the relationship, i.e. marriage to a Dutch man, was instrumental, a way to obtain legal status. This image is confirmed when she suggests that, although she knows little about Jirina's life in Bulgaria, she assumes that she was not happy there: '[…] of course she wasn't happy there, because otherwise she wouldn't have come here'. This contradicts what she said earlier, that Jirina's only reason to come to the Netherlands was 'to be with her love', and that she had no interest in coming to the Netherlands as such.

Another strategy used by interviewees to dissociate themselves from the images of migrant women in the media, is 'denial' or 'repression'. For Ellen, the main reasons for migration for women from east to west Europe are 'to get either a good education, that they can't get in their own country, or a good job'. After naming these two main reasons, she adds:

> And then I have a certain type of woman in mind. Of course, there are also women who come here to arrange a marriage.
> *What do you mean by 'arrange a marriage'?*

> Well, on the internet, there are these mail-order catalogues where you can select a Russian woman or a Bulgarian woman. I know they're there, but I kind of repress that when I think of Eastern European women who come here – for me, they are the people who are closer to me. The people who come for an education or a job. Yes, I can't understand them… I can understand very well that someone from Bulgaria who studied computer science, for example, and has had a good education at a good level but then can't use that because no company in Bulgaria or no institution has the money to buy good computers, then I can imagine that you would think well, I want to go abroad. I want to earn money and then, maybe, come back with my money and do something for my own country. I can understand that. Women who somehow are so desperate that they send a picture to a mail-order catalogue, they, well, it might be a logical step for them, but I can't understand it.
> 
> *You can't understand what they're looking for here or what they're trying to find?*
> 
> Yes, a better life and a steady income.

Ellen dissociates herself from women who 'come here to arrange a marriage' by 'repressing' the knowledge that they are there: she does not even want to think about it. She wants to think about women she can identify with, women who come here to get an education or find a job. However, while she repeatedly states that she cannot understand women who 'are so desperate that they send a picture to a mail-order catalogue', when I ask her, it turns out that she *can* understand them. They are looking for the same thing as the other women she described, the ones she understands: 'a better life and a steady income'. In her distinction between the two groups of women, identifying with one group and 'repressing' thoughts of the other group, there's a judgement: those who are different, whom she cannot understand, cannot be spoken of, and should be silenced and 'repressed'.

Hanneke tells a different story. She speaks about three of her friends whom she got to know through an international Masters course that took place in Amsterdam, in which many of the participants came from Eastern European countries. Most of them left after the year that the programme lasted, but three of the women stayed in the Netherlands.

> Yeah, I think that only the Hungarian woman was planning on staying here, even before the course … she was already engaged, after all. Umm, no that's not true, they broke up right before the course began, I remember now. So she was a little confused at the beginning of the year. But those other two, the Slovakian woman was not planning on staying here, but the Bulgarian was, she had already studied in England and I got the idea that she umm … wanted to get settled in a western country.

About her Bulgarian friend, who met a Dutch man and entered into a relationship with him during her time studying here, she says:

> Well, I suspect that that was what she was after, because for someone from her country, it's impossible to stay here without being coupled to someone, for legal reasons. And, well, of course she has a real relationship, it lasted for more than three years, after all, and she really also … well, I mean … had invested in that, emotionally. But I also think that it was practical.

Hanneke then goes on to describe in detail the developments after the year's course was over, when 'the time came when she [Hanneke's Bulgarian friend] needed a residence permit to be able to work here and stay here'. She goes into the legal arrangements and the position of her friend's boyfriend (who was not very co-operative). She recognizes the fact that if a non-EU citizen wants to stay in the Netherlands legally, there is a very limited number of available ways of doing this, and that a formal relationship is one of these ways. The difference between her, on the one hand, and Wilma and Ellen on the other hand, is that she acknowledges the fact that the Netherlands has restrictive policies and that she implicitly criticizes this, by representing any strategy that is employed to attain a legal status as legitimate. This is not only more representative of the reality that people are indeed 'forced' to develop new strategies in response to new restrictive policies, but it is also an effective way of countering the implicit moral judgement within this legal framework. Some of the respondents did not touch upon the issue of 'instrumental' marriages at all. They stated that their friends came to the Netherlands because of their relationships with Dutch men (where this was the case), without questioning or defending the relationships in any way.

A third reason for migration that was mentioned by some of the respondents was the desire 'to see the world'. Closely linked to this is the motive of self-realization (which is not necessarily linked to professional development, although this can be part of the process of self-realization). Hanneke, talking about her Bulgarian friend's reasons to come to the Netherlands, says: 'Probably because there are far more career opportunities. And because she was internationally orientated and wanted to see more than the Bulgarian environment.' This motive is typically evaluated positively by the interviewees, and often forms a basis for recognition, identification and bonding between the women.

## To Integrate or to be Integrated?

On the issue of 'integration', the need for it and what it consists of, it is striking that all interviewees use the term in a positive, affirmative way. This means that they take the necessity to 'integrate' in Dutch society as a given, even though the idea that immigrants should 'integrate' as such is relatively new, both in policymaking and in public opinion. On the exact content of 'integration' – in other words, what one should do in order to integrate into Dutch society – there is less consensus, and the concept remains quite vague. Most interviewees agree on the importance of learning the Dutch language as the first and most important sign of, or road towards, integration. Inge, a 31-year-old researcher at a technical university, says, in response to my question if she ever asks her colleague from Bulgaria about her migration to the Netherlands:

> No, I did ask her recently 'how long have you been in the Netherlands now?', I thought I'd like to know that and it was seven or eight years, and she speaks Dutch really well and she said, 'I worked really hard for that', so she really wanted to integrate. She did a lot for her Dutch course and I think she really profited from that.

She positively confirms the general opinion that learning to speak Dutch is both necessary to integrate in society, and beneficial for migrants themselves. This remark also exemplifies the direct link between immigration and the need for 'integration'. Wilma, a self-employed nutrition and health consultant, aged forty-one identifies what the obstacles are in the process of integration:

> Um, when they've made the decision to migrate, right, migration means to cross the border … but when you keep up your old habits and don't want to learn the language, then you migrate, but you don't integrate. You migrate with the thought 'I want to integrate' … that's what I assume. Because otherwise, you have another problem.
> *So you assume everyone does that, or is that what you see, or is that what you would do?*
> Yes, that's what I would do, but there are a lot of people, more the Islamic women, who don't integrate and who try to create a piece of foreign country in the Netherlands and then I think 'that doesn't help a bit'.

Jantina, who is the daughter of a Hungarian father and a Dutch mother, and who grew up in the South of the Netherlands where she still lives and where she works at a call-centre, makes a link between the presence of 'customs' from different countries and the loss of 'Dutch culture':

> Yes, but the Dutch culture is disappearing, of course, right… because you get all these customs from all these countries, but the Dutch culture itself is nowhere to be found anymore. Everything has been Americanized. So the real Dutch culture … what is that? Well, maybe in a really small village in Drenthe, you might still find it … I don't know, I get a little nostalgic.

Her discourse on what causes the loss of Dutch culture is slightly contradictory though: in the same sentence, she mentions 'Americanization' as well as the influence of customs from other countries that migrant populations bring with them. The 'Americanization' of culture is also mentioned by other interviewees, mostly to refer to the visible effects of global economy. This is also relevant in relation to the issue of 'Europeanness': a majority of the interviewees who state that they do feel 'European' in one way or another illustrate this by comparing Europe to the U.S.

There is a strong anti-Americanism present in these 'comparative' statements. 'Americanization' of culture stands for commercialization and the loss of cultural diversity – the effects of globalized capitalism are blamed on the U.S. Privatization and the decline of the welfare system are also covered under the heading of 'Americanization', as well as 'seeing the same shops everywhere'. A process of commercialization and privatization that is seen in almost all European countries is seen as not 'authentically' European but American. Ellen, a young researcher working on a project on Slavic history and literature and, in her own words, a strong supporter of the EU, sees a united Europe as a possible strategy for standing up to the influence of the U.S.:

> The Netherlands, but also a small country like Bulgaria, doesn't count in the world, not politically, not economically, and if you work together, you can make a bigger fist. Then you can, you put yourself on the map. [...] That's not the culture I feel at home in, and any country on its own can't compete against the influence of America, and the image everyone has that this is modern and this is hip and we have to do this and this works; you can't really put anything up against that, but as one Europe, you probably can.

Jantina, following on from her thoughts on the risks that Dutch culture will disappear, connects this to the need for everyone to abide by Dutch rules:

> You can always learn from other people, but if the Dutch culture itself gets snowed under, well, you have to think about that. Because what takes over then... because you still have to abide by the Dutch rules and if some groups think that the rules don't count for them, then you've got a problem. The Netherlands is much too soft. I'd like it to be stricter. People who ... you always have to keep to Dutch law and if you think 'That doesn't count for me, because I'm different', well, then you have a problem, I think.
> *And you don't have the feeling that that's happening in the Netherlands?*
> Yes, it is happening. A lot of people think that the Dutch rules don't count for them.

Exactly which Dutch rules Jantina is referring to remains vague. When I ask whether she means the law when she speaks of 'rules', she confirms, but in the example she later gives ('that they're rude'), the 'rules' seem to refer to something broader. This same mechanism can be observed in the national debate about 'Dutch norms and values': there is no definition of the norms and values referred to, but it is common practice to emphasize that it is crucial that everyone – including, and especially, immigrants – keeps to them.

In clarifying which groups 'think that Dutch rules don't count for them', Jantina explicitly mentions 'Islamic people' and Moroccans. This is not surprising, as those are the groups that are problematized in public discourse, especially with reference to their assumed lack of integration and their different 'culture'. Jantina is, in this respect, an exception in the sample of Dutch interviewees, in the sense that she seems to make no attempt to counter or resist the dominant discourses on migrants and integration, but directly adopts and affirms them. Other interviewees were more ambiguous in their ways of dealing with this, which shows both the power of a discourse that is so dominant, and their desire to resist it.

Within the current debate on the 'integration of minorities', a central place is given to the position of women from different 'cultures'. This is also true of the interviewees. Shared gendered experiences of motherhood or of being a wife were brought to the fore by many Dutch women in their accounts of their relationships with Hungarian and Bulgarian women. This functions both as a source of bonding, and as a sign of differentiation, between themselves and other women. In the former case, the emphasis on gender identity at certain moments functions to 'overcome' differences in identity that might be central in other contexts, even in other moments during the interview. Those who are, in the dominant discourse, defined as 'other' or 'outsider' on the grounds of one dimension of their identity, can be experienced as 'insiders' and as 'belonging' in other contexts, where the emphasis lies on another aspect of their identity. This process challenges the hegemonic tendencies of one identity category over others, showing how identity operates simultaneously within and across shifting boundaries of group formation (Brah, 1993). The (shared) identity as 'women' can thus 'overrule' the (differentiating) identity of the other woman as 'migrant', depending on the context.

On the other hand, femininity and gender relations also function as markers of differentiation: not as bridges between women but as boundaries. Different 'types' of femininity are often defined in a temporal scheme by interviewees: Eastern European women are less 'emancipated' than Dutch women, they embody a type of femininity that can no longer be found in Dutch women. Dutch women are 'further along' in the process of emancipation. The respondents illustrate this by referring to 'appearance', and to emancipation. Concerning appearance, it is often noted that women from Eastern Europe pay much more attention to their looks, the way they dress, their make-up, than Dutch women: they are more 'feminine'. When 'emancipation' is mentioned, the respondents refer to gender relations in the private sphere – where gender roles are perceived to be more 'traditional' in Dutch culture. Again, Dutch women come to the fore as being more emancipated. It is interesting to note that a lack of this is often presented as emancipation caused by the 'traditional' attitude of men, not by the women themselves: 'Bulgarian men are very traditional'; 'Bulgarian men expect their women to do everything'. Barbara, a Dutch woman married to a Bulgarian man, knows what Bulgarian women have to deal with: 'I am married to a Bulgarian man, so yes, I know firsthand what the expectations of a Bulgarian man of his wife are.' Nevertheless, she distinguishes herself from the majority of Bulgarian women because of the different way they deal with these expectations:

> Well, they handle it differently than I do. I think that Bulgarian women … it is, after all, a very macho culture, the Bulgarian culture, and Bulgarian women have been raised in it and, of course, have seen how their fathers and mothers interacted and they know what is expected of them. I don't know if, from some Bulgarian women I definitely hear it, well, maybe I'm jumping the gun, but … I do notice that it's different for Bulgarian women here in the Netherlands, because they, of course, see what's going on around them and come into contact with Dutch women and start to question who should be determining what in their lives. Should they, or their husband?

The way gender relations are organized in Dutch society functions here as an example for Bulgarian women: because they can see, here, how gender relations can be organized differently, it becomes possible to imagine a different life, a different role. On the other hand, when compared to yet other groups of women, East and West European women are described as being similar or equal as far as ideas of femininity and gender relations are concerned. Some respondents, when asked for similarities or differences between themselves and their Bulgarian or Hungarian friends or colleagues, make comparisons with other groups of women, specifically Muslim women. They state that they feel closer to women from Eastern Europe than to women from 'Islamic cultures' such as Turkey and Morocco, because of Turkish and Moroccan women's (perceived) different enactment of femininity and their different relationship to men. Women migrants are variously positioned in contemporary discourses. Combined with legal, normative and cultural practices – the dependent residence permit for married migrant women, and the fact that marriage is one of the few ways of entering the country legally – these material divergences and discourses produce a distinction between 'the European woman' and 'the other (migrant) woman'. Western/European women are portrayed as 'triumphant in the realisation of equal rights and social equality' (Lutz 1997) and are the measure against which others are judged – and predictably found lacking. The presumed absence of female autonomy in Muslim cultures is seen as one of many deviations from European femininity. Eastern European women, on the sliding scale of 'otherness' are represented as 'lagging behind' western women, but further along in the process of emancipation than other groups of women: they are 'western'. The idea of Eastern Europe being 'western' was articulated by several respondents in this context. This reflects the central (discursive) role of the Dutch Muslim community and Islamic 'culture' in the discourse on migration and integration, as well as the central role that 'women's emancipation' plays in this discourse: while the interview centres around relationships between Dutch and Eastern European women, there are only a few interviewees who do not refer to Muslim women or Islamic culture. The myth of equality between women and men in Western Europe can only hold if other groups of women are 'othered'. This is the same mechanism that functions in the debate on integration of minorities versus women's emancipation. The speech of minister de Geus is an example of this: for the declaration that Dutch women's emancipation has been successfully reached to hold, it has to be presented alongside the statement that there are other women who are 'not there yet'.

At the same time, it is remarkable how few references the respondents make to the position of women in the public sphere, especially in the labour market, when 'emancipation' is discussed. The Hungarian and Bulgarian interviewees in the Netherlands, on the other hand, emphasized this: many of them mentioned how shocked they were by the low labour market participation of Dutch women, and the poor arrangements that were in place for parental leave and the bad state of childcare facilities. Of course, amongst the Dutch respondents, there were also those who exposed the idea of the Dutch emancipation-ideal as a myth, as in the words of Hanneke:[5]

> My impression is that in theory it might be more free here, but in practice there is not much of a difference. It's less of a given there that one should be emancipated, but at the same time there are as many independent mothers and… yes, helping fathers, and I think that communism also created a kind of equality. For women there were also more legal arrangements, in a positive sense, compared to how it is here. They had, for example, two years maternity leave. If you had a baby you had a period of two years free of work, which gives you a certain kind of independence, and that is valued there, and that's better than here.

## Strategies of Resistance

The interviews illustrate the omnipresence of the current public debate around immigration and integration, in which Dutch Muslims are central, and in which the position of women also takes up a central role. It is almost impossible to speak about migration or migrant women without referring to the debate about integration, it seems. Hence, it is important to look into the ways the respondents position themselves *vis-à-vis* this debate. That public debates have an effect on 'reality' does of course not mean that everyone uncritically adopts the dominant discourses of the moment. Critical discourse analysis, in its orientation, topics, and in the issues that are tackled, studies 'the (abuse of) power in relations of gender, ethnicity and class, such as sexism and racism' (van Dijk 1987). The question is how discourse enacts, expresses, condones or contributes to the reproduction of inequality. This also opens possible effective strategies of resistance and dissent. What I show here is how difficult it is to resist completely the power of hegemonic discourses, even when the respondent has an interest in resistance, because of a personal engagement with those who are the object of these discourses. However, resistance is not impossible, and happens on different levels, with varying degrees of success, as proven by the interviews. The respondents make use of different 'strategies of resistance' – discursive strategies, that is – which may be more or less effective. There are three overall discursive strategies that can be distilled from the oral sources:

1. *The 'one exception'*: The respondent emphasizes the uniqueness of her friend/colleague/the women she knows: she is different from other Eastern European women in the Netherlands. A variant is the claim that Eastern European women (or Hungarian women, or Bulgarian women) are different from other groups of migrant women in the Netherlands. In both cases, the effect of this strategy in resisting stereotyped images or hegemonic discourse about immigrant women, is very limited, as the image itself is not criticized. Moreover, it is implicitly confirmed by the repetition of stereotypes and the denial that a specific person is 'like that', precisely by pointing to the 'uniqueness' of that person.
2. *Denial of dominant images*: This refers to the repetition of dominant images of migrants in the media, followed by an explicit statement that one does not share this image. In this case, the speaker presents *herself* as an 'exception': it is because of her specific characteristics – tolerance, openness towards others, 'naïveté' – that she has different ideas. The effect is the reproduction of the hegemonic discourse which is neither denied nor confirmed.

3. *Political and historical knowledge and consciousness* – and, importantly, accountability for one's own position within a specific geo-political setting – are crucial prerequisites for identification and bonding with 'others', and for resistance to stereotyping and 'othering' discourses. Consciousness of the different positions that migrant women have in Dutch society, which are not caused by 'cultural differences', but precisely by the system that qualifies them as 'migrant', as 'different', and attributes to them other – lesser – rights, is a starting point in resisting hegemonic discourses about 'foreigners'. This requires reflection on one's own position *vis-à-vis* the other, and knowledge of legal and historical frameworks that are part of the Dutch system. The knowledge of the histories of interethnic relations, and the identification of oneself as an inheritor of those histories forms the basis for the acknowledgement of the 'differences that matter' that are a result of these histories, and of the ways in which these histories mark the different positions of people in society today.

Dutch feminists in order to effectively counter the instrumentalization of feminist discourses and of the stepping stones towards the emancipation of women for which the women's movement struggled, should take this into account. Dutch feminism, as a movement, fails to resist adequately and clearly the 'divide and conquer' mechanism that is operative when, for example, minister de Geus, and with him other politicians and opinion makers, make use of the heritage of feminism to 'other' migrants and 'Islamic cultures'. If we cannot make alliances within the women's movement, and if white Dutch feminists do not publicly and insistently take their distance from the processes which announce Muslim women to be the losers in the race to 'emancipation', feminism will continue to be used for purposes which contradict its premises.

The historical and social dimensions of interethnic relations do not only come to the fore on the personal level, but are embedded in particular contexts. Acknowledging the context, and one's own as well as the other's position within this context is what Baukje Prins calls 'the loss of innocence', which is a prerequisite for the development of new, situated knowledge and skills. Members of minority or marginalized groups are more likely to develop those skills as they are 'forced' to do so through the confrontation with their position as 'other'. Members of majority groups have to learn these skills consciously, as they are more likely to perceive themselves as the normal, the natural, and thus not question their own position or identity. And while feminist theory can take credit for having raised these issues it often turns out to be more difficult to put these ideas into practice – it is still an ongoing process, and its urgency is illustrated by the situation in the Netherlands now.

A good example of this willingness to learn, is Hanneke, one of the interviewees. By acknowledging the problems that her friend had because she was a migrant woman in the Netherlands, she recognized that the strategies her friend used to overcome these problems qualify as modes of empowerment: strategies of resistance to a system that makes a difference between those who come from here and those who come from elsewhere, and through this, creates and sustains inequalities. At the same time Hanneke 'exposes' the constructed nature of certain images – notably images of Dutch society, and in particular, the image of the Dutch as the 'champions of emancipation' which is central to our national identity – and points out that these images, however widespread, do not necessarily represent 'reality'. Hanneke's representation of her friend's story, as well as of 'the Dutch', in turn, resists the hegemonic discourse about immigrant women and about 'Dutch culture', and manages to tell a different story – or the same story, from another perspective.

## Notes

1. The term 'integration policy' was introduced in the 1990s; preceding it were the 'minorities policies'. The term 'integration' was first introduced in the context of these policies, aiming at 'integration of minorities while holding on to one's own identity'.
2. More precisely, the new realist discourse is articulated around four main points. First, the claim on truth: the speaker presents him or herself as someone who dares to face the truth, and moreover, dares to 'call things by their name'. Taboos should be broken, everything should be said out in the open. Second, the new realist is a spokesperson of 'the common people' – that is, the common 'indigenous' people. This is also a claim for truth: the speaker claims to voice that which is thought by the majority, but is not spoken publicly, as these are people that have no voice in the public debate. Third, the 'sense of reality' is presented as a characteristic of Dutch identity. The Dutch, it is stated, need to return to the pre-Second World War situation, when an 'exaggerated caution' in dealing with (ethnic) difference was not yet a national habit. Fourth, resistance to 'the left' is a common characteristic. The so-called progressive elite have hijacked the debate with 'politically correct' ideas that have prevented taboos from being broken.
3. The Dutch term *schijnhuwelijk* refers, literally, to something that *appears* to be a marriage but in fact *is not* a marriage. Therefore the term 'fake marriage' is a more adequate translation than the more often used 'marriage of convenience'.
4. Richtlijn niet-reëel huwelijk, 1975.
5. Hanneke, 42, works for an environmental organization. She lives in Amsterdam and got to know women from Hungary and Bulgaria (as well as other European countries) during a one-year international Masters programme in environmental management. Several of these women stayed in Amsterdam after the programme and became her friends.

## References

Brah, A. 1993. 'Re-framing Europe. En-gendered Racisms, Ethnicities and Nationalisms in Contemporary Western Europe', *Feminist Review*, 45: 9–29.

Jessurun d'Oliveira, H.U. 1998. *Migratierecht en zijn dynamiek: het artefact van het 'schijnhuwelijk'*, Deventer, Kluwer.

Lutz, H. 1997. 'The Limits of European-ness: Immigrant Women in Fortress Europe', *Feminist Review*, 57: 93–111.

Prins, B. 2000. *Voorbij de onschuld. Het debat over de multiculturele samenleving*, Amsterdam, Van Gennep.

van Dijk, T.A. 1984. *Prejudice in Discourse: An Analysis of Ethnic Prejudice in Cognition and Conversation*, Philadelphia, J. Benjamins Publications.

van Dijk, T.A. 1987. *Communicating Racism: Ethnic Prejudice in Thought and Talk*, Newbury Park, Sage Publications.

Wodak, R. and T.A. van Dijk (eds.) 2000. *Racism at the Top. Parliamentary Discourses on Ethnic Issues in Six European States*, Klagenfurt, Drava Verlag.

*Chapter 10*

# Modernity versus Backwardness: Italian Women's Perceptions of Self and Other

*Enrica Capussotti*

> Historicism – and even the modern, European idea of history – one might say, came to non-European peoples in the 19th century as somebody's way of saying 'not yet' to somebody else.
> Dipesh Chakrabarty, *Provicializing Europe*

This chapter discusses the representation of Eastern European women migrants in the narratives of Italian women interviewees. Before presenting these narratives, it is important to underline briefly a few significant elements that shape the context in which they were elaborated and in which they negotiate their meanings. Firstly, the absence of public immigrants' voices in Italy: there are few public sites that immigrants can use to express their interests, experiences, and self-representations. Italy's immigrant population is fragmented (with forty-five nationalities having at least 5000 representatives in the country, King and Andall 1999: 142) and silenced within the national arena. Political responses are mainly articulated according to what is perceived as electoral interest, with the right-wing parties shaping the agenda and setting the tone by raising debates and creating anxieties about criminality, fear and repatriation; and, on the other hand, the centre-left wing parties which often oppose the rhetoric of the right with a vague and empty solidarity. In addition, while the forms of solidarity articulated within Catholic and socialist political cultures are important, they do not exclude an element of exoticism and tend to articulate a somewhat paternalistic view of immigrants. As Grillo and Pratt (2002) argue, the local arena offers the most important, if contradictory, forms of political and cultural mobilisation with which to deal with the politics of recognizing difference.

Secondly, there is the protagonist role played by the concept of 'national preference' (Balibar 1991) in driving public opinion, public rhetoric, politics and social policy. While globalization and transnational migrations have contributed to the redefinition of nation states, in terms of their functions, borders and sense of belonging, national citizenship – the 'last status privilege' (Ferraioli 1995) – has been reinforced to become the norm with which to gain access to state assistance, resources and rights (Scevi 2002). The narratives we analyse actively interact with the typical scenarios of Western European societies, in particular, the tenacious exclusion of the 'non-national' from social rights and the welfare state. 'Global migration management', at EU as well as at national levels, is organized around the key strategies of harmonization (at EU level), control (of EU borders), selection (of wanted/skilled migrants) and exclusion (of 'illegal' migrants). Migrants are constructed as the 'new dangerous classes' (Mezzadra and Petrillo 2000), and the tireless focus on 'illegal' immigration maintains and sustains exclusion and exploitation at various levels: it regulates the labour market and wages (offering 'illegal' workers at low cost to work in Western houses, in the construction sector, in agriculture, and in small industries); it provides the fear which is exploited by conservative politicians; and it justifies police control, restriction of rights, and the privatization of welfare systems.

Thirdly, it is essential to underscore the relevance of studying contemporary migration through an historical approach, which can locate in time and in space continuity and rupture in the history of diasporas, border crossings and movements. In the Italian context, its history of racial systems of classification helps one to interpret the cultural representations and mechanisms that sustain the racialisation of migrants today (Burgio 1998). In Italy, the 'racial question' was initially constructed around the differentiation between northerners and southerners. The classification of the peninsula's south as internal 'other' was crucial for the process of nation-building after unification in 1861 (Dickie 1999; Moe 2002); the difficulty of using skin colour and other phenotypic traits to justify racial distinction was resolved by essentializing cultural characteristics (Gibson 1998; Giacone 1998). This system of the classification of 'otherness', which is still operative today, includes diverse elements (social, cultural, geographical) which provide the basis for the naturalization of identities and the articulation of a racist discourse. Notions of national 'character', class belonging and education, gender roles and sexuality, and religion often act as substitutes for phenotypic characteristics as elements in the essentialization of identity and subjects.

The following pages focus on the mechanisms, images, contents and values which are used to construct different Eastern European women and different 'easts'. The narratives are constructed as part of mainly asymmetric relationships: while a few stories concern friendships, most of them are produced as an effect of the structure of employer/employee relations (in households and in agriculture), and of superficial acquaintances and of forms of social assistance. I argue that these representations are articulated through the cultural and ideological *repertoires* of Euro/Westerncentrism which are adopted and transformed within contemporary conjunctures. Ethnocentrism is a key element of the Italian women' narratives. Places, subjects and cultures are measured and valued with reference to a rich, developed, capitalistic and democratic system that is Italian, European and Western. In this context Eastern European women are used to renegotiate the self-representations of Italian women as modern and emancipated.

It is important to note the role played by the interviews themselves in constructing the 'other' as the object of the testimonies; in order to give space to the interviewees' images and words, we asked general questions about 'women migrants' and 'Eastern European', thus creating homogenous entities and using categories that incarnate the mechanisms of naturalization and of the processes of stereotyping. The term 'migrants' indicates a condition which fails to recognize the multiplicity of subject positions and experiences it contains and, in a similar fashion, 'Eastern Europe' is one of the internal 'others' constructed by Western Europe for the hegemonic affirmation of its model of civilization (Wolff 1994). Hence, the dialogue within the interviews influenced the narratives of sameness and otherness.

The binary categories of development-underdevelopment, modernity-backwardness, moderate-excessive (which, as Wolff stresses, was central to the Enlightenment conceptualization of west-east Europe), dominate the interviewees' image of the European east. This represents a continuity of symbolic classification that cannot simply be understood as the *long durée* of mental maps, but as cultural configurations adopted to accompany relationships of power and exploitation within the contemporary world. In the interviews the 'Eastern European' category was mainly deconstructed in term of national entities (Poles, Rumanian, Hungarian, etc.) or, more rarely, of geo-cultural areas: the Balkans, in which Bulgaria was located; Mitteleuropa, to trace a connection between Italy's north east and central Europe (mainly in terms of literary traditions); and central Europe itself, although this label seems to be more extraneous to the Italian geographic imagination.

Therefore the representations analysed here are the product of the Italian (and Western) imagination about east of Europe, more than they delineate a space of identification for women born in that area. Our research participates in an imaginative geography which proposes the east of Europe as a cultural space that is used as a point of comparison. Aware of these ambiguities, I will search for the axes along which similarity and difference are constructed and for the vocabulary used to deal with them.

## Gendered Perceptions: Sexuality and Work

On a first reading, the interviews with Italian women confirm the void which characterizes Italy's public sphere on many topics, including migration. The language is fragmented and the narratives advance with difficulty. Moreover, the discourse concerning women migrants does not refer to a repertoire of intercultural politics, a feature that seems to be aggravated by the specific focus on Eastern European women. When these Italian women were questioned about their first impressions of Eastern Europe, their answers were often hesitant:

> Well … I've never had much contact with … OK I travelled some, the last time was in Croatia, we could say that that's east, couldn't we? […] Then unfortunately sometimes on television you see these girls from the east who have been forced into prostitution. (Silvana)
>
> If I have ever travelled in Eastern Europe? No I really don't know anything about those countries … and if I already have some kind of idea of what she would be like? […] No, to be honest I've never thought about it … (Betta)
>
> You know, the east arrived fairly slowly, it didn't just appear overnight in one big bang. And so at the beginning, it could be that there was some confusion 'where are they coming from, how are they, who are they?' (Carlotta)
>
> How they could have been? I tell you I had no time to imagine them, they were here … (Margherita)

Uncertainty characterizes these attempts to answer questions about pre-existing expectations and ideas. The narrative mimics the absence of images and of thoughts before the speakers had actual experiences of arrivals, and therefore the imaginary dimension is not explicitly acknowledged, but flattened on direct experience. These hesitations might be interpreted as a cautious entrance onto a slippery terrain; intercultural relations, as well as migration, are understood as contested areas and the speaker can thus be prevented from assuming a definite and resolute position. Moreover, the discernment of having only a partial knowledge of the conversation matter influences the possible descriptions which are given. This is evident when eastern geography is involved and interviewees' declarations reveal both their lack of knowledge and a sort of disregard for the area. Silvana: 'She comes from there … […] she is Ukranian, Russian, from those areas'. And Patrizia: 'She is from those mountains… the Urals'.

But the encounter also stimulates curiosity and sustains a process of discovery; this interest is expressed by Roberta: 'They're from northern Russia, no, I meant northern Romania. We can look at an atlas and see … because I have only a vague idea of Romanian geography …' and also by Giovanna: 'I had to go look up Moldavia on the map, to see what countries it bordered, to see what kind of economy it has, because to be honest I had never even considered it'.

On one level, the testimonies reproduce the weaknesses in the shared representations through which intercultural relations and exchanges are constructed; and discomfort is expressed at Italian TV's dominant association of Eastern European women and prostitution (Patrizia, Silvana, Angela, Giovanna). In most national newspapers they are spoken of as sex workers, victims of trafficking and, in more recent year, as domestic workers and nurses in private houses.[1] This identification of these women as prostitutes and servants is shared with African and black women; but whilst for the latter these images are interpreted as a manifestation of racism, exoticism and of the legacy of Italian colonialism (Sorgoni 2002), for the Eastern Europeans, the rare analyses that have been conducted are based on quantitative data that supposedly confirm their consistent presence in Italy's streets and houses. The contents of the Italian prejudicial imagination of Eastern European women has still to be conceptualized, and an analysis of the various representations of 'otherness' in a comparative dimension could help towards an understanding of contemporary cultural prejudices and their historical and symbolic roots in Italy.

Giovanna articulates the centrality of gender and sexuality in determining the preconception against migrants from 'the east'. She recalls that:

> For the women arriving from the east, the Moldavians, Ukrainians, the Polish, well, at the beginning they were met with suspicion, partly because of how they dress and behave. The gold teeth, for example, they reminded people of gypsies. Then, they often brought these men trailing behind them, and they were drinkers, they seemed like trouble-makers, and so there was worry that they might ... people used to say 'don't trust them, don't you dare trust them or you'll come home one day to find that you've been cleaned out of everything you own, not by them, but by people they know, because they might be blackmailed, they're all here illegally' so there were some prejudices, and there were some incidents ...

In Giovanna's words the ingredients of the Slavic stereotype in Italy are listed: Slavs are negatively associated with gypsies; the men are conceived of as lazy, alcoholics and 'trouble-makers'; and the women as subjected to their will, power and violence. In trying to understand why they were perceived as a threat, Giovanna blames the mass media and common opinion for reinforcing a gendered resistance that was not operative with Filipino women, when they were employed in previous years:

> It's probably related to the fact that our television and newspapers talked about nothing else but prostitution in Eastern European countries, and how much *these women want to get their hands on our Italian husbands and sons*, how they want to snare an Italian husband! I'm not sure, but I imagine there was resistance on the part of women to accept people who seemed to so strongly threaten normal family life.

Women's sexuality and agency ('[they] want to get their hands on our Italian husbands and sons') are perceived as a threat to the position of Italian wives and mothers. Giovanna talks about a *vox populi* which was heard in Italy in the Seventies, which said to men who were interested in sexual intercourse: 'When you go [to Eastern European countries] take ten pairs of nylon stockings with you, they're really popular over there'.

The scene of beautiful young women entertaining Western men in hotels is one of the few memories of travelling east that emerges in the testimonies. (Giovanna, Silvana) The overwhelming presence of these images is recorded and reinforced by popular culture. The 1980 film *Un sacco bello* (*Fun is Beautiful*, Carlo Verdone) tells the story of a young Italian man who plans to go to Krakow and to pay for sex with packets of nylon socks, while the 1996 movie *Vesna va veloce* (Carlo Mazzacurati) represents the life of a young Czech in Italy who cannot find any jobs other than sex work. The two films reside between the reification of stereotypes and their reconsideration; on one hand they reproduce stories and characters that seem to be the only ones available in Italy's shared imagination about Eastern Europe women;[2] on the other, *Un sacco bello* is a parody of the working class *latin lover* who will never arrive in Krakow; and *Vesna va veloce* is centred on the protagonist's love for freedom which pushes her to escape from a traditional engagement with an Italian man, even if this is at the cost of becoming a prostitute.

It is difficult to interpret the lasting presence of these representations in Italy. Sex tourism is an old phenomenon that involves men from rich countries travelling to poor ones.[3] And Italy's economic position within global capitalism leads us to offer a first hypothesis: in the 1960s and 1970s east Europe offered a close and affordable place for male sexual practices and so reinforced the construction of the available sexuality of the women there; and the 1989 transition has further opened up the possibility of encounters, of selling and of buying, of movements in both directions. Furthermore, Larry Wolff's interpretation places sexuality at the centre of the Enlightenment construction of Eastern Europe; which suggests that more comparative research is needed to trace the permanencies and ruptures of the construction within contemporary Italian and Western European imagery.[4]

If the public sphere is perceived of as being unable to offer a shared reflection on contemporary immigration, interviewees move the focus to actual encounters. Italians have started to live and practice intercultural relations, which are challenging, both in positive and negative ways, the stereotypical representation which dominates the public realm. The narratives that emerge from the interviews are caught between these two realities: that of a dominant discourse governed by images and by categories frozen within the rhetoric of fear, of paternalism and of prejudice; and encounters with concrete women and men that produce experiences that resist, contest or reinforce dominant representations. This movement is evident in Giovanna's testimony; she condemns the mass media's exclusive focus on prostitution and on sexual exploitation, she mentions actual encounters between Italians and Eastern European and then she claims the existence of practices that are changing Italian views, but which do not of course challenge other axes of inequality (economic and social rights, citizenship, and the right to vote, amongst others): '*Do you think these prejudices have faded, or are they still strong?* I think they have probably faded a bit, with time. These immigrants have demonstrated that they are serious, that they are here to work hard, and they've found a market for themselves'. (Giovanna)

The interviews testify that spaces and occasions for meeting and exchanges are rare and confined; nevertheless there are the beginnings of a process of discovery, even if it is still inscribed in asymmetric relations. Equal work relations and friendships are significant exceptions within a discourse that is still shaped by social and economic discriminations. Carlotta maps various mechanisms she felt the Polish arrivals in Rome activated:

> I remember how it was about ten years ago, or maybe more, when the Poles first started arriving. At that time they almost seemed heroic to us, you would see them arriving in these early Polish cars. Underneath it all we were thinking 'the wall has fallen, they can get out, they can come here' the Poles in their stinky smoky cars taking a trip to see the West. Then, poor things, it's not that they found the promised land, they would hang around in the intersections to wash windshields ... and they seemed strange to us, kind of exotic ... 'they caused a revolution', and here they are washing windows. So you felt some pity for them ... then things started to change, people talked about their drinking, the Polish areas, the bottles, those kinds of things, and the feeling was more 'not all of them are good, not all of them struggled in the revolution'. Maybe in the beginning there was an over-reaction, which was then adjusted, and now we've found a way to meet each other half-way.

Carlotta describes a scenario conditioned by a residue of the Cold War system;[5] her description underlines a relevant shift that involves geopolitical, economic and global processes, as well as more specific social and cultural dynamics. If before 1989 and immediately after, Eastern European refugees were revered as important pawns in the ideological battle between the two blocs, in the 1990s they became 'simple' migrants, a cheap labour force for the production and reproduction of capitalist societies.[6] Moreover, the romantic picture of the transition drawn by the media further reinforced the otherness of Eastern European in Western eyes (Kideckel 1998). Curiosity, pity and apprehension are the emotions attached to the encounters in Carlotta's description.

If Carlotta talks of the possibility of meeting each other 'half-way' (suggesting that the divide us–them is enduring), Marta articulates her testimony around the positive experience of meeting Albanian women. Marta teaches Italian to migrants both in state schools and in a catholic organization; she proposes a positive view of intercultural encounters using her experience as a paradigmatic example. Although she did meet an Albanian woman who confirmed her 'prejudices against Slavs, that is the idea that women are subjugated', she is enthusiastic about other Albanians 'who seem to be extremely strong, determined, in many cases they were the ones who decided to come to Italy, for their children's futures, and they are the ones who work and keep the family together, the opposite of what I expected'.

Her discourse points to a widespread error in Italy, that is the identification of Albanians with Slavs. The Albanian mothers of her students helped her to question what she calls the 'prejudices about Slavs'; they are recognized as active subjects and their statuses as 'migrants' sustain a positive recognition. The association between migration and agency is evident in most of the interviews. Migrant women are admired because of their will, because they leave and work hard to give their children and families a better economic present and future. They are often described as the strongest members of the family and as being able to cope with emergencies and useless husbands. Recognition is evident on the basis of ideas of the feminine and of women's locations that are elaborated within a patriarchal system. This gendered identification is recalled by Giovanna who, remembering her travels to east of Europe, points to the fact that, 'well, the women had to work hard. I'm sixty years old, and women have always been the ones to toil…'.

She saw many similarities between Eastern European women and the women of her childhood who, in a rural division of labour, were expected to take care of the household, to have many children and to work in the fields. The image of the hard work done by women – that is part of female transmitted experience – reappears in the context of women's migration. Yet the recognition of migrant agency is not devoid of stereotypes and of prejudices; it uses rhetoric of sacrifice and it places women, although the image of the feminine is renegotiated, inside relations of exploitation (this is particularly evident when the migrants' hard work and agency is praised by their employers in agriculture and in the household).

## The Triumphant Italian Woman

In almost all the testimonies, Eastern European women are depicted as being the most similar to 'us' Italians: values, religion and physical appearances are shared, and therefore similarity is claimed.

> It isn't that there are certain physical characteristics that I expected to find strange, or that I would find a person very much different from myself, no, also because we are all Europeans, and we resemble each other in some ways, it isn't that we have different coloured skin. (Silvana)

Phenotypic traits still operate to signal similarity and belonging to Europe, while it is religion, namely Islam, that sanctions the 'other' *par excellence* (Angela, Carla, Rosaria). The interviewees recount the meanings and values shared by Italians and Eastern Europeans, concerning family and children, education and social status.[7] But this similarity is not absolute: class belonging, education and urban backgrounds condition the sense of similitude. These tropes are used to identify several women from Eastern Europe. The 'object' of these narratives is isolated and differentiated – because of her differences in terms of wealth, education, and gender behaviour – from the other member of an imagined community. Usually this strategy of distinction is sustained by experiences based on friendships, on voluntary work, on encounters within the household (between employer and employee) and it demands the depiction of a group which conforms to the 'real' and 'authentic' east. Whilst the group carries the weight of stigmatization and prejudices, the exceptional individual is recognized and can become a positive point of reference for the Italian interviewee. Similarity and sameness are thus produced through the vocabulary of exceptionalism and differentiation. Others – Eastern European women of the subaltern classes, who are less educated and from rural backgrounds, as well as other ethnic and religious diasporas (Muslims, but also South Americans and Filipinos) – are used to endorse this mapping of affinities and differences.

Patrizia – a young business consultant with a university degree, who is married and the mother of one child – talks of her similarities with Raissa, a Ukrainian woman in her fifties who is helping to take care of Patrizia's grandfather. Patrizia compares Raissa with a few women from Poland whom she had previously employed, by stressing the role of social backgrounds in tracing connections and understandings. While the Polish women did not know proper Italian – 'you could read fear in their eyes' – Raissa is 'more extroverted, in a good sense, that is, she's more open, less distrustful [...] she is more like us, is more like us also in terms of her actual background, I haven't noticed major differences ...'.

Later in her discourse, Patrizia stresses that the similarity is due to Raissa's former position as a white-collar worker during communism. Education, along with Raissa's long experience of immigration (seventeen years in Italy) and her knowledge of Italian, situate her closer to Patrizia. For this Italian woman, economic and social position is much more important than nationality in determining the possibility of understanding: 'Well, I don't think this is so much about nationality, it's more about one's upbringing, her social class, she is perfect, always neat and tidy, it's very, very important to her'.

Carlotta compares the mothers of two of her daughter's schoolmates. Agnés from Hungary, whom she knows, is a former athlete working in a national organization, who has been obliged to move to Rome with her husband because of their work, and are thus evidently middle class. The other is Ildico from Romania, who is probably working as a domestic helper close to her daughter's school. While she has an acquaintance with Agnés, mainly talking with her about the children and their education, she cannot talk with the other mother: 'With these others there's a complete wall. She has never allowed anyone to get any closer than 'Good morning' and 'Good afternoon' [...] In any case, you see a sort of outsider's attitude, not hostile, but they definitely keep to themselves'.

Carlotta defines Ildico as 'much more eastern' when asked to indicate any differences that there might be in the appearances of the two women; and she links this 'eastern' with 'something that we would probably call 'out of style'', that is a synonym of poverty. Agnés's wealth, education and cosmopolitanism provide the mirror for a positive similitude; and national backgrounds are reintroduced to suggest possible difference, because, in Carlotta's words, 'Romania is not Hungary'; according to her there are many 'easts', a legitimate claim that is moulded by the repertoire of Eurocentrism and the mix of pre- and post-1989 nation states.

> Czechoslovakia is a country that has an extremely strong cultural meaning for Europe, it is so central, so strong that it is difficult to identify it as being east. On the other hand, countries like the Ukraine, or Belarus or Romania, they are more remote for us, and we imagine them as being much much poorer, not only in material resources, but also in terms of culture and knowledge ... and in relations with us. [...] The differences increase when you go to more remote areas. These are really historical differences, very deep cultural differences. [...] If you compare those who come from Poland with those who come from countries east of Poland, you already see some differences.

Mechanisms of inclusion and distinction are at work also when the representative relationships are based on friendship. Angela is very fond of her Hungarian friend Csilla, who, like her, is a housewife, mother and wife of an Italian soldier. Both families live in an apartment block facing a barracks in the outskirts of Florence. In Angela's description, Csilla is presented as an exception in comparison to other Eastern European women, because of her economic wealth and emancipation. For Angela, her perception of the economic condition that obtains in Eastern Europe is fundamental in shaping her picture of the region. Although she has not been there, she has heard it reported that there is a lot of poverty there, which she associates with prostitution, the exploitation of children, India and Latin America. Questioned about her will to go to Eastern Europe, she answers:

> I can't stand to see people who are suffering, poverty. Because I've heard that... poverty, for example, to go to India, it would be hard to go to India. I'm not someone who would like to go there, I don't know if I could handle it, visiting India. [...] I don't like to see people suffering, to see little girls who prostitute themselves because they don't have... I can't stand it, it's too much.

> I would like to go to Eastern Europe, yes, but I don't want to see the poverty. [...] These people who travel in South America where there is so much poverty, I don't know if I could go there.

Hungary, Poland, Russia are confused within a sphere of global poverty, in which the exploitation of children and prostitution are the main symptoms and source of pity. The path followed by Angela's narrative, which is particularly interesting in terms of the associations it invokes, seems to confirm the image of the east as 'a zone of difficulty and of problems to be resolved. [...] Despite changes in the east, the transition furthers the objectification of east by the West and reproduces its utter otherness, even as it is reincorporated into the Western political and economic sphere of influence' (Kideckel 1998: 145).

Silvana's description of her friend Bori, whom she met during a period in hospital, adds a further element to the strategies of identification: the failure to recognize the 'coevalness' (Fabian 1983) of migrants, which is a fundamental pattern in the Eurocentric notion of 'otherness' and is dominant in the whole corpus of Italian interviews.

> At the beginning I didn't even understand that she was from the east. [...] Then, in terms of how I think, I don't think that they're very different from us. Really, I think that they are extremely devoted to their families, maybe even more than us Italians. [...] she's the one who decides what to make for dinner, she manages the household, in a very feminine way, it's like that. She strikes me as being like my mother was, here in Italy.

After noting how Bori could 'easily pass for an Italian', Silvana introduces the main element of differentiation between them: Bori is a more traditional housewife, so traditional that she resembles the model of femininity embodied by Silvana's mother. Although in later comments Silvana admits that the division of labour is unequal in her family, she blames objective circumstances – her husband is too busy, but he would like to help – and not her predisposition to be a housewife (she is working part-time at a university since her child was born). Silvana then returns to the parallels between Bori, in her early thirties, and her mother in her late sixties, and explains: 'I make the association between her and my mother because my mother lived through the 50s and 60s as a woman, when Italian society was completely different. We changed and I think that they changed too, but later than us and they also had the same immediate changes in male–female relationships. But that's just my impression.'

Silvana attributes the permanence of traditional gender roles to the 'dark and closed years' of the communist regime, which caused the crystallization of male–female relationship and a later entrance into modernity. What is problematic here is the location of her friend and her feminine model in the

Italian past (for an analysis of the work of gender during communism, which was based on a formal equality between sexes in the public sphere and a conservative politics in the private, see Nikolchina 2002). The position of the east and Eastern European women in the Italian past is to be found in most of the testimonies. In the case of Giovanna, who is in her early sixties (in other words, of the same generation as Silvana's mother), the reference to the past requires the introduction of yet another generation, that of her own mother. It is Eastern European women's ways of dressing that allows for the comparison, and which places them in Italy's 1960s again:

> They have lighter skin, and they are well-groomed, neat–like our mothers were in the 1960s, after the war, they have their hair styled, how can I explain it? Their hair is all in place, and even if they do follow the trends a little bit, they're not into this grunge, they might wear a bright blue top, but with a skirt, or jeans, clean and pressed.

She depicts a style that is situated before, and which has rejected, the novelties introduced by youth 'street fashion' during the 1960s. From Giovanna's political history and activism within the communist party, we deduce that she aligns herself with the rupture introduced by youth cultures and movements and that therefore she has to turn to her mother to find the right comparison that, moreover, assures her in her self-image.

The placing of migrant women in the Italian past is adjusted according to the age, class and education of the interviewee. According to Roberta, the Polish women employees in her house have a 'regard for men that I don't think exists anymore in Italian women […] that is like the way it was when we were little girls'. Then she recalls the 1940s and her mother teaching her daughters that 'when a marriage goes bad it is always the wife's fault. […] I see the same attitude amongst these girls […] among Italians there is stubbornness, no, not stubbornness, let's call it girls against men, absolutely'.

At stake there is the definition of Italian women's emancipation, which is being measured in a triangular relationship with Eastern European women and Italian men. Angela – discussing mixed heterosexual marriages – points to the predilection of Italians for women 'who are real women', meaning those who conform to traditional gender roles. She cites acquaintances who have married women from Cuba, South America and Eastern Europe, 'women who are in more desperate circumstances […] and who adjust more to the man'. On the contrary, Italian women are too emancipated and this could be the cause of the men's preference for foreigners. Angela's narrative reverses traditional stereotypes and suggests new ones. In her description, Swedish women are no longer the champions of emancipation. At least until the 1970s, Scandinavian women have been represented as the sexually liberated 'other' in opposition to repressed Italian women in films, magazines, novels; they were a mythical symbol in the construction of a national version of masculinity (for instance, the Latin lover of 1950s and 1960s). Angela articulates her counter-representation against this male 'myth' of 'the Swedes', and instead ascribes emancipation, liberation and freedom to Italian women; a new situation that even allows for a little revenge against Italian men who have been 'left behind'.

The renegotiation of women's position encompasses tensions that Angela translates into her concern that men could prefer non-Italian women. This preoccupation mirrors Giovanna's story of Eastern European women entering Italian families and 'robbing' the men; and it is reinforced by Patrizia's statement that 'Italian women have a more equal relationship with men anyway, and I would even say that we're overstepping our bounds a bit'. Patrizia compares herself with her colleague's wife, who is the same age as her and has a college degree, but with her husband has a 'very traditional relationship, like they were 50 years ago'.

Migrant women are used by Italian women for the renegotiation of their self-representations, as well their positions within contemporary Italy and Europe.[8] Their narratives illustrate 'the multiple articulations of the triumphant European/Western women versus 'the others" (Lutz 1997). This configuration presupposes a reference to backwardness that is overcome only by a few exceptional individuals. Eastern European migrants are placed in the Italian past because of the poverty of their countries; because of their approach to men and gender roles; because of the more authoritarian relationships between generations (Cristina); because of their style in dressing; because they seem 'naïve, childish' beside the entrepreneurial Italian mentality (Patrizia); and even because of their commitment to religion (this point was made by Orietta, the owner of a farm in the traditionally catholic north east of Italy).

Memories of Italian emigration are used also to construct the divide between Italian modernity and the backwardness of the 'others'. Polish domestic helpers remind Roberta of Italian country girls of the 1950s who migrated from rural areas to Rome; Cristina recalls a similar image but puts it even further back in the late-nineteenth and early-twentieth century. She explicitly refers to her memory of 'our' way of life many years ago – 'when our grandparents lived in the countryside' – in accounting for the better communication she has with Eastern European women compared with Filipino women. She also mentions the episode 'From the Apennines to the Andes', which is part of the book *Cuore*, one of the main texts in the education of the Italian masses of the values of the dominant national identity (Colombo 1998). In this episode, an Italian mother is forced by poverty to leave both Italy and her son to go to find work in Argentina as a servant. Eastern European domestic helpers remind Cristina of the fictional story and they overlap with the memory of Italy's diasporas. Contemporary migrants, although admired because they 'leave and go back, like a man', are perceived as the reincarnation of the same old story of poverty and of reactions to it. Cristina also traces a parallelism with her own experience of commuting 'for seven year as a teacher, I left with my suitcase, the first of my family [to go to work in another city]'.

Individual and collective memories are inevitably activated by transnational migration. But these are often marked by a rhetoric that flattens socio-historical specificity and which constructs a representation of an unchangeable history of the mobility of people. This pattern limits the understanding of the specific location of contemporary migrants within global relationships of power and exploitation, and of the migrants' actions and reactions to multiple forces that both oblige them to move and which prevent their movement. In addition, the appeal to the memory of Italian emigration and poverty can be used both to justify Italian women's positions of power (for instance Orietta refers to the harshness of her seasonal emigration to Germany as an ice-cream seller as a way of excusing the hard work she extracts from the seasonal Polish and Rumanian fruit-pickers on her farm); or to accommodate it (as in Cristina's comparison of her experience as a middle-class commuting teacher with the experiences of the maids who now work in her household).

The renegotiation of Italian women's self-identity occurs along different axes and multiple, interlocking perceptions: Italians and migrants; northerners and southerners, Italians and northern Europeans (see also Mai 2002). These self-representations continue to be built on duality and stereotypes: while Italians are much more open and friendlier than northern Europeans, the latter are much more organized and harder workers (Angela, in particular, uses the whole *repertoire* of self-denigration that is inseparable from Italian national identity) (Bollati 1983). Italy's southerners are lazier than northerners (Rosaria and others); and migrants are less developed and more backward than Italians (all).

The concepts and terms of modernity are largely used in Italian humanities and social science publications, and in mass media and political discourses, without the problematic implications they have in other national contexts (for a comparison with England and the USA see Mason 1988). The opposition of modernity to tradition has been – and sometimes still is – the dominant perception of the country in the eyes both of Italian and of foreign commentators (Agnew 1997). The image of a backward Italy and, above all, of backward Italian women caught in the network of religion, patriarchy and poverty, is today projected on to migrant women to sustain the alignment of the interviewees with modernity, emancipation and development. The presence of immigrants on the peninsula is the ultimate condition for Italians to feel part of Europe.[9] And while Eastern European women deserve to be addressed through the idiom of what Guha has called 'improvement' – signifying that they have the possibility of overcoming difference through imitation (Guha 1989) – other diasporic communities – identified as Muslim, Asian, Filipino, Nigerian – incarnate otherness. These dynamics regulate inclusion and exclusion, positive and negative recognitions, and the hierarchies through which immigrant communities are classified. The fact that Eurocentrism and ethnocentrism provide the vocabulary with which sameness, diversity, and intercultural encounters are named, confirms the difficulties of dealing with hybridity and liminality outside the spectrum of sedimented dichotomies and stereotypes.

## Notes

1. *Studi emigrazione*, n. 135, 1999 special issue 'Mass media, conflitti etnici e immigrazione'. In addition I looked at the newspaper, *La Repubblica*, in 1994, 1996, 1998 and 2000, which also contributes to the classification of Eastern European women as sex workers and losses.
2. In Italy the presence of a big communist party has undoubtedly shaped the perception of Eastern Europe. But the thematic of the women's free and available sexuality seems to be shared by people of different political position. For the Italian communists' imagery of USSR. See D'Attorre (1991).
3. At the time of the *Grand Tour* Venice was described as a 'large brothel' and in the early twentieth century Italian women were described as the main victims of *tratta delle bianche*. See Littlewood (2001).
4. Sexuality is not the main element used by Dutch women to identify Eastern European women; it is central in the English film *Birthday Girl* (Jez Butterworth 2001) which uses the presence of mail-order brides on the internet to reinforce the stereotype of eastern unreliability and of the women's 'available' sexuality.
5. In Italy, the paradigmatic case is the transformation of Albanians from anticommunist hero to dangerous 'invaders'. See Mai (2002).
6. Lisa Schuster (2003) explores this shift in the Western perception of refugees.
7. Former and neo-fascists, as well as exponents of the more conservative catholic groups, refer to Eastern Europeans as the more welcome Christian, as opposed to Muslim, immigrants. But even this racist classification does not prevent the exploitation and marginalization of many eastern women and men working in construction, agriculture, and domestic services.
8. For an analysis of the national collective 'self' that emerges in the discourse concerning migration see Mai (2002); Cotesta (1999). See Flesler (2003) and Nair (2003) for similar dynamics in Spanish culture.
9. In the 1990s Italian political discourse interconnected the country's growing role in the EU with an efficient control of Italian and European borders (Mai 2002).

## References

Agnew, J. 1997. 'The Myth of Backward Italy in Modern Europe', in B. Allen and M. Russo (eds.) *Revisioning Italy. National Identity and Global Culture*, Minneapolis, University of Minnesota Press.

Balibar, E. 1991. 'Es Gibt Keinen Staat in Europa: Racism and Politics in Europe Today', *New Left Review*, n. 186: 5–19.

Bollati, G. 1983. *L'italiano. Il carattere nazionale come storia e come invenzione*, Turin, Einaudi.

Burgio, A. 1998. *Nel nome della razza*, Bologna, Il Mulino.

———. 2001. *La guerra delle razze*, Rome, Il Manifesto.

Chakrabarty, D. 2000. *Provincializing Europe. Postcolonial Thought and Historical Difference*, Princeton, Princeton University Press.

Colombo, F. 1998. *La cultura sottile*, Milan, Bompiani.

Cotesta, V. 1999. 'Mass media, conflitti etnici e identità degli italiani', *Studi Emigrazione*, XXXVI(135): 443–70.

D'Attorre, P.P. (ed.) 1991. *Nemici per la pelle*, Milan, Franco Angeli.

Dickie, J. 1999. *Darkest Italy. The notion and stereotypes of the Mezzogiorno 1860–1900*, Basingstoke, Macmillian.

Fabian, J. 1983. *Time and the Other. How Anthropology Makes its Object*, New York, Columbia University Press.

Ferraioli, L. 1995. *La sovranità nel mondo moderno*, Milan, Anabasi.

Flesler, D. 2003. 'Differentialist Racism in Spanish Immigration Film', paper given at the conference *Hispanic Cinemas: the Local and the Global*, 28–29 Nov., Institute of Romance Studies (UL).

Gabaccia, D. 2002. 'Two Great Migrations: American and Italian Southerners in Comparative Perspective', in E. Dal Lago and R. Halpern (eds.) *The American South and the Italian Mezzogiorno. Essays in Comparative History*, New York, Palgrave.

Giacone, P. 1998. *Soli a Torino. La Stampa e L'Unità sull'immigrato meridionale (1960–61)*, Cavalermaggiore, Centro Stampa.

Gibson, M. 1998. 'Biology or Environment? Race and Southern 'Deviancy' in the Writings of Italian Criminologists, 1880–1920', in J. Schneider (ed.) *Italy's 'Southern Question'. Orientalism in One Country*, Oxford, Berg.

Kideckel, D. 1998. 'Utter Otherness: Western Anthropology and East European Political Economy' in S. Parman (ed.) *Europe in the Anthropological Imagination*, Upper Saddle River, NJ, Prentice-Hall.

King, R. and J. Andall 1999. 'The Geography and Economic Sociology of Recent Immigration to Italy', *Modern Italy*, 4(2): 135–58. Special Issue: *The Italian Experience of Migration*.

Kundnani, A. 2001. 'In a foreign land: the new popular racism', *Race and Class*, 43(2): 41–60.
Littlewood, I. 2001. *Sultry Climates. Travel and Sex since the Grand Tour*, London, John Murray.
Lutz, H. 1997. 'The Limits of European-ness: Immigrant women in Fortress Europe', *Feminist Review*, 57(1): 93–111.
Mai, N. 2002. 'Myths and Moral Panics: Italian Identity and the Media Representation of Albanian Immigration' in R. Grillo and J. Pratt (eds.) *The Politics of Recognizing Difference. Multiculturalism Italian-style*, Aldershot, Ashgate.
Mason, T. 1988. 'Italy and Modernization: a Montage', *History Workshop* (25): 127–47.
Mezzadra, S. and A. Petrillo (eds.) 2000. *I confini della globalizzazione*, Rome, Manifestolibri.
Moe, N. 2002. *The View from Vesuvio. Italian Culture and the Southern Question*, Berkeley, University of California Press.
Nair, P. 2003. 'Open to Wind and Fire: Globalization's Refugees, or the Politics of Class and Ethnicity in Poniente', paper given at the conference *Hispanic Cinemas: the Local and the Global*, 28–29 Nov., Institute of Romance Studies (UL).
Nikolchina, M. 2002. 'The Seminar: *Mode d'emploi.* Impure Spaces in the Light of Late Totalitarianism', *differences*, 15.
Scevi, P. 2002. 'La condizione giuridica dello straniero in Italia dopo la nuova legge sull'immigrazione', *Studi Emigrazione*, XXXIX(148): 907–20.
Schuster, L. 2003. *The Use and Abuse of Political Asylum in Britain and Germany*, London, Frank Cass.
Sorgoni, B. 2002. *Racist Discourses and Practices in the Italian Empire under Fascism*, in R. Grillo and J. Pratt (eds.) *The Politics of Recognizing Difference. Multiculturalism Italian-style*, Aldershot, Ashgate.
Wolff, L. 1994. *Inventing Eastern Europe. The Map of Civilization on the Mind of the Enlightenment*, Stanford, Stanford University Press.

*Chapter 11*

# Moral and Cultural Boundaries in Representations of Migrants: Italy and the Netherlands in Comparative Perspective

*Dawn Lyon*

## Introduction

This chapter analyses the interviews with native women in Italy and the Netherlands in comparative perspective, complementing the previous discussions by Esther Vonk and Enrica Capussotti. The chapter explores how the interviewees repeatedly make distinctions between themselves and those they feel are both similar to and different from them. Many of these distinctions are also judgements of worth, about whether another person, or group, is in some way better than or inferior to them. The particular contribution of this analysis is to disentangle different elements of the interviewees' discourse, in other words, to identify the components which underpin the construction of self and other. It takes inspiration from the work of Michèle Lamont and colleagues (Lamont 1992, 2000a, 2000b; Lamont and Thévénot 2000) and makes use of the concept of boundary-work.

Analysing boundaries (and borders), which have been at the centre of influential research in the social sciences and humanities in recent years, offers productive ways to think about mechanisms of inclusion and exclusion in everyday life through an emphasis on relational processes (Lamont and Molnár 2002). This chapter starts from the position that in everyday life we spent a good deal of time and energy engaged in making distinctions between ourselves and others – personally (self-other) and collectively (we-they). Through the construction of boundaries with respect to others, we make claims about who we are and how we wish to be recognized. In these processes, we secure dignity and honour, seek to avoid shame and 'maintain a positive self-identity by patrolling the borders of our groups' (Lamont 1992: 11). In addition, we acquire status, resources, resist threats, and legitimate social advantages (ibid: 13).

Lamont makes a distinction between different types of boundaries: moral, socio-economic and cultural. Moral boundaries are 'drawn on the basis of moral character; they are based around such qualities as honesty, work ethic, personal integrity, and consideration for others'. 'Cultural boundaries are drawn on the basis of education, intelligence, manners, tastes, and command of high culture.' Socio-economic boundaries are 'judgements concerning people's social position as indicated by their wealth, power, or professional success' (1992: 4).[1] With regard to the discourses and representations of migrants, the value of analysing the operation of boundaries in this way 'puts flesh on it [the relational dynamic of racism] by documenting inductively the building blocks of racism' (Lamont 2000a: 57). This chapter traces these distinctions in relation to the cultural repertoires and resources that people have to think with in the particular settings of this study, and evidences how certain repertoires are sustained over time and strengthened in the present climate through entrenched cultural practices and institutional arrangements.[2]

## Boundary Work

Reading the interviews through the concepts of moral and cultural boundaries in particular, it is remarkable how salient and productive they are for sorting through the narratives of the native women.[3] The analysis reveals points of connection for friendship, understanding and empathy, and, bases for social exclusion, prejudice and racism. Overall, what is striking is the extent to which moral boundaries figure in the accounts of many of the native women interviewees. Indeed, moral failings are often the grounds through which racism is expressed (Lamont 2000a). The emphasis on morality can be seen as evidence of the burden of suspicion migrant women are subject to – and in strikingly gendered ways, for instance around the issue of respectability/sexuality. Yet, the types of boundary-work one can trace in the narratives vary according to the nature of the relationship: employers tend to emphasise moral boundaries in their representations of migrant women, and friends more often refer to cultural as well as moral boundaries 'to incorporate the other into their own group' (Lamont 2000b: 44).

The Dutch and Italian women express some similar positions. Overall the Dutch voice moral boundaries less strongly than the Italians and they emphasize cultural boundaries slightly more than moral ones. The most striking difference however is in the components of anti-racist discourse present in the interviews. The Dutch talk about migration in terms of enrichment and openness, a vocabulary that is not heard in the Italian interviews.

The first part of the chapter discusses the most salient moral boundaries articulated by the native women interviewees. First, the discussion of hard work shows how migrants are represented against an implicit or explicit public narrative of laziness, or applauded for their willingness to labour without complaint. Second, in the discussions on respectability and traditional gender relations, women's bodies are seen as the measure of morality. The second part of the chapter discusses the ways in which native women invoke cultural boundaries when they talk about migrant women. In the first theme in this part, the boundaries of belonging to Europe, native women claim similarities with others on the basis of shared 'values'. Exclusion operates through Americanization/globalization, religious difference (Islam), and 'skin colour'. The second theme discusses how intelligence and manners operate as markers of distinction, both to exclude some from the dominant culture and to incorporate others, especially friends. The final section of the chapter discusses the interviewees' attempts to loosen boundaries through discourses of enrichment, openness, and universality.

## Moral Boundaries

### Hard Work as Moral Worth

Hard work is often evoked as a moral boundary in contemporary western culture (and especially so for men) (Lamont 2000a). It has a particular resonance in relation to migrants who, in Western Europe, are often perceived to gain from undue, or at least unearned, social benefits as reflected in the interviewees' images of migrants 'in search of golden mountains' or as an 'economic burden'. Inactivity is met with general disapproval – the idea that someone else is 'getting something for nothing' – notably by those who are themselves hard-working. And in some accounts, there is a quick leap from inactivity to criminality, especially in perceptions of men (e.g. Valeria, NL). In contrast then, hard work is the basis of moral approval by many of the native women interviewed.

In particular for the employers, hard work is used to distinguish between the 'good' and the 'undesirable' worker, the industrious and the lazy. In Italy this distinction is also applied to 1950s rural Italian women, whose strengths and capacities are celebrated, and opposed to young Italian women today (Capussotti, this book). Roberta is a middle-aged, middle-class woman who lives with her husband and (sometimes) her grown-up children in a wealthy suburb of Rome. She has employed a total of four domestic workers from Eastern Europe, three from Poland she claims, and one from Romania.[4] She especially appreciates those who labour without complaint: 'She was a classic farm girl like the country girls from our families in the very early 1950s, you know, very hearty, very capable, very robust and above all willing to do anything, without any complaints.' Giovanna, a teacher of Italian and history at a secondary school in Rome, who is careful not to ask too much of the domestic worker she employs, nevertheless comments: '… but they accept everything, and they just say 'I'm here to work, tell me what I need to do". In addition, employers emphasize honesty and straightforwardness. In so doing, they invoke the public narrative that domestic workers are not trustworthy; therefore honesty is a central and legitimate category of evaluation of them.[5] Within this, Roberta makes a distinction between different migrant groups, comparing the honesty of the Eastern European women she employs to Peruvian women, about whom she remarks: '[you] could never figure out what they were thinking …'

Generally Roberta talks about her domestic employees without personhood (Dal Lago 1999). They may have names or be one in a line of women, e.g. 'the second one' or one of 'these girls', from another place – she even confuses the cities and countries – remarkable for this or that particular competence or capacity. She even talks about 'exchanging our girls' with a colleague over the holiday period in terms such as 'you can have her …' or 'I'll use her …' – a resource reduced to her capacity for labour and without subjectivity, reminiscent of the practice of not using servants' real names but giving them generic substitutes (e.g., Hantzaroula 2002). Whilst this kind of attitude is not unusual in the Italian interviews, there are other forms of relationship. Giovanna describes points of genuine contact with the women she has employed, claiming a 'unique rapport' with each, and recounting exchanges which evidence recognition of them. In a rather more ambivalent appreciation, Adriana (It) (amongst others) recognizes one dimension of personhood of migrant women in their capacity to care. This celebration of their caring orientation in their work with the elderly makes them 'special', with 'more compassion, humanity' as they also work without complaint. However, Adriana remarks that they do so for just half the salary that an Italian woman would demand …

Similar distinctions to those voiced by Roberta operate in the account of Orietta, a farmer who employs mostly Romanian and Polish men and women as seasonal fruit-pickers. She very explicitly places herself on the positive side of the divide she makes between those with a work ethic (e.g. 'the Poles') and those without (e.g. 'the Romanians'). She recounts how she has done the work that she now employs others to do (fruit-picking), thus placing herself inside the schemas she invokes. She is still very much a farmer (within a traditional gendered division of labour), and her identification with their position opens up the possibility of solidarity,[6] in contrast to Roberta. In addition, as a young woman, she worked abroad for a summer (selling ice-cream in Germany) where, 'because there wasn't any work in my country, you tried to do a good job, because if they would hire you again you could earn something'. Decency and respect for the limits of oneself and others are linked to hard work and solidarity, in sharp contrast to the laziness that is so frowned upon.[7]

> *Do you feel like these women are like you, or different from you?*
> Mostly I feel like they are just like me, they help me, I help them, it's real co-operation between women. [...] Some of the young ones, you see right away they don't really care. [...] We have to make two or three trips to get the women over there [to their other plots of land]. You see who is first to get in the car, and who always stays here to wait, they're not even subtle about it.

Few of the Dutch women are direct employers of migrant women; rather they have friendships or collegial relationships with some migrant women. Still, hard work functions as an explicit basis for inclusion. For instance, Valeria discusses Hungarians in these terms: 'They work hard, they work long hours and they will do anything to have a better life [...] So they're not lazy at all as long as they know what they're doing it for. So they can come along, they can come along with Western Europe.' If in this case, they 'deserve' to be part of the West, in Janette's view they are 'useful for the Dutch, because they do jobs that would otherwise stay vacant.' Migrants are again applauded for accepting low-level work, echoing Roberta above. Taking this further, Wilma argues that the fit between service-based administrative work and a stance of servitude on the part of a Hungarian woman, Erica, employed in the organization is a valuable one, although her account does include her own encouragement of Erica to stand up to excessive demands. Amongst other interviewees, she also appreciates people who bring high-level skills to the Netherlands 'who just come here because they're good at their job, because we need them, too' (Petra). However, what is striking overall is the juxtaposition between assertive Dutch workers and servile migrant ones.

Finally, Esther, a social worker married to a Bulgarian man, has a less individualistic orientation, recognizing the conditions in which many migrants work, at times illegally: 'they work outrageously hard doing the most horrible jobs just to earn a lot of money and then they save that.'[8] What stirs Esther is not the question of legal status but the fact that the migrants she knows (she is mostly referring to Bulgarian men here) are compelled to work so hard and in the worst conditions. She makes no moral judgement about them as individuals for doing so, turning her criticism to a system which perpetuates this. The status of Esther's husband – who is now a practising psychotherapist – was not always legal. It may be that this gives her a bridge to connect to the difficulties legal regulation imposes, and inhibits her from making judgements of individual or collective worth on this basis.

### *Moral Boundaries Drawn on the Body: Respectability and Tradition*

Respectability is a central category of self-identity and evaluation by others of women in lower class positions (Skeggs 1997). In particular, the bodies of migrant women are sexualized and problematized through a moral gaze. The native women interviewees were largely critical of the media representations of migrant women as sex workers, yet they made numerous spontaneous comments on the dress, hygiene, and sexual politics of migrant women. The Dutch women referred to the excessive attention they claim migrant women give to appearance, expressed in terms of subordination to femininity (e.g. Esther), or a lack of body discipline (e.g. Norine). The Italian women drew parallels between the style of dress of migrant women and that of their own mothers (as discussed by Capussotti, this book).[9] Yet, the women migrants are made to tread a fine line between being considered old-fashioned or vulgar. Furthermore, these distinctions are articulated by contrasting different migrant groups, usually on the basis of nationality. For instance, Silvana (a friend of the Hungarian woman, Bori[10]) talks about a Ukranian woman, Raissa, who works for her aunt, and discusses her in contrast to South American women.

> In South America the fashion is different, women dress differently but then Raissa is really a woman of a different generation, she's 50 years old. So if she wears a skirt that I would never wear, or even my mother, it makes me think, maybe, because the skirts are a little bit old-fashioned, but you also realize that she doesn't have much money and she certainly wouldn't buy herself fancy clothes… But she's always nicely dressed, very neat, in a way that the Colombian isn't, it isn't that she doesn't dress neatly, she does pay attention, but while Raissa wears a little bit of make-up, not too much, just right, the other one I saw her last Sunday was completely painted up. But I think that's the style there … […] Yes, I think she [Raissa] is more formal, refined, not vulgar. While the other one could easily slide into vulgarity, instead Raissa is very refined.

Cristina (It), who at one time employed a Polish woman to care for her elderly mother, takes these distinctions further. Commenting on the style of the Russian women she has noticed, she says that there is 'something about them […] sort of peasant-like', that they can be identified by 'the way they move, how they hold themselves […] how they carry themselves' – Bourdieu's (1977) body hexis.

In several interviews, there is also an implicit connection between respectability and cleanliness in which hygiene signals moral purity.[11] Roberta recounts an episode in which one of the domestic workers she employs expresses her modesty (in a situation where she gets wet whilst cleaning and has to remove her clothes). She immediately goes on to applaud the cleanliness of the bathroom: 'I've never had such clean bathrooms, these girls get down on the floor and the clean the whole bathroom, all of the fixtures from down below.' The domestic worker performs the labour of decontamination, and from a position of inferiority, both literally and symbolically.[12]

In the accounts of friends, there is a celebration of respectability and an identification with the migrant women. Silvana recounts how Bori is very neatly dressed, as is her baby, 'very neat, perfect'. It matters to her, she says. She takes care over her body and about her clothes, 'not that she exaggerates' – exaggeration is defined as Armani – and, 'she's not at all flamboyant', meaning that she does not want to show off a label. In Silvana's view, none of this is related to her being from Eastern Europe; it is an expression of her investment in femininity, she says. Angela, who is friends with a Hungarian woman, Ildico,[13] makes very similar comments: starting from the inclusive 'we both dress fairly simply' she says 'it's not like we shop at Dolce & Gabanna ...'

In discussing sexual politics, the Italian women comment that women from Eastern Europe 'still show a complete dependence on men, absolute dependence', having 'a regard for men that in reality isn't returned or only to a very small degree ... like the way it was when we were little girls' (Roberta, Margherita). Italian women themselves, in contrast, 'don't settle for less than they want', and maybe 'look down a little on their men.' If these comments represent widely held views, there are some exceptions, for instance, Giovanna's remarks at her surprise at the lack of resistance of East European men to 'sending their women abroad. The men stay home and look after the children while their wives support them with the money they earn abroad.' Furthermore, distinctions are made between different groups of migrants, perceived to be more or less independent.[14]

It is the women interviewed in the Netherlands who have most to say about relationships and the gendered division of labour. Whilst Bulgarian women are very accepting of their (macho) culture when in Bulgaria, according to Esther (a social worker), and do 'what is expected of them', once in the Netherlands, they 'see what's going on around them and come into contact with Dutch women and start to question who should be determining what in their lives'. Previously, 'they [had] never learned to ask questions [...] you see them rebel here.' Paradoxically she talks at another point about how these women are interested in politics, something that features in many of their conversations. So, on the one hand, she is cognisant of them as thinking subjects and, on the other, gives Dutch women, through their example, the credit for opening their minds in the realm of relationships.[15] The distinction here between 'the European woman' and 'the other (migrant) woman' (Lutz 1997) can be read as a moral boundary.

## Cultural Boundaries

### *The Boundaries of Belonging to Europe*[16]

Many interviewees talk about their friends, or other migrant women they feel some connection to, on the basis of 'common cultural values'. Angela[17] claims that as a result of her upbringing she doesn't have any 'pre-conceptions' and her comments on migrants from Eastern Europe stress similarities: '[we have] the same attitudes, the same ways of thinking', which she summarizes as 'a Western mentality'. This orientation is echoed in many of the interviews: Valeria (NL) emphasizes how relationships are about understanding, recognition and communication with a person who can 'know immediately what you mean'. For Janette, Europe ends 'where you encounter people you can't understand, whose culture you can't understand' something which translates in geographical terms to 'the middle of Russia.' She claims to feel more connected to 'the Western countries, like America, and less with Eastern European countries. And that mostly has to do with, well, background, culture, I think.' Some women from further afield are, however, felt to be close as perceived cultural proximity can transcend geographical distance (e.g. Isabella, It, talking about Peruvian women).

Some of Janette's pro-European sentiment is concerned with standing up to America, a position echoed by Norine, Valeria and others who are also critical of the U.S. for its assumed cultural homogeneity, which is sometimes presented as threatening variety within Europe. It is interesting that the language used here is Americanization – a phenomenon discussed and feared since the 1950s – rather than the more contemporary term of globalization. Some indirect reference is made to the power and impact of global capital but the argument is not elaborated. If America as a global power is held responsible for what Italy and the Netherlands are losing, the women – and men – who move to the West, albeit from very different parts of the world, are seen to represent these global shifts.

However, the strongest distinctions made in the interviews are through religion and skin colour. Islam has been constructed as the nemesis of Christian Europe for more than a millennium, constructing Europeans in turn as the sole proprietors of civilization (Lamont, 2000a: 182). In recent years, the EU's defence of its external borders has further contributed to reinforcing the idea of Islam as being homogenous and other to Europe (ibid: 184). The interviews indicate a convergence in anti-Islam discourses and sentiments in both Italy and the Netherlands. The Western is often defined as Christian, and shared religious symbols, e.g. churches, are seen as significant points of mutual recognition: '[Women from Eastern Europe] are pretty European. Their churches might look different, but if they see a church in the middle of a city, they know what it is.' (Janette) These religious connections transcend Europe however so 'Africans' from Christian countries are also people to whom one can feel connected.

At the same time, colour is itself invoked as the marker of exclusion or belonging. For instance: '… we are all Europeans, and we resemble each other in some ways, it isn't that we have different coloured skin' (Silvana). In these kinds of discourses, shades of whiteness are rendered imperceptible as they are not seen to be significant. Indeed, whiteness is itself used to emphasise connection between Italians and Albanians in the face of prejudice towards the latter: 'I tell them "you are white, we are white, we are the same, I have the exact same eyes as you …"' (Isabella, It). Colour evidently functions as the visible sign of difference, naturalising racial difference grounded in the assumption of racial purity (Coombes and Brah 2000: 4).[18]

### Intelligence and Manners

The interviewees also make distinctions on the grounds of intelligence and manners. In talking about the farm workers she employs, Orietta mentions how the highly educated 'ones' learn more quickly, stating proudly that they have seasonal fruit-pickers who have university degrees, without any reference to the incongruence of this. Similarly, Roberta talks about one of the domestic workers she employs in terms which are appreciative of her high levels of education. In both cases, the value of the education is in its application to the present work. Roberta is impressed with her well-educated domestic worker, positively comparing her to ignorant 'country girls': 'And since she had studied chemistry, every time that she saw, I don't know, some kind of spot on the windowsill, or another kind on the parquet, she would examine the stain and say 'here we need this kind of solvent' and she could practically give the chemical formula for it [*laughs*].' Roberta applauds her capacity for thinking, using her head before her hands, even if the work is manual. Taking the initiative is praised elsewhere, be it in terms of studying, problem-solving, or managing difficult situations, by both Dutch and Italian interviewees. These are highly valued dimensions of individualism in the West, the acceptance of which in everyday conduct is met with approval and relief.

Language ability and competence features somewhere in almost every interview. Generally migrant women are applauded for learning Italian or Dutch, or criticized if they are not sufficiently conversant. Betta, talking about a Romanian woman who cared for a family member, commented, 'She spoke so well that I didn't really think of her as foreign'. Others expect such high levels of competence – a kind of quid pro quo for being granted residency (e.g. Suze). Only rarely did an interviewee comment on her own limitations of language: Giovanna regretted not being able to speak English or French as a medium of communication.

Many friends of migrant women, in the Netherlands and Italy alike, talk very positively about their intelligence and linguistic ability. For instance, Silvana talks in glowing terms about Orsola, whom she describes as 'highly educated', who 'speaks Italian very well' and for whom it is important to talk about books, and 'not just everyday practical things'. Valeria comments on the knowledge and intelligence of even the poorest Hungarians which she relates to the high standard of general education in Hungary. For the most part, the native women give little credit to the possibility of something in the East being better than the West, so this is an interesting exception. Indeed, they more often assume a position of superiority, in order to keep migrant women 'in their place', as Valeria relates: 'Hungarian women are higher educated than the Dutch women and sometimes they're ashamed of that ... [*Really?*] Really, I know a girl who doesn't dare to say that. She has a lower function than she was educated for but she doesn't want to insult her colleagues.'

In addition, what is notable in the Dutch interviews is the presence of distinctions made on the basis of discipline or civility.[19] Norine, a Dutch self-employed health consultant, describes migrant women as 'lax in taking the initiative to adapt their way of life', a claim made by other interviewees too. Norine considers herself to be a very open person for whom 'the world is my home' and claims not to distinguish between people on the basis of nationality or origin as 'I give everyone a chance and don't have a biased attitude.' However, she then exposes the limits to this stance in talking about women from Morocco, about whom she has become 'kind of wary' she says, '... I mean, you give them a finger and they want to take your arm.' She clearly perceives this as a break in the rules through the abuse of generosity (c.f. Lamont, 2000a: 177 on the 'over-extension of hospitality') which leaves her without recognition.

Petra, who is very open and generally positive towards migrants and migration, talks about some of the things that she finds difficult in her collegial relations, specifically with a Bulgarian women: 'Like we'll be talking about hierarchical relationships and then I sometimes think: well, we don't treat each other that way. And she, in her way, finds it normal to ... well, let's say the secretariat, to treat them rudely [...] sometimes I think, should I say something about that? ... I find that difficult.' The fact that Petra finds it hard to raise these issues with her friend/colleague suggests that they are deeply entrenched cultural practices. The lack of respect for others constitutes, for her, a 'breach of civility' (Lamont 2000a). She tries to resolve the tension by speaking up only to those people who are directly rude to her, shrugging off any broader responsibility – 'this isn't really my problem' she says. In this everyday encounter, we might read the playing out of bigger questions. Petra appears to feel caught between the recognition of difference and the imposition of universal conduct.

## Loosening Boundaries

In addition to the distinctions discussed so far, some interviewees seek to position themselves as generally inclusive and positive towards migrants. This takes three main forms in the interviews. There is a discourse of enrichment, which positively views the impact of migrants, albeit very selectively. Secondly, there is a stress on openness, which highlights the conduct of those in the receiving countries, and the efforts made to welcome others and gain understanding of their lives. Thirdly, there is recourse to universality, which tries to equalize difference. For some of the women interviewed, these expressions are attempts to position themselves as anti-racist; however the terms in which they do so are often problematic, 'containing' rather than confronting the politics of race (Essed 1991).

It is predominantly in the Netherlands that these sorts of views are articulated, a context where there is a ready language of anti-racism and an explicit public discourse about diversity, albeit one in which far right disourses have recently gained currency. In spite of this, there remains a political vocabulary to challenge these views. In Italy, in the context of 'populist strategies' which problematise migrants' personal characteristics (ter Wal, 1997), border controls and strict legislation on residence permits, challenges are voiced, amongst other things, through humanitarian norms, and the reformulation of racism through categories such as honesty, producing notions of good and bad migrants (ter Wal, 2000), and a weak anti-racist vocabulary.

Janette sees the presence of migrants in the Netherlands in terms of enrichment – but only in reference to the educated. She declares that she generally avoids topics of conversation that generate explicitly racist comments: 'I don't want to hear racist things, prejudice' she says, and she talks about Bulgarians and other migrant groups as 'deserving', not perceiving the distinctions she is making (if some are deserving, inevitably some others are not…). Petra also talks of the positive influence of migrant groups in the Netherlands – but then she conspicuously refers only to those from highly developed countries and regions (Scandinavia, America, Australia). One of the influences she notes is how it is becoming normal for women, like men, to work long hours (c.f. part-time practices in the Netherlands) – a notable reversal of the usual chain of influence. In another example, Norine explains how others are a source of interest to her: '… I think I'm relatively progressive to say that I approach everyone umm … positively in the beginning, like: wow, that's cool, you're from a different country with different cultures … tell me about yourself. Yes, that just captivates me. […] It's more an enrichment to me than thinking, 'yuck, a foreigner, with other habits, another language'.' This is what makes life interesting in her view, having learned from infancy that 'different is interesting'. However this may in effect be an instance of the 'overfriendliness' noted by Essed (1991: 181, Table 5.3).

In a second orientation, Petra emphasizes openness of the self and a willingness to help others: 'You [a newly arrived migrant] need the help of the people who live in the country, who have been here for a while. Because it's really hard to find your own way ...' The willingness to help, in principle at least (she comments that it is hard to find the energy for this), translates, into something more instrumental, a gain for her: 'I always think that every culture, however strange you might find things sometimes, if you don't block it right away, but if you're open to it, then you can always get something out of it.' Norine is more empathetic, showing solidarity in her claim to understanding:

> In the Netherlands, you naturally get into a situation where you are socially isolated. ... when you get here, you don't speak the language, you don't know the ways, then you need some perseverance to get through it and I know that that was very hard for Irina. You're walking on the edge, like: shall I go back to my country because it's a lot more familiar there?

Thirdly, the universality of human nature is what makes people fundamentally equal for some interviewees. For instance, in a discussion of similarities between Dutch and Eastern European culture, Petra, after grappling with the question for some time, comments: 'Everyone has the same insecurities and that's the same in every country. Like what's your attitude in life and how to interact with people, that kind of thing. I think that that's the same all over the world.' The universality of the human condition makes people equal in this perspective, not position, wealth or some other marker (c.f. Lamont's finding how in the U.S., money is seen to make people equal, 2000a: 171). This is also voiced through challenging distinctions between migrants, and by categorizing those from more privileged countries along with everyone else. In Petra's words: 'But really ... umm ... people from America or from Australia, they're migrants too but I think a lot of people don't see them as migrants'. Michaela is the one example amongst the Italian interviewees who expresses a similar view, standing out from the sample as she has a Bulgarian mother and an Italian father: 'We're all the same, aren't we? Why bother making all of these distinctions, because in the end, we're really the same.' However, material presented elsewhere in this chapter illustrates how these very same people are indeed making distinctions which expose the limits of their universal inclusion, and their criteria for belonging.

## Conclusions

This chapter has analysed representations of migrant women by native women in Italy and the Netherlands. The disentangling of the sub-categories of moral and cultural boundaries has added clarity to commonplace mobilizations of inclusion and exclusion. What is striking is the extent to which moral boundaries figure in the accounts of many of the native women interviewees, and are related to (and partially explained) by cultural repertoires and resources for sense-making. Whereas employers tend to emphasize moral boundaries in their representations of migrant women, friends more often refer to cultural as well as moral boundaries as a basis for inclusion. The Dutch women voice moral boundaries less strongly than the Italians, and they emphasize cultural boundaries slightly more than moral ones. In addition, whereas the Dutch talk about migration in terms of enrichment, openness, and universality, the Italians very rarely use this vocabulary.

Some of the orientations we have heard are linked to biographies in idiosyncratic ways in which some experiences appear to be able to create bridges to the other. From the interviews, it seems that two kinds of biographical experiences make a difference: a relationship with a non-native person; or an experience of migration, even within the same country, which is lived in a way which produces insight into processes of othering. Esther has both sets of experiences and goes through life feeling: 'we are always the outsiders who do and don't belong'. Angela has moved around Italy so much that she says she feels both '100% Italian' and 'a foreigner'. Travel in the accounts of some native women can be an experience of opening to the other; in others it marks the limits of openness, in the words of Suze: 'I perhaps feel more affinity for women who come from a country that I have visited myself and that I really quite enjoyed, perhaps.' Overall, there is some evidence from the interviews, albeit ambivalent, that connections across difference might give rise to new forms of relationship across Europe.

## Notes

1. Lamont first applied these ideas in her study of upper-class men in France and the U.S., published in *Money, Morals and Manners* (1992) – and more recently in a book on working-class men in France and the U.S., entitled, *The Dignity of Working Men* (2000).
2. The Netherlands, once noted for its tolerance, is now associated with the 'failure of multiculturalism'. The 'problem' of migration is constructed through a discourse of 'cultural incompatibility' which operates to naturalize difference. Italy in contrast was thought of as a country of emigration, and political recognition and policy measures concerning immigration are recent. Nowadays migrants are frequently depicted in the public sphere as being linked to criminality (men), and domestic work or sex-work (women), and are perceived as a source of social problems.

3. Socio-economic boundaries are also salient in the interviews but less prominent, so I do not discuss them here.
4. Italy now has a very large proportion of domestic workers relative to other EU countries – regular foreign domestic workers registered at INPS, 31.12.2000 = 136,619 (Ministero dell'Interno, in Caritas 2003: 299). There has been a shift from Italian women doing domestic and care work in their own homes, assisted in some cases by hired older rural women, to the employment of foreign domestic workers as a substitute for the labour of Italian women either as wives or workers (Salih 2001: 658). This new division of labour also implies that the patriarchal household and work structures and divisions of labour go unchallenged (Phizacklea 1997). The number of migrant domestic workers is regulated by a quota fixed annually, and permits are strictly tied to employment, making domestic workers highly dependent on the goodwill of employers and susceptible to exploitation by them.
5. There is a widespread idea, echoed by several interviewees, that illegal domestic workers will be blackmailed into letting thieves into the houses they clean.
6. In an Italian interview which stands out for its empathetic tone, Giovanna, puts herself in the situation of the Moldavian women she has employed, and asks aloud in the interview, '... if my life suddenly got turned upside down like that, what would I be capable of [laughter]?' She goes on to express her admiration of people who put themselves in situations where there is so much to learn, especially a new language, and local customs.
7. In the analysis by Enrica Capussotti, she reads the account of this experience as a way to justify the demands of hard work Orieta now places upon her employees.
8. They send money to their parents and families in Bulgaria and some also save with a view to returning and setting up a business, not that things work out this way very often, she says.
9. Examples include: 'They [women from the East] all dress alike' (Roberta); 'They are well-groomed, neat – like our mothers were in the 1960s, after the war' (Giovanna). Margherita talks about her embarrassment at how the dress of some Eastern European women, which she judged inappropriate for its overdone femininity, at a Christmas party she attended.
10. Silvana is an academic at a university in Tuscany, who through a hospital stay following a miscarriage, became friendly with a Hungarian woman, Orsola, who is married to an Italian and living in the vicinity.
11. Laura, a volunteer who teaches Italian to migrants, recounts how hygiene – dirt and smell – are elements of the prejudice Italian children express towards Romanian children in their class.
12. Giovanna also talks about the importance of getting things 'really clean' for the women she employs – whom she remarks use large quantities of detergents.
13. This friendship emerged through their husbands who both work in the military. Their husbands no longer work together but their relationship is now autonomous, like 'sisters', she says.
14. Margherita contrasts Albanian and Nigerian women with Moldavian, Russian and Ukranian. The latter grouping, she says, usually have some higher education and as a result are much more independent in their choices.
15. Throughout her interview many of her stories are about autonomy; making it on one's own in the face of adversity is the plot. In contrast, women who are reluctant to challenge, who 'just adapt to the life that their husband has here' without complaint, is something that makes her very uncomfortable – especially in the case of one woman who was evidently subject to domestic violence.

16. The question of European belonging is analysed in depth by Luisa Passerini in this book. In the section, I wish briefly to point to these expressions as different forms of boundary-work.
17. Extracts of Angela's interview are presented in the second *intermezzo*.
18. Laura recounts the story of a Senegalese boy who mocks a Somalian boy for the darkness of his skin, at the same time inventing a story about having white adoptive parents, suggesting the internalization of the racist hierarchies around him.
19. There are occasional references to rudeness in the Italian interviews, e.g. Daniela comments that Albanian women are argumentative.

# References

Bourdieu, P. [translated by Richard Nice] 1977. *Outline of a Theory of Practice*, Cambridge and New York, Cambridge University Press.

Brah, A. 2000. 'The Scent of Memory: Strangers, Our Own and Others' in A. Brah and A.E. Coombes (eds.) *Hybridity and its Discontents, Politics, Science, Culture*, London and New York, Routledge.

Caritas. 2003. *Immigrazione, Dossier statistico 2003*, Rome, Anterem.

Coombes, A.E., and A. Brah 2000. 'Introduction: The Conundrum of 'Mixing'', in A. Brah and A.E. Coombes (eds.) *Hybridity and its Discontents, Politics, Science, Culture*, London and New York, Routledge.

Dal Lago, A. 1999. *Non persone. L'esclusione dei migranti in una società globale*, Feltrinelli.

Essed, P. 1991. *Understanding Everyday Racism, An Interdisciplinary Theory*, Newbury Park, Sage.

Hantzaroula, P. 2002. 'The Making of Subordination: Domestic Servants in Greece, 1920–45', Ph.D. thesis, European University Institute.

Lamont, M. 1992. *Money, Morals, and Manners, The Culture of the French and the American Upper-Middle Class*, Chicago, University of Chicago Press.

Lamont, M. 2000a. *The Dignity of Working Men, Morality and the Boundaries of Race, Class and Immigration*, Russell Sage Foundation and Harvard University Press.

Lamont, M. 2000b. 'The Rhetorics of Racism and Anti-racism in France and the United States', in M. Lamont and L. Thévenot (eds.) *Rethinking Comparative Cultural Sociology, Repertoires of Evaluation in France and the United States*, Cambridge, Cambridge University Press.

Lamont, M., and V. Molnár 2002. 'The Study of Boundaries in the Social Sciences', *Annual Review of Sociology* 28: 167–95.

Lamont, M., and L. Thévenot (eds.) 2000. *Rethinking Comparative Cultural Sociology, Repertoires of Evaluation in France and the United States*, Cambridge, Cambridge University Press.

Lutz, H. 1997. 'The Limits of European-ness: Immigrant Women in Fortress Europe', *Feminist Review* 57: 93–111.

Phizacklea, A. 1997. 'Migration and Globalisation: A Feminist Perspective', in K. Khalid and H. Lutz (eds.) *The New Migration in Europe. Social Constructions and Social Realities*, London, Macmillan.

Salih, R. 2001. 'Moroccan migrant women: transnationalism, nation-states and gender', *Journal of Ethnic and Migration Studies* 27(4): 655–71.

Skeggs, B. 1997. *Formations of Class and Gender: Becoming Respectable*, London, Sage.

ter Wal, J. 1997. 'The Reproduction of Ethnic Prejudice and Racism through Policy and News Discourse: the Italian Case (1988-92)', Ph.D. thesis, European University Institute.

ter Wal, J. 2000. 'Italy: Sicurezza e Solidarità', in R. Wodak and van T.A. Dijk (eds.) *Racism at the Top, Parliamentary Discourses on Ethnic Issues in Six European States*, Austria, DRAVA.

*Chapter 12*

# Changing Matrimonial Law in the Image of Immigration Law

*Inger Marie Conradsen and Annette Kronborg*

## Introduction

Cross-border relationships, i.e. relationships where the partners originate from different countries, lie at the core of this research. From a legal perspective cross-border relationships imply a conflict between the state's interest in controlling who crosses its border and individuals' emotional desire to form relationships. The purpose of this chapter is to shed light on these relationships from two different angles – immigration law and family law. These two perspectives belong to different legal spheres, namely public law and private law. Public law is concerned with individuals' relationships to the state, and over the past decades it has ramified into a number of sub-disciplines reflecting the specialization of contemporary society. Immigration law is one such sub-discipline with roots in constitutional and administrative law. Immigration law itself has undergone radical changes over the past decades and due to the political attention attached to immigration it is now one of the disciplines with the rapidest changing legislation. Private law is concerned with the relations between individuals; within this, family law is concerned with the relations between partners, and parents and their children. The core of family law is matrimonial law, concerned with the relationship between spouses. Matrimonial law is, in contrast to immigration law, characterized as a legal discipline with a long tradition and enduring rules. The logic as well as the underlying values in public and private law thus differ fundamentally. By analysing the regulation of cross-border relationships from both perspectives we wish to demonstrate how the focus of the legislator has shifted from relationships to the crossing of borders. The consequence of this is that matrimonial law is reduced to an appendix to immigration law.

This chapter rests on a concrete story about Danish legislation. This story is of general interest to countries that have policies which restrict and control marriage as a tool to enter the country. The chapter is thematically linked to the interviews, but deals with the issues of migration and marriage at a general level. This level is highly relevant not only to the receiving countries of the project – Italy and the Netherlands – but also more generally in an enlarged Europe where not only Hungary and Bulgaria, but also a number of other countries will be controlling the external borders of the European Union. Furthermore, it is our claim that Denmark is particularly interesting as a legal case study because of the deep-rooted belief in the very possibility of controlling the administration through detailed legislation. Danish law is considered to be radical. Indeed, the Danish age-limit of twenty-four years for family-reunion has been described as draconian[1] (Kofman, 2002). This subordination of matrimonial law to immigration law is seen in a number of European countries and is closely related to the political gains of the extreme right. As family reunification is considered *the* migration generator then it is the most obvious target for governments wishing to curtail the influx of foreigners. So even if the present story is illustrative in a European context rather than exhaustive, it is not unique. (See also the contribution of Hanne Petersen to this volume for further contextualization of the Danish story.) The paper falls in two parts dealing with cross-border relationships from the perspective of immigration law and matrimonial law respectively. The final remarks bridge the two parts.

## Part I: Immigration Law

### Framing the Problem

The conflict between the state's interest in controlling who crosses its border and individuals' emotional desire to form relationships is well reflected in the following quotation from the Danish Minister for Refugee, Immigration and Integration Affairs: 'The Danish state cannot and will not interfere with the right of Danes to marry whom they choose. But it is quite natural for the state to interfere with who should be allowed to live in Denmark. Here a number of requirements exist such as: maintenance, dwelling, aggregate ties to Denmark and a minimum age of twenty-four years'.[2] On the face of it the public–private distinction expressed by the minister is exemplary, but it is quite clear that what the minister perceives as an absence of public interference has serious consequences for couples that do not meet the requirements: the possibility of living together is effectively excluded. The conflict manifests itself at two levels. First, there is the conflict that couples face when the spouse of foreign origin is refused the right of entry or stay. Numerous examples of this appeared during the parliamentary deliberations of the present Immigration Act as well as in the public debate following its passage through parliament. Second, we are concerned with the more general conflict between state and individual, a conflict that is neither new nor specific to immigration law. It is, however, pushed to the extremes here because it touches vital interests of the state, ultimately its security and economic future, as well as those of the individual, the possibility to live with whomsoever one desires.

The definition of a state comprises two notions: territory and people, and it is a well-established principle in international law that the state has a right to decide who should be allowed access to the territory, as well as who should be included in the citizenry. In contrast to the state's wish to control in great detail who is allowed access to the territory, love is anarchic: it does not have an eye to the geographic origin of the subject of affection, and marriage is by nature (at least semi-) permanent in character, implying that the stay of the spouse on the territory will also be so. As this paper is concerned with legislation concerning immigration, i.e. state produced regulation par excellence, the juxtaposition of love and law is not only valid but also vital. However, where a less state-centred starting point of the analysis is taken, as reflected in the revived discourse about natural law and ethics for instance, the juxtaposition may play a less prominent part.[3]

Cross-border relationships and their derivative legal complications are not new phenomena. A number of international instruments introduce special procedures regarding one spouse's access to residence in the country of the other spouse as well as regarding the acquisition of nationality for that spouse. Art. 8 of the 1950 European Convention on Human Rights protects the right to family life. Even if the article does not guarantee a general right to family reunification, the state cannot under certain conditions deny family reunification, and hence the spouse's access to the territory. As regards citizenship, a number of conventions, the earliest dating back to 1957, have introduced specially privileged naturalization procedures for married women.[4] These privileged procedures for spouses regarding both entry and citizenship may well be seen as attempts to meet the tension between the interest of the state and that of the individual in cases of cross-border relationships. As such, the conventions introduce a compromise between control and anarchy.

In an EU context the privileged procedures ascribed to spouses are of a different kind as they are based on the market logic of the European Community. The starting point is that workers are given a privileged position to move freely within the Union. Even if this starting point has been modified over the years and the number of persons that are allowed to live with their spouses in a Member State different from their own has been extended, the right remains founded in the market logic[5] (Ackers 1998, Foblets 1998, Jacqueson 2003).

## The Danish Immigration Reform

The meta-story in immigration law is one of exclusion and inclusion, one of 'them' and 'us'. This story varies in time and space – and in a EUropean context space in addition varies over time. As the temporal starting point of the research is pre-enlargement, the accession countries still belonging to the 'them' category, the relevant legal analysis is one of non-EU citizen migration to Denmark. The control of the Danish state with access to the territory is construed as an authorization system that has a qualitative as well as a quantitative dimension. The qualitative dimension is reflected in control over the geographic origin of the applicant as well as in the extension in time of the stay: depending on where you come from formal access may be more or less difficult just as the length of your stay may be more or less limited. The quantitative dimension is of course concerned with the numbers of foreigners allowed access to the territory. Here family reunifications together with asylum seekers make up important exceptions to a prevailing cessation of economic migration. Due to its built-in migration-generating quality, and hence uncontrollability, family reunification takes up an exceptional position.[6]

The Danish story, as it is expressed in the recently reformed immigration law, is concerned with curtailing the influx of foreign subjects coming to Denmark, and with better integrating those that are already here. The foundation of this story was laid in the late 1990s and reached its zenith during the 2001 election campaign. The story was written into the Government Platform of the elected liberal-conservative government and has subsequently been coined in the provisions of the Danish Immigration Act.[7] The following quote from the Government Platform sums the policy up in a remarkably clear way: 'The government finds it absolutely necessary to curtail the present influx of immigrants that arrive in Denmark. This will ensure the necessary time and free the necessary resources to a much better integration of the immigrants that are already in Denmark' (Regeringsgrundlag 2001). In addition to hardening the distinction between 'them' and 'us' by making it more difficult to gain access to the country, the distinction is softened as regards those who have already gained access in the interests of improved integration. In other words what the policy aims at is less 'them' and more 'us'.

The amendments introduced by the reform tell two sub-stories: one of refugees and one of family reunification. For the purpose of the present story we shall leave the story of refugees aside and concentrate on the strengthening regarding family reunification.[8] Characteristic of this story is that it is composed of a number of different measures that, when taken together, are intended to function as a multi-layer filter with a view to excluding as many applicants as possible. The first category of changes introduced by the reform is concerned with the quantitative dimension of controlling access to the territory. The most prominent provision is the change to the age limit for the reunification of spouses from eighteen to twenty-four years, which means that both spouses must now be twenty-four years of age before reunification is possible.[9] From the *travaux préparatoires* it is clear that the quantitative aim of a decline in family reunifications plays a prominent part in this change. Attention is drawn to how the marriage pattern of migrants has remained unchanged from 1994 to 1999: 27 percent married a Dane, 23 percent married an immigrant, 3 percent married a descendant of an immigrant and the remaining 47 percent married a person living abroad who subsequently moved to Denmark.[10] Against this background of close to 50 percent of immigrants marrying a spouse from abroad, the argument is linked to the goal of minimizing the risk of arranged and forced marriages with a view to obtaining family reunification. The older a person is, it is argued, the easier it is to resist family pressure in marriage matters.

A more qualitative innovation in the reformed Act, with strong quantitative undertones however, is the strengthening of the aggregate-tie criteria of 2000. The background to introducing the criteria in 2000 was that spouse reunification in some cases took place with persons living in Denmark who were poorly integrated into Danish society, the assumption being that reunification generates poor integration. In addition to emphasizing that the ties to Denmark must exceed those to another country (it used to be sufficient that the ties to the two countries were equally strong) the strengthening of this rule consists in extending the scope of the Act to (naturalized) Danish and Nordic citizens as well as to refugees. Apart from exceptional cases, family reunification can only take place if the spouses' aggregate ties with Denmark are stronger than their aggregate ties with another country.[11] This implies that a foreigner living in Denmark wishing to marry a woman from his home country is prevented from living in Denmark with his spouse. If the foreigner is a naturalized Dane he may also be excluded from living in Denmark if his wife comes from his country of origin.

More radically still the rule implied that a Danish citizen who has lived abroad and founded a family there might be prevented from returning to Denmark with his family. However, this particular aspect of the rule was modified in December 2003 so as to allow persons who have been Danish citizens, by birth or naturalization, for twenty-eight years, to return to live in Denmark with their foreign spouse even where they do not meet the criteria.[12] From the *travaux préparatoires* it follows that the twenty-eight year limit is intended to combine the twenty-four years limit with four years of the aggregate-tie criteria with a view to extending the protection of young persons at risk of entering forced marriages. In the 'them – us' context as outlined above, the provision is concerned with more 'us', albeit very subtly such that the extension to Danish citizens, that is the 'us' category, is meant to affect the 'them' among us only.

## The Right Marriage

Another essential measure in the Danish 'fight against family reunification' is the targeting of pro-forma marriages, arranged marriages and forced marriages.[13] We have already seen how the twenty-four year age limit targets this. The starting point of this effort is, following from the *travaux préparatoires*, a realization that the previous rules were based on modern western-European norms of family-building that had been exploited for migration purposes through pro-forma and forced marriages. The 'them–us' division reappears in the perception of marriage: read in this context it is revealed that Western European family life is based on love whereas 'elsewhere' (that is situated closer to the (Muslim) far-east thanEastern Europe) love is not a prerequisite and marriage is consequently reduced to the instrumental. The provisions may be seen as safeguarding what could be termed the subjective aspect of marriage, i.e. that the spouses live together not only for legal purposes but are motivated by a personal conviction, namely love. This presupposed link between law and love is crucial.

At this point it is useful to draw the attention to a proposal of the Danish opposition in Spring 2003 to introduce a 'love-card' (*kærestevisum*).[14] The purpose of the proposal was to mend the damage done to a number of mainly, but not only, young couples that the strengthened rules had prevented from living together in Denmark. The proposal allowed couples over the age of eighteen the possibility of testing their relationship for up to one year by living together in Denmark without the pre-condition of marriage. The parliamentary debate following the proposal shows in a convincing manner law's difficulties in handling love. Not surprisingly the government rejected the proposal with reference to the possibility of circumventing the twenty-four year age limit as well as the aggregate-tie criteria of the Act. As to the 'love without marriage' aspect of the proposal, the Minister focused on the absence of control in his speech: 'But there is no control with the duration of the relationship, no control with the seriousness of the relationship or on which background it is initiated, no subsequent control of whether the relationship exists when the foreigner with the love-card arrives in Denmark, and no one can blame the person living in Denmark if the love-relationship does not last in Denmark, when the daily round sets in, not even if the relationship breaks down after a week'. More polemically, but not irrelevant, the spokeswoman on migration of the Liberal Party called for a definition of *kæreste* (sweetheart), stressing that anyone could claim this status, and she problematized the fact that the proposal only allowed for the entrance of a new *kæreste* every three years, thus implying love's uncontrollability. The proposal's absence of control was emphasized, making the tension between the state's wish to control and love's uncontrollability clear.

The Christian Democrats drew attention to the fact that the proposal would discriminate against married couples, who would still be prevented from living together. The extreme right and the extreme left were more accommodating in their responses. The spokesman of the extreme right – otherwise renowned for his ruthless view on migration but a vicar by profession and perhaps therefore less shy towards love – termed the debate 'not as essential as the possibility of Danes living abroad to return to Denmark (that had been debated earlier the same day), but serious enough'. The spokeswoman of the extreme, and Euro-sceptic, left, on the other hand, focused on the contradiction in the government's policy that encouraged globalization, including a European federal state, while at the same time restricting the rights and possibilities of ordinary people in an internationalized world. This love-card 'counter-story' that was accompanied by proposals on simplified rules for family reunification and the improvement of foreign women's rights in Denmark, is one example of how the strengthening of the law intended to affect 'them' only, turned out to affect 'us' to an unacceptable extent and. Changes then called for were in part accommodated with the amendments passed in December 2003 as described above.

To return to pro-forma marriages and forced marriages, the provisions regulate that a residence permit cannot be issued if there are definite reasons to assume that the decisive purpose of contracting the marriage or establishing cohabitation is to obtain a residence permit.[15] And that unless exceptional reasons, noticeably obligations in international law, conclusively make it appropriate, a residence permit cannot be issued if it is considered doubtful that the marriage was contracted or the cohabitation was established at both parties' desire.[16] This was further emphasized with the introduction in December 2003 of the presumption that if the marriage takes place between close relatives it is an indication of the marriage not being established at both parties' desire.[17] The *travaux préparatoires* extend this presumption to apply to situations where family reunifications have already taken place within the close family, including (second) cousins, thereby introducing an extended version of 'original sin' into immigration law. The consequence of this presumption is that the onus of proof is reversed: it is for the couple to establish that their marriage is a result of their free will, and thus based on love, rather than for the administration to prove that it is not. This mechanism serves to overcome the law's difficulties in dealing with love as illustrated by the love-card episode above.

However, rather than overcoming this difficulty the mechanism serves to circumvent it by passing it on to the couple. Relevant criteria for proof are the duration and closeness of the relationship; whether or not the couple has arranged the wedding themselves; or whether or not they are cohabitants. The proof is established through simultaneous questioning of the partners or through witnesses. Underlying both provisions is dissociation from circumventing love as well as the privileged procedure that a love-relationship implies, namely access to the country in spite of a general immigration closure. The coupling of these provisions to the general conditions of marriage is conspicuous and is further underlined by the following quote from the *travaux préparatoires*: 'With a view to counteracting the risk of abusing the provisions in the Immigration Act it is proposed to change the Matrimonial Act so that it is a condition for entering marriage in this country that each party has either Danish citizenship or legal residence following the rules in the Immigration Act.' Changing marriage law in the image of immigration law in this way makes marriage instrumental. This has a certain irony as 'we' in the course of controlling 'their' circumvention of marriage become guilty of a similar disrespect of marriage. Matrimonial law has, in other words, become an appendix to immigration law.

Another radical change introduced by the reformed Act is the extension from three to seven years of stay on the same basis before permanent residence permit can be granted.[18] The underlying rationale of this change which is combined with intensified rules of revoking residence permits, is to preserve the possibility of revoking the permit and hence to force people to leave the country for an extended period. This may have severe consequences for women who have entered Denmark on the basis of family reunification, as divorce during the seven-year period generally implies a change in the basis of the stay and hence an obligation to leave the country. A proposal to ensure and improve the rights of foreign women in Denmark during the seven-year period especially in the case of divorce from a violent husband was unsuccessful.[19] Related to this proposal, but with a focus limited to future relations, is the government's proposed introduction of a waiting period of ten years in cases where the person living in Denmark applying for family reunification has been convicted of violence against a spouse or partner.[20]

It follows from this outline of the strengthening of the regulation of family reunification that the efforts centre on marriage. There is a dual reason for this. The first is one of necessity as family reunification is *the* migration generator. Hence if the influx of foreigners is to be curtailed it is necessary to staunch the possibility of reunifying spouses. The second is that the very complexity of marriage necessitates a multifaceted approach. However, in the course of curtailing the influx, it appears that the baby, understood as the family founded through marriage, is thrown out with the bath water, as marriage in the course of curtailing immigration is made instrumental.

## Part II. Matrimonial Law

In general, in European countries there has been what might be termed the 'individualization of the family', in which the family is viewed as comprising a number of isolated individuals with separate rights and duties. In traditional matrimonial law, the legislator acknowledged the already existing marital norms in society and considered it scandalous to have a relationship outside marriage. Today marriage has lost its authority as the exclusive way of founding a family. In contemporary Danish family law, marriage could be characterized as an *offer* to *autonomous partners* of a certain *distribution of risks* concerning their property and support in case of dissolution of their marriage in the future.[21] The European attempt to harmonize family law is in its initial stages. It is too early to tell whether a harmonization will happen and to what degree, but the work takes a starting point close to the Danish development. Against this background it is unlikely that the traditional understanding of marriage will be revived in law. [22]

The reform of immigration law[23] in 2002 contained alterations to the Marriage Act.[24] These consisted of: (1) two new conditions of marriage; (2) authorization for the person performing the marriage ceremony to inform the migration authorities if he suspects that the marriage is fake; and (3) a shortening of the period of validity of the certificate securing that the marriage conditions are satisfied.[25] The first modification, the addition of two marriage conditions, will be the focus of this section with the aim of describing the changing attitude towards marriage within the reform. In a context of the diminishing authority of marriage, post-Second World War legislation has sought to abolish or alter old regulations. In the same period, there have been no new regulations concerning general matrimonial norms of conduct up until the immigration reform.

One condition – the Marriage Act section 11a – is that both spouses need to have Danish citizenship or a residence permit. Thus, people who only remain in the country because their migration case is being tried by the Danish authorities are not allowed to marry in Denmark. This group of people is considered to represent a risk because they are suspected of abusing the rights of family reunion in order to enter the country by way of a 'fake' marriage. An exemption from the requirement of citizenship or residence permit may be granted by the marriage authorities if a marriage does not represent an abuse of the rights of family reunion but is considered to reflect an existing personal relationship between the partners. Relevant criteria for a permission to marry (according to section 11a) are the length of the period of time the applicant has already stayed in Denmark and whether or not the couple is expecting a child.[26] The second condition (the Marriage Act section 11b) is, that the spouses have to confirm that they are informed about the conditions of family reunion. The purpose of this condition is to make them aware that even though they marry they are not automatically entitled to live together in Denmark.

## *The Changing Legal Perception of Marriage and Family*

The new marriage conditions have purposes other than supporting and shaping the institution of marriage. The incorporation of these conditions in spite of their divergent character from family law was not seen as a problem in the legislative process. In parliament no concerns were expressed about the new legislation's possible violation of the values embedded in family law. This lack of critique is in line with the contemporary view of marriage. As a societal institution it has no value; spouses must create value for themselves. Indeed, the development of family law has meant that marriage is reduced to a matter between the spouses. At the same time, the definition of good family life has shifted from marriage as a formal institution to the welfare of the specific spouses.

These new conditions demonstrate a social and legal shift in the understanding of marriage. In 'traditional' law cohabitation was not considered acceptable and was even penalized. This view has now – if you are not a Danish citizen or do not have residence permit – been turned upside down. Today it is an advantage to demonstrate having 'practised' family life through cohabitation, before being allowed to marry and thereby enjoy the legal rights associated with the marital union. Cohabitation was, until the reform, linked to the agenda of emancipation from marriage through equality between spouses and cohabitants. The increased legal protection of cohabitants was a victory in the battle of diminishing the authority of marriage. Today, on the contrary, cohabitation is itself a marriage condition for some. Thus, immigration law has become a radical legal field in terms of the mutual relations of family and marriage within family law where lived family life overrules formal marriage arrangements.[27]

This radical position may be explained by the nature of immigration law. This legal field concerns people from outside the Danish society. These people are not legally comparable to people from inside the Danish society. Today distinctions on the basis of people's legal relationship to the state are considered very important by the new legislation. From a traditional point of view, getting married was considered good if the partners had the intention of founding a family, regardless of their legal position in immigration law. It was also considered an important social institution invested with legal authority. Within this perspective, the provision excluding some foreign or mixed couples from marrying in Denmark may be criticized. From an administrative point of view it is possible to investigate whether or not partners are already in a relationship as introduced in section 11a. However, it is not possible, in any meaningful manner, to carry out an administrative investigation of whether or not the partners have the right intentions. Thus, today's screening of cohabitants is too far-reaching compared to the traditional definition, where the right intention was sufficient as the relevant criterion. At the same time, from a modern point of view where family life is valued over formal marriage arrangements, it is more difficult to criticize the new requirements.

As described above, marriage has a different legal status in different European countries. An interpretation of its European status could be done on the basis of EHC Art. 12 concerning the right to marry, which states: 'Men and women of marriageable age have the right to marry and to found a family, according to the national laws governing the exercise of this right'. The activities of the European Court of Human Rights concerning marriage have mostly been related to Art. 8 about the right to family life, while the interpretation of Art. 12 has been of less interest (see van Dijk and van Hoof 1998). According to the *travaux préparatories* of the Danish immigration reform, the protection of human rights in Art. 12 is not expected to be better than in Art. 8. This is in line with the dissolution of the authority of marriage and the increasing importance of factual cohabitation and family life in its place. A critique of the new marriage conditions is that they presuppose a revitalization of traditional marriage.

### *Family Law as an Instrument of Immigration Law*

The new marriage conditions are different from those introduced with the Marriage Act of 1922. The influence of immigration law on the new conditions is easy to trace from their wording, which contains several references to the Immigration Act. Thus, the Marriage Act now appears as an instrument of a field of interest other than that of family law. This is not a new phenomenon. In the 1920s – intensified in the 1930s – marriage conditions served as an instrument of eugenics; and in the same period the Marriage Act served as an instrument of social policy, as men receiving social security were forbidden to marry. Nevertheless, these earlier conditions all related to the suitability of the partners to live married life and thus the conditions contributed to shape the institution of marriage.

The first mentioned new condition defines a group of people who is suspected of abusing the possibility of entering the country through family reunification, and the new rule prohibits them from marrying in Denmark. This sort of instrumentalization of the Marriage Act is new. The recent instrumentalization of the Marriage Act was repeated with the alteration of the Act following the immigration reform. In a Danish reform child abduction was introduced as a reason for divorce, but this reason was not related to marital norms. If that were the case, child abduction should be understood as a serious violation of marital norms. However, child abduction is now considered a reason for divorce as a reaction to the administrative experience of the difficulty in obtaining assistance from foreign authorities to return an abducted child if the abandoned parent is still married to the child-abductor. The instrumentalization of the Marriage Act means that there is no direct connection between the logic of the provisions and the corresponding aspects of society which the provisions are systematized to concern – in this case marriage. In short, the new provisions in the Marriage Act are not about marriage; they are about controlling national borders.

In the period of traditional matrimonial law the legislation aimed at constituting social life as such. This was also a period closer to natural law. The legislative systematization was in accordance with social practices. Today's legislation has new and different inclinations. The Danish reforms appear to seek the resolution of concrete problems with no ambitions of imposing general norms about marriage, as was the case earlier. The purpose of the new marriage conditions is to optimize their effect as a problem-solver – optimizing the control of the national borders. From a technical point of view, the conditions could be described as follow: the first condition about citizenship or residence permits views the couple as objects in the law; and the second about conditions for family reunion views them as subjects. The first condition prohibits certain people from marrying. The protection of marriage is weakened considerably. Marriage is conditioned on an admission – and thereby an administrative process. Marriage thus depends on a review of the specific couple's situation. The official authorities may interpret the couple's story in the light of strong national interests in limiting the numbers of foreigners in Denmark as long as the couple's human rights to family life are not violated. The second condition provides the basis for the authorities' information-giving role in relation to the couple informing them that marrying may not serve their interests, since marriage may not qualify them to stay in Denmark if their marriage should be considered as a fake. Thus, this condition may limit the numbers of marriage applications.

## Final Remarks

The analysis of the Danish immigration reform from the dual perspectives of immigration law and family law has exposed legislation aiming at a more efficient screening of who is allowed to cross the border, the purpose of this being to curtail the influx of immigrants. The means used to reach this goal is through an elaboration of immigration law in which the understanding of marriage plays an important part. Marriage is no longer seen as the formal frame of family life but, through a qualification of its meaning, it has been differentiated into sub-categories such as 'pro-forma marriage', 'forced marriage' and 'love marriage' putting the legal protection of women and love in a new context. This implies a shift from family law to immigration law which implies an instrumentalisation of matrimonial law. This has as a significant consequence that 'love' as opposed to 'marriage' has become the object of legal regulation. The Danish examples with the proposed introduction of a love-card as well as the recent resort to the technical reversal of the onus of proof in suspected cases of forced marriages convincingly demonstrate this. However, the examples also show the sheer difficulty in legally regulating love. Legal regulation, if it is to be successful, must be based on criteria that the immigration authorities are able to handle.

In a EUropean context, love is conspicuous by its absence in the proposed family reunification directive. It is clear from the preamble of the proposal that family life is protected, not because of its subjective, emotional basis, but because of its objective ability to create socio-cultural stability and to promote economic and social cohesion. Family reunification is, in other words, made an appendix to the functioning of the market. In this respect the European story echoes the Danish one, as the family is reduced to being an instrument in what is perceived as a greater cause. Concerning family-reunion with a partner, EU countries until now have agreed on marriage as the only relevant criterion. This is an agreement of doubtful content since marriage has lost its traditional meaning as known in family law. Indeed, the interviews of this research reflect that the law is not at the forefront of the decision-making of cross-border couples, neither as a potential obstacle nor, and this should be of interest to the legislator at various levels, as a strategic instrument.

## Notes

1. Letter to the Editor, *Berlingske Tidende,* 13 September 2002.
2. See for different perceptions of the relationship between love and law, Raes (1998) and Petersen (1998).
3. 1957 UN Convention on the Nationality of Married Women; 1979 UN Convention on Elimination of all Forms of Discrimination against Women; Council of Europe Resolution (77) 12 on the Nationality of Spouses of Different Nationality; 1997 Council of Europe Convention on Nationality.
4. van Krieken (2001) contends that in Europe family reunification and family formation is and will continue to be the one single main factor for immigration. He 'guesstimates' that the multiplier involved, i.e. the factor by which each residence permit in the Union results in an additional influx, is 2.5 meaning that 120 000 foreigners allowed to stay should be read as 300 000.
5. *Lov nr. 365 af 6. juni 2002 om ændring af udlændingeloven.* See now *Lovbekendtgørelse nr. 945 af 1. September 2006 af udlændingeloven,* as amended. An English version of the Act is available on www.inm.dk.
6. As regards refugees, see Kjær (2003).
7. Section 9 (1).
8. The respective figures in 1994 were 28 percent, 22 percent, 2 percent and 48 percent.
9. Section 9 (7).
10. Lov nr. 1204 af 27. december 2003 om ændring af udlændingeloven. Section 9 (7).
11. Section 9 (8), (9).
12. *Beslutningsforslag B 127 om indførelse af et kærestevisum af 27. marts 2003.* See also Conradsen (2003).
13. Section 9(9).
14. Section 9(8).
15. *Lov nr. 1204 om ændring af udlændingeloven af 27. december 2003.*
16. Section 11 (3).

17. *Beslutningsforslag B 126 af 27. marts 2003 om indsats til sikring og forbedring af udenlandske kvinders rettigheder.* The proposal was reintroduced as B 99, 19 December 2003.
18. *Udkast til lov om ændring af udlændingeloven, Ministeriet for flygtninge, indvandrere og integration,* 23 January 2003.
19. *Udkast til lov om ægteskabs indgaaelse og opløsning med tilhørende bemærkninger udarbejdet af den ved kgl. resolutioner af 25. juli 1910 og 19. juni 1912 nedsatte kommission, København 1913* (Kronborg, 2005).
20. The European project of harmonization is presented by the Commission on European Family Law (CEFL) on the following website: www.law.uu.nl/priv/cefl.
21. *Lovforslag nr. 152 til lov om ændring af udlændingeloven og ægteskabsloven med flere love.*
22. *Marriage Act (Lov nr. 276 af 30. juni 1922 om ægteskabets indgåelse og opløsning).*
23. Marriage Act section 11 a, 11 b, 19, 22 a.
24. FTA 2001–02, 2. saml., p. 4050-4051.
25. In the legal field of social security you will find a similar radical position of immigration law, see Olsen and Svendsen (2003).
26. FTA 2001–02, 2. saml., s. 3984.
27. COM (2002) 225 final. The scope of the proposal is family reunification of third-country nationals residing lawfully in the territory of a member state.

# References

Ackers, L. 1998. *Shifting Spaces. Women, Citizenship and Migration within the European Union,* Bristol, Policy Press.

Conradsen, I.M. 2003. 'Kærlighed og konventioner. Historien om et bebudet kærestevisum', in S. Jørgensen, H. Krunke, M. Hartlev and K. Ketscher (eds.) *Nye retlige design,* Copenhagen, Jurist- og Økonomforbundets Forlag (Love and Conventions. The Story of a Love-card Fporetold in *New Legal Designs*).

Foblets, M.-C. 1998. 'Family Reunification: Who Pays for Love in Europe?' in H. Petersen (ed.) *Love and Law in Europe,* Aldershot, Dartmouth.

Jacqueson, C. 2003. *The European Court of Justice's Strategy for European Community Integration,* Unpublished thesis, University of Copenhagen.

Kjær, K.U. 2003. 'Afskaffelse af de facto-begrebet – fup eller fakta?' *Juristen* 1: 3–14.

Kofman, E. 2002. 'Family-related Migration, a Critical Review of European Studies', *Journal of Ethnic and Migration Studies* 30(2): 243–62.

Kronborg, A. 2005. 'Ægteskabsbetingelser', *Juristen* 3: 88–95.

Olsen, C.B. and I.L. Svendsen 2003. 'Ændringer på det sociale forsørgelsesområde', CASA and *Socialpolitisk Forening's Annual Report.*

Petersen, H. 1998. 'The Language of Emotions in the Language of Law', in H. Petersen (ed.) *Love and Law in Europe,* Aldershot, Dartmouth.

Raes, K. 1998. 'On Love and Other Injustices. Love and law as Improbable Communications', in H. Petersen (ed.) *Love and Law in Europe*, Aldershot, Dartmouth.

van Dijk, P. and G.J.H. van Hoof 1998. *Theory and Practice of the European Convention of Human Rights*, Amsterdam, Kluwer Law International.

Regeringsgrundlag – Vækst, Velfærd, Fornyelse, VK Regeringen, 26. November 2001.

van Krieken, P. (ed.) 2001. *The Migration Aquis Handbook. The Foundation for a Common European Migration Policy*, The Hague, T.M.C. Asser Press.

*Intermezzo*

# In Transit: Space, People, Identities

*Andrea Pető*

*Edith Bruck was born in Hungary in 1932 in Tiszakarád to a very poor orthodox Jewish family. Her father was a butcher and a peddler; her mother was a housewife who gave birth to six daughters and two sons. Edith Bruck's formal education consisted of seven classes of elementary school. In 1944 she and her family, together with other Jews from the village, were deported to Auschwitz from where she was taken to Bergen Belsen. She later left for Czechoslovakia in 1945, and went to Israel in 1948. In 1954 she moved to Rome where she still lives today. Upon her arrival in Italy she worked in different professions (waiter, receptionist) before her first novel,* Who loves you that much, *was published in 1959 in Italian.[1] That brought her recognition and she has since become an acknowledged author of several books (translated also into several languages), and a film-maker. She has had three husbands: the first a Hungarian Jew whom she married in Czechoslovakia; the second a Hungarian Jew whom she married in Israel; and her present husband, an Italian whom she married in Italy. The interview took place in her apartment, which is filled with books, manuscripts, plants and a typewriter, in Rome on 4 January 2002.*

How did I get to Italy? Completely by accident, because I was wandering from one country to another after the war. I fled from Hungary over to Czechoslovakia, [along the route] those [returning Hungarian Jews] were unwelcome. There was no way of leaving Hungary officially. No way right up until 1989. [*Laughs*] Maybe, maybe I could emigrate to Israel, there may have been some organizations in Hungary, because my sister, for instance, left for Israel at once. Maybe this way, I don't know, maybe. But I didn't want to go there either. After a camp I didn't want to go to an institute. I will not enter a cinema even today where there are 200 people. I choose a seat where I can breathe, I hate crowds, I have a phobia. Same in the orphanage after the war, you know where I should have gone since I was underage. Living together with a lot of other people is very difficult. I lived in Czechoslovakia for two years. I don't know how to explain, where I was for almost a year, then I wandered off to Israel.

I first got married when I was 17 years old in Czechoslovakia and he was a Jew. The marriage lasted four years. That was a fictitious marriage and we went to Germany. It was a kind of transit for migrants. He said I was a peasant and abused me. I never in my life loved my first husband, I almost loathed him. I do not think very highly of Hungarian men. Not because he behaved like that, but because I've been to Hungary a million times since and have seen Hungarian men and husbands. They hurt and offend women very easily. They tell stories and show off and lie. I wouldn't say that, based on my experience, I would like to have a Hungarian husband. All the marital relations that we had were when we went to bed in the evening, I ran along the whole flat and he ran after me [*she laughs all the while*], and as I remember he set my clothes on fire by a so-called accident. He poured petrol over me and set it aflame. We got divorced in Israel and he got the room we had together. He nailed the door up so I couldn't get in.

[…] I think that Israel is a nervous country. A nervous situation, nervous people and a civilization quite alien to me. It is somehow distant from me. In a sense it's close, but distant at the same time. I understand the language, I perceive all the nuances, I understand where they come from, I know they're Jewish like me, and I'd like them to know that I'm Jewish like them, but there it doesn't count. Here it counts, maybe; there it doesn't. There were Jews before, too. My nephew says to me: I am not a Jew. I am not a Jew, I am Israeli. There's great difference between a diaspora Jew, for whom it matters that he's Jewish, and an Israeli who doesn't feel like a Jew but an Israeli. And he doesn't experience his Jewishness the way you do. Doesn't approach religion the way you do. Does not live in an environment where you're used to being a minority. You are a majority there. He doesn't have the feeling you may have had. So, how do you say, sticks up [out].[2]

Then I fell in love with my second husband. Then I said to myself, thanks, and asked myself but why? Because he had an evil spirit, that was the trouble with him. An evil spirit and I wanted this evil for myself. It passed fairly soon, quite fast, he behaved badly. There was this hot soup. In wintertime. Really hot soup. I said to him wait a little. And he poured it all over me. Right over me. Still he became a [violent] man in Israel. He tore up everything from my stockings to my dresses, and after two days he promised he wouldn't hurt me, then he came along and said honey, I brought you some pants. But something died inside me suddenly, you know? No, maybe

I didn't love him anymore or wasn't in love with him, I said no, and then he left and it was over. Later he came after me and begged me to forgive him. He didn't treat me carefully at all because I had survived Auschwitz, no, we can't say that, that I had spiritually really survived [...] I was very happy that I could make ends meet.

[In Israel] I had no money. I worked as a waitress and also worked in a military hospital, cleaning. I used to do the washing up, in these booths where they sold ice-cream and I ate what the patients left. If I could have saved a little, I would have lived a little better. Then I wouldn't have left, but I couldn't stand it any more. Maybe those who had more strength, a stronger will. [...] So I left in the end, through Greece, Switzerland, I arrived here in Italy and said I would move on to Argentina where a sister of mine lives, it was possible to go as a maid, someone was to send some paper to prove they would take me, [*laughs*], but nobody sent a thing, so I stayed.

I didn't speak any languages. I knew a little English, I knew a little Hebrew, but they didn't care about that in Italy [*laughs*] [*Really?*] and French but very poorly. I spoke each language very poorly. That is I stuttered in each foreign language, let's say I spoke only Hungarian correctly. Correctly, as much as I can, because I had left home a long time ago. I didn't get this letter of invitation, so I stayed in Italy; [it was] in 1954, in Rome, I arrived with an Israeli passport.

Yes, my third husband is Italian. Yes. The citizenship I got only after the wedding. We had lived together for eight years before we got married, and until then I had lived here with a residence permit for eight years, and after eight years, after we had got married, I got Italian citizenship then. Maybe he needed me. He deserved it, I didn't deserve it, I don't know, I think it was my problem. He was everything to me, he was my world, my father, my mother, my family, my relatives, my brothers, my sisters, he meant everything to me. Everything, I felt this absolutely overwhelming love which I can't get rid of [*laughs*], though I tried, but cannot. I love him, but it was difficult to try [*giggles*] to do something else.

*What has been the role of religion in your life?* My mother spoke only to God, not with us. She spoke to him as I speak with you now. My God I hope, please God, give me this, she looked up to the sky and always spoke to God. She spoke more to God than to her own child, to God. God didn't listen to her like he didn't listen to anyone. Then I said to Mum, why speak to God? "Get out!" She thought I was jealous of God. There was such a great social ... not class, class differences were, too, very great, because the poor could only marry the poor, and the rich could marry the rich, not like today when a prince marries a little actress or a ballerina, you know? Or a chorus girl. Then it was impossible for someone to court a poor girl who had no dowry. We lived in such an anti-Semitic atmosphere then.

At home I didn't want to be religious. Against religion, well not religion, not quite against religion, because I loved feasts, I loved Passover, they fasted for half a day, only half a day, but I loved all kinds of feasts, because there was a little more food, some cakes, maybe a re-done, new skirt or a real new skirt with straps and then I was so proud. A new pair of boots. Feasts always brought something. Even if it was just some ten nuts for everyone, for us children, these feasts brought us something really beautiful, I think. The joy of the day and this ritual, something, yes, that's it, my mother always thought by the Autumn feasts, by Spring, by Yom Kipur, at Chanuka, by them, in the past. By feasts, like peasants did with the moon and sunshine, what the weather will be like, my mother counted seasons by feasts. My mother was deeply religious. Her hair wasn't cut short but she wore a kerchief. And my father was a great liberal against religion, although he had grown up in a very religious family. He was quite normal, modern, let's say reformed. My husband is not christened, he is agnostic, a non-believer, the family doesn't care for that. He is not a believer, he says it's enough that I am one. […] Why does he say I am a believer? Because when I was very sad about something I said to him I wanted to pray and set out to look for my prayer-book. I stood there in front of the prayer-book, it's around here somewhere, it has a red cover, I know. If someone believes truly in any religion, I respect that, not if they do so fanatically, but deeply. But for you to say you believe, you have to behave as someone who believes. If someone says he believes, like everybody does, but his life doesn't reflect this belief, any belief, he doesn't even deserve it, I think. It doesn't have any depth. It is easy to say I believe. It is hard to believe and be just with mankind, with people and not to hate the others but to respect them, not to think that we're better than the others. I think this is religion. This is love. And not going out pounding your chest and praying and then cheating on someone, shooting someone and praying again. I don't think you can match war with religion, murder with religion. No, no, I don't know, I think the problem is that people do not believe in anything. They don't love and don't believe.

*Is migration more difficult for a single women?* It is more difficult, mainly because if the woman is beautiful the only thing men in Italy want is to go to bed with them. A foreign girl in Italy was absolutely considered a prostitute. A foreign girl, in 1954, 1955 and in 1956, 'til almost the 1970s, a foreign girl could be had, was free, because there was great hypocrisy and a self-righteous backwardness. Italian girls were brought up to do everything but to stay a virgin, whereas Hungarian women, or this Dutch girl[3] for example was a million times freer, and me, too. Because she lived at that time like we do here now. That is, she had this Italian boyfriend and she took him with her to the Netherlands. She took him home and he slept there, at their place. I was really surprised at this, you see, my upbringing and hers, that was two separate worlds. There were 200 years between the way I grew up in a little village with my parents and the way she grew up in Amsterdam with her bourgeois parents. So, it depends where you come from, what upbringing you've had, what they've put into your head, what they've put into your soul, what they've put into your blood, you know? You see, I felt that though she was the same age as me, I was full of complexes, I felt mistaken, exposed, a nothing, and she was a free, happy person. I was an old maid [*giggles*], inhibited, full of complexes, everything. And I remained one. And she a free, happy spirit who was flying for herself. Men with foreign girls: no matter where she came from, she could be had. Maybe she was longing for affection, maybe she was in need of dinner because she had no money, that's why she went to have dinner with someone. After that it was either over or the affair went on, all the same, everyone was after foreign girls.

At that time everyone accosted me in the street, everyone had compliments, everyone said dirty words and also offered food and compliments. It was easy to recognize me as a foreign girl because we acted differently. We didn't speak Italian for a start. They accosted us and saw we were foreigners from our clothes, from our behaviour. You could see from a mile's distance that we were foreigners. Now it's not so easy, because almost fifty years have passed, you see fashion and hairstyles are now homogenized. You can't tell the difference between a German girl and a Hungarian girl or between a Dutch girl and an Italian girl. Everyone's blond now [*laughs*]. At that time it was not like that. The world was very grey. You could still very much smell the war. You could feel it, you could see who were the haves and who were the have-nots, because everyone wore clothes from before the war, and coats and bags as well. It was a very small section of society who had [things]. You could see from the coats they were wearing that they were well off. And you could also see on the others that they had nothing. Immigrants, that's what was written on them. You could differentiate one person from the other, whereas today you can't differentiate one girl from another. Here you have the same hairstyle or the way they dress, one exactly like the other, you see, the world was not like this at that time when you were not even born [*laughs*]. There were such big differences. [...]

*What's the significance of you being a woman?* It would have been much easier to be a man. Because for a woman, if she is not really horrible or ugly, someone to whom nobody gives a look, say, if she's decent or beautiful, it is very difficult to defend herself. Defend herself, because it is only looks that count. She's not even considered a person, just a piece of meat. So just to make someone understand that you are a human being, not a woman, not a piece of meat, is a great effort. I mean, it was. It is easier now, because in the 1970s we made such scenes here, we were demonstrating for years, we had a theatre, a feminist theatre for years with my friends, with some eight friends. It is very difficult to make people understand that you are first and foremost a human being. And that you have a head you think with. Especially if you have a beautiful body. Then it's even more difficult, more difficult to get through this cover [*claps her hands*]. Very difficult. I think I took double pains to get where I wanted to. Or treble, yes treble or double pains at least. In my writing I don't have the feeling of discrimination: that because you're a woman, you don't get published. I never had any problems, only outside, in society. There was never anything wrong with publishers, only with men, with employers, and it was generally so with everyone, not just me. Believe me, I used to go to these peripheral districts in this civilized society, to talk to women, yes I used to go to all kinds of suburbs to have a look at how women lived, and they talked about how they were beaten and slapped by their husbands, and so we did a lot of social work for protecting women, for raising their consciousness about what their rights were and what they were entitled to do and that they did not have to let men, or their employers and husband do what they wanted.

We used to be active in raising such consciousness in women [in the Italian feminist movement], you see. There was nothing at all beforehand, they got their first training and right after that this feminist struggle started, and then slowly, slowly they got more and more conscious. It was a very long and very difficult job in the 1970s. After the American wave there then came the Italian wave of, let's say it was feminism. That was mostly why I left. I left the group because one of the women who were there, there were only women, I lived with them only, so she said she didn't believe in concentration camps. The other abused me as a Jew, another feminist made me come up eight steps and said I wouldn't set my foot in here any more. Because it was such a wild period of feminism that when a man came in they beat him up, and yelled, and wore men's hats, which is something I hate. I hate all extremist things. Moderate things – everything's fine that is civil and moderate. Everything that goes beyond the *equilibrio*, the balance, is not fine with me.

But I wasn't active, militant. Yet, it enriched me a lot, it was very important. I felt that what we did involved a lot of effort [...] Then I carried on doing the same things alone, because I always did the same, what I put into my work, [...] is women's problems, no, I didn't make feminist films but I created female figures. Or else I didn't make any difference, I never do, but there is a difference between a blind man and a blind woman, too. Because a man has rights. Men told stories about how they made love, about what great lovers they were. There was discrimination, too, much bigger than in a normal family. So, girls suffered much more from this discrimination than men. Men will be men. Men will be men even if blind. A girl is just a blind creature. Leaders were all men; it was very rare for a woman to be a leader in the blind people's association. The director and vice director were all men. It was difficult to find a girl among them. Girls were much more exciting, much more intelligent, much more sensitive, well, I think in general – I generalize, I know – I think women are stronger than men, more exciting and more interesting along with their mistakes, together with our mistakes. It is also a problem in work: a woman is supposed to do much more in her job than a man to demonstrate [that she is capable]. The problem is, for instance, that I had a woman boss, where I worked and she was much worse than a man. She was much stricter, much more disgusting and wanted to show that she's much better than a man. So, there was this period in the 1970s and before, if a woman was a leader, she was much meaner than a man.

Not to speak of the camps, where women behaved much worse than men. A woman was much more rotten and much nastier to another woman than any SS. In my view it comes from the fact that she wants to show him that she can exceed him in evil. For instance, nobody has ever written about it, well I have, for a conference, that women were stronger than men in the camps. More of them survived, they took better care of themselves, they deloused themselves more carefully and organized their lives better. I mean, men were a million times weaker and many more of them died and sooner. Because they were used to being served and being sucked up to. And what became of them? Helpless, disabled good-for-nothings. If male culture had existed, men would have endured much better what awaited them in the camps. I think there is still male culture, there is, but this way women force themselves that they are better, they are worth more, everyone says that now, you know? But to say and to see what percentage of them there are in Parliament, how many men and how many women, then you see it is still a male, male culture. There are a few more women, but it is still a long way from having minimal equality.

*You said you settled yourself in Italy?* Not through work, but mainly through my husband. This friend of mine, who found this job, then I got to know a lot of journalists, because her husband is a journalist, I got to know my husband at a conference. I went there, I didn't know her husband, I had known the girl before. I had two friends in the intelligentsia, and they were invited to China. When they returned we organized a conference in the whole of Italy. Through my husband, together with my husband, then everybody. So, there was not an intellectual or a writer in Italy whom I didn't know at that time. I learnt Italian among them, we lived among them, we had dinner among them, we were among them, we lived with them, in that, I believe, I was very privileged that I didn't have to, I could have ended up in a bank – how do you say that? As a cashier? You see, it was not my choice, it happened by accident. At least I was lucky, it was not my choice. I said I wanted to get to know these, I want to live with these. I saw my husband, I fell in love. Indeed, it could have turned out much worse. It was a virtue. But it was not my virtue. No, no.

[…] Feeling at home … I don't know what that means. This flat is my country. This flat is my home, but the question is not whether it is Italy or Hungary or Israel or America, it is my own, I feel that it is very difficult to live in the world as such, in the world in general. I feel at home when I go abroad from Italy and when the aeroplane finally lands, then I feel I am an Italian from Rome. Rome is mine. The Earth is mine and then I am happy and feel at home. I feel, maybe this is where my home is. I can hardly believe it when I come home. So this is home to me. Not home in a nationalistic kind of sense, maybe only because there is this plant and my desk, here a flower pot , there another one, over there [*points to a photo*] is my mother-in-law, my parents in the bedroom, so, for me, this is my homeland. I don't know in which sense, I cannot explain. I believe my identity is almost a house number, it exists through objects somehow. I feel strange everywhere. Strange and stranger. I feel at home only here. I love the little things if we speak about them, or if we can say happiness means anything. Let's say, pleasure. But I appreciate little things. I love children. I adore children. I'm happy when they hug me, I love cooking, I cook every day, I love cooking. I'm not surprised, but it still feels good if someone offers me a seat in the bus. I'm surprised to find that there are honest people. Things that should be normal every day, just these things. That you see this is human. It is worth living, hoping. That's why we've survived. We have survived because a German soldier left a little jam in the jar. That's why.

*Did you ever feel that you were lucky?* I think my life is well behind me, so I believe it turned out quite well for me. Let's say I survived that [Auschwitz] as well, I don't know if it's luck, I don't know yet. I survived because I was very poor. Added to that was the original hardness, the hardness of life that saved me in the camp. Let's say, we peasant Jews, or we can say proletarian Jews, endured the unendurable more easily than the lawyer's daughter. If you have plenty, that makes you weak. Scarcity, that makes you strong. Like young people today. So I'm stronger than young people. I think that thanks to my strong, poor roots I survived Auschwitz and the rest.

## Notes

1. *Who Loves You That Much* (Italian 1959, Hungarian 1964, German 1999, English 2001), *Transit* (Italian, 1978, Hungarian 1988*)*, *Nuda Proprietà*, (Italian 1993, Hungarian 1995), *Lettera alla Madre* (Italian, 1988), *L'attrice* (Italian 1995), *Il silenzio degli amanti* (Italian 1997).
2. Hungarian idom which signifies difference.
3. The Dutch girl is Edith Bruck's friend – they lived together in Rome when she arrived from Israel.

*Conclusions*

# Gender, Subjectivity, Europe: A Constellation for the Future

*Luisa Passerini*

### Acts of Intersubjectivity

The research we have presented in this book is based on the conviction that new ways of European subjectivity are made possible by the movements of migrant people and by their connections with native ones, terms that we have been trying to problematize. In a gendered perspective, the research has focused on women as subjects of such relationships. Since these forms of intersubjective relations are often ambivalent, I have engaged in an effort to make explicit what can be promising for the future of Europe in the exchanges between migrants and natives, without ignoring their negative or dark sides, that include continuing counterpositions between 'us' and 'them' and xenophobia at various degrees. In a consciously utopian perspective,[1] I will therefore try to find in our results the anticipations of some of the paths that lead to the future, especially those transformative pathways through which intersubjectivity and interconnectivity are growing.[2] At the same time, it would be naïve and misleading to expect to discover new forms of subjectivity ready to be projected into the future; any subjective formation we find today is encrusted with traces of 'old' subjectivity. I will try to see the old in tension with the new forms of identification and belonging, based not on opposition, but on openness, mutual collaboration and even attraction.

This research starts from an act of direct intersubjectivity, that generated other indirect such acts. The former consisted in the decision to interview women who have been and are subjects, in the double sense of being subjected to economic, legal and cultural processes,[3] for instance the various forms of migration from the East to the West of Europe, and of becoming fully conscious agents of such processes. We took this decision as researchers concerned with both women's studies and the analysis of new forms of Europeanness, being ourselves from different parts of Europe. This first intersubjective act, that presupposed our interest for and involvement in the relationships between women from the various parts of this continent, has been incorporated in the interviews, that themselves are the result of intersubjective relationships. Subsequently, indirect forms of intersubjectivity have been established through discourse: by interviewing not only women from Central and Eastern Europe, but also women from Western Europe, we have artificially reproduced encounters that did not take place empirically between those very individuals, but that are real on cultural grounds. In fact, the women who were called to represent the 'natives' most of the time never met the actual ones that represent the 'migrants', but the cultural encounter between women similar to them takes place every day in Europe. All this represents both the strength and the limitation of research, its separatedness, implying that it can never be conflated with daily experience.

Indeed, one of the aspects that we consider most important in this research is the insistence on the inter-subjective relationships between women from the four countries under consideration, especially between those who are labelled as 'migrant' and those who are called 'native', the former having moved in a literal sense and the latter having stayed resident in Italy and the Netherlands but being involved in the vast processes of cultural mobility that have been taking place through Europe recently. Intersubjectivity within a European horizon connects – at the scientific and analytical level – the women that have narrated their experiences and ourselves, who have undertaken this research with the aim of recognizing, among other things, new forms of European women's subjectivity.

These new forms must be seen against the background of the eroded boundary between subject and object.[5] While accepting the sense of this erosion, the reason for maintaining the analytical distinction between subject and object is that it allows a comprehension of individuality in progress, as a continuous creation of subjectivity from objectivity. This can mean the individuation of a person in contact with – sometimes against – a collective, or the transformation of obstacles into a new way of understanding the world and oneself. In both cases, objectivity is understood – on the lines of thought inaugurated by Siegfried Kracauer and Thomas Kuhn – as a form of intersubjectivity, from which – and in relationship with it – individuation and subjectivation take place. The areas designated as pertaining to 'subject' and 'object' are in this perspective osmotically connected along a continuum in which the position in one of the two fields can be transmuted into one in the other.

These are suggestions elaborated in contact with the narrations by the women that have been interviewed in the course of our research. But now, before listening more attentively to the voices from the present, we want to turn to yet another form of intersubjectivity, with women of the past who in various ways recognized themselves as Europeans.

## 'Mothers of Europe'

This title has two roots: the polemics against the exclusive insistence on the 'fathers of Europe' (i.e. the men who envisaged a united Europe in the past and/or undertook the creation of the European Community after the Second World War), and a more general sense of vindication, that surfaces even in our interviews. After Poly, the Bulgarian woman who replies when asked, *'And do you feel European?'* 'I do feel, yes, that I am a female ancestor of the first European civilization', we ask ourselves who our female ancestors are. There is still much research to be done on the many women who prefigured a united Europe, fighting as feminists and pacifists since the 1860s.[6] At the same time, we do not want to merely accept any united Europe and not even the present united Europe as it stands, rather to criticize and influence on cultural grounds the process of European construction. Thus the examples of women who added their own cultural dimension to a self-understanding as European can be particularly precious to us.

The historical dimension gives more meaning to the concept of constellation,[7] that is central to my approach here, i.e. to the cluster of three concepts: gender, subjectivity and Europe. I have adopted the term 'constellation' because I believe that this triangular connection is not only intellectual, between concepts and ideas, but also largely psychological and emotional, and therefore partially unconscious or semiconscious, a characteristic that is coherent with the implicit nature of Europeanness. The constellation is characterized by circularity, so that its three elements have to be considered in their unity and connection, although at times one of the three can act as a motor, as today it could well be the case for gender. The idea of constellation translates the simple sentence 'being a woman/a man in Europe' and its designation of a state of change; thus, the constellation was always in existence, but now it is in rapid motion – although not always immediately visible. The meaning of 'woman' is changing, the meaning of 'Europe' is changing, and the concept of 'being' or becoming a subject is also changing. There is a movement of each of these three terms, but there is also a concomitant change altogether, whereby the terms move as a configuration of stars over the ages, changing their respective place in relationship to one other and their location in wider space. The changes of the constellation in the past shed light on and give meaning to its present changes.

This is why in the present research we have chosen to study a particular group of European and Europeanist women, *Femmes pour l'Europe*,[8] that was created in Brussels in 1975 by Ursula Hirschmann,[9] uniting a cluster of women who shared the same intuition that women had an interest in Europe. The group was composed largely of the wives of Euro-bureaucrats, and some of them, like Hirschmann herself, felt unhappy or uneasy in the role of wife, in her case having previously been a militant, while others were engaged in politics at different levels. Thus, one of the stimuli to create the group was the perception of a tension between the private and the public. The group organized a conference in 1976 on the construction of Europe and its relation to women, and one member of the group, Fausta Deshormes, went on to oversee the production of a journal, *Femmes d'Europe*, within the European Commission. A prize was also created aimed at recognizing the 'mothers of Europe' rather than laying all the stress – as is often done even today – on the founding 'fathers'. What seems most interesting in our perspective is that some of the women who participated in this group defined themselves as 'femmes' in the ambivalent meaning that this term has in French, indicating not only women but also wives. It was on the basis of their condition as wives of men who were politically engaged in European affairs that some of them decided to make explicit their point of view as European women. In other words, they openly acted on the basis of gender, making their gendered condition the starting point of their reflections (*Des européennes* 1979).

*Femmes pour l'Europe* found alliance with conservative women's groups rather than radical feminist groups, because the former were more interested in Europe than the latter, so their relationships were either institutional or with groups and individuals situated on the moderate fringes of the new-wave feminism of the 1970s. In a publication dedicated to Ursula Hirschmann by her friends and colleagues, we find hints of Eurocentrism, which is totally consistent with that epoch and certainly present also in radical feminism. In spite of declarations in favour of 'femmes immigrées or 'femmes du quatrième monde', and of self-definitions as the 'European sisters of migrant women', the attitude was still that of giving voice to, or making justice for, the underprivileged (*Des européennes* 1979). However, a voice combining Europeanness and women's solidarity was at the end of the 1970s quite isolated, and its sound is very valuable to us today; the very definition of themselves as European women is relevant to our present effort. Altogether, the heritage from *Femmes pour l'Europe* is one that may be fertile for us, if accepted critically.

The experience of these women shows that Europeanness for them was not a choice made only on ideological grounds, rather it was relatively independent of their political ideas. Some went on identifying with Europe in the most difficult conditions, some acted consciously as Europeanist. All of them developed an identification with Europe on the basis of a deep passion that connected the private and the political, and that always involved some type of affection. Their contribution stresses explicitly the gendered quality of their subjectivity. There was still an element of subordination in this gendering, but the intersubjective nature of their enterprise contains positive aspects, to be rescued and elaborated.

## Expressing Europeanness

In the course of our interviews, a sense of belonging to Europe emerged spontaneously only in few cases, and therefore it was sometimes necessary to go back to the interviewees in order specifically to get reactions on this topic. Direct questions, however, elicited hesitations and even resistances. As it happens in oral encounters, the hesitations and resistances transmit meaning, because they call attention to the un-spoken or the not yet fully articulated. First of all, they probably reflect our own uncertainty in finding the right words to express our queries, as if we ourselves were not fully clear on what 'being European' means today and why it is relevant, due to the lack of a shared language in this respect. In any case, the initial uncertainty must be taken in consideration together with its opposite, i.e. the fact that in the subsequent development of the interview the replies of many interviewees were rather articulated and significant, as if feelings and ideas were there, ready to be expressed. The same Bulgarian woman who at first sounded perplexed: 'Oh my God! Well, attitude to Europe? I don't know …', when asked '*Do you feel European?*', replied: 'Of course I feel European. No doubt!' (Mina, Bu). Another one reacted to the question: '*What is Europe for you?*' laughing: 'Oh you're killing me with this question!' but, again, from her subsequent replies a strong sense of belonging to Europe emerged (Ana, Bu).

Similar reactions came from the Hungarian women. However, for what concerns them, one must remember that our questions were posed in the context of the preparation of Hungary's accession to the European Union, therefore they included a question on the meaning of the enlargement for the interviewees. In spite of this context, which should have made our questions more concrete, fewer replies came from the Hungarians. One explanation is that a Hungarian master narrative praises their country as a bastion of Europe against the Turks and therefore Hungarians consider themselves to be European *de jure*, so that posing this question might have created a short-circuit, in which the narrators were trying to understand how to relate to the interlocutor and whether the question was a provocation. In other words, a hypothesis could be that precisely because of a very loaded – overdetermined – context, the replies could not be easily articulated.

The Italian interviews[10] show at times an even deeper uncertainty: 'I hope that there is Europe' says Anna, who then stresses the tendency to mix, first of all between different Italian regions, and also in general. But most often it is rather an acceptance of being European in a given and stereotyped way that emerges under questioning, as we will see. The caution in speech could also be dictated, one might hypothesize, by intrinsic Eurocentrism and the fear of saying something wrong towards migrants in considering various Europeans as belonging to different categories, a fear based on a sort of partial awareness of a new political and cultural correctness.

The replies given by some Dutch women show the highest degree of elaboration in replying to questions on Europe and Europeanness. The difference in awareness between Dutch and Italians reflects the level of the political and media debates in their respective countries: in the Netherlands, parties, press and TV have posed the question of Europe and migrants with much more insistence and seriousness than in Italy. But the difference could also be due to more long-term disparities, such as the difference of national cultural heritage – possibly reflected also in the educational systems – i.e. the better possibility of conjugating Dutchness than Italianness with Europeanness, given the tradition of 'weak' Italian identity and democracy.[11] Therefore the replies of the Dutch women are particularly significant when showing that they share the problems of expressing Europeanness: 'I don't say "I'm European". I almost never say: "well I'm from Europe", "From the Netherlands", I say afterwards, but not European. […] I don't see anyone in my surroundings saying "I am European".' Through these words Petra (NL) is clearly voicing the unusualness of this type of verbalization. The difficulty may depend on the context, explains Ida (NL), stressing the situatedness and relativeness of the question: 'When I was in Morocco I felt a European and when I was in Turkey I also felt a European, but when I am in Spain I feel North European, and when I'm in Belgium I do not even think about that, neither in France and in Germany.'

This taken-for-grantedness is one of the obstacles to articulating a sense of belonging to Europe, also because it is coupled with the oppositional foundation of Europeanness, as this last quotation clearly shows and as we will see further on. Some Dutch women deny the use of the term 'European' in favour either of a more ancient form of internationalism, as they prefer to identify themselves as 'citizen of the world' (Norine, NL), or of a transatlantic sense of belonging, defining themselves as 'Western' (Petra, NL). This latter example is the result of a wider sense of identification, while in other cases 'European' and 'Western' are used in an interchangeable way, as in the case of Angela (It).

Such reactions point to the implicitness of being European, *de facto* moving and exchanging ideas in Europe much more than elsewhere, but without expressing a full awareness of this. The hypothesis of implicitness is confirmed by the contemporaneous presence of hesitation and verbalization. The reasons for this implicitness might be disparate: suspicion and embarrassment (possibly semi-conscious) for what Europe was in the past, with its history of colonialism, imperialism, genocides of various types; but also diffidence towards the present EU bureaucracy. And last, but not least, the confusion between Europe and the Union.

The oscillation of meaning between 'Europe' and the 'European Union' is very widespread in public discourse at all levels. On the accession of ten countries to the EU on the 1 May 2004, President Prodi said in the course of the Slovenian celebration: 'Welcome to Europe!' One cannot help thinking that it would have been more appropriate to say: 'Welcome to the European Union', as many of the people interviewed in the 'new' countries had rightly pointed out that they were 'rejoining Europe'. It is no wonder that this recurrent confusion is present in our interviews, without a consistent difference between the countries of origin.

This is not to mean that the narrators do not understand the difference, on the contrary. For instance, when Europe is presented as a place advantageous for women, where they might find better opportunities of professional realization and social welfare, it is transparent that the reference is to the EU and the possible accession to it (Victoria, Bu/I; Ralica, Bu/I). However, as it has been observed in other situations,[12] some women – especially those coming from a long history of welfare such as that of the Scandinavian countries or from a socialist tradition – hesitate in front of a Europeanization that might not guarantee their conquests in terms of emancipation. Victoria (Bu) for instance says: with reference to women's situation, I claimed, and still do, that in the recent past Bulgarian women had better opportunities for professional realisation and more social privileges which enabled them to develop professionally, in spite of the general lower standard of living [...] although I see this Europeanization as a very positive factor of development, which opens new opportunities ahead.

This can also be worded in terms of diffidence towards the presumed advantages offered by a wider Europe, although not necessarily in terms of gender.

In principle, an idea of cultural Europe as distinct from the Union is useful in order to be able to criticize the present European construction. This meaning could be attributed to an ethical statement by one of the Dutch narrators, that asserts the responsibility of the EU towards the Eastern European countries: 'you can't leave them out in the cold [...] you can't let them down now. That's irresponsible' (Valeria, NL). Implicitly, she is counterposing a wider idea of Europe and Europeanness to the narrow one that might be represented by the EU. Similarly, Annet (NL) stresses the positive value of a Europe larger than '... the EU. But for me, Europe is more ... I think it's really special that since 1989, that wall has come down and we have that part of Europe as well. Yes, I think that's a big enrichment.' At the same time, for what concerns citizens of the countries from the former Communist bloc, the possibility of acceding to the Union might enforce and make more immediate the desire of being European in a more general sense, as even some of the native women recognize (Petra, NL).

Whatever the roots of the hesitations and verbal difficulties in expressing a sense of belonging to Europe – and as we have seen they can be many different ones – I am convinced that we should treasure this moment of suspension before expressing an allegiance to Europe. It indicates a substantive problematicity for women in general to feel fully European, because of the inherited lack of recognition as full citizens. It also implies that one cannot declare oneself European – and especially not a European woman – so easily of these days, without going through a complex path, of de-construction and re-construction.

## De- and Re-Territorializing Europe[13]

A stereotype implanted in our research from the beginning has been the assumption of the division between an East and a West of Europe, a stereotype that the research came to radically challenge. This division appeals to our imaginary and is a legacy of shared political and cultural ideas. It is a heritage of the Enlightenment, which however reunited the various parts of the continent in a *République des Lettres* (Voltaire) where scholars and ideas could freely travel from the Atlantic to the Urals. But the borders between East and West in Europe were always vague and contested, as Voltaire himself did not consider European the Balkan peninsula, then under the Turks, and Montesquieu did not include Russia in Europe. At the symbolic level, the East has always been a site of the liminal, the different, and even the dangerous.[14]

During the period of the national independence struggles and until the second world war, the claim to a specificity of 'Mitteleuropa'[15] or central Europe was recurrent, as a way of stating a complex identity of its own. In our interviews with Bulgarians and Hungarians, a claim reappears to challenge the East–West divide by affirming a sense of belonging to a 'central' location mediated by nationality: 'It's rather coming from the fact that I'm Bulgarian that I feel European. Because I'm like that! I'm like that. As a Bulgarian I feel European' (Ana, Bu/I). A central entity is 'needed' in order to redefine Europe, says Noemi (Hu/NL), otherwise Europe would be 'mutilated', as happened during the cold war and under the communist regimes. Mina (Bu/I) introduces the theme of the double or hyphenated identity, explaining that the Bulgarian women abroad even make themselves known as 'Bulgarian–Europeans', that is to say, there is no difference between being a Bulgarian and being a European.

This attitude may foster a way of cumulating identifications perceived not as antagonist to each other, on the contrary as shedding reciprocal light and pride, in a mixture that the single individual manages to keep together and alter with time. On such a basis, a whole string of identifications can take place, from the local to the regional, the national, the continental, and eventually the global sense of belonging to a world community that has 'glocal' meanings. On the other hand, the same attitude could also be used to exclude others, who do not have the same nationality or 'centrality'.

On the basis of other interviews too, both Bulgaria and Hungary appear to be considered by their citizens as being European by excellence, due to their central location in the continent and 'in-betweenness' between East and West. The attitude of being 'central' to Europe is highly significant at the symbolic level, because of its double sense, geographical and cultural. The metaphor of the 'heart' of Europe, often used to indicate various countries (a recurrent case is Switzerland, also for its federal structure), is another example of the search for affirming centrality, first of all in a physical sense, that becomes immediately symbolic.[16] Understood geo-symbolically,[17] centrality is very relevant. It is a way of redefining East and West, that implies the existence of an Eastern Europe, Russia, whose Europeanness is often denied of these days. Besides this territorial sense, the metaphor of inbetweenness has a double meaning in a gendered context: it also alludes to the activities of mediation that women have performed for a long time, for instance between the public and the private or between various social groups, as anthropological research has pointed out. We can imagine that this activity of mediation is now being transformed, being no longer closely coupled with subordination.

The claim to centrality emerges conjugated with one of the typical attributes of identity in the old sense, i.e. naturalness or the sense of 'being born such and such', an attribute hardly compatible with the new forms of open subjectivity that seem to be developing now. For instance, we find the feeling of being 'naturally European' expressed by Teri (Hu/NL): 'I find it natural that I am European'. As noticed at the beginning, we are bound to find combinations of old and new forms of subjectivity; it is easy to see how this 'naturalness' could be employed in an exclusionary way, but which final configuration will prevail in the future will depend on many factors.

Meanwhile, the discursive insistence on centrality, as well as the experiences of mobility and of exchange between mobile and native women, re-territorialize Europe in the sense of designing a possible European territory that does not yet fully exist, but is a possibility, after the de-territorialization provoked by migration. The territory on which the migratory itineraries are carved is already European, but not in a simple sense. It is still burdened by former hierarchies between periphery and centre, between East and West, South and North, all charged with value judgments that establish different levels of Europeanness. This territory can become European in new senses, as this term takes up new meanings. Various processes of redesigning culturally the European territory seem to take place; such could be the links between regional and local areas rather than nations. (This appears for instance in the close connection between the Balkans and Puglia established by Michaela (It), a very different approach than the traditional insistence on the national intra-European stereotypes (for instance talking about the Germans, 'they are much more repressive there', and the French, 'they are much more strict and perhaps much less politically correct [about minorities and migrants]').

The issue of 'central' Europe is not present in the interviews with Dutch and Italian women, who however often adopt the East/West divide in a critical way. Some Dutch women criticize this divide as not really relevant (Janette) or 'unnatural', i.e. enforced only in the last fifty years, during the era of the communist regimes (Ida). At the same time, others state that 'the border [of Europe] stops at the Russian border', since the Russians 'don't have the "European culture"', as for instance the Poles do (Annet, NL). The Italian interviews bear the effect of the collective amnesia in Italian public discourse regarding the era of communism and the cold war; this is just one of the reasons of the denial, in these interviews, of differences between the East and West of Europe, but it should be kept in mind as an important component. It is more accentuated in Italy than in other Western European countries because of the specific vicissitudes of the Italian Communist Party and its international role, as well as its links with the anti-fascist Resistance and the social movements in the national context – elements which amount to a complex ambivalence.

When spoken, the denial of differences between Eastern and Western Europeans and the claim to recognize them as similar and united by a common European background often reveals Eurocentric roots and an exclusionary orientation. Some Italians introduce rather heavily the observation that the specificity uniting Western and Eastern Europeans in comparison with other women, marks a difference not only with Northern Americans but even more with Africans and South Americans. The difference is sometimes expressed not in geographical terms, on the basis of continents, but of religious culture, Islam being the site of the deepest one (Carla, It).[18] This attitude is shared by some Dutch women (for instance, Annet). Thus, the denial of difference with the internal other is used as a way of reaffirming distance with the external other (as the European positivistic anthropology did in treating the Jews, an example of internal other, and the blacks, an example of the external, in very different ways), except reintroducing the internal difference when the discrimination based on it becomes useful, at another stage of power relationships.

Indeed, a convergence between the women from the four countries is the difference that they establish between European women, on the one hand, and American women (meaning the United States), on the other: the images of the U.S. women are highly stereotyped and mediated from TV and cinema.[19] Historically, it is in the European tradition that Europeanness is defined by contrast and opposition, so much so that the traditional European identity used to be at the same time essentialist and vague, when there was no other with which to confront oneself and on which to project one's dark sides.[20] The 'other' women, in the interviews with Dutch and Italian women, are those who 'look' different, and the contrast with them becomes the basis for a precarious unity between Easterners and Westerners. In this perspective, the reference to the 'European' values maintains its potential essentialism.

This reference can be found in many interviews. Hilda (Hu/NL) includes among the reasons that make her feel European that she 'can freely move among countries and speak a few European languages'. Diversity in languages and food, and tolerance, democracy, freedom of speech are for Brigi (Hu/NL) all indicators of Europeanness. Some Italian interviewees seem to understand Europeanness as the combination of a wide diversity and of tolerance towards this diversity. There are also passing references to the common historical basis represented by the heritage from the Romans and by Christianity (Patrizia, It; Annet and Janette, NL), that seem to represent more feeble echoes of ongoing debates and school education than deeply shared opinions. Many Dutch women show the sense of belonging to a communal civilisation (Janette), insist on the variedness of European languages and cultures (Norine), and on the sense of freedom of women contrasted with men's attitudes in South American countries (Valeria).

This is why the reference to the European values must be de-essentialized (and here we can give a contribution as researchers). There is no longer anything essentially European in the values of tolerance and diversity, except for their historical genesis. It is rather the artificial nature of a European identification that must emerge as a positive aspect.[21] A Europeanness that is being constructed 'artificially', as a result of will and determination. This construction can employ elements from a previous repertoire, such as the rhetoric tradition of European values of tolerance, freedom and democracy, but it is possible that they become concrete resources to be used for a future narration informed by a critique of their exclusionary implications.

De-territorialization, in the sense of not being connected exclusively with a territory, can be an individual and collective experience, but it can also be a cultural operation. Such would be a proposal of dissociating Europe from its traditional boundaries, and envisaging its connections with Mediterranean, African and Middle-Eastern countries: to be European *entre autre*, in the words of Derrida (1991), might be true also of countries and cultures. It is no longer of interest to discuss whether Turkey or Morocco belong exclusively to Asia or to Europe, but it is important to keep opening up an idea of Europe, according to which countries which are geographically not considered part of the structure of Europe can be considered *also* European. Cultures too might be European *entre autre*, i.e. African, European, gendered, generational, without hierarchies established among these identitarian terms.

For the migrants, this might be equivalent to the development of a 'third' and post-nationalistic point of view,[22] going beyond the logic of moving between two or three or more nation states, and adopting a stance that is not determined solely by the sense of belonging to any of these states. In practical terms, this 'third' point of view can be cosmopolitan in the old sense or European or even combine a traditional cosmopolitanism, a new sense of globality and Europeanness, depending on a series of circumstances in which migration takes place as well as on the previous life experience of the subject involved. This new perspective, often defined as transnational, promises to redesign the boundary East–West in Europe.

## 'Une Europe du Sentiment'

Historically, the link between a European sphere understood as public and the private sphere has been established by many Europeanists, perhaps the best known being Denis de Rougemont. It is to him that we owe the expression 'Europe du sentiment', literally, a Europe of sentiment. But it was Ursula Hirschmann who gendered the concept, insisting on the link between the public and the private, feeling at the same time a subject of Europeanness and of love.[23] As we have seen, some of the women of *Femmes pour l'Europe* also established a link between the two spheres. It is significant that we find variations on this theme in our interviews.[24]

Altogether, the perceptions of Europe presented by the Dutch and Italian women are widespread and varied, but associated with the sphere of private emotions (or better, the 'intimate' in Habermasian terms) only occasionally.[25] This may be due to the type of narrative that is coherent with their situation, most of them having been faced less frequently and directly with the possibility of establishing relationships with foreigners. On the contrary, the intimate is very present in the narratives of Bulgarian and Hungarian women, often in connection with the question of being European. In the Bulgarian interviews, meaningful replies to the questions on Europe are given in correspondence with contemporary political events, but also on the basis of personal bonds. For instance Boyana (Bu/NL), whose husband is French: 'I feel European more than ever especially now, when France is against the war with Iraq, and I feel sad because my own country supports the war' (she is referring to the axis Chirac/Schroeder against the war in Iraq).

The private is present in the new sense of belonging that can be evinced from some replies, either in the form of allegiances linked with marriage and love – as in the preceding example – or on the basis of the ancient self-representation of woman as mother that seems to solve or overcome the problematic nature of the European rhetoric of unity, such as in the quotation from Poly (Bu/NL) claiming to be one of the female ancestors of a new generation of Europeans. While this type of link is rarely uttered, the love of the couple on the contrary is very present in the narratives of the Bulgarian and Hungarian women as a reason for migration, either with a husband or with a boyfriend. Other times love is introduced as the consequence of migrating and a reason for staying on. The discourse on love emerges as a constant element of these narratives even through declarations *ex negativo*, that presuppose an expectation in this sense even when they deny the actual taking place of a love relationship. Julia (Bu/NL): 'My goal was obviously to see, to learn, to visit. I haven't met my great love', as if the imaginary around migration necessarily included love in one way or other. In real life, sometimes migration induces a break-up, as happened to Tanya, whose Bulgarian boyfriend tried to follow her when she migrated to Italy; he went to Nice but could not adjust there and after two years they broke up.

In this context, love and marriage are linked with the question of citizenship, since for instance the authorities in the Netherlands try with various procedures to ascertain and counteract the possibility of 'fake marriages' made in order to obtain citizenship. Mónika (Hu/NL) tells that after many difficulties with getting a visa because of the procedures, she finally married the Dutch man with whom she was in love, and she now lives in Amsterdam. It is all too coherent with this life narrative that she claims a 'cosmopolitan' identity rather than a European one, a narrative step that allows her to jump over the limitations that bureaucracy wanted to impose on her, trying to prevent her to become a 'European'. For our purposes, it is relevant to notice the penetration into the intimate sphere done by the bureaucratic agency emanating from a democratic government, asking for a formal declaration from the couple involved as well as from their parents on the existence of 'true love' between two people of different national origin.[26]

It should be noted that in our narratives nationalities are present, even if love changes the role of national boundaries. Comparisons are made by some of the interviewees between the men of various countries, that are often classified on the basis of the double stereotype pertaining to masculinity and nationality; often Bulgarians and Hungarians are portrayed negatively as jealous and oppressive, while Dutch and Italians seem to be 'way ahead'. However, critical remarks over the type of masculinity displayed by other nationals can also be repeatedly found; for instance, Tanya again: 'look, although it might sound rude, I think Italians are dull'; and Kremena (Bu/NL): 'the younger Italians are mummies (*mammoni*) and completely disoriented until 30–35'. At the same time as finding such rigid and essentialist classifications, most interestingly we encounter rather often a refusal to typify the beloved one. Christina (Hu/NL) says of her man: 'I do not think he is a typical Dutchman' (she had migrated to the Netherlands 'for love', and now both of them live in Hungary). Norine (NL): 'my husband would say that I am not a typical Dutch woman, because he could never have endured that'. Love individualizes each person, making her/him unique, and therefore it contrasts some of the stereotypes presiding to national divides.

On the link between the public and the private, the interviewees show a certain lack of ideology. Especially for what concerns love, there are no general declarations, rather a flexible attitude emerges, in the sense of a capacity to move, intertwined with love relationships, and at the same time to learn languages, find new jobs, bridge cultural differences. Love appears in a certain sense to be a European force, although often paired with nationality. This does not mean that other emotions, such as pride, and other themes, such as work, do not figure prominently in the interviews. In fact, one should bear in mind that the background to our analysis is a situation where multiple subject positions, with 'contradictory discourses and opposing needs', are being configured, as Salih (2003: 126) has observed. However, it seems relevant to give space to love, both in view of the contribution that this can bring to envisaging migrant women as subjects of emotions besides ideas and attitudes, and because of the recent re-discovery of emotions in feminist scholarship.[27]

For what concerns Europe, the interviews with Bulgarians and Hungarians seem to confirm at a simpler level of expression what the experience of *Femmes pour l'Europe* had suggested: tentative new ways of feeling European are possible, in part linked with new developments in emotional life, and capable of bringing the contribution of the private into the public. The interviews offer many instances of a love that is a driving force in overcoming or bridging cultural differences, but rather realistically oriented, as one of the forces that move people towards changing, at the same time informed by previous and new loyalties. This approach is apt to changing situations: pragmatic but not without principles, attentive to personal feelings and to cultural traditions of different countries. In other words, it can be seen as a possible basis for new forms of Europeanness, understood as new forms of intersubjectivity.

## Gendering the European Subject

In a post-colonial world, the subject of Europeanness is no longer understood exclusively as male, white and Christian (even layness was defined as antagonistic mainly to Christianity), a view that resulted in ignoring the plurality of European cultural traditions and/or subjecting them to a rigid hierarchy. That vision of subjectivity favoured a conception of life in which emotions were extolled but not integrated with intellectual values, where women and men were only formally equal, and the fulfilment of a love relationship was either confused with the sexual act or completely detached from it. The concept of identity related to this vision was monolithic and hierarchical, subordinating the richness of psychic life to a pyramidal system of values. Conceptualizing European identity in this way was part of a tradition of dogmatic ethnocentrism that privileged the dominating role of Europe and isolated it. Indeed, the arrogance of that form of subjectivity went together with its defensive character.

The new subjectivities that are in the process of being formed no longer claim to be superior to any other one, whilst retaining the specificity which derives from place and tradition (and in the end that of the individual in its multiple connections). This is one reason why 'identification', 'belonging', 'allegiance'[28] are better terms than identity, because they allow us to deal with an idea of Europeanness in which the women we encountered can be seen as contributing to the construction of feelings rather than seen as negotiating objectified identities. In this light, we can understand better the potential contribution of the attitudes expressed in some interviews to develop and spread feelings of belonging to Europe (in terms inspired by Raymond Williams, to contribute to create a European 'structure of feeling'), not without criticism, and to problematise this sense of belonging, taking a distance from any conception of Europe as a fortress.

The self recognition as European, if it does not undergo the critique induced either by the experience of exclusion or by a political choice, runs the risk of being taking for granted, with the legacy of undiscussed Eurocentrism and racism. Help might come from the intersubjective encounter between women of different identifications that establish other bases for reciprocal recognition. A significant example is that of Giovanna (It), a teacher, who was induced to look at a map, and find out where Moldavia is, after she met a woman from there. In this case, the inter-subjective and inter-cultural contact contributed to enlarge and deepen her vision of Europe. Therefore, the construction of a 'new other European woman' as Central or Eastern European (Regulska 1998) is being challenged by the possible exchanges between women in Europe that such an attitude seems to promise for the future — at least as a potentiality of new forms of intersubjectivity.

Intersubjectivity is at work in everyday life in the fields of friendship, love, and work, and especially in the areas of connection between the public and the private. We have hinted only at some of the many intersubjective links generated by the experience of migration. What is most interesting to us is the type of intersubjectivity that emerges as a site of recognizing each other as gendered; we have seen inter- and intra-gender examples. All this implies gendering various forms of intersubjectivity, especially if we envisage

Europeanness as an intersubjective construction in which women have a crucial role.

In general, gendering the European subject cannot mean simply adding women to Europe (or to migration)[29] and men to gender. While on the one hand Europe is in the process of becoming, at least under certain aspects, a gendered space, on the other hand there is not and there cannot be one 'woman's way' of being European. The multiplicity of women's forms of subjectivity is paralleled by the recognition of the multiple ways of combining the public and the private, to some extent a novelty in women's lives. We can recognize as antecedents the women who were part of the group *Femmes pour l'Europe*; for them Europe was not a mere sum of nationalities, nor simply a framework for bi- or tri-lateral relationships, but a reality in process that included everybody who came in contact with it.

I see two directions in which one can gender the European subject avoiding the trap of essentialism in conceiving either gender or Europeanness. The first direction is that of combining the traditions of nihilism and feminism in order to configure a new position of the subject of historical change. In the history of Europeanness, 'Europe' has sometimes been characterized as a void, to be filled by projections, expectations, utopian hopes. This line of meaning is much more promising than the essentialist one, attributing to this continent some fixed attributes that imply its superiority towards other parts of the world or, within Europe itself, to peoples considered as being 'more European' than others, treated as 'peripheral' or marginal. The absence of Europe has indicated in time the incapability of this continent to oppose Fascism and Nazism and later on to develop a foreign policy autonomous from the United States. This 'absence' is even more evident today, when a European Union exists, but divisions and contrasts in it make Europe as a force peace hardly visible (Balibar 2003).

This critical or 'negative' line can be found in Nietzsche and his ironical treatment of the good European, portrayed as a wandering shadow. We can pick up the nihilist tradition and transform it in a positive way, while at the same time not losing its negativity – i.e. its capacity to negate the present in order to prepare something else. The new subjects – among them women – are no longer privileged in the old affirmative sense, such as the notion of a working class that emancipates at the same time itself and all the other oppressed. The new subjects are privileged[30] in a negative way, in the sense that they do not claim for themselves any particular privilege; but, de-essentializing themselves, they contribute to a general task of de-essentializing identity and sense of belonging. This platform of negativity is useful for the effort to find new forms of identification with Europe that can correspond with new forms of subjectivity.[31]

Negativity becomes particularly fruitful when conjugated with the positive and substantive women's traditions concerning peace and European federalism. Positiveness was imbued with essentialism, before the 1960s, insofar as women claimed to be able to contribute to a new and higher organization of the continent as bearers of social words of order: peace, welfare, home territory, equal rights for all, precisely on the basis of their nature of mothers, naturally peaceful. If we take off any element of feminine essence – that is also the basis of subordination – from the subject, these attributes are no longer given in an almost biological way, on the contrary they are the result of choices, whether individual or collective. This 'negative' Europeanness would therefore go against the grain of identity politics as the latter developed in the period after 1989.

The second direction has to do with a movement of intersubjectivity. One of the outcomes of our project, and of the experience of inter-subjective exchange within it, is that one cannot feel European unless she has encountered the Eastern and Central dimensions of Europe. In other words, it is no longer sufficient – in order to contribute to new and open forms of Europeanness – to feel European only on the basis of a Western positionality. At the same time, I see a crucial possibility of taking up a positionality in Central and Eastern Europe in terms of a critique of Eastern Eurocentrism (as it emerged in some of the interviews, for instance in the traditional narrative on Central Europe as a bastion against the Turks). Such a critique is very much needed in order to configure new ways of belonging to Europe. And the link between the various parts of Europe is especially indispensable for what concerns women. Going back to the constellation 'gender, subjectivity, Europe', in other terms to the situation of being a European woman today, it is really impossible to say either 'I am a European woman', or 'I want to become a European woman' unless there is some sort of a dialogue between women from different parts of Europe.

Today the constellation is moving, but it is not yet seen by many people. For instance the mass media, such as most daily newspapers and TV, either do not see it or consider it in vulgar and banal ways or notice only some aspects of it, and therefore do not give space to one of the manifestation of the change of this constellation, i.e. the positions on Europeanness which various feminist scholars have taken. The consequence is a typical separatedness of the initiating European public sphere into two public spheres, a supposedly general one inhabited by male intellectuals, and a gendered one, where feminist scholarship concerning Europe and Europeanness is being developed. This is partially due to the nature of the processes the constellation involves and to the biased and gendered nature of the media and the public sphere, but it may also be due to our insufficient effort to connect the issues of feminism and Europeanness in a clear and understandable way. I think that we could do more in this direction, establishing further ways of intellectual communication between women from various parts of Europe, as a part of the enterprise of cultural de- and re-territorialization.

## Notes

1. Discourses on utopia understood in a positive sense have reappeared and intensified in Europe in the recent decades. See for instance Rüsen *et al.* (2004) and Passerini (2002).
2. I owe some of this terminology to Escobar and Harcourt (2003). I agree with them that trying to see multiple futures in the present contrasts the type of imaginary connected with the system of power, and favours different ways of imagining. However, as the three editors notice, visions of the future do not necessarily lead to the overthrow of the present state of power and domination, as it was the case with the imaginary connected with the old type of politics, and appeal to other ways for change.
3. Of the many meanings for 'subject' listed by the Oxford English Dictionary, 2nd edition, these two refer respectively to nos. 2 ('a subordinate') and 9 ('a thinking or cognizing agent'). Treating migrant women as subjects goes together with recognizing the role of gender in their subjectivity. See Phizacklea (2003) on gender blindness in migration studies and the configuration of women exclusively as victims, and Fortier (2000) on the primacy of gender as a key stabilising principle in Italian emigré culture. For the nexus subject/gender based on the concept of the body as site of gendered subjectivity, see among others Braidotti (1994).
5. On which not only feminism has insisted. Elias (1997) developed a critical view of the traditional division between subject and object, a hypothesis characterised according to him by the egocentrism of humankind and by the polarisation of what is in fact a continuum between involvement and detachment.
6. Cf. Passerini (2003a). While many of the women's associations in Europe from the last decades of the nineteenth century were pacifists and Europeanists, the study of women's contributions to Europeanism is still underdeveloped. Among recent publications, see Pisa (2003).
7. Constellation in Jungian terms is a cluster of psychic elements that show an affinity among one another, around a content that is partially or predominantly unconscious. A constellation is characterized by an energetic charge that acts like a magnet; it has a nucleus, with energetic value, that activates a complex, grouped in a figure or constellation. Cf. Galimberti (1999). I am grateful to Fabrice Olivier Dubosc for clarifications on this concept. I would like to apply the term and concept to the situation of gendered subjectivity in Europe today because it has the advantage of underlining two elements: the emotional aspect (one's self-recognition either as a woman or as a European cannot take place without emotions) and the implicitness of feeling European Europeans are often more 'European' than they consciously think or declare they are, since they are moving, exchanging ideas and objects and goods in Europe more than anywhere else, enacting a high degree of interconnectivity, both material and spiritual/cultural, without expressing a full awareness of this – see Kaelble (2001).
8. This section anticipates briefly a future publication on the history of *Femmes pour l'Europe* and Ursula Hirschmann. The section owes much to Dawn Lyon's research in Brussels and in the Archives at the EUI, that have recently been given the papers associated with the publication *Femmes d'Europe* (see Previti Allaire 2003), and to her interviews with the donor of these papers, Fausta Deshormes, on 29 April 2003 in Rome, and with Jacqueline de Groote on 15 December 2003 in Brussels, as well as to the interview with Edoardo Paolini, conducted by Enrica Capussotti on 24 March 2004 in Rome. I would like to express deep thanks to Dawn Lyon and Enrica Capussotti for their work, and to the interviewees for their contributions.

9. Ursula Hirschmann was born in Berlin in 1913, to a Jewish family, and migrated with her brother Albert (now Hirschman), when the Nazis took power in Germany, first to France and then to Italy. She had an important role in the creation and diffusion of the Ventotene Manifesto in 1941. During her life, she married two anti-Fascists and Europeanists, first Eugenio Colorni and then Altiero Spinelli, who later became a European Commissioner.
10. For what concerns the interviews with the women of the receiving countries, let us remember that they are different in that the questions to them were mainly, although not only, related to attitudes towards the 'other' women, the ones coming into their countries from Bulgaria and Hungary.
11. The difference might also be partially due to the construction of the sample. See Appendix. Let us note that, although the national differences are quite important in structuring the testimonies, the nation is by no means the only form of cohesion among the interviewed women: age and class appear to be grounds for collective recognition as well as self-recognition.
12. The reference is to Ulrike Liebert's observations on Greek and Danish women who saw the accession to the European Union as endangering their social and political achievements in the respective countries, quoted by Passerini (2000).
13. For these terms, see Deleuze and Guattari (1980), but with the modifications introduced by Fortier (2000: 13n), in order to reduce the exclusive emphasis on movement and to pay attention to both movement and attachment. Of course, de-territorialization does not necessarily imply the development of a sense of belonging to Europe; it could well be the origin of different senses of belonging.
14. Historically, in the European tradition, and even today, the East is understood as a limit, an extreme pole, dangerously close to the Other, with sexual undertones. We can contribute to deconstruct this idea of the East by de-territorializing our idea of Europe.
15. On this concept and term cf. Schultz and Natter (2003).
16. The concept has many applications in the field of migration. For instance, Fortier refers to the 'potency of betweenness' in the formation of migrant belonging (2000: 16).
17. Cf. Ivekovic's (1999) concept of 'psycho-political' geography; see also Ivekovic (1995: 44) on the European habit to self-define by tracing a frontier with the East.
18. The difference can be expressed in terms of space or of time: in the Italian interviews, as shown by Capussotti, the denial of difference between Western and Eastern Europeans is coupled with admitting a difference of temporality, in the sense of considering the West some twenty or thirty years 'ahead' of the East, although the East is supposed to be able to catch up with rapid integration (Fausta, Silvia, Anna, who are all Italians). This attitude is also shared by some Dutch, for instance Petra.
19. One wonders, although there are no open traces of this, whether this strong divide originated not only from the media and the recent developments in world politics that have fostered anti-Americanism, but also from the experience of relationships between American feminists and women of Eastern and Central Europe. Immediately after the fall of the communist regimes, a series of initiatives were generously started by feminists in the United States in order to establish contacts with women and potential feminists in post-communist countries. For these therefore, during quite a time, there was more exchange with American than with Western European feminists. This must be admitted as a heavy responsibility for us Western European feminists. In general, there is now a concrete danger that the dialogue between European women from various parts of Europe becomes an obstacle to the relationships with other women of the world, either with Northern American women or with

women of other continents. On the contrary, the sense of unity among European women should never be understood as a way of differentiating ourselves from 'other' women, rather a basis for wider sense of unity. On a possible dialogue between East and West women's movements, based on the analysis of the nature and limits of women's emancipation under state socialism, see Einhorn (1993) and Funk (1993); what has not been discussed in comparing women's heritages is the extent to and the form in which they have embarked in a critique of the symbolic aspects of subordination, a crucial aspect for any movement in post-modernity.

20. Cf. the volume edited by Lutz, Phoenix, and Yuval-Davis (1995) that introduced the concept of Europism as an updating of Eurocentrism. However, I believe that we are no longer in the stage of Europism for what concerns ideological stereotypes that now include an undifferentiated multiculturalism. See the difference established by Salih (2003) between interculturalism, that includes exchange, and multiculturalism, that indicates mere coexistence.

21. Michelet: 'ce qu'il y a de moins simple, de moins naturel et de plus artificiel, c'est à dire de moins fatal, de plus humain et de plus libre dans le monde, c'est l'Europe', quoted by Morandi (1952: 1875). One should also notice that the artificiality can be present either as a self-reflective aspect of cultural construction or as an imposed aspect of a bureaucratic construction.

22. There can exist a non-oppositional duality – see Passerini (2003b: 51–2). Some of the observations by Salih (2003) on the deconstruction of binary oppositions and reconfigurations done by Moroccan women in Italy, going beyond the alternative hybrid/assimilated, suggest a complex identity that is more than a simple 'double belonging'. See also Favell (1999) referring to 'another Europe', beyond the context of nationalities.

23. Cf. Rougemont (1995); the writing included in the book *Le paysan du Danube* that mentions 'une Europe du sentiment' was written in 1932. Ursula Hirschmann, in her unfinished autobiography, *Noi senza patria,* gives a lucid description of what happened, privileging a 'subjective' form such as love: 'I want to observe here, without false modesty, that perhaps I deserve the highest mark in love. This does not mean that I did not make one hundred mistakes. But I am happy with my man, I love my children, I am loved by them with that quantity of hatred that is inevitable, I have avoided big blunders, I know how to behave with the naturalness acquired during long years of apprenticeship. But for all this, what a high price I paid! Practically all my life has been a continuous effort around 'love', i.e. around nothing. Had I become a doctor or an architect, I would have used all the treasure of my inventiveness, my instinct and my intellect for this goal outside myself. Such an objectivization of my person would have taught me directly that detachment and balance that I pursued with such immense effort through the wrong way, the 'feminine' one' (1993: 87-8).

24. See chapter by Nadejda Alexandrova in this book.

25. Cf. Habermas (1989), and the consequent discussion, especially by Fraser (1991), on the subsumption under the public sphere of various public spheres for women, blacks, and others.

26. The reference is to a portfolio put together by a Hungarian interviewee on her relationship with a Hungarian man in Holland, who had a work permit and a residence permit, so that he actually could take responsibility for her as his partner and she could stay with him legally. The couple had to present letters by the parents of both, stating that they had 'witnessed the development of true love' (woman's parents) and that they had known of 'a serious long-term affiliation, which has been based on true

love' (man's parents). On the legal aspects of the conflation between public and private in this field see Conradsen and Kronborg in this volume.
27. The reference to emotions has become more important for feminist scholars in recent times, in contrast with the relative lack of interest of the 1970s. For instance, the emotional element is central in Slapšak's definition of mobility, while Yuval-Davis (2003) considers emotions, along the lines of Crowley (1999), as crucial for preferring 'belonging' to 'citizenship'. For Slapšak (2003), the term 'mobility' stretches not only to the mobility of the body (travel, change, communication), but also to culturally recognizable (and defined) emotions: in what ways, when, and by what are women 'moved', emotionally 'mobile' and 'motivated' (she observes that all three terms have the same etymology) and which context can make this mobility political. For Yuval-Davis, who refers to Crowley (1999), 'belonging' is a thicker concept than that of citizenship, because it is not just about membership, rights and duties, but also about the emotions that such memberships evoke. Nor can belongings be reduced to identities and identifications, which are about individual and collective narratives of self and others, presentation and labelling, myths of origin and myths of destiny. Belonging can be considered as a deep emotional need of people, formatted during infancy and/or even already in the womb.
28. Crowley (1999) notes that 'belonging' is useful precisely because it is vague. Indeed, these terms are often ambivalent: 'belonging' can have a normative sense in public discourse, especially in the use made of the term by nationalists and xenophobic politicians in the sense of stigmatising non-belonging (cf. Favell and Geddes 1999), while it can also be used to indicate a non-prescriptive global or transnational belonging (Blom 1999).
29. On both additions see Andall (2003: Introduction).
30. I use the concept of privileged subject in a different sense than Hanne Petersen in her essay in this volume, because her concept belongs to the tradition of studies on human and legal rights, while I am using it here in the political sense of the subjects of change within the tradition of socialist and Marxist thought. On Nietzsche's concept of the 'good European' as the shadow see Passerini (2003c: 26).
31. See Griffin and Braidotti (2003: 234). In the effort to situate the issue of whiteness in the geo-historical space of Europe, the authors draw a feminist political strategy of developing a post-nationalist understanding of European identity and of flexible citizenship forms.

# References

Andall, J. (ed.) 2003. *Gender and Ethnicity in Contemporary Europe*, Oxford and New York, Berg.
Balibar, E. 2003. *L'Europe, l'Amerique, la Guerre,* Paris, La Découverte.
Blom, A. 1999. 'Is There Such a Thing as 'Global Belonging'? Transnational Protest during the 'Rushdie Affair'', in A. Geddes and A. Favell (eds.) *The Politics of Belonging: Migrants and Minorities in Contemporary Europe,* Aldershot, Ashgate.
Brah, A. 1993. 'Re-Framing Europe: En-gendered Racisms, Ethnicities and Nationalisms in Contemporary Western Europe', *Feminist Review* 45: 9–29.

Braidotti, R. 1994. *Nomadic Subjects. Embodiment and Sexual Difference in Contemporary Feminist Theory*, New York, Columbia University Press.

Caine, B. and G. Sluga 2000. *Gendering European History*, London and New York, Leicester University Press.

Crowley, J. 1999. 'The Politics of Belonging: Some Theoretical Considerations', in A. Geddes and A. Favell (eds.) *The Politics of Belonging: Migrants and Minorities in Contemporary Europe*, Aldershot, Ashgate.

Deleuze, G. and F. Guattari 1980. *Mille Plateaux. Capitalisme et schizophrénie*, Paris, Minuit.

Derrida, J. 1991. *L'autre cap. La démocratie ajournée*, Paris, Minuit.

*Des européennes parlent de l'Europe. Réflexions rassemblées par le groupe 'Femmes pour l'Europe'*, 1979. Ministère des Affaires Etrangères, du Commerce Extérieur et de la Coopération au Développement, Brussels.

Einhorn, B. 1993. *Cinderella Goes to Market. Citizenship, Gender and Women's Movements in East Central Europe*, London and New York, Verso.

Elias, N. 1997. *Involvement and Detachment*, Oxford, Basil Blackwell.

Escobar, A. and W. Harcourt 2003. 'Conversations Towards Feminist Futures', in K.-K. Bhavnani, J. Foran and P.A. Kurian (eds.) *Feminist Futures*, London, Zed.

Essed, P. 1995. 'Gender, Migration and Cross-Ethnic Coalition Building', in H. Lutz, A. Phoenix and N. Yuval-Davis (eds.) *Crossfires. Nationalism, Racism and Gender in Europe*, London and East Haven, Pluto Press.

Favell, A. 1999. 'To Belong or Not To Belong: The Postnational Question', in A. Geddes and A. Favell (eds.) *The Politics of Belonging: Migrants and Minorities in Contemporary Europe*, Aldershot, Ashgate.

Fortier, A.-M. 2000. *Migrant Belongings. Memory, Space, Identity*, Oxford and New York, Berg.

Fraser, N. 1991. 'Rethinking the Public Sphere: A Contribution to the Critique of Actually Existing Democracy', in C. Calhoun (ed.) *Habermas and the Public Sphere*, Cambridge, MA: MIT Press.

Funk, N. (ed.) 1993. *Gender Politics and Post-communism. Reflections from Eastern Europe and the Former Soviet Union*, London and New York, Routledge.

Galimberti, U. 1999. *Dizionario di Psicologia*. Milan, Garzanti.

Geddes, A. and A. Favell (eds.) 1999. *The Politics of Belonging: Migrants and Minorities in Contemporary Europe*, Aldershot, Ashgate.

Griffin, G. with R. Braidotti 2003. 'Whiteness and European Situatedness', in G. Griffin and R. Braidotti (eds.) *Thinking Differently. A Reader in European Women's Studies*, London, Zed.

Habermas, J. 1989. *Structural Transformation of the Public Sphere*, Cambridge, MA, MIT Press.
Hirschmann, U. 1993. *Noi senza patria*, Bologna, Il Mulino.
Ivekovic, R. 1995. *La balcanizzazione della ragione*, Rome, manifestolibri.
Ivekovic, R. 1999. *Autopsia dei Balcani. Saggio di psico-politica*, Milan, Cortina.
Kaelble, H. 2001. *Europäer über Europa. Die Entstehung des europäischen Selbst-verständnisses im 19. und 20. Jahrhunder*, Frankfurt and New York, Campus.
Lutz, H., A. Phoenix and N. Yuval-Davis (eds.) 1995. *Crossfires. Nationalism, Racism and Gender in Europe*, London and East Haven, Pluto Press.
Morandi, C. 1952. 'L'Idea dell'Unità Politica d'Europa nel XIX e XX Secolo', in Marzorati, C. (ed.) *Questioni di Storia Contemporanea*, Milan, 3 vol: 1875.
Passerini, L. 1999. *Europe in Love, Love in Europe. Imagination and Politics between the Wars*, London, I.B. Tauris.
Passerini, L. 2000. 'The Last Identification: Why Some of Us Would Like to Call Ourselves Europeans and What We Mean by This', in B. Strath (ed.) *Europe and the Other and Europe as the Other*, Brussels, P.I.E.-Peter Lang.
Passerini, L. 2002. 'Utopia and Desire. Measuring the distance from 1968', *Thesis Eleven* (68): 11–30.
Passerini, L. 2003a. *Women in Europe, Women in Love: Searching for New Forms of Subjectivity*, The Ursula Hirschmann Annual Lecture Series on Gender and Europe, Florence, Robert Schuman Centre for Advanced Studies, European University Institute.
Passerini, L. 2003b. 'Diventare Soggetto nell'Epoca della Morte del Soggetto', in L. Passerini (ed.) *Memoria e Utopia. Il Primato dell'Intersoggettività*, Turin, Bollati Boringhieri.
Passerini, L. 2003c. 'Dimensions of the Symbolic in the Construction of Europeanness', in L. Passerini (ed.) *Figures d'Europe. Images and Myths of Europe*, Brussels, Presses Interuniversitaires Européennes.
Phizacklea, A. 2003. 'Gendered Actors in Migration', in J. Andall (ed.) *Gender and Ethnicity in Contemporary Europe*, Oxford and New York, Berg.
Pisa, B. (ed.) 2003. *Cittadine d'Europa. Integrazione Europea e Associazioni Femminili Italiane*, Milan, Franco Angeli.
Previti Allaire, C. 2003. "Femmes d'Europe': Un Nouveau Fonds aux AHCE', *EUI Review*, Spring: 13–15.
Regulska, J. 1998. 'The New 'Other' European Woman', in V. Ferreira, T. Tavares and S. Portugal (eds.) *Shifting Bonds, Shifting Bounds. Women, Mobility and Citizenship in Europe*, Oeiras, Celta.

de Rougemont, D. 1995. *Le Paysan du Danube,* Clamecy, L'Age d'Homme.

Rüsen, J., M. Fehr and A. Ramsbrock (eds.) 2004. *Die Unruhe der Kultur. Potentiale des Utopischen,* Weilerswist, Velbrück Verlag.

Salih, R. 2003. *Gender in Transnationalism. Home, Longing and Belonging among Moroccan Migrant Women,* London and New York, Routledge.

Schultz, H.-D. and W. Natter 2003. 'Imagining *Mitteleuropa.* Conceptualisations of 'Ist' Space In and Outside German Geography', *European Review of History* 10(2): 273–92.

Slapšak , S. 2003. 'Theorising Women's Mobility: Women Activists' Cross-Border Actions', in G.G. Deschaumes and S. Slapšak (eds.) *Balkan Women for Peace,* Paris, Transeuropeans.

Yuval-Davis, N. 2003. "Human Security' and the Gendered Politics of Belonging', Paper given at the Workshop *Politics of Belonging: Transnationalism, Migration and Gender,* 16 May, Ruhr-Universität, Bochum.

# Appendix 1: Summary of Individual Interviewees

## Bulgarians in Italy

| Interview code | Date of interview | Place of interview | Pseudonym | Age | Nationality | Place of origin | Main places of residence in life | Family of origin | Religious affiliation | Education (level) | Occupation in 'home' country |
|---|---|---|---|---|---|---|---|---|---|---|---|
| **Bul01** | 30.12.2001 | Ruse (BG) | IRENA | 33 | Bulgarian | Ruse (BG) | Ruse (BG); Medelin (Columbia); Padua (I) | Father: engineer; mother: dressmaker | No | College | Student |
| **Bul02** | 10.01.2002 | Sofia (BG) | RALICA | 34 | Bulgarian/ Italian | Sofia (BG) Florence (I) | Sofia (BG); | - | No | High school | Folklore dancer |
| **Bul03** | 24.02.2002 | Plovdiv (BG) | NONA | 33 | Bulgarian/ Italian | Yambol (BG) | Plovdiv (BG); Venice (I) | Mother: midwife | No | High school | Student |
| **Bul04** | 21.03.2003 | Pisa (I) | VICTORIA | 60 | Bulgarian/ Italian | Sofia (BG) Prague (CZ); Pisa (I) | Sofia (BG); | - | Christian orthodox | PhD | Student |
| **Bul05** | 08.03.2002 | Florence (I) | MINA | 29 | Bulgarian | Sofia (BG) | Sofia (BG); Florence (I) | Father: rehabilitation specialist; mother: engineer | No | MA | Student |
| **Bul06** | 11.03.2002 | Florence (I) | JELISAVETA | 27 | Bulgarian/ Italian | Sofia (BG) | Sofia (BG); Florence (I) | Father: truck driver | No | High school | Student |
| **Bul07** | 12.03.2002 | Near Florence (I) | YANA | 40 | Bulgarian/ Italian | Biala Slatina (BG) | Biala Slatina (BG); near Florence (I) | - | No | High school | Cashier in electric company |
| **Bul08** | 16.03.2002 | Pisa (I) | ANA | 40 | Bulgarian | Vidin (BG) | Vidin (BG); Florence (I), Pisa (I) | Father: writer; mother: teacher | No | High school | Professional dancer |

## Appendix 1

| Interview code | Date of interview | Place of interview | Pseudonym | Age | Nationality | Place of origin | Main places of residence in life | Family of origin | Religious affiliation | Education (level) | Occupation in 'home' country |
|---|---|---|---|---|---|---|---|---|---|---|---|
| Bul09 | 13.03.2002 | Mestre (I) | ANGELNIA | 30 | Bulgarian | Sofia (BG); Mestre (I) | Sofia (BG) | - | No | High school | Student |
| Bul10 | 19.03.2002 | Rome (I) | MARINA | 34 | Bulgarian/ Italian | Sofia (BG) | Sofia (BG); Prague (C Czech Republic); Moscow (Russia); Rome (I) | Father: teacher; mother: doctor | No | MA | Student |
| Bul11 | 20.03.2002 | Rome (I) | CAROLINA | 58 | Bulgarian/ Italian | Krivodol Vratza (BG) | Vratza (BG); Rome (I) | Father: national railway employee | Christian orthodox | MA | Student |
| Bul12 | 19.03.2002 | Rome (I) | KRISTINA | 42 | Bulgarian | Sofia (BG) | Sofia (BG); Ljublana (SL); Florence (I); Rome (I) | Father: economist; mother: chemist | No | High school | Amateur theatre actress |
| Bul13 | 25.03.2002 | Sofia (BG) | MAYA | 42 | Bulgarian | Pernik (BG) | Sofia (BG); Florence (I) | - | No | MSc | Engineer; unemployed; tradeswoman |
| Bul14 | 17.07.2002 | Pancharevo village (BG) | ADELA | 56 | Bulgarian/ Italian | Pancharevo village (BG) | Rieti (I) | - | No | High school | Student |
| BulRe01 | 29.05.2002 | Plovdiv (BG) | OLGA | 38 | Bulgarian | Plovdiv (BG) | Central Italy | Father: businessman | No | High school | Worker |

## Appendix 1

| Interview code | Present family situation | Husband's nationality | Children | Previous migration experience | Date of first entrance to I/NL | Individual/ collective migration | First job in I/NL | Current job | Sequence of employment | Character of stay |
|---|---|---|---|---|---|---|---|---|---|---|
| BuI01 | Married | Italian | 2 | No | 1990 | In family | Housewife | Works at her husband's office | - | Permanent |
| BuI02 | Italian partner | N/A | No | No | 1990 | Individual | Dancer | Sales manager | Dancer; sales manager | Permanent |
| BuI03 | Married | Italian | No | No | 1990 | Individual | Dancer | Housewife | - | Permanent; frequent visits to BG |
| BuI04 | Married | Italian | 1 | No | 1968 | In family | Student | Retired | University professor | Permanent |
| BuI05 | Single | - | - | - | 1993 | Individual | Student | Radio journalist | Guide; waitress; radio journalist | Permanent |
| BuI06 | Married | Italian | - | No | 1998 | Individual | Dancer | Bridge referee | Dancer; Saleswoman; bookshop-owner; referee | Permanent |
| BuI07 | Cohabitation | Italian | 2 | No | 1990 | Individual | Dancer | Cook | Dancer; cook | Permanent |

# Appendix 1

| Interview code | Present family situation | Husband's nationality | Children | Previous migration experience | Date of first entrance to I/NL | Individual/ collective migration | First job in I/NL | Current job | Sequence of employment | Character of stay |
|---|---|---|---|---|---|---|---|---|---|---|
| BuI08 | Divorced | Bulgarian | - | No | 1990 | In family | Dancer | Shop owner | Dancer; shop owner | Permanent |
| BuI09 | Cohabitation | Italian | - | No | 1990 | Individual | Dancer | Hairdresser | Dancer; bartender; hairdresser | Permanent |
| BuI10 | Married | Italian | - | No | 1989–90 | In family | Journalist | Journalist | Journalist | Permanent |
| BuI11 | Married | Italian | 1 | No | 1971 | In family | Translator | Part-time TV journalist | Translator; journalist | Permanent |
| BuI12 | Divorced | Bulgarian | - | No | 1990 | Individual | Actress in a circus | Theatre director | Actress; Director | Permanent |
| BuI13 | Divorced | Bulgarian | 2 | No | 1999 | Individual | Manager in pizzeria | - | - | Temporary |
| BuI14 | Married | Italian | 2 | No | 1967 | In family | Worker | - | - | Permanent |
| BuIRe01 | Divorced; cohabitation | Bulgarian | 1 | No | 1990 | Individual | Dancer | Shop owner | Worker (BG); dancer (I); shop owner (BG) | Return |

Data is missing from two Bulgarian interviewees in Italy. In one case, we were not able to obtain consent for the inclusion of details, in another, the poor recording limited the use of the interview.

## Bulgarians in the Netherlands

| Interview code | Date of interview | Place of interview | Pseudonym | Age | Nationality | Place of origin | Main places of residence in life | Family of origin | Religious affiliation | Education (level) | Occupation in 'home' country |
|---|---|---|---|---|---|---|---|---|---|---|---|
| BuNL01 | 21.06.2002 | Utrecht (NL) | PLAMENA | 24 | Bulgarian | Pleven (BG) | Pleven (BG), Blagoevgrad (BG), Rosmalen (NL) | Father: military servant; mother: engineer | No | BA (BG); MA (NL) | Student |
| BuNL02 | 23.06.2002 | Delft (NL) | POLY | 28 | Bulgarian | Haskovo (BG) | Haskovo (BG), Delft (NL) | Father: private business; mother: economist | No | MSc | Student, part-time jobs |
| BuNL03 | 22.06.2002 | Den Haag (NL) | ALENA | 27 | Bulgarian | Sofia (BG) den Haag (NL) | Sofia (BG), | Mother: engineer | No | Secondary school, unfinished BA | Part-time jobs, housewife |
| BuNL04 | 22.06.2002 | Delft (NL) | KALINA | 38 | Bulgarian | Sofia (BG) | Sofia (BG), Lebanon, Delft (NL) | Parents: private business | No | MA | Computer firm, private business; IMF projects |
| BuNL05 | 23.06.2002 | Delft (NL) | EVA | 25 | Bulgarian | Sofia (BG) | Sofia (BG), Delft (NL) | Parents: engineers | No | MSc | Student |
| BuNL06 | 24.06.2002 | Amsterdam (NL) | TEODORA | 44 | Bulgarian | Varna (BG) | Varna (BG), Sofia (BG), Prague (CZ), Amsterdam (NL) | Father: navy captain; mother: accountant | No | MA | Translator, teacher |

*Appendix 1*

| Interview code | Date of interview | Place of interview | Pseudonym | Age | Nationality | Place of origin | Main places of residence in life | Family of origin | Religious affiliation | Education (level) | Occupation in 'home' country |
|---|---|---|---|---|---|---|---|---|---|---|---|
| **BuNL07** | 24.06.2002 | Amsterdam (NL) | LUBOMIRA | 28 | Bulgarian | Hisar (BG) | Plovdiv (BG), Amsterdam (NL) | Mother: nurse | No | MSc | Engineer-technologist |
| **BuNL08** | 27.06.2002 | Zeist (NL) | ALBENA | 43 | Bulgarian/Dutch | Vladimirovo Montana (BG) | Montana (BG), Sofia (BG), Zeist (NL) | Father: employee in a shop; mother: weaver | No | MA | Translator |
| **BuNL09** | 22.07.2002 | Sofia (BG) | BOYANA | 63 | Bulgarian/French | Sofia (BG) | Sofia (BG), Tunisia France, NL | – Academy | No | Musical | Violinist |
| **BuNL10** | 29.06.2002 | Delft (NL) | KREMENA | 48 | Bulgarian/Dutch | Vratza (BG) | Vratza (BG), Troyan (BG), Plovdiv (BG), Delft (NL) | – | No | Art College | Painter at a medical factory, free-lance painter |
| **BuNL11** | 28.06.2002 | Enschede (NL) | KATE | 38 | Bulgarian/Dutch | Plovdiv (BG) | Plovdiv (BG), Sofia (BG), New York (USA), Amsterdam (NL), Enschede (NL) | Mother: ethnologist | No | MA | PhD student |
| **BuNL12** | 01.07.2002 | Schiphol (NL) | VIOLETA | 42 | Bulgarian | Pazardzhik (BG) | Pazardzhik (BG); Eindhoven (NL) | Father: economist; mother: teacher | No | MA | Teacher of English, translator, guide |
| **BuNL13** | 04.07.2002 | Den Haag (NL) | VESELA | 22 | Bulgarian | Shumen (BG) | Shumen (BG), Varna (BG), the Hague (NL) | Parents: military service | No | Secondary school | Student |

Appendix 1                                                                                              281

| Interview code | Date of interview | Place of interview | Pseudonym | Age | Nationality | Place of origin | Main places of residence in life | Family of origin | Religious affiliation | Education (level) | Occupation in 'home' country |
|---|---|---|---|---|---|---|---|---|---|---|---|
| BuNL14 | 6.07.2002 | Kroneberg (NL) | JOANNA | 31 | Bulgarian/ Dutch | Rousse (BG) | Ruse (BG), Veliko Turnovo (BG), Maastricht (NL), Kroneberg (NL) | Father: engineer; mother: social worker | No | MA; post graduate studies (NL) | Working in NGO |
| BuNLPo15 | 2.07.2002 | Assen (NL) | RENETA | 55 | Bulgarian/ Dutch | Martinovo (BG) | Montana (BG) (in 1987 in prison for illegally crossing border) | – | Christian Orthodox | Secondary school | Worker |
| BuNLPo16 | 26.06.2002 | den Haag (NL) | ROSA | 53 | Bulgarian/ Dutch | Sofia (BG) | Sofia (BG), Trieste (I), Paris (FR), den Haag (NL) | – | Christian Orthodox | Secondary school | Dancer |
| BuNLPo17 | 17.07.2002 | Sofia (BG) | LILIA | 75 | Bulgarian/ Australian | Pancharevo (BG) | Pancharevo (BG), Trieste (I) | – | No | Secondary school | Worker |
| BuNLRe01 | 16.07.2002 | Sofia (BG) | NIKOLETA | 57 | Bulgarian | Sofia (BG) | Sofia (BG), Austria, Australia | – | Christian Orthodox | MSc | Engineer |
| BuNLRe02 | 19.05.2002 | Ruse (BG) | JULIA | 27 | Bulgarian | Ruse (BG) | Ruse (BG), Boskoop (NL), Ruse (BG) | – | No | College | Student |
| BuNLRe03 | 19.05.2002 | Ruse (BG) | LORA | 66 | Bulgarian | Karanvyrbovka (BG) | Ruse (BG), NL | – | No | Medical Academy | Vice director of a Medical School |

# Appendix 1

| Interview code | Present family situation | Husband's nationality | Children | Previous migration experience | Date of first entrance to I/NL | Individual/ collective migration | First job in I/NL | Current job | Sequence of employment | Character of stay |
|---|---|---|---|---|---|---|---|---|---|---|
| BuNL01 | Married | Dutch | No | - | 2000 | In family | Housewife | Trainee private banking | - | Permanent |
| BuNL02 | Married | Bulgarian | 1 | No | 2001 | Family reunification | Housewife | Housewife | - | Temporary |
| BuNL03 | Married | Bulgarian | 1 | No | 1999 | Family reunification | Housewife | Housewife | - | Temporary |
| BuNL04 | Married | Bulgarian | 2 | Lebanon | 1998 | Family reunification | Programmer | Expert economic planning | Programmer consultant; expert economic planning | Permanent |
| BuNL05 | Cohabitation | - | - | No | 2001 | Individual | PhD student | PhD student | - | Temporary |
| BuNL06 | Married | Dutch | No | Prague (CZ) | 2001 | In family | Cashier at supermarket | Cashier at supermarket | - | Permanent |
| BuNL07 | Co-habitation with male partner | Dutch | No | No | 2001 | In family | Cashier at supermarket | Cashier at supermarket | - | Temporary |
| BuNL08 | Married | Dutch | 2 | No | 1987 | In family | Teacher translator | Teacher translator | - | Permanent |
| BuNL09 | Married | French | No | Yes | 1979 | In family | Violinist | Violinist | - | Plans for permanent return |
| BuNL10 | Married | Dutch | 1 | No | 1997 | In family | Free-lance painter | Painter | - | Commuting |

# Appendix 1

| Interview code | Present family situation | Husband's nationality | Children | Previous migration experience | Date of first entrance to I/NL | Individual/ collective migration | First job in I/NL | Current job | Sequence of employment | Character of stay |
|---|---|---|---|---|---|---|---|---|---|---|
| BuNL11 | Married | Dutch | 1 | New York (student) | 1994 | In family | Housewife | Center for Higher Education Policy Studies | – | Permanent |
| BuNL12 | Married | Dutch | N/A | Traveled to Moscow, Morocco, Western Europe | 1998 | In family | Part-time job in administration translator | Translator | Part-time jobs; phone-advertising; | Temporary |
| BuNL13 | Co-habitation with male partner | N/A | N/A | No | 2000 | Joined her boyfriend | Selling newspapers | Selling newspapers | – | Temporary |
| BuNL14 | Married | Dutch | N/A | USA (student) | 1997 | In family | Student | Marketing communications | Marketing communications | Permanent |
| BuNLPo15 | Divorced | Dutch | 2 | No | 1990 | Individual | Housewife | Social worker | Housewife; social worker | Commuting |
| BuNLPo16 | Divorced | Dutch | 1 | Italy; France | 1986 | In family | Dancer | Coffee-shop and bakery owner | Dancer; unemployed; shop-owner | Permanent |
| BuNLPo17 | Married | Bulgarian (political emigrant) | 2 | Istanbul Trieste (I) Australia | 70s | Family reunification | Retired | N/A | N/A | Permanent |
| BuNLRe01 | Married | Bulgarian | 3 | Austria; Australia; Austria; Bulgaria | 1982–90 | In family | Editor in a publishing house | N/A | N/A | N/A |
| BuNLRe02 | Single | – | No | No | 1999 | Au-pair | Babysitter | Unemployed | Babysitter; part-time secretary | Temporary |
| BuNLRe03 | Married | Bulgarian | 2 | Lebanon | 1998–2000 | In family | N/a | Retired | N/a | Temporary |

## Hungarians in Italy

| Interview code | Date of interview | Place of interview | Pseudonym | Age | Nationality | Place of origin | Main places of residence in life | Family of origin | Religious affiliation** | Education (level) | Occupation in 'home' country |
|---|---|---|---|---|---|---|---|---|---|---|---|
| **HuIPo01** | 04.01.2002 | Rome (I) | EDIT | 72 | Hungarian/Italian | Hungary | Czechoslovakia, Germany, Israel, Greece, Switzerland | Peasant | Jewish origins | 4 years of schooling | Child |
| **HuIPo02** | 06.03.2002 | Florence (I) | RÓZSA | 59 | Hungarian/Italian | Budapest (HU) | Budapest (HU), Florence (I) | Professionals | Catholic | Unfinished MA; Italian and library degrees | Clerical work, librarian |
| **HuIPo03** | 04.03.2002 | Florence (I) | BORI | 33 | Hungarian/Italian | Budapest (HU) | Budapest (HU), Pécs (HU), Florence (I) | Teachers | – | University degree | Language teacher, translator, interpreter, entrepreneur |
| **HuIPo04** | 11.03.2002 | Florence (I) | VALI | 49 | Hungarian/Italian | Budapest (HU) | Budapest (HU), Florence (I) | Father: high profile civil servant and communist party secretary; mother: head of office at a state company | – | Secondary school | Secretary |

# Appendix 1

| Interview code | Date of interview | Place of interview | Pseudonym | Age | Nationality | Place of origin | Main places of residence in life | Family of origin | Religious affiliation** | Education (level) | Occupation in 'home' country |
|---|---|---|---|---|---|---|---|---|---|---|---|
| **HuIPo05** | 11.03.2002 | Florence (I) | CSILLA | 32 | Hungarian/Italian | Budapest (HU) | Budapest (HU), Teramo* (I), Rome (I), Florence (I) | Father: technician; mother: professional | – | College of catering; student in College of Finance and Business | Restaurant manager, tourist guide, accountant |
| **HuIPo06** | 12.03.2002 | Florence (I) | IRÉN | 53 | Hungarian/Italian | Budapest (HU) | Budapest (HU), Florence (I) | Technicians | – | Secondary school | – |
| **HuIPo07** | 13.03.2002 | Florence (I) | ZSUZSA | 33 | Hungarian (waiting for Italian citizenship) | Debrecen (HU) | Debrecen (HU), Rome (I), Dublin (IRL), Florence (I) | Teachers | Protestant | MA | Teacher, interpreter, librarian |
| **HuIPo08** | 13.03.2002 | Florence (I) | KAMILLA | 57 | Hungarian | Born in Germany (in HU when 3 years old) | Budapest (HU), travelling as a singer | War orphan; Step parents: father foreman in factory; mother: nurse | – | Secondary school; music performer school | Secretary, singer, dancer, music performer |
| **HuIPo09** | 08.05.2002 | Rome (I) | JULI | 42 | Hungarian | Budapest (HU) | Budapest (HU), Rome (I) | Father: technician; mother: tailor | – | Law Degree | – |
| **HuIPo10** | 10.05.2002 | Rome (I) | EMESE | 21 | Ethnic Hungarian in Rumania | Cluj* (Rumania) | Cluj* (Rumania), Rome (I) | Mother: worker; | Catholic | Secondary school | Team leader at an Electric Wiring Systems |

| Interview code | Date of interview | Place of interview | Pseudonym | Age | Nationality | Place of origin | Main places of residence in life | Family of origin | Religious affiliation** | Education (level) | Occupation in 'home' country |
|---|---|---|---|---|---|---|---|---|---|---|---|
| **HuIPo11** | 13.05.2002 | Rome (I) | SAROLTA | 34 | Hungarian (waiting for Italian) | Maglód* (HU) | Maglód* (HU), Rome (I) | Father: in building trade; mother: housewife | Catholic | Teacher College; English Russian degree | Secretary |
| **HuIPo12** | 13.05.2002 | Rome (I) | LILI | 69 | British | Budapest (HU) | Budapest (HU), Moscow (Russia), London (UK), Oxford (UK), Italy, London (UK), Rome (I) | Parents: intellectuals | Jewish origins | University degree at the Lenin Academia in Moscow | University professor |
| **HuIPo13** | 13.05.2002 | Rome (I) | PETRA | 30 | Hungarian/Italian | Budapest (HU) | Budapest (HU), Pécs* (HU), Rome (I) | Mother: Engineer | – | University degree; Post graduate course in palaeography and archive studies | – |
| **HuIPo14** | 15.05.2002 | Florence (I) | IVETT | 29 | Hungarian | Budapest (HU) | Budapest (HU), Florence (I) | – | – | University degree (HU); degree in political science (I); MA (I) | Teacher, translator, interpreter |

Appendix 1

| Interview code | Date of interview | Place of interview | Pseudonym | Age | Nationality | Place of origin | Main places of residence in life | Family of origin | Religious affiliation** | Education (level) | Occupation in 'home' country |
|---|---|---|---|---|---|---|---|---|---|---|---|
| HuIPo15 | 18.05.2002 | Caprarola (I) | EMMA | 39 | Hungarian/Italian | Miskolc (Hu) | Miskolc (HU), Moscow (Russia), Budapest (HU), Rome (I) | Father: factory worker; mother: cook | – | University degree (Russia) | Teacher |
| HuIPo16 | 21.08.2002 | Budapest (HU) | SZOFI | 23 | Hungarian | Budapest (HU) | Budapest (HU), Bolzano (I) | – | – | Secondary school | – |
| HuIRe01 | 14.09.2002 | Budapest (HU) | GYÖNGY | 43 | Hungarian/Italian | Budapest (HU) | Budapest (HU), Italy | – | No | University degree | English teacher |
| HuIRe02 | 18.05.2002 | Budapest (HU) | JANKA | 42 | Ethnic Hungarian in Rumania | Romania | Hungary (HU), South Tirol (I) | – | No | Degree | Working in agriculture |
| HuIRe03 | 23.04.2003 | Budapest (HU) | ANGÉLA | 30 | Hungarian | Budapest (HU) | Italy | Mother: music teacher | No | University degree | Student and teacher |

\* anonymised name
\*\* Religious affiliation is stated when it is specifically mentioned. Most Hungarians are baptised but are not religious.

| Interview code | Present family situation | Husband's nationality | Children | Previous migration experience | Date of first entrance to I/NL | Individual/ collective migration | First job in I/NL | Current job | Sequence of employment | Character of stay |
|---|---|---|---|---|---|---|---|---|---|---|
| HuIPo01 | Married | Italian | No | Czechoslovakia Israel | 1954 | Political | Director of a hairdresser salon | Writer, artist | Freelance writer, journalist, novelist | Permanent |
| HuIPo02 | Married | Italian | 2 | No | 1968 | Individual (for love) | None | None | None | Permanent |
| HuIPo03 | Married | Italian | 1 | No | 1997 | Individual (for love) | Part-time Hungarian teacher at Hungarian Association | Teacher | – | Permanent |
| HuIPo04 | Married | Italian | 1 | No | 1971 | Individual (for love) | Secretary in her husband's firm | Secretary | – | Permanent |
| HuIPo05 | Married | Italian | 2 | No | 1991 | Individual | Restaurant manager | Housewife, voluntary work Hungarian at Association | Restaurant manager, housewife | Commuting |
| HuIPo06 | Married | Italian | 2 | No | 1971 | Individual (for love) | Workshop assistant | Part time seamstress at home | – | Permanent |

Appendix 1

| Interview code | Present family situation | Husband's nationality | Children | Previous migration experience | Date of first entrance to I/NL | Individual/ collective migration | First job in I/NL | Current job | Sequence of employment | Character of stay |
|---|---|---|---|---|---|---|---|---|---|---|
| HuIPo07 | Married | Italian | No | Dublin | 1998 | Individual (for love) | – | None | Housewife, unemployed | Permanent |
| HuIPo08 | Divorced | Italian | No | – | 1974 | – | Singer | Art gallery assistant | Singer, dancer, art gallery assistant | Permanent |
| HuIPo09 | Married | Italian | No | No | 1989 | Student | Nurse | Works for her husbands journal | Baby sitter, nurse, cleaner, theatre stunt, editor | Permanent |
| HuIPo10 | Single | – | No | No | 2002 | Individual | Cleaner | Cleaner | – | Tourist visa (3 months) |
| HuIPo11 | Married | Italian | 2 | No | 1995 | Individual (for love) | None | Housewife | – | Permanent |
| HuIPo12 | Married | Hungarian | 2 | UK (1956) | Since 1997 permanent | With her husband after retiring | Retired | – | – | Permanent |
| HuIPo13 | Married | Italian | 1 | Student | 1995 | Individual (for love) | – | Head of office | – | Permanent |

| Interview code | Present family situation | Husband's nationality | Children | Previous migration experience | Date of first entrance to I/NL | Individual/ collective migration | First job in I/NL | Current job | Sequence of employment | Character of stay |
|---|---|---|---|---|---|---|---|---|---|---|
| HuIPo14 | Married | Italian | | Student | 1998 | Individual (for love) | Student | Coordinator of an urban project for tourist purposes | Baby sitter, interpreter, trade union internship | Permanent |
| HuIPo15 | Married | Italian (divorced from Hungarian) | 2 | Student | 1991 | Individual (for love) | Work in documentary-making company | Same | – | Permanent |
| HuIPo16 | Single | – | No | – | 1998 | Student | Part time jobs for students | Waitress | – | Temporary |
| HuIRe01 | Married | Italian | 2 | No | 1987 | Individual (for love) | English teacher | English teacher | Teaching | Return |
| HuIRe02 | Co-habitation with male partner | Hungarian | No | From Transylvania (Rumania) to Hungary | 1990 | Individual | Au pair | – | – | Return |
| HuItRe04 | Co-habitation with male partner | Hungarian | No | – | 1992 | Individual | Au pair | Teacher | – | Return |

Data missing from one interview as consent not obtained for inclusion of details.

## Hungarians in the Netherlands

| Interview code | Date of interview | Place of interview | Pseudonym | Age | Nationality | Place of origin | Main places of residence in life | Family of origin | Religious affiliation | Education (level, subjects) | Occupation in 'home' country |
|---|---|---|---|---|---|---|---|---|---|---|---|
| HuNL01 | 28.06.2002 | Utrecht (NL) | EMÍLIA | 44 | Hungarian/ Dutch | Budapest (HU) | Budapest (HU), Bladel (NL) | Father: technical assistant mother: administrator | – | MA | IT expert |
| HuNL02 | 28.06.2002 | Rotterdam (NL) | MAGDA | 40 | Hungarian/ Dutch | Szeged (Hu) | Szeged (HU), Rotterdam (HU) | Father: engineer; mother: teacher | | Doctor | Doctor |
| HuNL03 | 29.06.2002 | Amersfort (NL) | ROZIKA | 32 | Hungarian/ Dutch | Kaposvár (Hu) | Kaposvár (HU), Budapest (HU), Amsterdam (NL), Amersfort (NL) | Father: engineer; mother: director of school | – | MSc (HU); MSc (NL) | Environmental advisor in a Dutch company in Hungary |
| HuNL04 | 29.06.2002 | Utrecht (NL) | HENRIETTA | 37 | Hungarian/ Dutch | Csömör (HU) | Csömör (HU), Budapest (HU), Utrecht (NL) | Father: printer; mother: financial administrator | Catholic | MA | University teacher |
| HuNL05 | 30.06.2002 | Amsterdam (NL) | MARI | 30 | Hungarian/ Dutch | Pécs* (HU) | Pécs* (HU), Switzerland, Amsterdam (NL) | Father: carpenter; mother: social worker | – | BA; College for Social Pedagogy (NL) | – |

| Interview code | Date of interview | Place of interview | Pseudonym | Age | Nationality | Place of origin | Main places of residence in life | Family of origin | Religious affiliation | Education (level, subjects) | Occupation in 'home' country |
|---|---|---|---|---|---|---|---|---|---|---|---|
| HuNL06 | 01.07.2002 | Eindhoven (NL) | ILA | 46 | Hungarian/ Dutch | Budapest (HU) | Budapest (HU), Las Palmas (SP), Amsterdam (NL), Eindhoven (NL) | Father: conductor and composer; mother: musician, singer, music critic | Catholic | Music Academy | Musician |
| HuNL07 | 02.07.2002 | Amsterdam (NL) | ÁGI | 47 | Hungarian/ Dutch | Budapest (HU) | Budapest (HU), near Amsterdam (NL) | Father: literary scholar; mother: historian | – | MSc | Researcher |
| HuNL08 | 03.07.2002 | Amsterdam (NL) | PIROSKA | 41 | Hungarian/ Dutch | Jászberény (HU) | Jászberény (HU), Eger (HU), Brabant (NL), Amsterdam (NL) | Parents: workers | – | College degree | Secretary, teacher, professional folk dancer |
| HuNLPo09 | 04.07.2002 | Badhoevedorp (NL) | ILONA | 60 | Hungarian/ Dutch | Budapest (HU) | Budapest (HU), Badhoevedorp (NL) | Father: protestant pastor; mother: teacher | Protestant | BA | – |
| HuNLPo10 Dutch | 05.07.2002 | Hague (NL), Jerusalem, (HU) | ELLA protestant | 71 | Hungarian/ | Budapest | Budapest (HU), Hague (NL) | Father: pastor; – | Protestant | BA | – |
| HuNLPo11 | 05.07.2002 | Hague (NL) | EUFROZINA | 69 | Hungarian/ Dutch | Budapest (HU) | Budapest (HU), Belgium, Hague (NL) | Father: engineer; mother: housewife | Catholic | Degree | Kindergarten teacher |

## Appendix 1

| Interview code | Date of interview | Place of interview | Pseudonym | Age | Nationality | Place of origin | Main places of residence in life | Family of origin | Religious affiliation | Education (level, subjects) | Occupation in 'home' country |
|---|---|---|---|---|---|---|---|---|---|---|---|
| HuNL12 | 06.07.2002 | Amsterdam (NL) | MÓNIKA | 33 | Hungarian/ Dutch | Zalaegerszeg (HU) | Zalaegerszeg (HU), Helsinki (FL), UK, Utrecht (NL) | Parents: dentists | New Protestant community | MA | Teacher, translator, interpreter, boarding school teacher |
| HuNL13 | 08.07.2002 | Utrecht (NL) | KLÁRI | 36 | Hungarian/ Dutch | Budapest /HU) | Budapest (HU), Utrecht (HU) | Father: military officer; mother: accountant | Catholic | BA (HU); MBA (NL) | Head of Treasury at a bank |
| HuNL14 | 25.06.2002 | Hague (NL) | ERZSÉBET | 37 | Hungarian/ Dutch | Budapest (HU) | Budapest (HU), Utrecht (NL), Hague (NL) teacher | Father: photographer; mother: Protestant | Protestant | MA in a firm | Works for a Protestant gathering, administrator |
| HuNL15 | 25.06.2002 | Utrecht (NL) | BRIGI | 30 | Hungarian/ Dutch | Budapest (HU) | Budapest (HU), London (UK), Malta, Roosendaal (NL), Utrecht (NL) | Father: fireman; mother: administrator | – | BA | Baby sitter |
| HuNL16 | 23.06.2002 | Amsterdam (NL) | ANETT | 24 | Hungarian | Budapest (HU) | Budapest (HU), Amsterdam (NL) | Parents: entrepreneurs | – | BA | Works for telephone company |

Appendix 1

| Interview code | Date of interview | Place of interview | Pseudonym | Age | Nationality | Place of origin | Main places of residence in life | Family of origin | Religious affiliation | Education (level, subjects) | Occupation in 'home' country |
|---|---|---|---|---|---|---|---|---|---|---|---|
| HuNL17 | 24.06.2002 | S'Hertogen-bosch (NL) | TERI | 29 | Hungarian/Dutch | Komárom-Komarno (Slovakia) | Komarno (SLK), Nemesócsa, Nagymegyer, Prague (CZ), Eindhoven (NL), Hertogenbosch (NL) | Parents: teachers | – | MA (CZ) | – |
| HuNL18 | 20.06.2002 | Utrecht (NL) | HILDA | 38 | Hungarian/Dutch | Near Győr* (HU) | Near Győr* (HU), Pécs (HU), Deventer (NL) | Father: veterinary; mother: economist | – | Doctor of Law | Works in international company |
| HuNLRe01 | 31.05.2002 | Budapest (HU) | MARGIT | 44 | Hungarian | Budapest (HU) | Leuven (NL), - London (UK) | – | – | MA | – |
| HuNLRe02 | 27.10.2002 | Budapest (HU) | SÁRA | 29 | Hungarian | Budapest (HU) | England, Israel | – | – | – | – |
| HuNLRe03 | 24.04.2002 | Budapest (HU) | NOÉMI | 36 | Hungarian | Budapest (HU) | – | – | – | – | – |

# Appendix 1

| Interview code | Present family situation | Husband's nationality | Children | Previous migration experience | Date of first entrance to NL | Individual/ collective migration | First job in NL | Current job | Sequence of employment | Character of stay |
|---|---|---|---|---|---|---|---|---|---|---|
| HuNL01 | Married | Dutch | 2 | – | 1988 | Individual (for love) | – | Freelance translator, editor, teacher, volunteer for Autism Foundation | – | Permanent |
| HuNL02 | Married | Dutch | – | – | 1995 | Student | Doctor | Doctor | Doctor | Permanent |
| HuNL03 | Married | Dutch | – | Amsterdam (NL) | 1997 | Individual (for love) | Baby sitter | Employee in a company | Baby sitter, employee | Permanent |
| HuNL04 | Married | Dutch | – | – | 1998 | Individual (for love) | Secretary | Project manager in University | Secretary, project manager | Permanent |
| HuNL05 | Married | Dutch | 1 | Au pair in Switzerland, England | 1995 | Individual (for love) | Cleaner | Social worker | Cleaner, baby sitter, social worker | Permanent |
| HuNL06 | Divorced/ Married | Dutch (divorced from Hungarian) | 3 | Las Palmas (with first husband) | 1992 | Individual (for love) | Musician | Musician | – | Permanent |
| HuNL07 | Divorced/ Married | Dutch (divorced by Hungarian) | 1 | – | 1990 | Individual (for love) | – | Computer animation design | – | Temporary |

| Interview code | Present family situation | Husband's nationality | Children | Previous migration experience | Date of first entrance to NL | Individual/ collective migration | First job in NL | Current job | Sequence of employment | Character of stay |
|---|---|---|---|---|---|---|---|---|---|---|
| HuNL08 | Co-habitation | Dutch | 2 | – | 1990 | Individual (for love) | Taxi driver | Kindergarten teacher | Taxi driver, post office clerk, baby sitter, dance teacher | Permanent |
| HuNLPo09 | Married | Dutch | 4 | – | 1964 | Individual (for love) | In hospital | Translator, interpreter | – | Permanent |
| HuNLPo10 | Married | Hungarian | 4 | Jerusalem (with her father) | 1950 | Political | – | – | – | Permanent |
| HuNLPo11 | Widow | Widow | 5 | Belgium | 1960 | With her fiancée | Social services | – | – | Permanent |
| HuNL12 | Married | Dutch | 3 | Finland, England, Scotland | 1995 | Individual (for love) | – | – | – | Permanent |
| HuNL13 | Divorced | Dutch | 2 | – | 1997 | Individual (for love) | Bank employee | Investment analyst | – | Permanent |
| HuNL14 | Married | Hungarian | 1 | – | 1990 | Student | Editor | – | Editor, American IT company, Dutch insurance company | Permanent |

# Appendix 1

| Interview code | Present family situation | Husband's nationality | Children | Previous migration experience | Date of first entrance to NL | Individual/ collective migration | First job in NL | Current job | Sequence of employment | Character of stay |
|---|---|---|---|---|---|---|---|---|---|---|
| HuNL15 | Married | Dutch | – | – | 1992 | Individual | Baby sitter | Web-mistress | Baby sitter, car-lease company, SWOT analysis, web-mistress | Permanent |
| HuNL16 | Co-habitation with male partner | Dutch | – | – | 2002 | Individual (for love) | Commercial editor in a TV show | Same | – | Temporary |
| HuNL17 | Married | Dutch-Indonesian | | – | 1998 | Individual (for love) | Volunteer in a social-cultural community house | Receptionist at a college | – | Permanent |
| HuNL18 | Married | Dutch | 2 | – | 1992 | Individual (for love) | – | – | – | Permanent |
| HuNLRe01 | Single | – | – | – | 1993 | Individual (for love) | Student | English teacher | – | Return |
| HuNLRe02 | Single | – | – | – | 1997 | Individual | Au-pair | Administrator | – | Return |
| HuNLRe03 | Married | Dutch | 2 | – | 1992 | Student | Student | Research Institute | – | Return |

## Italian women

| Interview code | Date of interview | Place of interview | Pseudonym | Age | Education | Place of origin | Nationality | Main places of residence in life | Migration experience | Current occupation | Present family situation | Child | Character of relation with migrant women |
|---|---|---|---|---|---|---|---|---|---|---|---|---|---|
| It1 | 2.4.2002 | Sesto Fiorentino (Florence) | ANGELA | 40 | Secondary school (scientific stream) | Naples | Italian | Rome, Belgium, Gaeta (I), Tarquinia (I), Sesto Fiorentino (I) | As a child (Belgium) | Housewife | Married | 1 | Friendship |
| It2 | 8.4.2002 | Florence | MARIA | 29 | Secondary school; university (architecture) | Taranto | Italian | Taranto, Florence | No | Student | Single | No | Daughter of a mixed couple (Italian and Bulgarian) |
| It3 | 15.4.2002 | Florence | LINA | 53 | Secondary school (administration) | Florence | Italian | Florence | No | Private agency | Married | 1 | Colleague and friend |
| It4 | 17.4.2002 | Rome | ROBERTA | 68 | Secondary school (humanities) 5 years of university (political science without final degree) | Florence Rome | Italian | Florence, | No | Retired from administrative work | Married | 3 | Employer of domestic workers |

# Appendix 1

| Interview code | Date of interview | Place of interview | Pseudonym | Age | Education | Place of origin | Nationality | Main places of residence in life | Migration experience | Current occupation | Present family situation | Child | Character of relation with migrant women |
|---|---|---|---|---|---|---|---|---|---|---|---|---|---|
| It5 | 18.4.2002 | Rome | BETTA | 70 | MA | Rome | Italian | Rome | Student (Grenoble, FR) | Retired from teaching | Widow | 3 | Acquaintance |
| It6 | 18.4.2002 | Rome | CARLOTTA | 42 | Secondary school (Restorer) | Rome | Italian | Rome | No | Housewife | Co-habitation with male partner | 1 | Acquaintance |
| It7 | 19.4.2002 | Rome | CRISTINA | 73 | MA | Rome | Italian | Rome | No | Retired from PR job | Married | 2 | Employer of domestic workers |
| It8 | 23.4.2002 | Florence | FRANCESCA | 44 | Professional school (beautician) | Florence | Italian | Florence | No | Worker in Beauty-Salon | single | no | Friendship |
| It9 | 19.4.2002 | Rome | GIOVANNA | 62 | MA (humanities) | Udine | Italian | Rome | Internal migration from Udine to Roma (with her parents) | Retired from teaching | Married | 3 | Employer of domestic workers |
| It10 | 22.4.2002 | Florence | SILVANA | 39 | MA (political science) | Florence | Italian | Florence | No | University assistant | Married | 1 | Friendship |
| It11 | 8.5.2002 | Florence | MARGHERITA | 27 | MA (humanities) | Florence | Italian | Florence | No | Social worker | Single | No | Social worker |
| It12 | 8.5.2002 | Florence | DANIELA | 29 | MA (architecture) | Florence | Italian | Florence | No | Social worker | Co-habitation with male partner | No | Social worker |

| Interview code | Date of interview | Place of interview | Pseudonym | Age | Education | Place of origin | Nationality | Main places of residence in life | Migration experience | Current occupation | Present family situation | Child | Character of relation with migrant women |
|---|---|---|---|---|---|---|---|---|---|---|---|---|---|
| It13 | 24.4.2002 | Florence | ROSARIA | 66 | MA (psychology and law) | Milan | Italian | Florence | Internal migration from Milan to Florence (with her husband) | Secretary | Married | 1 | Assistance |
| It14 | 13.6.2002 | Florence | MARTA | 33 | MA (humanities) | Naples | Italian | Florence | Internal migration from Naples to Florence (with her parents) | Teacher | Single | No | Teacher of Italian to migrants |
| It15 | 22.6.2002 | Trento* | ORIETTA | 51 | Compulsory education | Arco | Italian | Trento* | No | Agriculture | Married | 1 | Employer in agriculture |
| It16 | 22.06.2002 | Trento* | PATRIZIA | 35 | MA (economics) | Arco | Italian | Trento* | No | Manager | Married | 2 | Employer of domestic workers |
| It17 | 23.6.2002 | Trento* | CARLA | 59 | Professional school | Arco | Italian | Trento* | No | Agriculture | Married | 3 | Employer in agriculture |
| It18 | 22.6.2002 | Trento* | ADRIANA | 66 | Compulsory education | Arco | Italian | Trento* | No | Housewife | Married | 2 | Voluntary work in catholic church |

* Indicates the interview took place in a nearby rural area

# Appendix 1

## Dutch women

| Interview code | Date of interview | Place of interview | Pseudonym | Age | Education | Place of origin | Nationality | Main places of residence in life | Migration experience | Current occupation | Present family situation | Child | Character of relation with migrant women |
|---|---|---|---|---|---|---|---|---|---|---|---|---|---|
| NL01 | 07.06.02 | Utrecht | BARBARA | 29 | Social work | Lunteren | Dutch | Lunteren and Ede, Amsterdam | No | Social worker in Jewish organisation | Married to Bulgarian | – | Friendship |
| NL02 | 10.06.02 | Utrecht | ELLEN | 27 | Teacher training | Sint Maartensbrug | Dutch | Wormerveer, Amsterdam | No | PhD student | Co-habitation with male partner | – | Colleague |
| NL03 | 28.06.02 | Amsterdam | MAAIKE | 24 | University student | Vroomshuis | Dutch | Leiden | Student | Student | Single | – | Friendship |
| NL04 | 19.07.02 | Leiden | WILMA | 43 | MBA | Geldrop | Dutch | Japan, USA, Germany, France | As a child: Japan USA; student in Germany, France | Self-employed 'food and health' advisor | Married | 2 | Colleague |
| NL05 | 18.10.02 | Leiderdorp | DIANA | 29 | Pedagogy | Hengelo | Dutch | Nijmegen; Den Haag | Student | Community worker | Lives in shared house | – | Friendship |
| NL06 | 18.10.02 | Den Haag | JANTINA | 30 | 1-year secretarial education | Den Bosch | Dutch | Maastricht | As a child (Germany) | Call-centre employee | Single | – | Friendship and daughter of a mixed couple (Hungarian father and Dutch mother) |

# Appendix 1

| Interview code | Date of interview | Place of interview | Pseudonym | Age | Education | Place of origin | Nationality | Main places of residence in life | Migration experience | Current occupation | Present family situation | Child | Character of relation with migrant women |
|---|---|---|---|---|---|---|---|---|---|---|---|---|---|
| NL07 | 20.10.02 | Maastricht | INGE | 31 | Public administration | Barsingerhorn | Dutch | Leeuwarden, | No Hengelo | University research staff | Single | – | Colleague |
| NL08 | 29.10.02 | Hengelo | JACQUELINE | 41 | Psychology | Leiden | Dutch | Nigeria, Voorschoten, Leiden | As a child (Nigeria) | Social worker and psychologist | Single | – | Colleague and voluntary work in support group for migrants without documentation |
| NL09 | 25.05.03 | Leiden | MARJON | 33 | Law | Amsterdam | Dutch | Amsterdam | – | Jurist | Single | – | Acquaintance |
| NL10 | 11.06.03 | Utrecht | ILSE | 42 | Anthropology | Brabant | Dutch | Amsterdam, Utrecht | – | Manager in post-doc education | Co-habitation with male partner | 3 | Employer |

Appendix 1

| Interview code | Date of interview | Place of interview | Pseudonym | Age | Education | Place of origin | Nationality | Main places of residence in life | Migration experience | Current occupation | Present family situation | Child | Character of relation with migrant women |
|---|---|---|---|---|---|---|---|---|---|---|---|---|---|
| NL11 | 21.06.03 | Amsterdam | DEBORAH | 35 | Compulsory education | Laren | Dutch | Almere, Amsterdam | No | Entrepreneur (runs shop and information centre on prostitution) | Married | 1 | Colleagues and clients |
| NL12 | 01.11.02 | Amsterdam | HANNEKE | 41 | Degree in translation; European masters (environmental management) | Hilversum | Dutch | Krimpen a/d Yssel, Boxtel, Amsterdam | UK | Project-staff environmental organisation | Male partner lives separately | 1 | Friendship |
| NL13 | 26.05.03 | Rotterdam | SUZE | 32 | Social work | Zoetermeer | Dutch | Zoetermeer, Gorinchem | No | Coordinator social work project with prostitutes | Co-habitation with male partner | – | Colleagues and clients |

Data missing from one interview as consent not obtained for inclusion of details.

# Appendix 2: Summary of interviewees' characteristics by nationality

## Bulgarian migrant women[1]

| Age cohort[2] | 20–29 | 30–39 | 40–49 | 50–59 | 60–69 | 70+ |
|---|---|---|---|---|---|---|
| | 9 | 9 | 8 | 5 | 4 | – |
| Highest educational level attained[3] | Primary School | Secondary school | Technical/professional | University first degree | University masters degree | PhD |
| | – | 11 | 6 | – | 16 | 2 |
| Place of origin[4] | Capital | City (More Than 500,000) | City (100,000–500,000) | City (20,000–100,000) | Town (2,000–20,000) | Village (less than 2,000) |
| | 13 | – | 8 | 10 | – | 4 |
| Family status[5] | Married | Single | Divorced | Co-habitation | Widowed | |
| | 21 | 2 | 5 | 7 | – | |
| Children[6] | No | Yes | | | | |
| | 16 | 19 | | | | |
| Religion[7] | None | Orthodox | Catholic | Muslim | Protestant | Jewish |
| | 30 | 5 | – | – | – | – |
| Migration[8] | Pre 1989 | Post 1989 | | | | |
| | 6 | 29 | | | | |

# Appendix 2

| Occupation in receiving country[9] | Housewife | Unemployed | Retired | | | |
|---|---|---|---|---|---|---|
| | 3 | 1 | 2 | | | |
| | Professional | Associate professional | Small business owner | Clerical | Service/sales | Low/unskilled |
| | 11 | 4 | 2 | 2 | 6 | 1 |
| Social mobility arising from migration | Upward mobility | Downward mobility | | | | |
| | 18 | 17 | | | | |
| Previous migration experience | Yes as a child | Yes as a student | Yes as a political refugee | Yes as a worker | Family migration | No |
| | – | 6 | 2 | 3 | 2 | 22 |
| Character of stay[10] | Permanent | Commuting/temporary | Return | | | |
| | 20 | 11 | 4 | | | |

*Notes*

1. The tables here are intended to contextualize the results of the research presented in this volume. Material for Bulgaria is taken from "Migration Trends in Selected EU Applicant Countries. Volume I – Bulgaria. The Social Impact of Seasonal Migration" (IOM-Sofia: September 2003). This publication considers seasonal migration and offers an analysis of more general migration based on various sociological data collected in the last 15 years. Whilst it is rich in terms of information on the numbers of actual and potential migrants, it barely addresses the phenomenon of intercultural relationships and mixed marriages. In this respect, the present research is perhaps the only one of its kind in Bulgaria.

2. The older migrant women came to the target countries before 1989. They were either political migrants or well-educated women, mostly philologists, who had married Italian or Dutch men in their professional spheres. According to the IOM publication: 'in 1992-3 the scope and structure of the emigration flow changed' (2003: 17). Before that, in 1989-91 Bulgarian Turks accounted for 90 per cent of emigration, mainly to Turkey. Later the average emigrant became older than 30, and predominantly of Bulgarian nationality. In 1995-6, further transformations of the migration flow were detected: 60 per cent of the emigrants were between 30-49 years old and the majority of them were from urban areas. Our research sample does not differ from this profile.

3. During the 1990s the average Bulgarian migrant 'became older and of better educated' (ibid.). A study of potential migration conducted by IOM-Sofia, shows further that the percentage of high-skilled Bulgarians willing to migrate amounts to nearly 35 per cent of all potential migrants. Perhaps this number shows the tendency to mobility of high-qualified personnel which is widespread at present.

4. These numbers correspond to the tendency detected of migration of educated persons from urban areas. Many of the interviewed migrant women who were born in smaller cities have moved to bigger cities or the capital before emigrating from the country. The unemployment and lack of career possibilities in small cities can be the motive for both internal and external migration. However, the economic reasons for migration (which are referred to by 89.5 per cent of the potential Bulgarian migrants in 2001) are rarely pointed out as significant for the interviewed Bulgarian women who married a westerner. (The data are from the sample study of potential external migration of IOM-Sofia. The 2001 data was gathered during the census of 1 March 2001, the size of the sample is 25,542 persons aged 16-60. This is helpful in indicating the attitude to intercultural relationships amongst the other possible motives for emigration.)

5. The target group in the sample included married women or women who live on co-habitational terms with their partners.

6. No research has been done so far on the children of mixed marriages.

7. The reason for this large negative answer to the question of religion refers to religion as practice and as a strong belief in God. Otherwise most of the interviewed women belong to the Eastern Orthodox Christian Church. The questionnaire did not include a specific question about religion and practice, therefore only those interviewees who emphasized their strong religious affiliations were placed in a separate category, "orthodox". Religion can be potential reason for migration for only 1.3 per cent of all Bulgarians including minority groups (ibid.: 38).

8. The target group of interviewees were women who migrated after the fall of Communism, and some pre-1989 political migrants.

9. Most of the Bulgarian women who migrate legally are well-educated persons, who seek achievement in their professional lives.

10. The IOM survey on potential migration (quoted in the IOM-Sofia, 2003: 24-25) shows that among the most attractive countries for potential migration, Italy ranks at fourth place if it is a temporary migration, and at the seventh place if the migrant chooses to become a permanent resident. As for the Netherlands, in this list it ranks on eighteenth place for both temporary and permanent character of stay. In both cases, Germany is the most preferred country for migration, followed by USA and Greece if temporary migration is concerned, and by Australia and Canada if a person decides to leave Bulgaria permanently.

## Hungarian migrant women[1]

| Age cohort[2] | 20–29 | 30–39 | 40–49 | 50–59 | 60–69 | 70+ |
|---|---|---|---|---|---|---|
| | 6 | 16 | 10 | 3 | 3 | 2 |
| Highest educational level attained[3] | Primary School | Secondary school | Technical/professional | University first degree | University masters degree | PhD |
| | – | 4 | – | 18 | 16 | 2 |
| Place of origin[4] | Capital | City (More Than 500,000) | City (100,000–500,000) | City (20,000–100,000) | Town (2,000–20,000) | Village (less than 2,000) |
| | 26 | – | 6 | 5 | 2 | – |
| Family status[5] | Married | Single | Divorced | Co-habitation | Widowed | |
| | 27 | 4 | 3 | 5 | 1 | |
| Children[6] | No | Yes | | | | |
| | 17 | 23 | | | | |
| Religion[7] | None | Orthodox | Catholic | Muslim | Protestant | Jewish |
| | 30 | 5 | – | – | – | – |
| Migration[8] | Pre 1989 | Post 1989 | | | | |
| | 12 | 28 | | | | |
| Occupation in receiving country[9] | Housewife | Student | Unemployed | Retired | Volunteer | |
| | 3 | 8 | 1 | 0 | 1 | |
| | Professional | Associate professional | Small business owner | Clerical | Service/sales | Low-/unskilled |
| | 9 | 8 | 0 | 5 | 5 | 0 |

| Social mobility arising from migration | Upward mobility | Downward mobility | | | |
|---|---|---|---|---|---|
| | 24 | 14 | | | |
| **Previous migration experience** | Yes as a child | Yes as a student | Yes as a political refugee | Yes as a worker | Family migration | No |
| | | 2 | 4 | 3 | 7 | – |
| **Character of stay**[10] | Permanent | Commuting/temporary | Return | | | |
| | 34 | – | 6 | | | 24 |

*Notes*

1. Unfortunately, there does not exist a similar document for Hungary as for Bulgaria. The IOM Hungary published the country reports on migration trends only of six countries. (The country reports on Migration Trends form part of a publication series of six volumes - Bulgaria, Czech Republic, Poland, Romania, Slovakia, Slovenia - which have evolved under the European Commission funded project "Sharing Experience: Migration Trends in Selected Applicant Countries and Lessons Learned from the 'New Countries of Immigration' in the EU and Austria " managed by the International Organization for Migration Mission with Regional Functions for Central Europe in Vienna, Austria – IOM, Hungary.) The contextual material presented here is based on a document entitled: "The Labour Market and Migration: Threat or Opportunity? – The Likely Migration of Hungarian Labour to the European Union" (TÁRKI Social report Reprint Series No. 15. Ágnes Hárs, Bori Simonovits, Endre Sík). The document deals not only with seasonal migration but offers a more thorough general analysis of migration and migration potential collected over the last years, and focusing on the likely trends in migration. It is informative in terms of numbers of actual and potential migrants, but it hardly addresses the volume of migration in Hungary. Hárs et al. noted that in the last 20 years the Hungarian migration potential was low in comparison to other Central and Eastern European countries, and Hungarians had the lowest score in Central and Eastern Europe. Comparable migration potential data for Central and Eastern Europe in the new millennium strengthen this tendency; in that, regionally, Hungarian migration potential is relatively low, at a level roughly equivalent to Bulgaria and the Czech Republic. Migration was nevertheless at higher levels than through the period before 1989, when migration was officially and politically difficult. It is for this reason that there is not more detailed research concerning Hungarian migration to Italy and the Netherlands in the period of our research. In this respect, our research is perhaps the only one in Hungary of its kind.

2. The older migrant women came to the target countries before 1989. They were mostly well-educated women, some of them political migrants, mostly with some kind of university degree, who had married Italian or Dutch men.

3. "The social and demographic characteristics of migration potential – ignoring the influence of educational level – can be seen as constant. There is a general tendency for men, the younger age groups, the unemployed, students… to be more inclined to take work abroad." (ibid.: 270.) Our research sample does not differ from this profile as most migrated young, in their twenties. During the 1990s the planned migration target did not change. This is probably simply the continuation of a long-standing trend governed by historical and geographical considerations. First and foremost, Hungarians seek to realize their worth on the German and Austrian labour market, while the most common planned destination for emigration, besides these two countries, is the U.S. Looking at the evolution in time of migration potential (ibid.: 266) we see that, compared to the situation in the 1990s, the chances that someone would go abroad to work roughly doubled between 1993 and 2003. According to an EU source, 11.3 per cent of qualified Hungarians plan to live or work within five years in the old EU member states (ibid.: 268). Perhaps this number shows the tendency to mobility of high-qualified personnel which is widespread at present.

4. These numbers correspond to the detected tendency of migration of educated persons from urban areas. Many of the interviewed migrant women who were born in a village or a smaller cities have moved to bigger cities or the capital mostly to study before emigrating. The unemployment and lack of career possibilities in small cities can be the motive for both internal and external migration. However, the economic reasons for migration are rarely pointed out as significant for the interviewed Hungarian women who married a westerner.

5. The target group in the sample included married women or women who live on co-habitational terms with their partners.

6. No research has been done on the children of mixed marriages.

7. The reason for this large negative answer to the question of religion refers to religion as practice and as a strong belief in God. Otherwise most of the interviewed women belong to the Catholic and Protestant Church. The questionnaire did not include a specific question about religion and practice, therefore only those interviewees who emphasized their strong religious affiliations were placed in separate categories: 'Catholic', 'Protestant' and 'Jewish'. There is no information concerning religion as a potential reason for migration.

8. The interviewees were mostly women who migrated after the fall of Communism; in addition, we interviewed 12 women who emigrated before 1989.

9. Most of the Hungarian women who migrate legally are well-educated persons, who seek achievement in their professional lives.

10. The surveys on potential migration (Migration Potential Research Series 2001, 2002) show that among the most attractive countries for potential migration Italy ranks on fourth place if it is a temporary migration, and also on the fourth place if the migrant chooses to become a permanent resident in 2001. As for the Netherlands, in this list it is mentioned together with other counties for both temporary and permanent character of stay. It means that this country is not preferred so strongly than the bigger West-European countries. In both cases, Germany and Austria are the most preferred countries for migration, followed by U.S. and U.K. if temporary migration or permanent resident is concerned.

## Native Italian Women

| Age cohort[2] | 20–29 | 30–39 | 40–49 | 50–59 | 60–69 | 70+ |
|---|---|---|---|---|---|---|
| | 3 | 3 | 3 | 3 | 4 | 2 |
| **Education**[1] | Compulsory school | High school | Professional/Technical | University first degree | University masters degree | PhD |
| | 2 | 5 | 2 | – | 9 | – |
| **Family situation** | Married | Living with partner | Alone | Shared household with friends | Living with parents | Single parent |
| | 12 | 2 | 2 | 1 | 1 | – |
| **Mixed marriage** | Yes | No | | | | |
| | – | 12 | | | | |
| **Migration experience**[2] | In family of origin | Student | Work | | | |
| | 4 | 2 | – | | | |
| | Abroad | Abroad | | | | |
| | 1 | 1 | | | | |
| **Occupational position** | Social/community work sector | Educational, research sector and student | Self-employed | Agriculture | Employee | Housewife | Retired |
| | 2 | 3 | 2 | 2 | 2 | 3 | 4 |
| **Relationship to migrants**[3] | Friendship | Acquaintance | Employer | Colleagues | Social work | Voluntary assistance |
| | 4 | 3 | 7 | 1 | 2 | 2 |

## Notes

1. For what concerns the social status of the Italian interviewees (age, education, family situation) we have tried to be wide-ranging. Most age groups have been included: most women are married but the younger ones illustrate the range of new living choices (co-habitation with partner, with friends, alone). If we compare these data with the Dutch women's sample we find a greater number of married couples within the Italian sample which we can explain in two ways: referring to the typical figures that indicate a consistent number of married couples in Italy; stressing the role of the 'snow ball' as an instrument for contacting women to be interviewed. The 'snow ball' method has also had a role in shaping the educational level of our sample; in fact most of the women contacted in Rome belong to the educated bourgeoisie not only in terms of educational level, but also in their family situation, and economic conditions.
2. Stories and images of Italian emigration are constantly recollected within the public discourse when contemporary immigration to Italy is addressed. Although this feature was not specifically looked for, several women in the sample referred to their memories of 'movement' in order to give sense to immigrant experiences in Italy.
3. Three main characteristics of our sample have been shaped in relation to the main representations of migration in Italy:

- First of all, the literature stresses, in Italy and more widely in Europe, that most women migrants from Eastern Europe are employed as care workers in Italian household. In order to have a picture able to narrate the 'other side of the coin', we have contacted several Italian women employers of migrant 'care' or domestic workers. Moreover, in the employer category, Italian women working in agriculture are present due to the important role of this sector for migrants' seasonal labour.
- Secondly, in Italy the State's inability to deal with migrant needs and rights has encouraged the development of a voluntary care sector which tries to substitute for public intervention in education, housing, health, and other areas of fundamental rights. Therefore, in our sample we included Italian women working in this sphere.
- Thirdly, we contacted Italian women who have a relationship of friendship with migrant women (including some of those interviewed). In this way we sought narratives of experiences which are potentially outside of the power relations associated with work and assistance.

## Native Dutch Women[1]

| Age cohort[2] | 20-29 | 30-39 | 40-49 | 50-59 | 60-69 | 70+ |
|---|---|---|---|---|---|---|
| | 4 | 5 | 4 | – | – | – |
| Education[1] | Compulsory school | High school | Professional/Technical | University first degree | University masters degree | PhD |
| | 1 (primary only) | 2 (one still a student) | – | 2 | 8 | – |
| Family situation | Married | Living with partner | Alone | Shared household with friends | Living with parents | Single parent |
| | 3 | 3 | 4 | 2 | 1 | |
| Mixed marriage | Yes | No | | | | |
| | 2 | – | | | | |
| Migration experience[2] | In family of origin | Student | Work | | | |
| | 3 | 5 | 2 | | | |
| Occupational position | Social / community work sector | Educational and research sector | Self-employed | Student | Other (jurist; NGO project staff; call centre staff) | |
| | 4 | 3 | 2 | 1 | 3 | |
| Relationship to migrants[3] | Friendship | Acquaintance | Employer | Colleagues | Social work | Voluntary assistance |
| | 5 | 1 | 1 | 3 | 3 | 3 |

*Notes*

1. The Dutch women in this sample were engaged in the research in three ways, the majority directly via the Bulgarian and Hungarian women who were part of the research, who recommended colleagues, friend, acquaintances and other Dutch women from their surroundings. Secondly, two women responded to a call placed on a Dutch-Bulgarian bulletin board on the Internet. Thirdly, a minority of women were contacted directly, independently of the Hungarian and Bulgarian women involved. This was to construct a sample which included a broader range of relationships between Dutch and migrant women. These were, most importantly, women who work with migrant women (not exclusively, but including women from Eastern Europe) in their profession as social workers. No comparable research on the relationships between native Dutch and migrant women from Hungary and Bulgaria has been done. Similar, oral history based research and other, non-scientific projects have been carried out with native Dutch and migrant women, mainly from Turkey and Morocco. Government funded research usually focuses on groups of migrant women that have the highest numerical presence in the Netherlands and, are the most visible (often because their position and/or behaviour are problematised in terms of lack of integration). Women from Eastern Europe are not included in these categories.

2. Age, education and profession: the range represented in the sample of Dutch women is narrower than in the Italian sample. An explanation for this might be the method of finding Dutch interviewees: contacts were mostly volunteered by Hungarian and Bulgarian women who participated in the research; those women who were interested in giving us contacts were usually women who were in good relationships with Dutch women and generally managing their lives in the Netherlands to their satisfaction; and they tended to give details of women with whom they are on good terms.

3. Some of the respondents lived abroad for several reasons in different periods of their lives. 5 interviewees have never lived abroad; 8 had some 'migration experience' ranging from spending three months abroad whilst studying to living in another country during their childhood or as adults for extensive periods. Only one of them called her childhood experiences of mobility 'migration'.

4. Represented in the table is the category in which the relationship that was most discussed during the interview falls, even though in some cases respondents referred to different women to whom they had different relationships (e.g., both colleagues and friends). The method of migrant women suggesting native women to interview explains the nature of the relationships, i.e., mostly friends or co-workers were recommended, instead of employers or social workers. Moreover, comparing the Dutch sample to the Italian one, the category of employer in the situation of employer-migrant domestic or care worker, is absent; few women from Hungary or Bulgaria work as domestic workers in the Netherlands. Migrant domestic workers are usually from the South or from other Eastern European countries, and the practice of live-in domestic or care work is less widespread than in Italy.

# Notes on Contributors

**Nadejda Alexandrova** is Assistant Professor in literature in the Department of Slavic Studies at Sofia University 'St. Kliment Ohridski'. She is also a member of the Gender Studies Centre at Sofia University and a researcher in a number of international projects concerning gender and feminism.

**Rosi Braidotti** former Professor of Gender Studiesis now Distinguished Professor in the Humanities at Utrecht University. She set up and directed until 2005 ATHENA: the European Socrates Thematic Network for Women's Studies. Amongst her most widely read publications are *Nomadic Subjects: Embodiment and Sexual Difference in Contemporary Feminist* Theory (New York: Columbia University Press, 1994); *Metamorphoses: Towards a Materialist Theory of Becoming* (Cambridge: Polity Press, 2002); her most recent book is *Transpositions: On Nomadic Ethics* (Cambridge: Polity Press, 2006).

**Enrica Capussotti** is Researcher at the Department of History, Siena University. She obtained her Ph.D. at the European University Institute and was subsequently a Marie Curie Fellow at the Institute of Romance Studies (University of London). She is currently working on two projects, the first concerning internal migration in Italy in the 1950s, and the second focusing on contemporary European cinema and European belongings. She is the author of *Gioventù perduta. Gli anni cinquanta dei giovani e del cinema in Italia* (Florence: Giunti, 2004).

**Inger Marie Conradsen** studied law at University of Copenhagen (cand.jur.), University of Edinburgh (LL.M) and the European University Institute (Ph.D.). She now works at the Danish Ministry of the Interior and Health. She has published nationally and internationally on health law, in particular reproductive rights, and immigration law.

**Anna Hortobagyi** graduated from the University of Economics in Budapest in 2003 specializing in EU studies, German and pedagogy. In 2003–04 she worked at the Strategic and International Department of Government Office of Equal Opportunities, and from 2004 in the Department of Development and Strategy of the Ministry of Youth, Family, Social Affairs and Equal Opportunities.

**Annette Kronborg**, LL.M, Ph.D., is Associate Professor in the Legal Faculty, Cophenhagen University, Denmark. She teaches family law and international family law and researches in these areas. Her publications are mainly in Danish.

**Ioanna Laliotou** is Assistant Professor in Contemporary History at the University of Thessaly, Greece, and a Fullbright Visiting Scholar at Columbia University (2006). Her research interests concern the history of contemporary migrations, the history of subjectivity, and cultural theory and criticism. She is author of *Transatlantic Subjects: Acts of Migration and Culture of Transnationalism between Europe and America* (Chicago: Chicago University Press, 2004). She is also a member of the editorial committee of the journal Historein (www.historein.gr).

**Dawn Lyon** is Lecturer in Sociology at the University of Kent, UK. She completed her Ph.D. in the sociology of careers at the European University Institute where she co-ordinated the Gender Studies Programme in the Robert Schuman Centre for Advanced Studies (2000–04). From 2004–06 she was Senior Research Officer on the 'Transformations of Work' research programme at the University of Essex. Her research interests and publications focus on work and employment and gendered processes and identities at work, especially in comparative perspective.

**Miglena Nikolchina** is Professor and Head of the Department of Theory and History of Literature, Sofia University, Bulgaria. She is the author of *Matricide in Language: Writing Theory in Kristeva and Woolf* (New York: The Other Press, 2004), which has also appeared in Bulgarian (1997), Macedonian (2000), Russian (2003) and Hungarian (2004). Her other books include *Born from the Head: Plots and Narratives in Women's Literary History* (Sofia, 2002), and *The Utopian Human Being* (Sofia, 1992).

**Luisa Passerini** is Professor of Cultural History at the University of Torino and External Professor at the European University Institute, Florence. She has been Director of the research group 'Europe : Emotions, Identities, Politics' at the Kulturwissenschaftliches Institut, Essen, as the recipient of the Research Prize of Nordrhein–Westfalen, 2002–04. Among her recent publications are: *Europe in Love, Love in Europe. Imagination and Politics Between the Wars* (London and New York, 1999); *Il mito d'Europa. Radici antiche per nuovi simboli* (Florence, 2002); *Memory and Utopia* (London, 2007), and, as editor: *Across the Atlantic: Cultural Exchanges between Europe and the United States* (Brussels, 2000); *Figures d'Europe. Images and Myths of Europe* (Brussels, 2003); (with Ruth Mas), Special Issue of the *European Review of History* on 'Europe and Love – L'Europe et l'amour', 11(2) Summer 2004.

**Hanne Petersen** received her doctoral degree in law at the University of Copenhagen in 1991 and spent a year as a Jean Monnet Fellow at the EUI from 1993–94. From 1995–99 she was Professor in the Sociology of Law and Legal Science at the University of Greenland in Nuuk. Having returned to the University of Copenhagen she took up a Professorship in Greenlandic Sociology of Law from 2001–06. She has published in the areas of labour law, women's law, indigenous legal issues, legal theory, legal culture, as well as on *Home Knitted Law* (Dartmouth: Ashgate, 1996). She has edited several books, amongst them *Love and Law in Europe* (Aldershot: Ashgate, 1998).

**Andrea Pető** is Associate Professor at the University of Miskolc, where she directs the Equal Opportunity and Gender Studies Centre; she is also Assistant Professor at the Department of Gender Studies at the Central European University, Hungary. Publications include: *Nohistóriák. A politizáló magyar nok története* (1945–51) (Seneca, 1998), translated as *Women in Hungarian Politics* 1945–51 (Columbia University Press/East European Monographs, 2003); a biography of Rajk Júlia (Balassi, Budapest, 2001); *Napasszonyok és Holdkisasszonyok. A mai magyar konzervatív noi politizálás alaktana*, (Women of Sun and Girls of Moon. Morphology of Contemporary Hungarian Women Doing Politics) (Balassi, 2003); and six edited volumes in Hungarian, seven in English, and two in Russian.

**Esther Vonk** has an MA in Women's Studies and Dutch language and literature from Utrecht University, the Netherlands. She has worked as coordinator of the International Office of Women's Studies at Utrecht University. She currently works as European programme officer for Mama Cash, a Fund for Women in Amsterdam. She is also involved in different feminist groups and initiatives in the Netherlands.

# Index

about this book
  communication, migration and 15
  everyday life of migrants 16
  focus 2
  'food talk' 16
  imaginary geographies 15
  integration of minorities 17
  intermezzos 15, 16, 18
  intersubjectivity 19
  legal subjectivity 14
  love in migrant accounts 16
  methodological choices 5–13
  mobility and subjectivity 14
  modernity and backwardness 17–18
  moral and cultural boundaries 18
  progressive potential of Europe 13–14
  structure 13–19
  transformations and subjecthood 14
  work, 3, 5, 7–8, 10, 12, 16, 18
Ackers, Louise 230
adaptation 46, 139, 143, 147, 149, 150, 159
Adorno, Theodor 24
affective relationships 51–2, 126
Agnew, J. 208
airports 100–101
Al-Ali, N. and Koser, K. 108n2
Alexandrova, Nadejda 9, 12, 15, 16, 84–91, 95–107, 138–50, 273n24, 314
alternative subjectivities, range of 28
Andall, J. 123, 274n29
Anderson, B. 37
Angelov, Angel 116, 118
Anthias, F. and Lazaridis, G. 96
anti-Americanism 187
anti-Europeanism 25, 26
anti-feminism 65n10
anti-Semitism 25
Anzaldua, G. 40n1
Appadurai, Arjun 25
Armstrong, A. and Welshman, N. 71
aspiration and work 128
assimilation 48, 64n2, 64n7
asylum seekers 180–81
asymmetric relationships 196–7, 201
Athanasiou, Athina 64
Augé, Marc 100, 150n1
Australia 33

authenticity and truth 180–85

backwardness *see* modernity and
Bade, K.J. 4
Bakhtin, Mikhail 116, 118
Balibar, E. and Wallerstein, I. 66n2
Balibar, Étienne 24, 37, 196, 266
Barthes, Roland 152–3
Bell, D. and Binnie, J. 50
belonging
  and attachment to place 95–107
  boundaries, moral and cultural 219–20
  *see also* home
Benería, L. and Roldán, M. 135n2
Benhabib, S. 25, 36–7
Berns, Sandra 76–7
Bhabha, Homi K. 37, 64n1, 100, 101
Bhavnani, K. 36
Binnie, J. 50
Binnie, J. and Valentine, G. 50
black subjectivity 32–3
Blom, A. 274n28
Bogdanov, B. 118
Boiadjiev, T. 117
Bollati, G. 208
Bommes, M. and Morawska, E. 11
border crossings 96–9
border-places and 'home' 95–107
Borris, E. and Prügl, E. 135n2
Botev, Hristo 108n8, 108n10
boundaries, moral and cultural 212–27
  belonging to Europe, boundaries of 219–20
  boundary expansion in Europe 217–18
  boundary work 213–14
    cultural boundaries 219–21
    hard work as moral worth 214–16
    intelligence 220–21
    loosening boundaries 222–3
    manners 220–21
    moral boundaries 214–18
    respectability and self-identity 217–18
    tradition and nationality 217–18
Bourdieu, Pierre 217
Brah, Avtar 35–6, 40n2, 102, 188
Braidotti, Rosi 11, 12, 13, 23–40, 64n3, 270–71n4, 314
British Nationality Act (1948) 81n2

British Nationality Acts (1948 and 1981) 81n2
Brodkin Sacks, K. 33
Bruck, Edith 18, 103, 243–50, 284, 288
Buck-Morss, S. 57
Bulgaria
  Adela, Bulgarian/Italian migrant in Italy 143, 149, 276, 278
  Albena, Bulgarian/Dutch migrant in Netherlands 102, 104, 108n14, 141, 143, 145, 148, 156, 157, 280, 282
  Alena, Bulgarian migrant in Netherlands 100, 101, 102, 112, 114, 130, 131, 148, 149, 279, 282
  Ana, Bulgarian migrant in Italy 46, 102, 106, 119, 148–9, 255, 258, 275, 278
  Angelina, Bulgarian migrant in Italy 102, 105, 146, 147, 148, 276, 278
  Boyana, Bulgarian/Dutch migrant in Netherlands 47, 55, 59, 60, 104, 105, 108n14, 114, 115, 119, 143, 262, 280, 282
  Carolina, Bulgarian/Italian migrant in Italy 144, 145, 276, 278
  Eva, Bulgarian migrant in Netherlands 100, 102, 108n14, 142, 148, 279, 282
  Irena, Bulgarian migrant in Italy 102, 108n14, 112, 119, 135n6, 141, 143, 146, 275, 277
  Jelisaveta, Bulgarian/Italian migrant in Italy 15, 84, 101, 102, 107, 108n14, 130, 144, 146–8, 275, 277
  Joanna, Bulgarian/Dutch migrant in Netherlands 102, 114, 120, 148, 281, 283
  Julia, Bulgarian migrant in Netherlands 114, 263, 281, 283
  Kalina, Bulgarian migrant in Netherlands 108n14, 113, 115, 123, 124, 126, 149, 279, 282
  Kate, Bulgarian/Dutch migrant in Netherlands 280, 283
  Kremena, Bulgarian/Dutch migrant in Netherlands 108n14, 112, 113, 114, 142, 143, 144, 148, 155, 262, 280, 283
  Kristina, Bulgarian migrant in Italy 124, 135n6, 145, 147, 148, 149, 276, 278
  Lilia, Bulgarian/Australian migrant in Netherlands 281, 283
  Lora, Bulgarian migrant in Netherlands 145, 148, 281, 283
  Lubomira, Bulgarian migrant in Netherlands 127, 128, 129, 280, 282
  Marina, Bulgarian/Italian migrant in Italy 47, 54, 98, 99, 101, 105, 106, 108n5, 108n14, 115, 124, 136n7, 141, 143, 158, 276, 278
  Maya, Bulgarian migrant in Italy 276, 278
  migrants from 1, 10, 275–83
    characteristics of 304–6
  Mina, Bulgarian migrant in Italy 100, 102, 142–3, 147–8, 154, 156, 255, 258, 275, 277
  Nikoleta, Bulgarian migrant in Netherlands 281, 283
  Nona, Bulgarian/Italian migrant in Italy 101, 108n14, 113, 144, 146, 148, 275, 277
  Olga, Bulgarian migrant in Italy 101, 115, 148, 276, 278
  Plamena, Bulgarian migrant in Netherlands 102, 112, 114, 115, 124, 144, 157, 160, 279, 282
  Poly, Bulgarian migrant in Netherlands 135n6, 149, 253, 263, 279, 282
  Ralica, Bulgarian/Italian migrant in Italy 108n14, 148, 257, 275, 277
  Reneta, Bulgarian/Dutch migrant in Netherlands 102, 105, 112, 113, 114, 129, 149, 281, 283
  Rosa, Bulgarian/Dutch migrant in Netherlands 51–2, 97, 98, 108n16, 129, 149, 151n8, 281, 283
  Teodora, Bulgarian migrant in Netherlands 100, 127–8, 129, 141, 143, 145, 279, 282
  Vesela, Bulgarian migrant in Netherlands 280, 283
  Victoria, Bulgarian/Italian migrant in Italy 106, 108n12, 130, 257, 275, 277
  Violeta, Bulgarian migrant in Netherlands 104, 105, 113, 114, 115, 133, 145, 280, 283
  Yana, Bulgarian/Italian migrant in Italy 142, 143, 144, 146, 147, 148, 275, 277
Burgio, A. 196
Burke, Peter 140
Butterworth, Jez 209n4

Canada 33
Capussotti, Enrica 1–19, 122–35, 165–74, 195–211, 214, 217, 225n7, 271n8, 272n18, 314
caring and work 131
Caritas (2003) 225n4
Casey, Catherine 136n12
Castells, M. 29
Catholicism 77, 173, 174, 195
Certeau, Michel de 139, 150n1
Chakrabarty, Dipesh 195
Cheak, P. and Robbins, B. 64n5
choice
  agency and 79
  of countries for research 7–8
  of exile 52
  'force' vs 'choice' distinction 180–81
  of method of oral history 5
  of work 123–6
Christianity 29, 32, 34, 69, 79, 80, 108n9, 209n7, 219–20, 261, 264, 306n7
citizenship 31, 86–7
  democratic citizenship 36–7
  European Union (EU) 36
  flexibility in 35–7, 38
  modern citizenship 76–7
  politics of 36–7
  post-nationalistic identity and 35–6
  'transversal citizenship' 49
  'unencumbered' 76–7
civilization 24
  Europe as 'cradle' of 30

# Index

Clifford, James 30
Clough, P. 134
Coelho, Paulo 141
cohabitation 237
Cohn-Bendit, Daniel 31
collective enterprises 74
Colombo, F. 207
Colorni, Eugenio 271n9
communication 111–20
   conversation 116–19
   crisis in 57
   culture as 114–16
   dialectical communication 117–19, 120
   dialogism 116–19
   inadequacies of 113–14, 115, 129
   language and 114
   loneliness and failure in 115
   oral communication 117–18
   reciprocity and 111–12
   spontaneous interaction and 112–13
   'stereo' effects of 114–15, 120
   togetherness and 111–12
   tolerance, indifference and 115
   types of 111–14
   unwritten communication 119–20
   written communication 119–20
communism 56, 116, 119, 258, 260
   activism under 206
   anti-feminism after 65n10
   collapse of 124, 272n19
   equality under 190, 206
   heterotopia of 57
   isolation during 15, 205
   Italian communist party 209n2, 260
   migration and 7, 47
   national belonging under 103–4
   religion under 161
   restrictions on mobility under 47, 106, 124
   *see also* post-communism
comparative design 7–8
Conradsen, Inger Marie 17, 18, 228–42, 273n26, 314
consciousness 39
   forms of 30–31
constant mobility 29–30
conversation 116–19
Coombes, A.E. and Brah, A. 220
Corrin, C. 55
cosmopolitanism 39, 47, 204
Cotesta, V. 209n8
Cotterrell, Roger 77–8
Couhnihan, C. and Esterik, P. van 152, 158–9
courting 141
Cresswell, T. 29
Crowley, J. 273n27, 274n28
culture
   boundaries, moral and cultural 219–21
   as communication 114–16
   conflicts and food-talk 153–4, 156–7, 157–8
   cultural identity in Europe 34–5
   cultural incompatibility 46, 224n2
   homogenization of 38
   integration and threat to 187–8
   intercultural dialogues 5
   intercultural relations 198–9, 201–4

   legal culture of Europe in transformation 68–70, 75–6
   moral and cultural boundaries 18
   socio-cultural mutation 29
   trans-culturality and location 28–9
   US legal culture 78–9
   *see also* multiculturalism

Dahl, T.S. 70
Dahrendorf, Ralf 29
Dal Lago, A. 215
D'Attorre, P.P. 209n2
de Geus, Aart Jan 177, 190, 192
de Groote, Jacqueline 271n8
De Lauretis, T. 40n1
de-territorialization 258–62
Deleuze, G. and Guattari, F. 23, 25, 33, 48, 64n4, 272n13
Deleuze, Gilles 24
democratic citizenship 36–7
democratization 56
Denmark
   age limit criteria for reunification of spouses 232
   aggregate-tie criteria 232
   cohabitation in 237
   family law 235–9
   family reunification, immigration law on 231–2
   immigration reform 231–2, 239–40
   legal perception of marriage and family, change in 236–8
   legal system in 72–3, 80–81
   matrimonial law 229, 239–40
dependency 90
Derrida, Jacques 24, 47, 261
Desai, J. 51
Deshormes, Fausta 254, 271n8
destination countries, attitudes towards 53–5
Dia, Biatriz de 150n5
dialectical communication 117–19, 120
dialogism 116–19
diaspora
   diasporic identity 36
   narratives of 30
   queer diaspora studies 50–51
Dickie, J. 196
'difference' and 'exclusion' 37–8
differentiation, tradition and 205–6
dignity through work 129–30
discovery, process of 198–9
discrimination 173
   at work 132–4
dissociation, repression and 183–4
Douglas, Mary 152, 157, 162
Dübeck, I. 74
Dubosc, Fabrice Olivier 271n7
Dyer, Richard 32–3

economics
   advantage in 180
   burden of 214
   capitalism 49, 130
   conventional assumptions 136n12
   developed countries 133

drive of economic need 63
economic future 230
economic maintenance 69
economic marriages 144–5
economic migrants 180–81, 231
economic transitions 2–5
emancipation and wealth 204
food, economy with 155–6
global economy 23, 30, 37, 187, 201
Italian economy 200
legal and economic status 74
market economy 25
means, lack of 78, 81
migrant and native labour 133
and morals of family unit 56
political or economic exiles 52
post-communist 45
power and authority in 160
pragmatism in 139
present conditions 124, 202
professional and economic opportunity 124
rationality of 113
social and economic cohesion 240
social and economic rights 201
socio-economic boundaries 213, 225n3
US and European hegemony in 32
Ehrenreich, B. and Hochschild, A. 135n2
Einhorn, B. 55, 272n19
Eisenstein, Z. 25
emancipation and integration 177–93
  affirmation of need for 185–90
  asylum seekers 180–81
  authenticity and truth, preoccupation with 180–85
  cultural threat of integration 187–8
  denial of dominant images 191
  discourse in context, 'integration of minorities' in Netherlands 178–80
  dissociation, repression and 183–4
  empowerment strategies 193
  'fake marriage' 182–3
  gender relations and femininity 188–90
  historical consciousness 192
  instrumentalization of feminist discourse 191–2
  interethnic relations 192–3
  labour market and 'emancipation' 190
  legal status, attainment of 185
  migration, reasons for 180–82
  minorities, integration in Netherlands 178–80, 188–90
  Netherlands emancipation policy 177
  new realist discourse 178–9
  nostalgia 180
  permission to reside 182–3
  political consciousness 192
  'self' and 'other' in discourse of 179–80
  stereotypes and 'one exception' 191
  strategies of resistance to hegemonic discourse on 191–3
emotional relationships 59, 62–3
empiricism 3
empowerment 24, 193
Eng, D.L. 50
Eng, D.L. and Hom, A.H. 50, 65n8

enlargement of European Union (EU) 34, 79, 109n19
equality
  under communism 190, 206
  equal rights, citizen as subject of 76–7
Escobar, A. and Harcourt, W. 270n2
Essed, Philomena 32, 40n2, 222–3
ethnic cooking 162
ethnicity 32–3
Eurocentrism 5, 32, 204
Europe 23–40, 45–64
  airports as 'non-places' 100–101
  belonging and attachment to place 95–107
  border crossings 96–9
  boundary expansion in 25
  citizenship 'unencumbered' 76–7
  contemporary construction of 5
  cultural identity in 34–5
  'difference' and 'exclusion' in mind-set of 37–8
  equal rights, citizen as subject of 76–7
  Europeanness and belonging 4
  gender relations, interdisciplinary research 70–74
  geo-political space of 4–5
  history of 32
  identity and passport 99
  landscapes 101–3
  late modern forms of emergent legal subjectivity 77–9
  legal culture in transformation 68–70, 75–6
  legal subjectivity 68–81
    emergent late modern forms of 77–9
    mobility, privilege and 68–9
  legal subordination of women 74–6
  modern citizenship 76–7
  multiple belonging and limits of 103–6
  multiple selves in complex legal contexts 79–81
  non-places 99–101
  objects, place of 101–3
  passport, sanctity of 96–9
  post-nationalist identity in 35–6, 38, 39–40
  post-nationalist space in 25, 26, 35
  re-grounding of 31–5
  social imaginary, lack in 39
  space, creation of 101–3
  subjectivity, pre-modern privileged 74–6
  subjectivity, towards privileged legal 68–70
  train stations as 'non-places' 100, 101
  transition and first impressions 99–101
  unification of 26–7, 31
  universalism of 26
  visas and documentation 98–9
  white migrants, experience of 33–4
European Convention on Human Rights (1950) 230
European Court of Justice (ECJ) 78–9
European Union (EU) 23, 31
  accession of Bulgaria and Hungary 109n19
  black subjectivity in 32–3
  citizenship 36
  constitution of 74
  democratic citizenship 36–7
  enlargement of 34, 79

*Index* 321

identity 37
immigration law 230
legal subject-hood in 72–4
national identity 36, 37, 103, 157, 178–80, 193, 207–8
nationality 36
ongoing process of 37
opposition to 25
origins of 25–6
progressive potential 23–4, 26
racialized hierarchy of 34
social agenda 30
trans-national space in 37
Europeanness 53
belonging and 4
expression of 255–8
in narratives of migration 262–3
*Des européennes* 254
Europism 32
exclusion, legitimization of 80–81
exile status 105, 106
economic or political exiles 52
identification as of 51
romanticization of 46
subjectivity in 50
expectations and ideas, uncertainty in 198
experiences of mobility 53–5, 61–2
exploitation 209n7
discrimination at work and 133–4

Fabian, J. 205
'fake marriage' 182–3
family bonding 155, 162
family law as instrument of immigration law 238–9
family life and work 130–32
family situations of interviewees
cohabiting women
Anett (Hungarian) in Netherlands 126, 257, 260, 261, 293, 297
Angéla (Hungarian) in Italy 287, 290
Angelina (Bulgarian) in Italy 102, 105, 146, 147, 148, 276, 278
Carlotta (Italian) in Italy 198, 201, 203, 204, 299
Daniela (Italian) in Italy 226n19, 299
Ellen (Dutch) in Netherlands 183, 184, 185, 187, 301
Eva (Bulgarian) in Netherlands 100, 102, 108n14, 142, 148, 279, 282
Ilse (Dutch) in Netherlands 302
Janka (Hungarian/Rumanian) in Italy 287, 290
Lubomira (Bulgarian) in Netherlands 127, 128, 129, 280, 282
Olga (Bulgarian) in Italy 101, 115, 148, 276, 278
Piroska (Hungarian/Dutch) in Netherlands 15, 59, 87, 88, 91, 161, 162, 292, 296
Ralica (Bulgarian/Italian) in Italy 108n14, 148, 257, 275, 277
Suze (Dutch) in Netherlands 220, 224, 303
Vesela (Bulgarian) in Netherlands 280, 283

Yana (Bulgarian/Italian) in Italy 142, 143, 144, 146, 147, 148, 275, 277
divorced women
Ági (Hungarian/Dutch) in Netherlands 59, 108n14, 112, 292, 295
Ana (Bulgarian) in Italy 46, 102, 106, 119, 148–9, 255, 258, 275, 278
Ila (Hungarian/Dutch) in Netherlands 292, 2957
Kamilla (Hungarian) in Italy 60, 61, 62, 109n17, 285, 289
Klári (Hungarian/Dutch) in Netherlands 293, 296
Kristina (Bulgarian) in Italy 124, 135n6, 145, 147, 148, 149, 276, 278
Maya (Bulgarian) in Italy 276, 278
Olga (Bulgarian) in Italy 101, 115, 148, 276, 278
Reneta (Bulgarian/Dutch) in Netherlands 102, 105, 112, 113, 114, 129, 149, 281, 283
Rosa (Bulgarian/Dutch) in Netherlands 51–2, 97, 98, 108n16, 129, 149, 151n8, 281, 283
married women
Adela (Bulgarian/Italian) in Italy 143, 149, 276, 278
Adriana (Italian) in Italy 215, 300
Ági (Hungarian/Dutch) in Netherlands 59, 108n14, 112, 292, 295
Albena (Bulgarian/Dutch) in Netherlands 102, 104, 108n14, 141, 143, 145, 148, 156, 157, 280, 282
Alena (Bulgarian) in Netherlands 100, 101, 102, 112, 114, 130, 131, 148, 149, 279, 282
Angela (Italian) in Italy 16, 159, 170, 171, 173, 199, 203, 204, 205, 206, 207, 208, 218, 219, 224, 227, 256, 298
Barbara (Dutch) in Netherlands 16, 165, 169, 189, 301
Bori (Hungarian/Italian) in Italy 131, 205, 217, 218, 284, 288
Boyana (Bulgarian/Dutch) in Netherlands 47, 55, 59, 60, 104, 105, 108n14, 114, 115, 119, 143, 262, 280, 282
Brigi (Hungarian/Dutch) in Netherlands 153, 261, 293, 297
Carla (Italian) in Italy 159, 203, 260, 300
Carolina (Bulgarian/Italian) in Italy 144, 145, 276, 278
Cristina (Italian) in Italy 207, 208, 217, 299
Csilla (Hungarian/Italian) in Italy 105, 145, 158, 161, 170, 172, 204, 285, 288
Deborah (Dutch) in Netherlands 303
Edith (Hungarian/Italian) in Italy 18, 103, 243–50, 284, 288
Ella (Hungarian/Dutch) in Netherlands 161, 292, 296
Emília (Hungarian/Dutch) in Netherlands 62, 63, 108n14, 141, 143, 291, 295
Emma (Hungarian/Italian) in Italy 95, 105, 108n4, 108n14, 115, 130, 131, 132, 142, 143, 148, 286, 290

Erzsébet (Hungarian/Dutch) in Netherlands 136n10, 152, 293, 296
Giovanna (Italian) in Italy 198, 199, 200, 201, 202, 206, 207, 215, 218, 220, 225n6, 265, 299
Gyöngyi (Hungarian/Italian) in Italy 133, 134, 155, 160, 287, 290
Henrietta (Hungarian/Dutch) in Netherlands 125, 126, 291, 295
Hilda (Hungarian/Dutch) in Netherlands 261, 294, 297
Ila (Hungarian/Dutch) in Netherlands 292, 295
Ilona (Hungarian/Dutch) in Netherlands 292, 296
Irén (Hungarian/Italian) in Italy 108n14, 112, 119, 137, 141, 143, 146, 285, 288
Irena (Bulgarian) in Italy 102, 108n14, 112, 119, 135n6, 141, 143, 146, 275, 277
Ivett (Hungarian) in Italy 286, 289
Jelisaveta (Bulgarian/Italian) in Italy 15, 84, 101, 102, 107, 108n14, 130, 144, 146–8, 275, 277
Joanna (Bulgarian/Dutch) in Netherlands 102, 114, 120, 148, 281, 283
Juli (Hungarian) in Italy 108n14, 285, 289
Kalina (Bulgarian) in Netherlands 108n14, 113, 115, 123, 124, 126, 149, 279, 282
Kate (Bulgarian/Dutch) in Netherlands 280, 283
Kremena (Bulgarian/Dutch) in Netherlands 108n14, 112, 113, 114, 142, 143, 144, 148, 155, 262, 280, 283
Lili (Hungarian/British) in Italy 286, 289
Lilia (Bulgarian/Australian) in Netherlands 281, 283
Lina (Italian) in Italy 298
Lora (Bulgarian) in Netherlands 145, 148, 281, 283
Magda (Hungarian/Dutch) in Netherlands 159, 291, 295
Mari (Hungarian/Dutch) in Netherlands 154, 160, 161, 291, 295
Marina (Bulgarian/Italian) in Italy 47, 54, 98, 99, 101, 105, 106, 109n5, 108n14, 115, 124, 136n7, 141, 143, 158, 276, 278
Mónika (Hungarian/Dutch) in Netherlands 99, 108n14, 141, 142, 143, 155, 263, 293, 296
Nikoleta (Bulgarian) in Netherlands 281, 283
Noémi (Hungarian) in Netherlands 258, 294, 297
Nona (Bulgarian/Italian) in Italy 101, 108n14, 113, 144, 146, 148, 275, 277
Orietta (Italian) in Italy 159, 207, 208, 215, 220, 300
Patrizia (Italian) in Italy 198, 199, 203, 207, 261, 300
Petra (Hungarian/Italian) in Italy 216, 221, 222, 223, 256, 257, 272n18, 286, 289

Plamena (Bulgarian) in Netherlands 102, 112, 114, 115, 124, 144, 157, 160, 279, 282
Poly (Bulgarian) in Netherlands 135n6, 149, 253, 263, 279, 282
Roberta (Italian) in Italy 198, 206, 207, 214, 215, 216, 217, 218, 220, 225n9, 298
Rosaria (Italian) in Italy 203, 208, 300
Rozika (Hungarian/Dutch) in Netherlands 141, 143, 154, 291, 295
Rózsa (Hungarian/Italian) in Italy 284, 288
Sarolta (Hungarian) in Italy 285, 289
Silvana (Italian) in Italy 198, 199, 200, 202, 205, 206, 217, 218, 220, 225n10, 299
Teodora (Bulgarian) in Netherlands 100, 127–8, 129, 141, 143, 145, 279, 282
Teri (Hungarian/Dutch) in Netherlands 141, 143, 155, 259, 293, 297
Vali (Hungarian/Italian) in Italy 106, 284, 288
Victoria (Bulgarian/Italian) in Italy 106, 108n12, 130, 257, 275, 277
Violeta (Bulgarian) in Netherlands 104, 105, 113, 114, 115, 133, 145, 280, 283
Wilma (Dutch) in Netherlands 181, 182, 183, 185, 186, 216, 301
Zsuzsa (Hungarian) in Italy 285, 289
single women
 Diana (Dutch) in Netherlands 301
 Emese (Hungarian/Rumanian) in Italy 285, 289
 Francesca (Italian) in Italy 299
 Hanneke (Dutch) in Netherlands 184, 185, 190, 193, 194, 303
 Inge (Dutch) in Netherlands 156, 181, 186, 302
 Jacqueline (Dutch) in Netherlands 302
 Jantina (Dutch) in Netherlands 186, 187, 188, 301
 Julia (Bulgarian) in Netherlands 114, 263, 281, 283
 Maaike (Dutch) in Netherlands 301
 Margherita (Italian) in Italy 198, 218, 225n9, 225n14, 299
 Margit (Hungarian) in Netherlands 294, 297
 Maria (Italian) in Italy 115, 298
 Marjon (Dutch) in Netherlands 302
 Marta (Italian) in Italy 201, 300
 Mina (Bulgarian) in Italy 100, 102, 142–3, 147–8, 154, 156, 255, 258, 275, 277
 Sára (Hungarian) in Netherlands 294, 297
 Szofi (Hungarian) in Italy 286, 290
widowed women
 Betta (Italian) in Italy 198, 220, 299
 Eufrozina (Hungarian/Dutch) in Netherlands 292, 296
Fanon, Frantz 24
Favell, A. 273n22
Favell, A. and Geddes, A. 274n28
Felstead, A. and Jewson, N. 134
feminism

Anglo-Saxon feminist jurisprudence 71
anti-feminism 65n10
feminist theory 29, 32
   'figurations' of alternative feminist subjectivity 28
   and historicity, challenge of 57–8
   instrumentalization of feminist discourse 191–2
   state feminism 56
   Western feminism 56–7
*Femmes pour l'Europe* 253–4, 262, 264, 266, 271n8
Ferraioli, L. 196
Ferreira, V. *et al* 35
Finch, J. and Hayes, L. 102
Flesler, D. 146, 209n8
Foblets, M.-C. 230
Foblets, M.-C. and Dupret, B. 78
   food-talk 152–63
   cultural conflicts and 153–4, 156–7, 157–8
   economy with food 155–6
   family bonding 155, 162
   food systems, conflicting traditions in 153–7
   functionalist approach to food 154
   identity and 152, 157–9
   intergenerational connections 160–61
   Italian tradition 156, 159
   'other' marking of 157–9, 162–3
   power and food 160–62
   'self' marking of 157–9
   social functions of 152–3, 154, 158, 162
   structuralist approach to food 158–9
   transformations in cooking 158
forced migration 2–3, 9, 47, 53
Fortier, A.-M. 102, 104, 107, 108n1, 109n18, 270–71n3, 272n13, 272n16
Fortuyn, Pim 178
Foucault, Michel 24, 33
Frankberg, R. 33
Fraser, N. 273n25
Freud, Sigmund 24
Fuentes, A. and Ehrenreich, B. 135n2
*Fun is Beautiful* (Carlo Verdone film) 200
functionalist approach to food 154
Funk, N. 272n19
Funk, N. and Mueller, M. 55

Galimberti, U. 271n7
Gazsi, Judit 9
Geddes, Andrew and Favell, Adrian 108n1
gender
   Europe and subjectivity 253–5
   gendered subjectivity and Jungian constellation 271n7
   gendering the European subject 264–8
   legal equality and 75
   migration and 2
   political transformation and 56
   relations, interdisciplinary research 70–74
   relations and femininity 188–90
   stereotype and preconception 199–200
   transnational mobility and 2
geographies
   geo-political space of Europe 4–5
   histories and geographies, embeddedness in 30

imaginary geographies 95–6
location and geographical characteristics 102
topographical mapping of love 138–40
Giacone, P. 196
Gibson, M. 196
Giddens, Anthony 139–40, 143, 150n2
Gilroy, Paul 32, 36, 38, 40n2, 64n1
Ginzburg, Carlo 140
Glants, M. and Toomre, J. 152
global poverty, perceptions of 204–5
globalization 14, 25, 49, 64n6, 69, 72, 196, 214, 219, 234
g-local change 29
Goody, Jack 153, 157, 159, 160, 163n1
Grewal, I. and Kaplan, C. 27, 28
Griffin, G. and Braidotti, R. 274n31
Grillo, R. and Pratt, J. 195–6
Gross, N. and Simmons, S. 139, 146
Guha, Ranajit 208–9

Habermas, Jürgen 24, 39, 262, 273n25
Hadzhikosev, S. and Vagenstein, S. 142, 150n4
Hale, Liz 150n5
Hall, Stuart 25, 38, 40n2, 64n1
Hantzaroula, P. 215
Haraway, Donna 26–7, 40n1
Harding, Sandra 26–7
Hardt, M. and Negri, A. 25
Hárs, Ágnes, *et al* 308n1
Hasselaar, Kenau Simonsdochter 174n1
Hellum, A. 70
heteronormativity 48–51
heterotopia of communism 57
Hirschman, Albert 26
Hirschmann, Ursula 26, 253–4, 271n8, 271n9, 273n23
historical consciousness 192
histories and geographies, embeddedness in 30
history of Europe 32
Hoerder, D. 4
Holleman, J.F. 73
home
   and homeland 50
   homelands, attitudes towards 53–5
   intimacy of 87
   laboured creation of 102
   place of objects and 103
homelessness 29–30
homesickness 46, 53, 105
hooks, bell 33
Hortobagyi, Anna 84–91, 315
Human Rights, European Court of (ECHR) 78–9
Hungary
   Ági, Hungarian/Dutch migrant in Netherlands 59, 108n14, 112, 292, 295
   Anett, Hungarian migrant in Netherlands 126, 257, 260, 261, 293, 297
   Angéla, Hungarian migrant in Italy 287, 290
   Bori, Hungarian/Italian migrant in Italy 131, 205, 217, 218, 284, 288
   Brigi, Hungarian/Dutch migrant in Netherlands 153, 261, 293, 297
   Csilla, Hungarian/Italian migrant in Italy 105, 145, 158, 161, 170, 172, 204, 285, 288

Edith, Hungarian/Italian migrant in Italy 18, 103, 243–50, 284, 288
Ella, Hungarian/Dutch migrant in Netherlands 161, 292, 296
Emese, Hungarian/Rumanian migrant in Italy 285, 289
Emília, Hungarian/Dutch migrant in Netherlands 62, 63, 108n14, 141, 143, 291, 295
Emma, Hungarian/Italian migrant in Italy 95, 105, 108n4, 108n14, 115, 130, 131, 132, 142, 143, 148, 286, 290
Erzsébet, Hungarian/Dutch migrant in Netherlands 136n10, 152, 293, 296
Eufrozina, Hungarian/Dutch migrant in Netherlands 292, 296
Gyöngyi, Hungarian/Italian migrant in Italy 133, 134, 155, 160, 287, 290
Henrietta, Hungarian/Dutch migrant in Netherlands 125, 126, 291, 295
Hilda, Hungarian/Dutch migrant in Netherlands 261, 294, 297
Ila, Hungarian/Dutch migrant in Netherlands 292, 295
Ilona, Hungarian/Dutch migrant in Netherlands 292, 296
Irén, Hungarian/Italian migrant in Italy 108n14, 112, 119, 137, 141, 143, 146, 285, 288
Ivett, Hungarian migrant in Italy 286, 289
Janka, Hungarian/Rumanian migrant in Italy 287, 290
Juli, Hungarian migrant in Italy 108n14, 285, 289
Kamilla, Hungarian migrant in Italy 60, 61, 62, 109n17, 285, 289
Klári, Hungarian/Dutch migrant in Netherlands 293, 296
Lili, Hungarian/British migrant in Italy 286, 289
Magda, Hungarian/Dutch migrant in Netherlands 159, 291, 295
Margit, Hungarian migrant in Netherlands 294, 297
Mari, Hungarian/Dutch migrant in Netherlands 154, 160, 161, 291, 295
migrants from 1, 10, 284–97
characteristics of 307–9
Mónika, Hungarian/Dutch migrant in Netherlands 99, 108n14, 141, 142, 143, 155, 263, 293, 296
Noémi, Hungarian migrant in Netherlands 258, 294, 297
Petra, Hungarian/Italian migrant in Italy 216, 221, 222, 223, 256, 257, 272n18, 286, 289
Piroska, Hungarian/Dutch migrant in Netherlands 15, 59, 87, 88, 91, 161, 162, 292, 296
Rozika, Hungarian/Dutch migrant in Netherlands 141, 143, 154, 291, 295
Rózsa, Hungarian/Italian migrant in Italy 284, 288
Sára, Hungarian migrant in Netherlands 294, 297

Sarolta, Hungarian migrant in Italy 285, 289
Szofi, Hungarian migrant in Italy 286, 290
Teri, Hungarian/Dutch migrant in Netherlands 141, 143, 155, 259, 293, 297
Vali, Hungarian/Italian migrant in Italy 106, 284, 288
Zsuzsa, Hungarian migrant in Italy 285, 289
Husserl, Edmund 24
hybridity 65–6n2
hyperrealism 178

idealization of origins 104
identity 37
  cultural identity in Europe 34–5
  diasporic identity 36
  dis-identification 38
  European Union (EU) 37
  and food-talk 152, 157–9
  identification as of exile status 51
  national identity 36, 37, 103, 157, 178–80, 193, 207–8
  and passport 99
  post-nationalist identity in Europe 35–6, 38, 39–40
  professional identity 123–6
  respectability and self-identity 217–18
  self-identity, renegotiation of 207–8
immigration law 228–35, 239–40
  age limit criteria for reunification of spouses 232
  aggregate-tie criteria 232
  Danish immigration reform 231–2, 239–40
  European Convention on Human Rights (1950) 230
  European Union (EU) context 230
  family reunification 231–2
  framing the problem 229–30
  international instruments 230
  marriage exploitation for migration purposes 233–5
  state, definition of 230
inclusion and distinction, mechanisms of 204–5
inequalities 65n10, 201
  reproduction of 191, 193
  social inequalities 5
integration 64n7
  forced integration 46
  integration policy 193n1
  of minorities 17
  and threat to culture 187–8
  *see also* emancipation and integration
intelligence 220–21
intercultural dialogues 5
intercultural relations 196, 198–9, 201–4
interethnic relations 192–3
intergenerational connections 160–61
intersubjectivity 251–3
interviewees
  Adela (Bulgarian/Italian) in Italy 143, 149, 276, 278
  Adriana (Italian) in Italy 215, 300
  Ági (Hungarian/Dutch) in Netherlands 59, 108n14, 112, 292, 295

# Index

Albena (Bulgarian/Dutch) in Netherlands 102, 104, 108n14, 141, 143, 145, 148, 156, 157, 280, 282
Alena (Bulgarian) in Netherlands 100, 101, 102, 112, 114, 130, 131, 148, 149, 279, 282
Ana (Bulgarian) in Italy 46, 102, 106, 119, 148–9, 255, 258, 275, 278
Anett (Hungarian) in Netherlands 126, 257, 260, 261, 293, 297
Angéla (Hungarian) in Italy 287, 290
Angela (Italian) in Italy 16, 159, 170, 171, 173, 199, 203, 204, 205, 206, 207, 208, 218, 219, 224, 227, 256, 298
Angelina (Bulgarian) in Italy 102, 105, 146, 147, 148, 276, 278
Barbara (Dutch) in Netherlands 16, 165, 169, 189, 301
Betta (Italian) in Italy 198, 220, 299
Bori (Hungarian/Italian) in Italy 131, 205, 217, 218, 284, 288
Boyana (Bulgarian/Dutch) in Netherlands 47, 55, 59, 60, 104, 105, 108n14, 114, 115, 119, 143, 262, 280, 282
Brigi (Hungarian/Dutch) in Netherlands 153, 261, 293, 297
Bulgarian migrants, characteristics of 304–6
Carla (Italian) in Italy 159, 203, 260, 300
Carlotta (Italian) in Italy 198, 201, 203, 204, 299
Carolina (Bulgarian/Italian) in Italy 144, 145, 276, 278
characteristics by nationality 304–13
Cristina (Italian) in Italy 207, 208, 217, 299
Csilla (Hungarian/Italian) in Italy 105, 145, 158, 161, 170, 172, 204, 285, 288
Daniela (Italian) in Italy 226n19, 299
Deborah (Dutch) in Netherlands 303
Diana (Dutch) in Netherlands 301
Dutch natives, characteristics of 312–13
Edith (Hungarian/Italian) in Italy 18, 103, 243–50, 284, 288
Ella (Hungarian/Dutch) in Netherlands 161, 292, 296
Ellen (Dutch) in Netherlands 183, 184, 185, 187, 301
Emese (Hungarian/Rumanian) in Italy 285, 289
Emília (Hungarian/Dutch) in Netherlands 62, 63, 108n14, 141, 143, 291, 295
Emma (Hungarian/Italian) in Italy 95, 105, 109n4, 108n14, 115, 130, 131, 132, 142, 143, 148, 286, 290
Erzsébet (Hungarian/Dutch) in Netherlands 136n10, 152, 293, 296
Eufrozina (Hungarian/Dutch) in Netherlands 292, 296
Eva (Bulgarian) in Netherlands 100, 102, 108n14, 142, 148, 279, 282
Francesca (Italian) in Italy 299
Giovanna (Italian) in Italy 198, 199, 200, 201, 202, 206, 207, 215, 218, 220, 225n6, 265, 299
Gyöngyi (Hungarian/Italian) in Italy 133, 134, 155, 160, 287, 290

Hanneke (Dutch) in Netherlands 184, 185, 190, 193, 194, 303
Henrietta (Hungarian/Dutch) in Netherlands 125, 126, 291, 295
Hilda (Hungarian/Dutch) in Netherlands 261, 294, 297
Hungarian migrants, characteristics of 307–9
Ila (Hungarian/Dutch) in Netherlands 292, 295
Ilona (Hungarian/Dutch) in Netherlands 292, 296
Ilse (Dutch) in Netherlands 302
Inge (Dutch) in Netherlands 156, 181, 186, 302
Irén (Hungarian/Italian) in Italy 108n14, 112, 119, 137, 141, 143, 146, 285, 288
Irena (Bulgarian) in Italy 102, 108n14, 112, 119, 135n6, 141, 143, 146, 275, 277
Italian natives, characteristics of 310–11
Ivett (Hungarian) in Italy 286, 289
Jacqueline (Dutch) in Netherlands 302
Janka (Hungarian/Rumanian) in Italy 287, 290
Jantina (Dutch) in Netherlands 186, 187, 188, 301
Jelisaveta (Bulgarian/Italian) in Italy 15, 84, 101, 102, 107, 108n14, 130, 144, 146–8, 275, 277
Joanna (Bulgarian/Dutch) in Netherlands 102, 114, 120, 148, 281, 283
Juli (Hungarian) in Italy 108n14, 285, 289
Julia (Bulgarian) in Netherlands 114, 263, 281, 283
Kalina (Bulgarian) in Netherlands 108n14, 113, 115, 123, 124, 126, 149, 279, 282
Kamilla (Hungarian) in Italy 60, 61, 62, 119n17, 285, 289
Kate (Bulgarian/Dutch) in Netherlands 280, 283
Klári (Hungarian/Dutch) in Netherlands 293, 296
Kremena (Bulgarian/Dutch) in Netherlands 108n14, 112, 113, 114, 142, 143, 144, 148, 155, 262, 280, 283
Kristina (Bulgarian) in Italy 124, 135n6, 145, 147, 148, 149, 276, 278
Lili (Hungarian/British) in Italy 286, 289
Lilia (Bulgarian/Australian) in Netherlands 281, 283
Lina (Italian) in Italy 298
Lora (Bulgarian) in Netherlands 145, 148, 281, 283
Lubomira (Bulgarian) in Netherlands 127, 128, 129, 280, 282
Maaike (Dutch) in Netherlands 301
Magda (Hungarian/Dutch) in Netherlands 159, 291, 295
Margherita (Italian) in Italy 198, 218, 225n9, 225n14, 299
Margit (Hungarian) in Netherlands 294, 297
Mari (Hungarian/Dutch) in Netherlands 154, 160, 161, 291, 295
Maria (Italian) in Italy 115, 298
Marina (Bulgarian/Italian) in Italy 47, 54, 98, 99, 101, 105, 106, 108n5, 108n14, 115, 124, 136n7, 141, 143, 158, 276, 278

Marjon (Dutch) in Netherlands 302
Marta (Italian) in Italy 201, 300
Maya (Bulgarian) in Italy 276, 278
Mina (Bulgarian) in Italy 100, 102, 142–3, 147–8, 154, 156, 255, 258, 275, 277
Mónika (Hungarian/Dutch) in Netherlands 99, 108n14, 141, 142, 143, 155, 263, 293, 296
Nikoleta (Bulgarian) in Netherlands 281, 283
Noémi (Hungarian) in Netherlands 258, 294, 297
Nona (Bulgarian/Italian) in Italy 101, 108n14, 113, 144, 146, 148, 275, 277
Olga (Bulgarian) in Italy 101, 115, 148, 276, 278
Orietta (Italian) in Italy 159, 207, 208, 215, 220, 300
Patrizia (Italian) in Italy 198, 199, 203, 207, 261, 300
Petra (Hungarian/Italian) in Italy 216, 221, 222, 223, 256, 257, 272n18, 286, 289
Piroska (Hungarian/Dutch) in Netherlands 15, 59, 87, 88, 91, 161, 162, 292, 296
Plamena (Bulgarian) in Netherlands 102, 112, 114, 115, 124, 144, 157, 160, 279, 282
Poly (Bulgarian) in Netherlands 135n6, 149, 253, 263, 279, 282
Ralica (Bulgarian/Italian) in Italy 108n14, 148, 257, 275, 277
Reneta (Bulgarian/Dutch) in Netherlands 102, 105, 112, 113, 114, 129, 149, 281, 283
Roberta (Italian) in Italy 198, 206, 207, 214, 215, 216, 217, 218, 220, 225n9, 298
Rosa (Bulgarian/Dutch) in Netherlands 51–2, 97, 98, 108n16, 129, 149, 151n8, 281, 283
Rosaria (Italian) in Italy 203, 208, 300
Rozika (Hungarian/Dutch) in Netherlands 141, 143, 154, 291, 295
Rózsa (Hungarian/Italian) in Italy 284, 288
Sára (Hungarian) in Netherlands 294, 297
Sarolta (Hungarian) in Italy 285, 289
Silvana (Italian) in Italy 198, 199, 200, 202, 205, 206, 217, 218, 220, 225n10, 299
Suze (Dutch) in Netherlands 220, 224, 303
Szofi (Hungarian) in Italy 286, 290
Teodora (Bulgarian) in Netherlands 100, 127–8, 129, 141, 143, 145, 279, 282
Teri (Hungarian/Dutch) in Netherlands 141, 143, 155, 259, 293, 297
Vali (Hungarian/Italian) in Italy 106, 284, 288
Vesela (Bulgarian) in Netherlands 280, 283
Victoria (Bulgarian/Italian) in Italy 106, 108n12, 130, 257, 275, 277
Violeta (Bulgarian) in Netherlands 104, 105, 113, 114, 115, 133, 145, 280, 283
Wilma (Dutch) in Netherlands 181, 182, 183, 185, 186, 216, 301
Yana (Bulgarian/Italian) in Italy 142, 143, 144, 146, 147, 148, 275, 277
Zsuzsa (Hungarian) in Italy 285, 289
intimate relationships 59, 62–3

Irigaray, Luce 24, 138
isolation
  during communism 15, 205
  and differentiation 203
Italy
  Adela (Bulgarian/Italian) in 143, 149, 276, 278
  Adriana, native interviewee in 215, 300
  Ana (Bulgarian) in 46, 102, 106, 119, 148–9, 255, 258, 275, 278
  Angela, native interviewee in 16, 159, 170, 171, 173, 199, 203, 204, 205, 206, 207, 208, 218, 219, 224, 227, 256, 298
  Angéla (Hungarian) in 287, 290
  Angelina (Bulgarian) in 102, 105, 146, 147, 148, 276, 278
  Betta, native interviewee in 198, 220, 299
  Bori (Hungarian/Italian) in 131, 205, 217, 218, 284, 288
  Carla, native interviewee in 159, 203, 260, 300
  Carlotta, native interviewee in 198, 201, 203, 204, 299
  Carolina (Bulgarian/Italian) in 144, 145, 276, 278
  Cristina, native interviewee in 207, 208, 217, 299
  Csilla (Hungarian/Italian) in 105, 145, 158, 161, 170, 172, 204, 285, 288
  Daniela, native interviewee in 226n19, 299
  domestic workers in 225n4
  Edith (Hungarian/Italian) in 18, 103, 243–50, 284, 288
  Emese (Hungarian/Rumanian) in 285, 289
  Emma (Hungarian/Italian) in 95, 105, 109n4, 108n14, 115, 130, 131, 132, 142, 143, 148, 286, 290
  Francesca, native interviewee in 299
  Giovanna, native interviewee in 198, 199, 200, 201, 202, 206, 207, 215, 218, 220, 225n6, 265, 299
  GyöngyGyöngyi (Hungarian/Italian) in 133, 134, 155, 160, 287, 290
  Irén (Hungarian/Italian) in 108n14, 112, 119, 137, 141, 143, 146, 285, 288
  Irena (Bulgarian) in 102, 108n14, 112, 119, 135n6, 141, 143, 146, 275, 277
  Italian communist party 209n2, 260
  Italian tradition in food 156, 159
  Ivett (Hungarian) in 286, 289
  Janka (Hungarian/Rumanian) in 287, 290
  Jelisaveta (Bulgarian/Italian) in 15, 84, 101, 102, 107, 108n14, 130, 144, 146–8, 275, 277
  Juli (Hungarian) in 108n14, 285, 289
  Kamilla (Hungarian) in 60, 61, 62, 109n17, 285, 289
  Kristina (Bulgarian) in 124, 135n6, 145, 147, 148, 149, 276, 278
  Lili (Hungarian/British) in 286, 289
  Lina, native interviewee in 298
  Margherita, native interviewee in 198, 218, 225n9, 225n14, 299
  Maria, native interviewee in 115, 298

Marina (Bulgarian/Italian) in 47, 54, 98, 99, 101, 105, 106, 108n5, 108n14, 115, 124, 136n7, 141, 143, 158, 276, 278
Marta, native interviewee in 201, 300
Maya (Bulgarian) in 276, 278
migrants to 1, 10, 275–8, 284–90
Mina (Bulgarian) in 100, 102, 142–3, 147–8, 154, 156, 255, 258, 275, 277
native Italian interviewees, characteristics of 310–11
Nona (Bulgarian/Italian) in 101, 108n14, 113, 144, 146, 148, 275, 277
Olga (Bulgarian) in 101, 115, 148, 276, 278
Orietta, native interviewee in 159, 207, 208, 215, 220, 300
Patrizia, native interviewee in 198, 199, 203, 207, 261, 300
Petra (Hungarian/Italian) in 216, 221, 222, 223, 256, 257, 272n18, 286, 289
Ralica (Bulgarian/Italian) in 108n14, 148, 257, 275, 277
Roberta, native interviewee in 198, 206, 207, 214, 215, 216, 217, 218, 220, 225n9, 298
Rosaria, native interviewee in 203, 208, 300
Rózsa (Hungarian/Italian) in 284, 288
Sarolta (Hungarian) in 285, 289
Silvana, native interviewee in 198, 199, 200, 202, 205, 206, 217, 218, 220, 225n10, 299
Szofi (Hungarian) in 286, 290
Vali (Hungarian/Italian) in 106, 284, 288
Victoria (Bulgarian/Italian) in 106, 108n12, 130, 257, 275, 277
women native to 1, 10, 298–300
Yana (Bulgarian/Italian) in 142, 143, 144, 146, 147, 148, 275, 277
Zsuzsa (Hungarian) in 285, 289
Ivekovic, R. 272n17

Jackson, P.A. 50, 65n8
Jacqueson, C. 230
Joerges, C. and Ghaleigh, N.S. 70
journey narratives 138–40, 150
Judaism 16, 18, 25, 32–3, 77, 158, 165–6, 170, 173, 243–4, 248, 250, 260, 271n9
Juhász, Borbála 9
Jungian constellation 271n7

Kaelble, H. 271n7
Kershenovich, Paulette 158
Kideckel, D. 201, 205
King, R. and Andall, J. 195
Kjaer, K.U. 239n6
Kofman, E. et al 135n2
Kofman, Eleonor 64, 229
Konstantinov, Aleco 108n11
Koser, K. and Lutz, H. 2, 135n2
Kracauer, Siegfried 252
Kristeva, Julia 119, 140, 162
Kronborg, Annette 17, 18, 228–42, 273n26, 315
Kuhn, Thomas 252
Kulumdjiev, K. 117
Kussmaul, A. 4

labour market 130, 132–3, 190
Laclau, Ernesto 29
Laliotou, Ioanna 1–19, 45–64, 122–35, 315
Lamont, M. and Molnár, V. 212
Lamont, M. and Thévénot, L. 212
Lamont, Michèle 212, 213, 214, 219, 221, 223, 224n1
landscapes 101–3
  of postmodernity 28
language
  and communication 114
  of interviews 9
  presumption of commonality in 65n13
Lash, S. and Friedman, J. 105
legal culture in transformation 68–70, 75–6
legal perspective on migration 72–3
legal status, attainment of 185
legal subject-hood in EU 72–4
legal subjectivity
  collective enterprises and 74
  in Europe 68–81
    emergent late modern forms of 77–9
    mobility, privilege and 68–9
  exclusion, legitimization of 80–81
  'intersectional self' and 78
  multiple belonging and 105–6, 107
  power relations 80
  pregnancy and 78
  rights and privileges 74–5
  security issues 80
  subordination and 79–80
legal subordination of women 74–6
Lévi-Strauss, Claude 158–9
Levski, Vassil 108n10
Liebert, Ulrike 272n12
life stories see interviewees
Littlewood, I. 209n3
Lloyd, Genevieve 26
location
  construction of 27–8
  facilitation of relationships 60
  feminist theory 29, 32
  geographical characteristics and 102
  home and homeland 50
  landscapes of postmodernity 28
  politics of 27–31
  situated politics of 35
  trans-culturality and 28–9
loneliness 115
love 138–50
  courting 141
  distance and drive of 140–41, 142
  driving-force of 142–3
  legitimization of marriage and migration 144–6
  love-letters 141
  love relationships 60–61
  marriage and migration 144–6
  as mediator, topographical mapping of concept 138–40
  negation of 149
  romantic motifs and plots 140–43, 144, 145, 148, 149
  self-improvement and 146–50
  separation and 142–3

spatial stories of 141–2
'topos' of 138, 141, 146–7, 148, 150
transnational intimacies, stigmatization of 139
'true love' stereotype of 144
Lowe, W. 4
Lutz, Helma 189, 207, 218
Lutz, Helma *et al* 40n2, 135n2, 272n20
Lyon, Dawn 1–19, 95–107, 122–35, 212–27, 271n8, 315

Mackie, V. 50, 65n8
Mai, N. 208, 209n5, 209n8, 209n9
manners 220–21
Márai, Sándor 163n4
marginalization 209n7
marriage
  exploitation for migration purposes 233–5
  'fake marriage' 182–3
  legal perspective on 72–3
  love and 139
  love relationship in 146
  mixed marriages 144–6
masculization of property 56
Mason, T. 208
matrimonial law 228–9, 235–40
  cohabitation in 237
  Danish family law 235–9
  Danish legislation 229, 239–40
  family law as instrument of immigration law 238–9
  legal perception of marriage and family, change in 236–8
  religious underpinning 69
Mehdi, R. and Shaheed, F. 71
memories
  individual and collective 207–8
  and narratives of migration 27
Mény, Y. 39
Mezzadra, S. and Petrillo, A. 196
Michelet, Jules 273n21
migrants
  Adela (Bulgarian/Italian) in Italy 143, 149, 276, 278
  Ági (Hungarian/Dutch) in Netherlands 59, 108n14, 112, 292, 295
  Albena (Bulgarian/Dutch) in Netherlands 102, 104, 108n14, 141, 143, 145, 148, 156, 157, 280, 282
  Alena (Bulgarian) in Netherlands 100, 101, 102, 112, 114, 130, 131, 148, 149, 279, 282
  Ana (Bulgarian) in Italy 46, 102, 106, 119, 148–9, 255, 258, 275, 278
  Anett (Hungarian) in Netherlands 126, 257, 260, 261, 293, 297
  Angéla (Hungarian) in Italy 287, 290
  Angelina (Bulgarian) in Italy 102, 105, 146, 147, 148, 276, 278
  Bori (Hungarian/Italian) in Italy 131, 205, 217, 218, 284, 288
  Boyana (Bulgarian/Dutch) in Netherlands 47, 55, 59, 60, 104, 105, 108n14, 114, 115, 119, 143, 262, 280, 282

  Brigi (Hungarian/Dutch) in Netherlands 153, 261, 293, 297
  Carolina (Bulgarian/Italian) in Italy 144, 145, 276, 278
  Csilla (Hungarian/Italian) in Italy 105, 145, 158, 161, 170, 172, 204, 285, 288
  Edith (Hungarian/Italian) in Italy 18, 103, 243–50, 284, 288
  Ella (Hungarian/Dutch) in Netherlands 161, 292, 296
  Emese (Hungarian/Rumanian) in Italy 285, 289
  Emília (Hungarian/Dutch) in Netherlands 62, 63, 108n14, 141, 143, 291, 295
  Emma (Hungarian/Italian) in Italy 95, 105, 109n4, 108n14, 115, 130, 131, 132, 142, 143, 148, 286, 290
  Erzsébet (Hungarian/Dutch) in Netherlands 136n10, 152, 293, 296
  Eufrozina (Hungarian/Dutch) in Netherlands 292, 296
  Eva (Bulgarian) in Netherlands 100, 102, 108n14, 142, 148, 279, 282
  Gyöngyi (Hungarian/Italian) in Italy 133, 134, 155, 160, 287, 290
  Henrietta (Hungarian/Dutch) in Netherlands 125, 126, 291, 295
  Hilda (Hungarian/Dutch) in Netherlands 261, 294, 297
  idealization of origins by 104
  Ila (Hungarian/Dutch) in Netherlands 292, 295
  Ilona (Hungarian/Dutch) in Netherlands 292, 296
  Irén (Hungarian/Italian) in Italy 108n14, 112, 119, 137, 141, 143, 146, 285, 288
  Irena (Bulgarian) in Italy 102, 108n14, 112, 119, 135n6, 141, 143, 146, 275, 277
  Ivett (Hungarian) in Italy 286, 289
  Janka (Hungarian/Rumanian) in Italy 287, 290
  Jelisaveta (Bulgarian/Italian) in Italy 15, 84, 101, 102, 107, 108n14, 130, 144, 146–8, 275, 277
  Joanna (Bulgarian/Dutch) in Netherlands 102, 114, 120, 148, 281, 283
  Juli (Hungarian) in Italy 108n14, 285, 289
  Julia (Bulgarian) in Netherlands 114, 263, 281, 283
  Kalina (Bulgarian) in Italy 108n14, 113, 115, 123, 124, 126, 149, 279, 282
  Kamilla (Hungarian) in Italy 60, 61, 62, 109n17, 285, 289
  Kate (Bulgarian/Dutch) in Netherlands 280, 283
  Klári (Hungarian/Dutch) in Netherlands 293, 296
  Kremena (Bulgarian/Dutch) in Netherlands 108n14, 112, 113, 114, 143, 144, 148, 155, 262, 280, 283
  Kristina (Bulgarian) in Italy 124, 135n6, 145, 147, 148, 149, 276, 278
  Lili (Hungarian/British) in Italy 286, 289
  Lilia (Bulgarian/Australian) in Netherlands 281, 283

# Index

Lora (Bulgarian) in Netherlands 145, 148, 281, 283
Lubomira (Bulgarian) in Netherlands 127, 128, 129, 280, 282
Magda (Hungarian/Dutch) in Netherlands 159, 291, 295
Margit (Hungarian) in Netherlands 294, 297
Mari (Hungarian/Dutch) in Netherlands 154, 160, 161, 291, 295
Marina (Bulgarian/Italian) in Italy 47, 54, 98, 99, 101, 105, 106, 109n5, 108n14, 115, 124, 136n7, 141, 143, 158, 276, 278
Maya (Bulgarian) in Italy 276, 278
Mina (Bulgarian) in Italy 100, 102, 142–3, 147–8, 154, 156, 255, 258, 275, 277
Mónika (Hungarian/Dutch) in Netherlands 99, 108n14, 141, 142, 143, 155, 263, 293, 296
Nikoleta (Bulgarian) in Netherlands 281, 283
Noémi (Hungarian) in Netherlands 258, 294, 297
Nona (Bulgarian/Italian) in Italy 101, 108n14, 113, 144, 146, 148, 275, 277
Olga (Bulgarian) in Italy 101, 115, 148, 276, 278
Petra (Hungarian/Italian) in Italy 216, 221, 222, 223, 256, 257, 272n18, 286, 289
Piroska (Hungarian/Dutch) in Netherlands 15, 59, 87, 88, 91, 161, 162, 292, 296
Plamena (Bulgarian) in Netherlands 102, 112, 114, 115, 124, 144, 157, 160, 279, 282
Poly (Bulgarian) in Netherlands 135n6, 149, 253, 263, 279, 282
Ralica (Bulgarian/Italian) in Italy 108n14, 148, 257, 275, 277
Reneta (Bulgarian/Dutch) in Netherlands 102, 105, 112, 113, 114, 129, 149, 281, 283
Rosa (Bulgarian/Dutch) in Netherlands 51–2, 97, 98, 108n16, 129, 149, 151n8, 281, 283
Rozika (Hungarian/Dutch) in Netherlands 141, 143, 154, 291, 295
Rózsa (Hungarian/Italian) in Italy 284, 288
Sára (Hungarian) in Netherlands 294, 297
Sarolta (Hungarian) in Italy 285, 289
Szofi (Hungarian) in Italy 286, 290
Teodora (Bulgarian) in Netherlands 100, 127–8, 129, 141, 143, 145, 279, 282
Teri (Hungarian/Dutch) in Netherlands 141, 143, 155, 259, 293, 297
Vali (Hungarian/Italian) in Italy 106, 284, 288
Vesela (Bulgarian) in Netherlands 280, 283
Victoria (Bulgarian/Italian) in Italy 106, 108n12, 130, 257, 275, 277
Violeta (Bulgarian) in Netherlands 104, 105, 113, 114, 115, 133, 145, 280, 283
Yana (Bulgarian/Italian) in Italy 142, 143, 144, 146, 147, 148, 275, 277
Zsuzsa (Hungarian) in Italy 285, 289
migration
  affective relationships and 51–2
  assumptions attached to 3
  communism and 7, 47
  concept of 2–3
  contemporary form 3
  desire to move 53
  destination countries, attitudes towards 53–5
  dialectical communication 117–19, 120
  dissidence of 52–3
  emotional relationships and 59, 62–3
  experiences of mobility and 53–5, 61–2
  forced migration 2–3, 9, 47, 53
  homelands, attitudes towards 53–5
  immigrant itineraries 30
  immigrant population in Italy, fragmentation of 195–6
  intercultural dialogues and 5
  intimate relationships and 59, 62–3
  legal perspective on 72–3
  love, marriage and 144–6
  personal relationships and 59–62
  physical disruption of 58–9
  physical movement of 58–9
  plurality of reasons for 46
  political refugees 51–2
  pre-1989 migrants 51–2
  reasons for 180–82
  reflection on properties of migrant subjectivity 46–7
  relationships, maintenance and reclamation of 59–63
  studies of 2, 3
  subjective movement of 58–9
  subjectivity and 63–4
  Third Country Nationals 79
  transnational 45–6
  women migrants, increase in numbers of 2
Mill, John Stuart 75, 76
Minh-Ha, Trinh 40n1
mobility 1, 45–64
  centrality of 50
  circulation and multiple axes of 29
  communist restrictions on 47, 106, 124
  constant mobility 29–30
  effects of 49–50
  encounters, new forms of 2
  experiences of mobility 53–5, 61–2
  heteronormativity, movement and critique of 48–51
  immigrant itineraries 30
  objectification of process 63
  personal 'dissidence' as constitutive in 51–5
  political space, mobility and redefinition of 55–8
  prerequisite for comfort and well-being 105
  privilege, legal subjectivity and 68–9
  relationships that move you 58–64
  technology and distance in 105
  transnational spaces and 50
Moch, L.P. and Tilly, L. 4
modern citizenship 76–7
modernity, backwardness and 195–209
  asymmetric relationships 196–7, 201
  cosmopolitanism 204
  differentiation, tradition and 205–6
  discovery, process of 198–9

Eurocentrism 204
expectations and ideas, uncertainty in 198
gender, stereotype and preconception 199–200
global poverty, perceptions of 204–5
immigrant population in Italy, fragmentation of 195–6
inclusion and distinction, mechanisms of 204–5
inequalities 201
intercultural relations 198–9, 201–4
memories, individual and collective 207–8
'national preference' and public opinion 196
'other,' construction as object of testimonies 197
phenotypic traits 203
racialisation of migration 196
self-identity, renegotiation of 207–8
sex tourism 200
sexual exploitation 200–201
sexuality and work, gendered perceptions 198–202
symbolic classification, continuity of 197
triumphant Italian woman 202–9
Moe, N. 196
Moghadam, V. 55
Mohanty, C. 27–8
Montanari, M. 163n2
moral boundaries 214–18
Morandi, C. 273n21
Morin, E. 39
Morley, D. 105
Morrison, Toni 32
motherhood 130–32
'mothers of Europe' 253–5
Mouffe, C. 29
multiculturalism 8, 17, 23, 32, 35–6, 78–9, 95–6, 116, 178, 180, 224n2, 272–3n20
multidisciplinarity 12, 13
multiple belonging 105–6, 107
multiple selves 79–81
Muslims 32, 69, 71, 77, 79, 173, 189–90, 191–2, 203, 209, 209n7

Nair, P. 209n8
narratives of migration 6–7, 13, 15, 18, 195, 273–4n27
asymmetric relations in 196–7
border-places and 'home' in 95–107
boundary work 213–14
breaking loose from fixed narratives 180
communicative deficiency in 115
contradictory nature of 106
'dance through life' in 84–91
ethnic cooking and belonging in 162
Europeanness in 262–3
histories and geographies, embeddedness in specific 30
interaction with Western scenarios 196
isolation and differentiation in 203
journey narratives 138–40, 150
as maps of imaginary geographies 95–6
memory and 27
nostalgia and homesickness in 53
passion and suffering in 143
romantic plots in 149

sameness and otherness in 197
sexuality and work, gendered perceptions 198–202
traditional narratives 46, 52
triumphant Westernism and 207
vacillation in 47
see also interviewees
national identity 36, 37, 103, 157, 178–80, 193, 207–8
nationality 36, 140, 146, 182, 203, 217–18, 221, 230, 258–9, 263–4
British Nationality Act (1948) 81n2
naturalization 33, 196, 197, 230, 232
Nazi persecution, anti-fascism and 25–6
Netherlands
Ági (Hungarian/Dutch) in 59, 108n14, 112, 292, 295
Albena (Bulgarian/Dutch) in 102, 104, 108n14, 141, 143, 145, 148, 156, 157, 280, 282
Alena (Bulgarian) in 100, 101, 102, 112, 114, 130, 131, 148, 149, 279, 282
Anett (Hungarian) in 126, 257, 260, 261, 293, 297
Barbara, native interviewee in 16, 165, 169, 189, 301
Boyana (Bulgarian/Dutch) in 47, 55, 59, 60, 104, 105, 108n14, 114, 115, 119, 143, 262, 280, 282
Brigi (Hungarian/Dutch) in 153, 261, 293, 297
Deborah, native interviewee in 303
Diana, native interviewee in 301
Ella (Hungarian/Dutch) in 161, 292, 296
Ellen, native interviewee in 183, 184, 185, 187, 301
emancipation policy 177
Emília (Hungarian/Dutch) in 62, 63, 108n14, 141, 143, 291, 295
Erzsébet (Hungarian/Dutch) in 136n10, 152, 293, 296
Eufrozina (Hungarian/Dutch) in 292, 296
Eva (Bulgarian) in 100, 102, 108n14, 142, 148, 279, 282
Hanneke, native interviewee in 184, 185, 190, 193, 194, 303
Henrietta (Hungarian/Dutch) in 125, 126, 291, 295
Hilda (Hungarian/Dutch) in 261, 294, 297
Ila (Hungarian/Dutch) in 292, 295
Ilona (Hungarian/Dutch) in 292, 296
Ilse, native interviewee in 302
Inge, native interviewee in 156, 181, 186, 302
Jacqueline, native interviewee in 302
Jantina, native interviewee in 186, 187, 188, 301
Joanna (Bulgarian/Dutch) in 102, 114, 120, 148, 281, 283
Julia (Bulgarian) in 114, 263, 281, 283
Kalina (Bulgarian) in 108n14, 113, 115, 123, 124, 126, 149, 279, 282
Kate (Bulgarian/Dutch) in 280, 283
Klári (Hungarian/Dutch) in 293, 296
Kremena (Bulgarian/Dutch) in 108n14, 112, 113, 114, 142, 143, 144, 148, 155, 262, 280, 283

*Index* 331

Lilia (Bulgarian/Australian) in 281, 283
Lora (Bulgarian) in 145, 148, 281, 283
Lubomira (Bulgarian) in 127, 128, 129, 280, 282
Maaike, native interviewee in 301
Magda (Hungarian/Dutch) in 159, 291, 295
Margit (Hungarian) in 294, 297
Mari (Hungarian/Dutch) in 154, 160, 161, 291, 295
Marjon, native interviewee in 302
migrants to 1, 10, 279–83, 291–7
Mónika (Hungarian/Dutch) in 99, 108n14, 141, 142, 143, 155, 263, 293, 296
multiculturalism in 224n2
native Dutch interviewees, characteristics of 312–13
Nikoleta (Bulgarian) in 281, 283
Noémi (Hungarian) in 258, 294, 297
Piroska (Hungarian/Dutch) in 15, 59, 87, 88, 91, 161, 162, 292, 296
Plamena (Bulgarian) in 102, 112, 114, 115, 124, 144, 157, 160, 279, 282
Poly (Bulgarian) in 137n6, 149, 253, 263, 279, 282
Reneta (Bulgarian/Dutch) in 102, 105, 112, 113, 114, 129, 149, 281, 283
Rosa (Bulgarian/Dutch) in 51–2, 97, 98, 108n16, 129, 149, 151n8, 281, 283
Rozika (Hungarian/Dutch) in 141, 143, 154, 291, 295
Sára (Hungarian) in 294, 297
Suze, native interviewee in 220, 224, 303
Teodora (Bulgarian) in 100, 127–8, 129, 141, 143, 145, 279, 282
Teri (Hungarian/Dutch) in 141, 143, 155, 259, 293, 297
Vesela (Bulgarian) in 280, 283
Violeta (Bulgarian) in 104, 105, 113, 114, 115, 133, 145, 280, 283
Wilma, native interviewee in 181, 182, 183, 185, 186, 216, 301
women native to 1, 10, 301–3
new realist discourse 178–9, 180
 emancipation and integration 178–9
 main points of 193n2
Nietzsche, Friedrich 24, 35, 274n30
Nikolchina, Miglena 12, 15, 64, 65n14, 111–20, 206, 315
nomadism 30, 40, 48–9, 61–2
non-places 99–101
nostalgia 46, 53, 180
Nousiainen, K. *et al* 70, 71, 72

occupations of interviewees
 agent
  Lina (Italian) in Italy 298
 agricultural workers
  Carla (Italian) in Italy 159, 203, 260, 300
  Orietta (Italian) in Italy 159, 207, 208, 215, 220, 300
 beautician
  Francesca (Italian) in Italy 299
 call-centre employee
  Jantina (Dutch) in Netherlands 186, 187, 188, 301

 cashiers
  Lubomira (Bulgarian) in Netherlands 127, 128, 129, 280, 282
  Teodora (Bulgarian) in Netherlands 100, 127–8, 129, 141, 143, 145, 279, 282
 cleaner
  Emese (Hungarian/Rumanian) in Italy 285, 289
 company employee
  Rozika (Hungarian/Dutch) in Netherlands 141, 143, 154, 291, 295
 cook
  Yana (Bulgarian/Italian) in Italy 142, 143, 144, 146, 147, 148, 275, 277
 designer
  Ági (Hungarian/Dutch) in Netherlands 59, 108n14, 112, 292, 295
 doctor
  Magda (Hungarian/Dutch) in Netherlands 159, 291, 295
 economic planner
  Kalina (Bulgarian) in Netherlands 108n14, 113, 115, 123, 124, 126, 149, 279, 282
 entrepreneur
  Deborah (Dutch) in Netherlands 303
 hairdresser
  Angelina (Bulgarian) in Italy 102, 105, 146, 147, 148, 276, 278
 homeworker
  Irén (Hungarian/Italian) in Italy 108n14, 112, 119, 137, 141, 143, 146, 285, 288
 housewives
  Adriana (Italian) in Italy 215, 300
  Alena (Bulgarian) in Netherlands 100, 101, 102, 112, 114, 130, 131, 148, 149, 279, 282
  Angela (Italian) in Italy 16, 159, 170, 171, 173, 199, 203, 204, 205, 206, 207, 208, 218, 219, 224, 227, 256, 298
  Carlotta (Italian) in Italy 198, 201, 203, 204, 299
  Csilla (Hungarian/Italian) in Italy 105, 145, 158, 161, 170, 172, 204, 285, 288
  Nona (Bulgarian/Italian) in Italy 101, 108n14, 113, 144, 146, 148, 275, 277
  Poly (Bulgarian) in Netherlands 137n6, 149, 253, 263, 279, 282
  Sarolta (Hungarian) in Italy 285, 289
 investment analyst
  Klári (Hungarian/Dutch) in Netherlands 293, 296
 journalists
  Carolina (Bulgarian/Italian) in Italy 144, 145, 276, 278
  Juli (Hungarian) in Italy 108n14, 285, 289
  Marina (Bulgarian/Italian) in Italy 47, 54, 98, 99, 101, 105, 106, 109n5, 108n14, 115, 124, 136n7, 141, 143, 158, 276, 278
  Mina (Bulgarian) in Italy 100, 102, 142–3, 147–8, 154, 156, 255, 258, 275, 277
 jurist
  Marjon (Dutch) in Netherlands 302

management
   Ilse (Dutch) in Netherlands 302
   Patrizia (Italian) in Italy 198, 199, 203, 207, 261, 300
   Ralica (Bulgarian/Italian) in Italy 108n14, 148, 257, 275, 277
musicians
   Boyana (Bulgarian/Dutch) in Netherlands 47, 55, 59, 60, 104, 105, 108n14, 114, 115, 119, 143, 262, 280, 282
   Ila (Hungarian/Dutch) in Netherlands 292, 295
office worker
   Irena (Bulgarian) in Italy 102, 108n14, 112, 119, 137n6, 141, 143, 146, 275, 277
painter
   Kremena (Bulgarian/Dutch) in Netherlands 108n14, 112, 113, 114, 142, 143, 144, 148, 155, 262, 280, 283
PhD students
   Ellen (Dutch) in Netherlands 183, 184, 185, 187, 301
   Eva (Bulgarian) in Netherlands 100, 102, 108n14, 142, 148, 279, 282
professionals
   Emma (Hungarian/Italian) in Italy 95, 105, 108n4, 108n14, 115, 130, 131, 132, 142, 143, 148, 286, 290
   Hanneke (Dutch) in Netherlands 184, 185, 190, 193, 194, 303
   Ilona (Hungarian/Dutch) in Netherlands 292, 296
   Inge (Dutch) in Netherlands 156, 181, 186, 302
   Ivett (Hungarian) in Italy 286, 289
   Jelisaveta (Bulgarian/Italian) in Italy 15, 84, 101, 102, 107, 108n14, 130, 144, 146–8, 275, 277
   Joanna (Bulgarian/Dutch) in Netherlands 102, 114, 120, 148, 281, 283
   Kamilla (Hungarian) in Italy 60, 61, 62, 109n17, 285, 289
   Kate (Bulgarian/Dutch) in Netherlands 280, 283
   Noémi (Hungarian) in Netherlands 258, 294, 297
   Petra (Hungarian/Italian) in Italy 216, 221, 222, 223, 256, 257, 272n18, 286, 289
   Plamena (Bulgarian) in Netherlands 102, 112, 114, 115, 124, 144, 157, 160, 279, 282
   Sára (Hungarian) in Netherlands 294, 297
   Silvana (Italian) in Italy 198, 199, 200, 202, 205, 206, 217, 218, 220, 225n10, 299
   Violeta (Bulgarian) in Netherlands 104, 105, 113, 114, 115, 133, 145, 280, 283
project manager
   Henrietta (Hungarian/Dutch) in Netherlands 125, 126, 291, 295
psychologist
   Jacqueline (Dutch) in Netherlands 302
receptionist
   Teri (Hungarian/Dutch) in Netherlands 141, 143, 155, 259, 293, 297
retailers
   Ana (Bulgarian) in Italy 46, 102, 106, 119, 148–9, 255, 258, 275, 278
   Olga (Bulgarian) in Italy 101, 115, 148, 276, 278
   Rosa (Bulgarian/Dutch) in Netherlands 51–2, 97, 98, 108n16, 129, 149, 151n8, 281, 283
   Vesela (Bulgarian) in Netherlands 280, 283
retired
   Cristina (Italian) in Italy 207, 208, 217, 299
   Giovanna (Italian) in Italy 198, 199, 200, 201, 202, 206, 207, 215, 218, 220, 225n6, 265, 299
   Lili (Hungarian/British) in Italy 286, 289
   Lora (Bulgarian) in Netherlands 145, 148, 281, 283
   Roberta (Italian) in Italy 198, 206, 207, 214, 215, 216, 217, 218, 220, 225n9, 298
   Victoria (Bulgarian/Italian) in Italy 106, 108n12, 130, 257, 275, 277
secretaries
   Rosaria (Italian) in Italy 203, 208, 300
   Vali (Hungarian/Italian) in Italy 106, 284, 288
self-employed
   Wilma (Dutch) in Netherlands 181, 182, 183, 185, 186, 216, 301
social workers
   Barbara (Dutch) in Netherlands 16, 165, 169, 189, 301
   Daniela (Italian) in Italy 226n19, 299
   Diana (Dutch) in Netherlands 301
   Jacqueline (Dutch) in Netherlands 302
   Margherita (Italian) in Italy 198, 218, 225n9, 225n14, 299
   Mari (Hungarian/Dutch) in Netherlands 154, 160, 161, 291, 295
   Reneta (Bulgarian/Dutch) in Netherlands 102, 105, 112, 113, 114, 129, 149, 281, 283
   Suze (Dutch) in Netherlands 220, 224, 303
students
   Maaike (Dutch) in Netherlands 301
   Maria (Italian) in Italy 115, 298
teachers
   Albena (Bulgarian/Dutch) in Netherlands 102, 104, 108n14, 141, 143, 145, 148, 156, 157, 280, 282
   Angéla (Hungarian) in Italy 287, 290
   Bori (Hungarian/Italian) in Italy 131, 205, 217, 218, 284, 288
   Emília (Hungarian/Dutch) in Netherlands 62, 63, 108n14, 141, 143, 291, 295
   Gyöngyi (Hungarian/Italian) in Italy 133, 134, 155, 160, 287, 290
   Margit (Hungarian) in Netherlands 294, 297
   Marta (Italian) in Italy 201, 300
   Piroska (Hungarian/Dutch) in Netherlands 15, 59, 87, 88, 91, 161, 162, 292, 296

# Index

theatre director
   Kristina (Bulgarian) in Italy 124, 135n6, 145, 147, 148, 149, 276, 278
unemployed
   Julia (Bulgarian) in Netherlands 114, 263, 281, 283
waitress
   Szofi (Hungarian) in Italy 286, 290
web-mistresses
   Anett (Hungarian) in Netherlands 126, 257, 260, 261, 293, 297
   Brigi (Hungarian/Dutch) in Netherlands 153, 261, 293, 297
writer
   Edith (Hungarian/Italian) in Italy 18, 103, 243–50, 284, 288
Olsen, C.B. and Svendson, I.L. 240n25
Olsen, F.E. 71
Olwig, K.F. and Sorensen, N.N. 126–7
Ong, Aiwa 4, 40n4, 49
oral communication 117–18
oral history 1, 5–13
Ørsted, A.S. 75
'other'
   construction as object of testimonies 197
   marking of in food-talk 157–9, 162–3

Paasilehto, S. 69
Panova, N. 119
Paolini, Edoardo 271n8
Parrenas, R.S. 2, 134, 135n2, 136n13
Passerini, Luisa 1–19, 39, 150, 150n3, 226n16, 251–74, 316
passport, sanctity of 96–9
Petersen, H. and Zahle, H. 79
Petersen, Hanne 12, 14, 68–81, 274n30, 316
Petö, A. and Szapor, J. 154
Petö, Andrea 9, 12, 16, 152–63, 243–50, 316
phenotypic traits 203
philosophy
   connection making 24
   continental 24–5
   poststructuralist 24
Phizacklea, A. 2, 123, 225n4, 270–71n3
Phizacklea, A. and Wolkowitz, C. 135n2
Pisa, B. 271n6
Plato 116, 117, 118, 119
political consciousness 192
political refugees 51–2
political space, mobility and redefinition of 55–8
politics
   of labour and work 134–5
   of location 27–31
*The Politics of Jurisprudence* (Cotterrell, R.) 77–8
Porsdam, H. 78
Portes, A. *et al* 107
Posadskaya, A. 55
post-communism 2, 35, 45, 48, 50, 55, 57–8, 65n12, 272n19
   post-communist movements from East to West 45–6
post-nationalist space in Europe 25, 26, 35
postmodernism, jurisprudence and 79
poststructuralism 24

Powell, John 78, 79
power
   and food 160–62
   power relations
      and legal subjectivity 80
   power-relations 23, 28, 40
*Powers of Horror* (Kristeva, J.) 162
pregnancy 78
Preuss, Ulrich 36
Previti Allaire, C. 271n8
Prins, Baukje 178, 192
privilege, legal subjectivity and 68–9
Probyn, E. 29
professional identity 123–6
Provenza Gardensa, Countess de 150n5

qualifications and employment 133

racialisation of migration 196
racialized hierarchy of EU 34
racism 7, 14, 18, 25, 26, 28, 191, 199, 213, 222, 265
Raes, K. 239n2
re-grounding of Europe 31–5
re-territorialization of Europe 258–62
Reading, A. 55
reciprocity and communication 111–12
Regeringsgrundlag 231l
Regulska, Joanna 34, 265
relationships
   asymmetric relationships 196–7, 201
   facilitation of 60
   intercultural relations 196
   intimate relationships 59, 62–3
   love relationships 60–61
   maintenance and reclamation of 59–63
   mobility and 58–64
   personal relationships 59–62
   work as impediment to fulfilled 131–2
religion under communism 161
religious underpinning of matrimonial law 69
*La Repubblica* 209n1
*République des Lettres* (Voltaire) 258
research considerations
   analysis 11–12
   assumptions attached to migration 3
   choice of countries 7–8
   comparative design 7–8
   contemporary mobility 3
   empiricism 3
   Europe and Europeanness 4–5
   gender relations, interdisciplinary research 70–74
   geographical locations 11
   interpretation 10–13
   interviews with native women 7. 9–10
   language of interviews 9
   life stories and interviews 6
   methodological choices 5–13
   multidisciplinarity 12, 13
   oral history 1, 5–13
   sampling method 9
   selection of women migrants 6–7, 9, 10
   subjectivity and transnationalism 4
   techniques 8–9, 10–11

testimonies of migrant and native women 2
    see also interviewees
respectability and self-identity 217–18
Riccio, Bruno 103
Rich, A. 27
romantic motifs and plots 140–43, 144, 145, 148, 149
romanticization of exile status 46
rootlessness 29–30
Rothstein, H. and Rothstein, R.A. 154
Rougemont, D. de 140, 273n23
Rueschemeyer, M. 55
Rüsen, J. *et al* 270n1
Russia 47

Salih, R. 103, 104, 225n4, 264, 272–3n20, 273n22
*Les Samourais* (Kristeva, J.) 119
Sassen, Saskia 2, 23, 28, 122
Scevi, P. 196
Scheffer, Paul 178
Schultz, H.-D. and Natter, W. 272n15
Schuster, LIsa 209n6
Scrinzi, F. 122
'self'
    marking of in food-talk 157–9
    and 'other' in discourse of emancipation 179–80
    self-fulfillment and work 127–8
    self-identity, renegotiation of 207–8
    self-improvement and love 146–50
    sense of self and work 122–3
separation and love 142–3
sex tourism 200
sexual exploitation 200–201
sexuality and work, gendered perceptions 198–202
Shah, P.A. 81
Shohat, E. and Stam, R. 38
Simeon I, King of Bulgaria 108n9
Sinfield, A. 51
Skapska, Grazyna 81
Skeggs, B. 217
Slapšak, S. 273n27
social agenda of EU 30
social bonds, work creation through 126–8
social functions of food-talk 152–3, 154, 158, 162
social homeostasis 81
social imagery 37–40
social imaginary, lack in Europe 39
social interaction 60
social rights and work 130–31
socialization and work 127
socio-cultural mutation 29
Soeteman, A. 79
solidarity in work 132–4
Sorgoni, B. 199
Soviet Union 25, 39
Spinelli, A. and Rossi, E. 26
Spinelli, Altiero 25–6, 271n9
Spivak, Gayatri 40n2
Staples, David 64, 134
state, definition of 230
status and work 129–30

'stereo' effects of communication 114–15, 120
stereotypes 144, 191
Stewart, J. and Armstrong, A. 71
Stoyanov, Tsvetan 116–20
structuralist approach to food 158–9
Stychin, C.F. 50
subject, usage of term 73–4
*The Subjection of Women* (Mill, J.S.) 75, 76
subjectivity 1, 45–64, 68–81, 270–71n3
    alternative subjectivities, range of 28
    de-territorialization of Europe 258–62
    Europeanness, expression of 255–8
    in exile status 50
    'figurations' of alternative feminist 28
    gender, Europe and 253–5
    gendered subjectivity and Jungian constellation 271n7
    gendering the European subject 264–8
    intersubjectivity 251–3
    late modern forms of emergent legal 77–9
    legal perspective on 72–3
    libertory forms of 96
    and migration 63–4
    motherhood, work and 130–32
    'mothers of Europe' 253–5
    pre-modern privileged 74–6
    re-territorialization of Europe 258–62
    reflection on properties of migrant subjectivity 46–7
    sentiment, Europe of 262–4
    subjective movement of migration 58–9
    towards privileged legal Europe 68–70
    transnational forms of 2, 4
    and transnationalism 4
    usage of term 73–4
    valorization of 49
subordination 79–80
Svensson, E.M. *et al* 72
*Symposium* (Plato) 116, 117

ter Wal, J. 222
Toomre, Joyce 163n3
tradition
    in narratives 46, 52
    and nationality 217–18
train stations 100, 101
trans-culturality 28–9
trans-national space 37
transnational forms of subjectivity 2, 4
transnational intimacies, stigmatization of 139
transnational migration 45–6
transnational spaces and mobility 50
transnationalism 4, 107, 108n2
'transversal citizenship' 64n6
truth, authenticity and 180–85
Turner, V. 96

unification of Europe 26–7, 31
United States 33, 39
    US legal culture 78–9
universalism of Europe 26
unwritten communication 119–20

van Dijk, P. and van Hoof, G.J.H. 238
van Dijk, T.A. 179, 191

van Krieken, P. 239n4
Vassileva, B. 8
Ventadorn, Maria de 150n5
Ventotene Manifesto 271n9
*Vesna va veloce* (Carlo Mazzacurati film) 200
visas and documentation 98–9
Voltaire 258
Vonk, Esther 9, 16–17, 151n6, 165–74, 177–94, 316
Voutira, Effi 64

Walker, A. 40n1
Walzer, Michael 32
Ware, V. 33
Watson, Peggy 56, 58, 65n12, 65n10
Weston, K. 50
white migrants, experience of 33–4
Williams, Raymond 265
Wittig, M. 40n1
Wlocevski, S. 4
Wodak, R. and van Dijk, T.A. 179
Wolff, Larry 197, 200
Women Living under Muslim Law (WLUML) 71
Woolf, Virginia 33
work 122–35
   affective relationships of the workplace 126
   aspiration and 128
   caring and 131
   channelling in 125
   choice of 123–6
   context of 126–7
   dignity through 129–30
   discrimination 132–4
   exploitation and discrimination 133–4
   family life and 130–32
   as impediment to fulfillment of relationships 131–2
   labour market discourses 132–3
   labour market 'feminization' 130
   motherhood and 130–31
   politics of labour and 134–5
   professional identity and 123–6
   qualifications and employment, disparity between 133
   self-fulfillment and 127–8
   sense of self and 122–3
   social bonds, creation through 126–8
   social rights and 130–31
   socialization and 127
   solidarity 132–4
   status and 129–30
world-migration 28–9
written communication 119–20

xenophobia 1, 14, 25, 26, 28, 46, 251

Young, Robert 33, 64n1
Yuval-Davis, N. and Anthias, F. 40n2
Yuval-Davis, N. and Stoetzler, M. 95
Yuval-Davis, Nira 64n6, 95, 273n27

Zhechev, T. 116–17